CONTEMPORARY MUSICIANSHIP

CONTEMPORARY MUSICIANSHIP

Analysis and the Artist

JENNIFER STERLING SNODGRASS
Hayes School of Music, Appalachian State University

New York Oxford
OXFORD UNIVERSITY PRESS

Oxford University Press is a department of the University of Oxford.
It furthers the University's objective of excellence in research,
scholarship, and education by publishing worldwide.

Oxford New York
Auckland Cape Town Dar es Salaam Hong Kong Karachi
Kuala Lumpur Madrid Melbourne Mexico City Nairobi
New Delhi Shanghai Taipei Toronto

With offices in
Argentina Austria Brazil Chile Czech Republic France Greece
Guatemala Hungary Italy Japan Poland Portugal Singapore
South Korea Switzerland Thailand Turkey Ukraine Vietnam

For titles covered by Section 112 of the US Higher Education Opportunity Act, please visit www.oup.com/us/he for the latest information about pricing and alternate formats.

Published by Oxford University Press
198 Madison Avenue, New York, New York 10016
http://www.oup.com

Library of Congress Cataloging-in-Publication Data
Snodgrass, Jennifer.
Contemporary musicianship : analysis and the artist / Jennifer Sterling Snodgrass, Hayes School of Music, Appalachian State University.
pages cm
Includes bibliographical references and index.
ISBN 978-0-19-999087-0 (pbk. : alk. paper) 1. Music theory—Elementary works. I. Title.
MT7.S674 2015
781—dc23
2015001207

Printing number: 9 8 7 6 5 4 3 2 1

Printed in the United States of America
on acid-free paper

CONTENTS

PREFACE

What is musicianship? Musicianship cannot be defined in one simple sentence. It is the knowledge of music theory; the mastery of aural skills; the curiosity and creativity that leads to composition; and the informed performance of classical masterpieces, musical theater, popular music, and jazz songs. In short, it is the development of true artistry. This book seeks to help the student and amateur musician gain the tools and knowledge necessary to achieve a high level of musicianship. By studying performances, analyzing musical scores and charts, practicing aural skills, and learning a bit about the background of the finest musicians in history, you can begin the journey toward true musicianship.

APPROACH

Contemporary Musicianship: Analysis and the Artist presents traditional music theory and analysis in an innovative manner, combining music history, popular culture, aural skills, and composition to reach a broader audience that includes the amateur musician, music therapist, performer, and the music business/industry student. This book teaches students both basic and advanced principles of music theory while incorporating the great works of classical performers and popular artists. Each chapter is designed around a specific theoretical topic, similar to many current theory textbooks. However, the approach presented here allows for in-depth study of the performances or songwriting techniques and how a specific theoretical principle is used in the music. Each chapter highlights an artist in residence, including his or her basic biography, chart history, interviews, and effect on popular culture. This gives students the opportunity to really understand the background and performance style of one particular artist, while relating the theoretical and aural skills to his or her music.

This instructional approach has proven to be successful for the amateur musician. Musical analysis comes alive for many students when they are given the context for which a piece of music is written. Today's generation is very visual, and the YouTube channel designed for this text will enable students to see live performances and critique music videos while analyzing the musical score. In terms of harmony, equal importance is given to both Roman numeral analysis and lead sheet symbols. Students are encouraged to play progressions and excerpts on their guitar as well as use the traditional keyboard method. The pop trivia accompanying each chapter provides great insight into the artists presented in the text. As a result of this approach, theory is no longer just notes on the page and math problems. It becomes a musical experience evolving throughout the life of an artist.

LAYOUT

The structure of the book will align with a yearlong course syllabus, although an instructor could use opening chapters for a semester-long course. The text is split into two main sections. Chapters 1–11 deal primarily with the fundamentals of music, diatonic harmonies, lead sheet notation, and non-chord tones. Chapters 12–15 are more advanced and include the study of chromatic harmonies and modulation. For students enrolled in a music industry program, Appendixes 1 and 2 include chapters on the Nashville Number System and the perspective of the songwriter. Additional supplemental chapters in advanced theoretical topics—such as extended triads, Neapolitan chords, augmented sixth chords, and classical form—are all available on the course site for download.

Each chapter contains the following information:

1. List of chapter objectives
2. Concise and accessible discussion of theoretical principles, all highlighted with extensive examples both in and out of a musical context
3. Background of artist in residence, including chart history, reviews, and effects of the artist on popular culture
4. Score study based on performances and songs written or performed by the artist in residence
5. Written exercises for theoretical study
6. Analysis of larger excerpts from both classical and popular literature

Several chapters contain additional materials for study, including the following:

"The Final Note: Real-World Perspective": This section includes an interview with a person currently working in the music business. Each artist answers a series of questions pertaining to either the specifics of the chapter or their journey in music, whether in performing, writing, or industry.

Chapter 1: Sharon Corbitt-House (studio director and artist manager)
Chapter 2: Mark O'Connor (performer, composer, educator)
Chapter 5: Gregg Lohman (drummer for Kellie Pickler)
Chapter 6: Frank Babbitt (violist for Chicago Lyric Opera and Chicago Symphony)
Chapter 7: Layng Martine (songwriter, wrote number 1 song for Elvis Presley)
Chapter 8: Amy Bishop Greene (operations coordinator at Lyric Opera of Chicago)
Chapter 10: Jeff Watson (executive at Warner Brothers Records)
Chapter 13: Renée Fleming (international opera star)
Chapter 14: Pat McMakin (director of operations for Ocean Way Recording Studio)
Chapter 15: Courtney Gregg (general manager at Carnival Publishing)
Appendix 1: Brian Yak and Christa Yak (songwriters and lead singers of For the Fatherless)
Michael Alvarado and Carissa Rae (songwriters and lead singers for Us The Duo)
Ashton Lee (songwriter)
Appendix 2: Sarah Hurst (songwriter)
Jeremy Johnson and Paul Marino (songwriters)
James Isaac Elliot (songwriter and educator)
Tom Douglas (songwriter)
Ben Folds (songwriter and touring musician)
Online Chapter 1: Barbara Hendricks (international opera star)

"Aural Skills Conditioning" (Chapters 1–15): The word *conditioning* is a verb, and in this context, we believe that aural skills acquisition is an active process. The aural skills conditioning sections are found at the end of the first 15 chapters. Each chapter includes exercises in solfège, Takadimi rhythmic counting, melodic and rhythmic dictation, contextual listening, and collaborative performance opportunities. Although aural skills develop slower than written theory, there is enough subject overlap between the parallel chapters of theory and aural skills allowing incorporation of ear training in the classroom. Students are also encouraged to practice on their own by using the audio files made available on the course website.

Composition Projects: Written in a manner to allow students a good deal amount of freedom, these projects encourage students to employ some of the theoretical principles taught in the form of creative composition. Composition is encouraged throughout the text, including improvisation. While only a few formal composition projects are included within the text, students and instructors are urged to create their own composition projects.

Chapter 8: Composition using basic chord progressions and diatonic melodies

Chapter 11: Composition using non-chord tones in the melody, diatonic harmonies, and specified cadences

Chapter 12: Songwriting using secondary dominants and pop melody

Chapter 15: Songwriting/composition using various types of modulations and borrowed chords

Appendix 2: Free songwriting using proper song form. Students are encouraged to co-write using all techniques taught throughout the text.

SUPPLEMENTAL MATERIALS

For Instructors

- **Ancillary Resource Center:** Access a wealth of teaching resources, including an instructor's manual with answers to exercises in the book, sample syllabii, chapter outlines, and more.
- **Music Theory Skill Builder for *Contemporary Musicianship*:** Help your students practice and master basic music theory skills with Oxford's online Music Theory Skill Builder. Specially priced packages are available for this text. Package with text (to come) or order Access Card ISBN 978-0-19-999091-7. Contact your Oxford University Press representative for more information.

For Students

- **Companion Website** (www.oup.com/us/snodgrass) includes additional chapters on extended chords, chromatic chords, modulations, and classical forms; and audio recordings of musical examples from the book
- **Author's YouTube channel** features performances linked to key examples in the text. By watching musical performances on YouTube, students will be encouraged to discuss performance, marketing, and the overall style of each artist presented. The YouTube channel can be accessed via the Companion Website or by entering the author's name and book title in the YouTube search field.

  Playlist 1: Chapters 1–9

  Playlist 2: Chapters 10–14

  Playlist 3: Chapters 15–Appendix 2

  Playlist 4: Supplemental chapters

In rare instances, the YouTube channel may occasionally need to be updated by the author. Oxford University Press cannot guarantee that videos hosted on YouTube will always be available.

- **Music Theory Skill Builder for *Contemporary Musicianship*:** Provides hundreds of exercises in an interactive environment keyed to this text where students can practice and master core concepts that they need for success in Music Theory. A built-in, live grade book allows instructors to track student progress. Music Theory Skill Builder can be packaged with the text for $10.00 (see package ISBNs to come) or purchased separately for $34.95. To have your bookstore stock individual access cards for separate purchase, order Music Theory Skill Builder Access Card ISBN 978-0-19-999091-7.

ACKNOWLEDGMENTS

I am extremely grateful to the many people who helped in the development of this book. Special appreciation goes to the many instructors who reviewed the initial prospectus of this text, including the following:

Patricia Burt, *Valparaiso University*
Robert Chamberlin, *Webster University*
Mark Crawford, *Tennessee State University*
Christine Gengaro, *Los Angeles City College*
Celinda Hallbauer, *Central Texas College*
Donna Ham, *South Plains College*
Richard Hoffman, *Belmont University*
Luke Hubley, *Houston Community College*
Rebecca Jemian, *University of Louisville*
Brenda Luchsinger, *Alabama State University*
Shafer Mahoney, *Hunter College CUNY* and *The Juilliard School*
Paul Musso, *University of Colorado–Denver*
Scott Phillips, *University of Alabama at Birmingham*
David Runner, *Milligan College*
Katherine Strand, *Indiana University*
Adriana Tapanes-Inojosa, *Harold Washington College*
Bryan Heath Vercher, *Lamar State College–Port Arthur*
Mark Zanter, *Marshall University*

I am indebted to my editor Richard Carlin, who took a chance on an idea that was a bit different from conventional theory textbooks on the market. He has been an exceptional guide in assisting with copyrights, overall scope, and layout of this project. Editorial assistant Meredith Keffer and project editor Marianne Paul have been exceptional in assisting me with copyrights, editing, and permissions. I appreciate their attention to detail, quick responses, and dedication to this project.

My appreciation goes to the University Research Council at Appalachian State University for their financial support of this project and to members of the graduate school and Dr. Edelma Huntley for their commitment to the Graduate Research Associate and Mentoring program. Specific mention should be given to The Hubbard Center for Faculty Development and my scholarly writing team of Gordon Hensley, Scott Rice, Ben Strickland, and Gail York, who supported me in the early stages of this manuscript. I am grateful for the financial support from the Textbook and Academic Authors Association to cover some costs of copyrights. I am indebted to the dean of the Hayes School of Music, Dr. William Pelto, for his endorsement of a semester-long sabbatical and his constant excitement and belief in my research agenda.

Many students and alumni have helped to compile information, locate musical examples, edit early manuscripts, and finalize copyrights for this text. I am forever humbled by their willingness to work alongside me to see this project to completion. My heartfelt thanks and appreciation go to David Wilson, Alex Boatright, Sean McBride, Cam Haas, RJ Wuagneux, Will Fortune, Rachel Mullins, Alex Alberti, Kenneth Kennedy, AJ McCurry, Elizabeth Chapa, Georgina Welch, Aaron Saidizand, and Brooke Bacot. I also am grateful for the talented performers who took the time to provide audio recordings for the aural skills exercises, including Tyler Stark, Oran Dickens, Erica Spear, Patrick Jones, David Marvel, Molly Reid, Neil Shaw, Alex Travers, Stephen Taperek, Nora Naughton, David Wilson, and recording engineer Greg Herndon.

Other individuals have been invaluable in terms of helping me to make connections with members of the music industry, connections I would not have been able to make without their assistance. Many thanks to Keith Mason of Belmont University, Lynsey Delp and Amy Little of Lifeway Worship, Lewis Jones at the University of Miami, and Joseph Howard at Hal Leonard Publishing.

One of the greatest experiences in writing this text has been in the conversations with the music professionals and others in the field. I am forever changed by their words and their experiences. My gratitude and admiration goes to the SaraCare Fund, Mark O'Connor, Bob Crumwell, Ashton Smith, Barbara Hendricks, Sharon Corbitt-House, Paul Batsel, Gregg Lohman, Layng Martine, Jeff Watson, Frank Babbitt, Amy Bishop Greene, Pat McMakin, Courtney Gregg, Brian Yak, Christa Yak, Michael Alvarado, Carissa Rae Alvarado, James Isaac Elliot, Sarah Hurst, Tom Douglas, Matt Faulkenbury, Paul Marino, Jeremy Johnson, Renée Fleming, and Ben Folds.

Without the encouragement and support of my friends, this project would never have been realized. My gratefulness is extended to Reeves Shulstad, Lisa Runner, Mary Gayle Greene, Steve Laitz, William Harbinson, Tom Licata, Hannah Price, Amy Bishop Greene, Lowell White, Andy Page, Scott Wynne, and Nick Webb. I must also give special thanks to the most astounding circle of cyber colleagues who have guided me throughout this entire project with gracious wisdom and laughter, including Melissa Hoag, Jena Root, Leigh Van Handel, Barbara Wallace, Cynthia Gonzales, Jana Millar, Jan Miyake, Charlene Baughan Romano, Elizabeth Sayrs, and Nicole Molumby.

I was first encouraged to write this book by students enrolled in the music industry program in the Hayes School of Music at Appalachian State University. It took me over 6 years to better understand their needs and to develop a curriculum that had them excited about musicianship. My thanks goes out to all of my MIS students, past, present, and future. My strongest encourager was Adam Sensenbrenner, alumnus and current music industry executive. Adam worked with me to develop the initial prospectus for Oxford University Press and has been invaluable in terms of helping me to think clearly about the pedagogical needs of today's music student.

Four students worked beside me through the many phases of this project. For each of them I must give special recognition. I am indebted to Meredith Anderson for helping me to choose and analyze music, Sarah Renshaw for helping me to select pictures and develop the YouTube channel, Molly Reid for writing and assisting me with all of the aural skills units, and Bradley Green for assisting with analysis and notation of all of the graphics. This was a true team effort, and your enthusiastic spirits and your excitement for learning and music forever humble me. Thank you for being an essential part of this experience.

Finally, I am grateful to my family, who always support me in my efforts, both inside and out of the classroom. My parents, Richard and Linda Sterling, instilled within me a love of music from a very early age. My mother would rock me to sleep each night singing the greatest hits of James Taylor. It was also my mother who read to me excerpts from Beverly Sills's book *Bubbles* before I could really read. My father would drive me to classical voice lessons while we listened to the Eagles, Billy Joel, Garth Brooks, and Michael Jackson. Throughout my childhood, my parents encouraged me to explore all genres of music and for that I am eternally grateful. I will forever be indebted to them for filling our home with music.

My husband, Greg, and daughter Katie bring an immense amount of joy to my life. I am thankful for a husband who encourages my passion for teaching, and I appreciate his calm disposition in times of excitement and stress. My daughter Katie has taught me more about priorities and love than anyone before. I will always take a moment away from writing in order to dance with her and experience pure happiness.

Ernest Hemingway once said, "It is good to have an end to journey toward; but it is the journey that matters, in the end." The writing of this book has been in itself a journey, one for which I am deeply grateful.

CONTEMPORARY MUSICIANSHIP

CHAPTER 1

THE BASICS OF PITCH AND RHYTHMIC NOTATION

Artist in Residence: The Music of the Movies

Chapter Objectives

- Identify pitches when given treble, bass, and C clefs
- Define and recognize all accidentals
- Notate and recognize whole and half steps
- Identify note and rest values
- Insert barlines in order to show correct meter

WEBSITE

VIDEO TRACK 1

Music has the ability to evoke emotions of hope, patriotism, anger, love, and fear, among others. It is safe to say that every emotion has been expressed in music at some point in time. Take a few minutes to watch the opening scene from *The Shining*: the first time, watch the clip with the sound off; the second time, watch with the audio.

The scene opens with a beautiful lake surrounded by mountains. A Volkswagen Beetle weaves through the dense forest and the rocky cliffs. The background music could easily be "America the Beautiful" or "Holiday Road." However, this is Stephen King's *The Shining*, and the use of "Dies Irae" alerts the audience that this is not going to end well for the man in the car.

The "Dies Irae," or "Day of Wrath," melody is taken from a 13th-century Latin hymn used in the Roman Catholic Mass for the Dead. Talk about spooky! It has been used extensively in music, including clear shout-outs in Berlioz's *Symphonie Fantastique* and

Holst's *The Planets*. For fun, listen to these pieces to hear how each composer integrates the ancient melody.

PITCHES AND CLEFS

The melody of "Dies Irae" is notated on a **staff**, a grid of five lines and four spaces. Noteheads are positioned on the staff in order for a performer to know the exact pitches to perform. Pitches notated higher on the staff are higher in sound, while those lower on the staff produce a lower sound. We use seven letter names to distinguish between each of the pitches: A, B, C, D, E, F, and G (the musical alphabet). The **clef**, found at the beginning of each staff, alerts the performer as to the specific placement of one pitch.

There are three main clefs used in music notation: treble clef, bass clef, and C clef.

The **treble clef** is used for higher pitches and identifies the pitch G as being on the second line. It is sometimes identified as the G clef. Notice how the treble clef actually wraps around the second line.

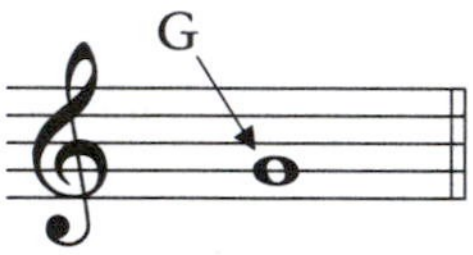

The **bass clef** is used for lower pitches and is sometimes known as the F clef. Notice how the two dots are located above and below the line indicating the pitch F.

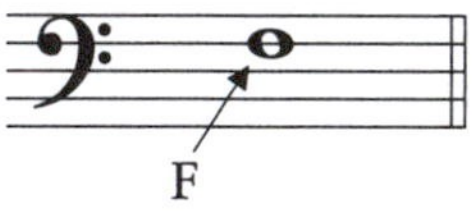

C clefs were some of the earliest clefs in music notation and identify the location of the pitch commonly identified as middle C. They may occur on any of the five lines of the staff, but the following three are the most common.

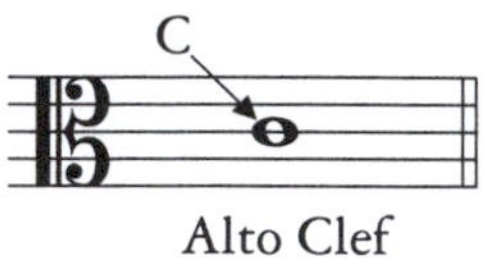

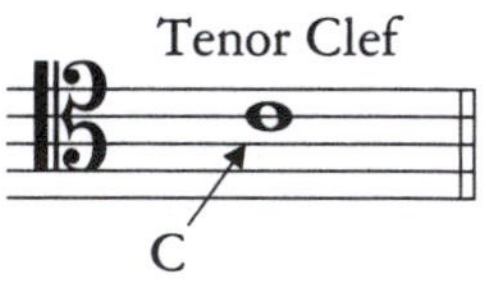

Knowing this, it is now relatively simple to figure out the names of the pitches used in the "Dies Irae" melody. Because the bass clef is given, we are able to find the location of the pitch F. The names of the other pitches are based on this placement. Study the names of the pitches in the bass clef, and then relate these to the "Dies Irae" melody.

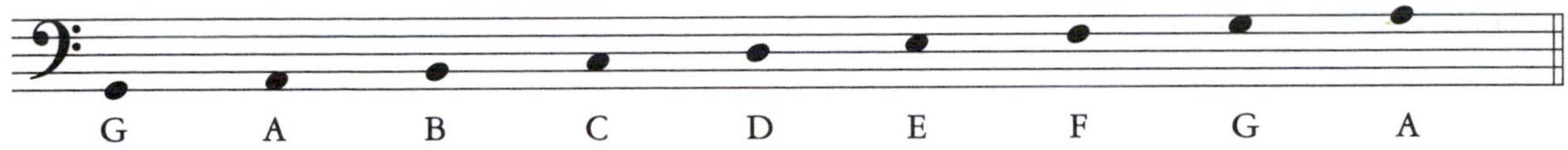

THE GRAND STAFF AND OCTAVE IDENTIFICATION

Most music, unlike "Dies Irae," includes instruments or voices that use both the pitches of the bass clef and treble clef simultaneously. The grouping together of these staves is called the **grand staff**. The pitch C is placed in the middle of the two staves and notated on a ledger line. Ever heard of middle C? Well, that's how this particular pitch got its name!

When you look at the grand staff, you can see several instances where the pitch C can be identified. This is why we use something called octave identification in order to specify a particular register. The octave identification number changes each time the C is repeated in a new octave. All pitches found within that octave use the same number designation. Middle C is always labeled as C4. The first graphic below shows all of the octave registers; the second shows the names for various pitches, including octave identifications.

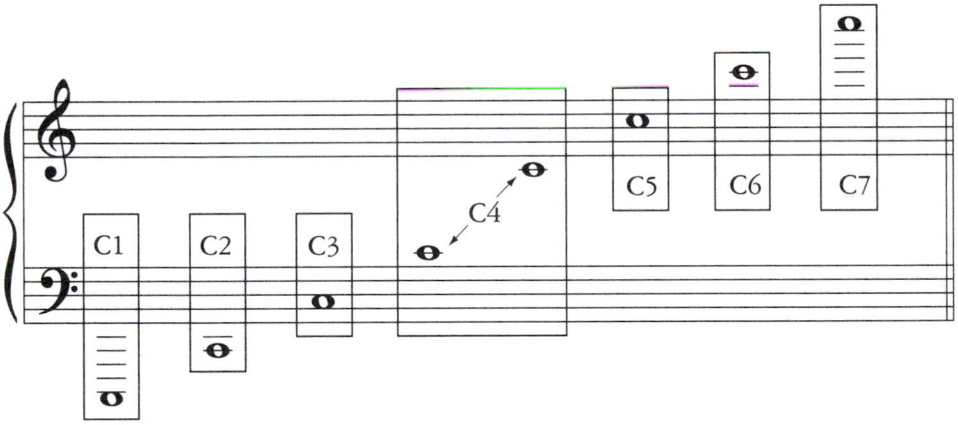

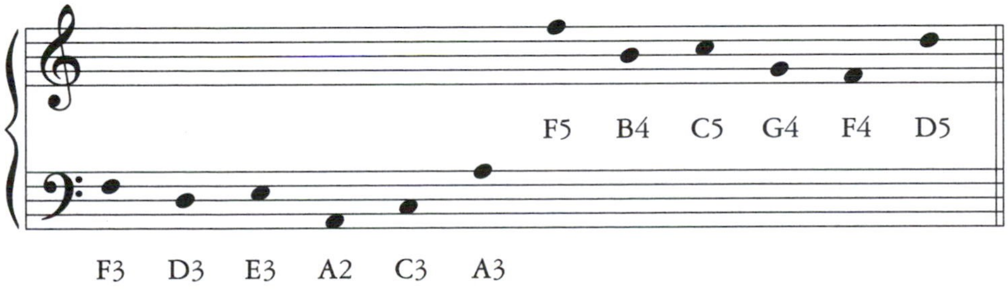

LEDGER LINES

Music would be pretty limited if it contained only the pitches notated within the grand staff's lines and spaces. We can extend the staff up or down to accommodate pitches outside the standard five-line staff by using **ledger lines**. Study the following grand staff in order to better understand the identification and placement of ledger lines.

The Truman Show (1998) chronicles the life of a man who is unaware that his every move is being filmed as a reality show. The film was nominated for several Oscars, including Best Director. In this excerpt, a light falls from the sky, and Truman is becoming increasingly aware that things are not exactly as they seem. As Truman begins his commute to work, the radio station begins to play Wolfgang Amadeus Mozart's "Rondo Alla Turca" from *Piano Sonata No. 11 in A Major* to help "calm down its listeners."

WEBSITE

VIDEO TRACK 2

The notation of the excerpt is shown below. Notice that the music for the piano is written on the grand staff. Several pitches are identified for you, both in terms of pitch name and octave identification.

Mozart, *Sonata No. 11 in A Major*, K. 331, Mvt. III

THE KEYBOARD

The standard keyboard is based on the seven pitches of the musical alphabet: A, B, C, D, E, F, and G. The black keys and white keys are arranged to help to identify the pitch placement on the keyboard. In any octave, the pitch C is always to the left of two black keys, while the pitch F is always to the left of the three black keys.

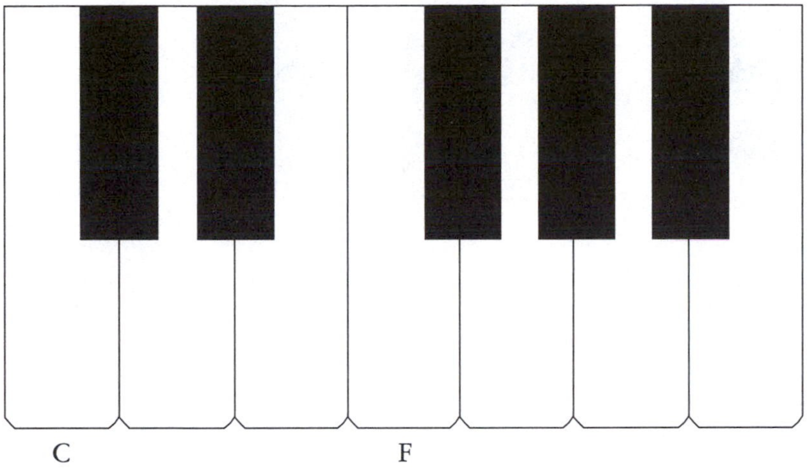

The other pitches are arranged sequentially over the white keys based on these two placements.

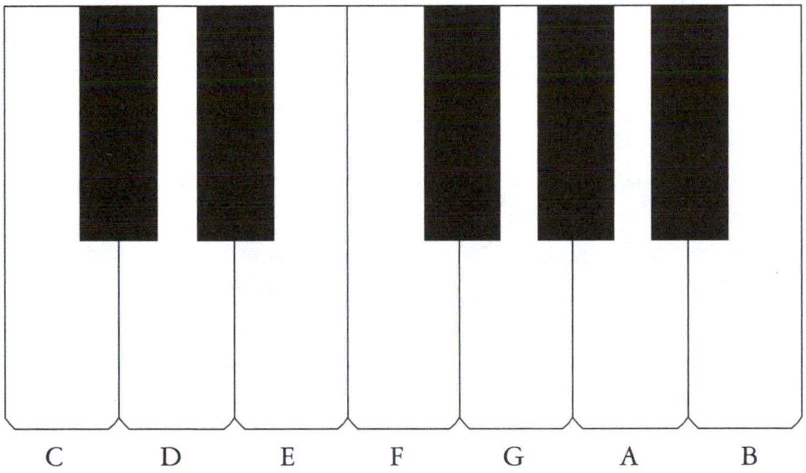

ACCIDENTALS

You may also notice in the Mozart example that several pitches are marked with accidentals. **Accidentals** are symbols that alter a pitch by a half or whole step. All of the possible accidentals are listed below.

Accidental	𝄫	♭	♮	♯	𝄪
Name	Double Flat	Flat	Natural	Sharp	Double Sharp
Action	Lowers a pitch a whole step	Lowers a pitch a half step	Cancels out an accidental	Raises a pitch a half step	Raises a pitch a whole step

Let's look at a keyboard to help us better understand this concept. In Western music, a **half step** is the shortest distance between two pitches; it can also be thought of as two adjacent keys on the keyboard. All of the black keys are named in relationship to the white keys in terms of half steps.

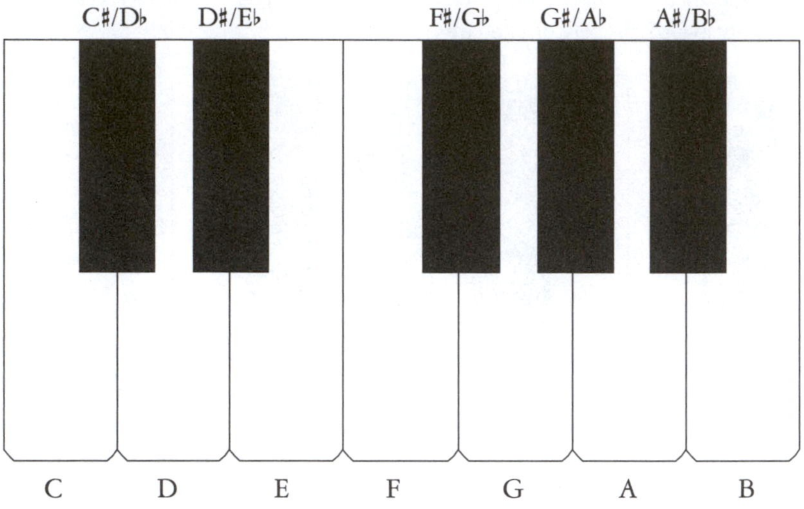

Using the keyboard, we can determine that F to F♯ is a half step, D to D♯ is a half step, and so on. Within each octave there are two half steps found on white keys, E–F and B–C. A **whole step** is comprised of two half steps so F–G is a whole step, and E–F♯ is a whole step, as is B–C♯.

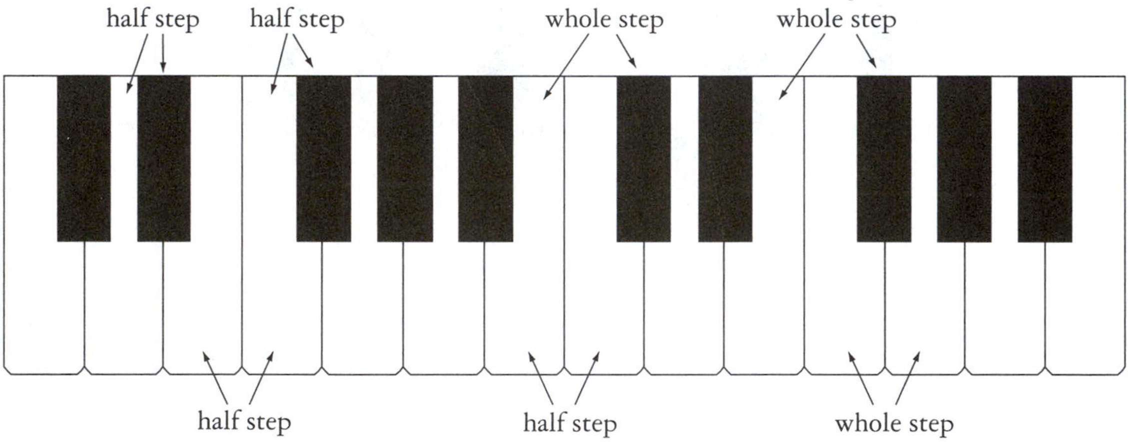

Return to the score for *Sonata No. 11 in A Major,* K. 331. The first accidental notated by Mozart is a G♯. Seeing the sharp, the performer would play the pitch one half step above the G key. Notice how several keys on the keyboard sound exactly the same but are spelled with two different letter names? These are called **enharmonic pitches**, such as C♯ and D♭.

It is important for musicians to have a basic understanding of how the pitches on the staff relate to the pitches on their perspective instrument. The following figure includes various pitches on the staff and their placement on the piano and guitar.

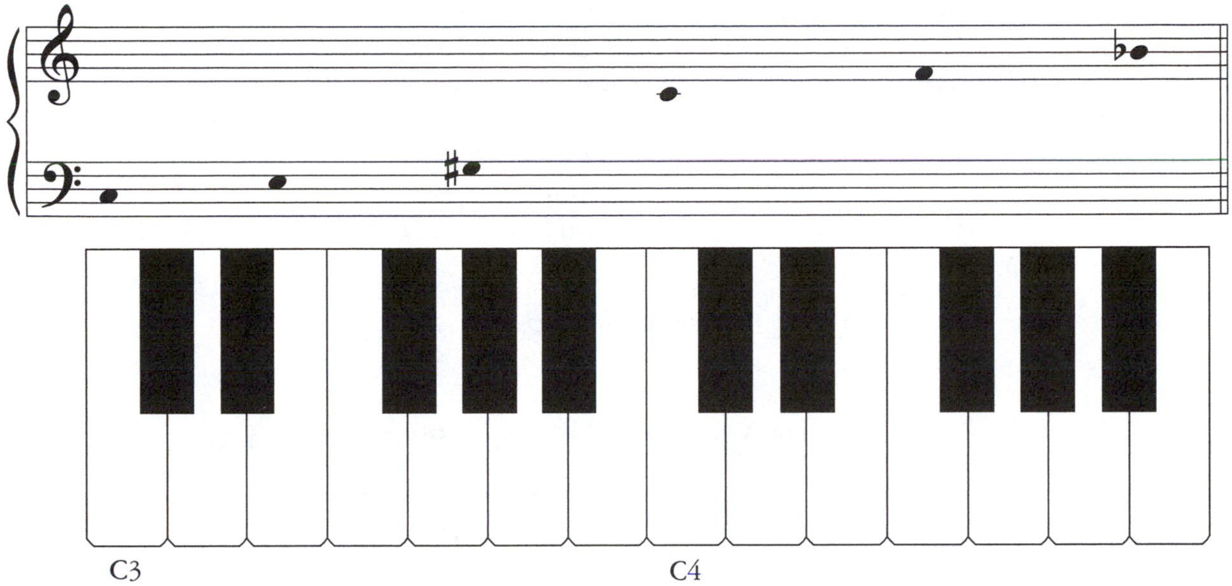

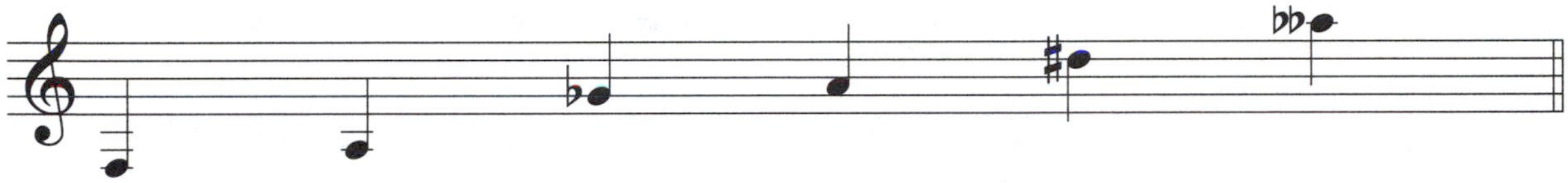

```
E ---------------------------------------------------------------------- 3 -------------
B ---------------------------------------------------------- 4 ---------(8)-------------
G -------------------------------------------------- 2 ---------(8)---------(12)-------------
D ---------------------------------- 4 ---------(7)---------(13)---------(17)-------------
A ----------------- 0 ---------(9)---------(12)---------(18)---------(21)-------------
E -- 1 --------------------------(14)---------(17)---------(23*)--------------------------
```

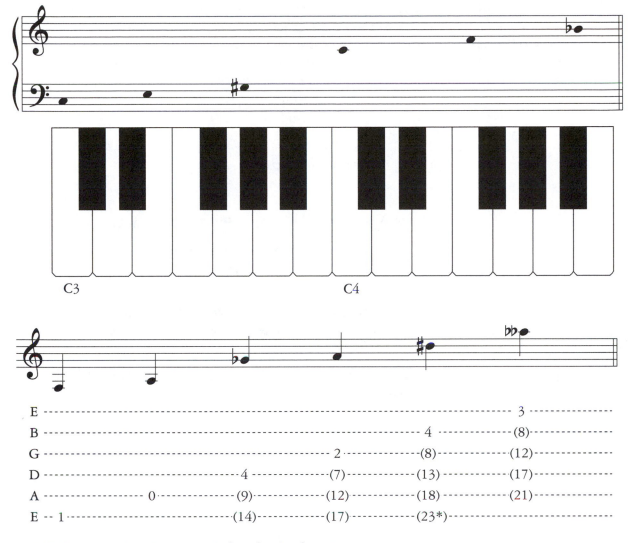

* Only some guitars have enough frets for this fingering.

RHYTHM AND METER

VIDEO TRACK 3

In 2011, it was assumed that *The King's Speech* was going to dominate the Academy Awards. The film ended up winning four Oscars, including Best Picture. Based on the true story of King George VI, the movie chronicles the king's treatment for speech impediment and England's eventual involvement in World War II. In the film's climatic scene, the king is delivering the radio address to millions of listeners around the country declaring war on Nazi Germany. The music in the background is taken from the second movement of Ludwig van Beethoven's *Symphony No. 7.* How does this particular composition add to the emotion of this scene?

The main melody almost sounds like a slow march, and the beats are regular and in some ways predictable. Tap along with the music as you watch the excerpt. What you are tapping is the beat. Rhythm is measured in terms of beats, or a regular pulse. The **meter** is the grouping of strong and weak beats, while the **tempo** is the speed of the beat. These patterns are grouped together and collected into measures, separated by barlines.

We use various types of noteheads and rests to indicate different rhythms, whether indicating sounds (notes) or silence (rests). All of the notes and rests are in proportion to one another. The largest single note value used most in music today is the whole note. Study the charts below to better understand the proportion of each note value. Durations of silence (rests) share the same value as their corresponding note value.

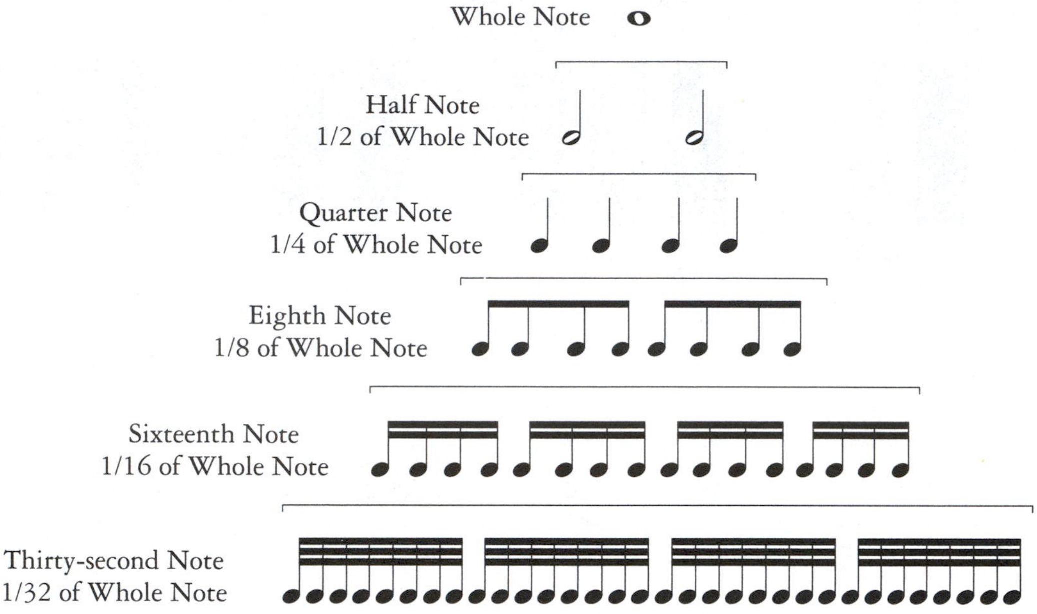

Name of note/rest	Note	Rest	Note Value
Whole	𝅝	𝄻	1
Half	𝅗𝅥	𝄼	1/2 of whole note
Quarter	♩	𝄽	1/4 of whole note
Eighth	♪	𝄾	1/8 of whole note
Sixteenth	𝅘𝅥𝅯	𝄿	1/16 of whole note
Thirty-second	𝅘𝅥𝅰	𝅀	1/32 of whole note

So how do we know how long to hold each rest or pitch and the organization of the meter? Well, that is indicated by the time signature. The **time signature** is a pair of numbers that indicate the meter, what note value = 1 beat, and the number of beats per measure. We separate these measures using barlines.

SIMPLE METER

As you were tapping along to the music from *The King's Speech*, you probably noticed that you could divide your taps into two equal parts. The basic premise for music in **simple meter** is just that: the main beat can be divided into two equal parts. The top number of a time signature in simple meter will typically be 2, 3, or 4.

Study the time signatures shown. In simple meter, the top number tells the performer how many beats occur per measure, while the bottom number indicates which note value receives 1 beat. All of the other note values are in proportion to the note value indicated by the bottom number.

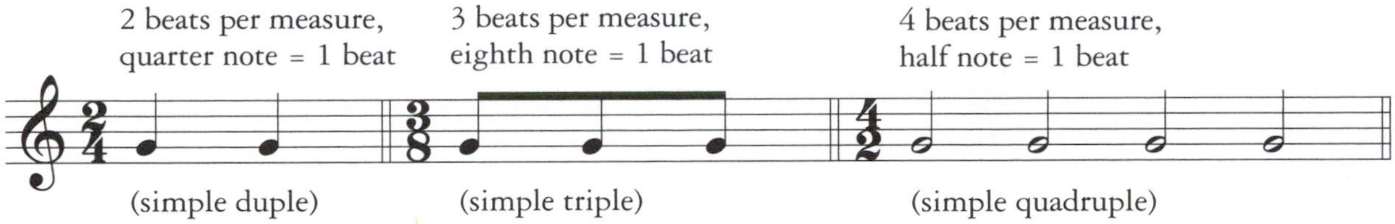

Study the score excerpt from the second movement of Beethoven's *Symphony No. 7*. The time signature tells us that there are two beats per measure and that the quarter note is receiving the beat. That means that the second violins in measure 27 would play the pitch E for 1 full beat followed by a pair of Es for a half a beat each (2 beats total for the measure). A barline precedes the first beat of every measure, helping the performer to clearly see the beat groupings; in this case, 2 beats per measure.

VIDEO TRACK 3

Beethoven, *Symphony No. 7*, Mvt. II

There are several other notational issues you might notice in the excerpt that deserve discussion.

Dotted notes: A **dotted note (dot)** extends the value of a note or rest by one-half of its original value. Take, for instance, the dotted quarter note in measure 29 in the cello line. The quarter note is 1 beat, and the dot adds ½ of a beat. The total duration of the pitch D4 would be for 1½ beats.

Beaming: A **beam** is used to connect two or more note values that contain flags. Look at measure 32 in the viola line. The note values used are all eighth notes, but the pairs are all beamed together in order to convey the two beat groups.

COMPOUND METER

Compositions or songs written in **compound meter** have a beat that is divided into three equal parts. The main beat in compound meter is always a dotted note because dotted notes divide naturally into three equal parts.

The top number of a time signature for a piece of music written in compound meter is typically a 6, 9, or 12; however, the top number indicates the number of divisions in the measure, not the number of beats. The bottom number is the note value receiving the division, not the actual beat.

To better understand the actual note value receiving the beat, follow this formula:

1. Divide the top number by 3 to determine the number of beats per measure.
2. Double the note value on the bottom and add a dot. This note value is the true beat.

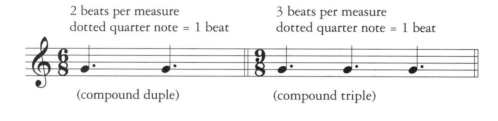

2 beats per measure
dotted quarter note = 1 beat

3 beats per measure
dotted quarter note = 1 beat

(compound duple)

(compound triple)

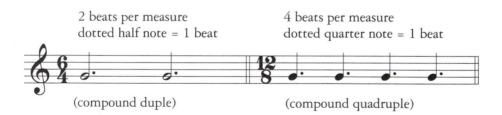

2 beats per measure
dotted half note = 1 beat

4 beats per measure
dotted quarter note = 1 beat

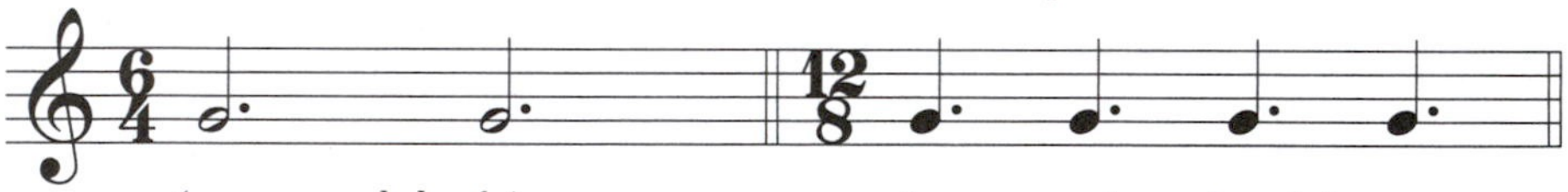

(compound duple)

(compound quadruple)

"Belle Nuit" from Jacques Offenbach's opera *Les Contes d'Hoffmann* has been used in many TV commercials and films. The director's choice to use it in this particular scene in *La Vita È Bella* is quite deliberate because there is absolutely no dialogue and all we hear is the music for the first 2 minutes. We know exactly what is happening without any subtitles or text. How does this particular piece evoke a sense of hope in the characters?

WEBSITE
VIDEO TRACK 4

The time signature tells the performer that there are six eighth notes per measure, but the main beat is the dotted quarter note, of which there are two per measure. As you listen to the excerpt, try to tap both the main beat and the three divisions per beat.

Offenbach, "Belle Nuit" from *Les Contes d'Hoffmann*

Watch how movie directors programmed Claude Debussy's "Clair de Lune" in *Ocean's 11* (2001) while you follow along with the score. The time signature indicates that there are three beats per measure and the dotted quarter note is the main unit of beat. This excerpt is not as easy to "tap along to." Why is that? What liberties does the orchestra take in relation to the piano reduction shown in the following figure?

WEBSITE
VIDEO TRACK 5

Debussy, "Clair de Lune" from *Suite Bergamasque*, Mvt. III

Debussy, "Clair de Lune" from *Suite Bergamasque,* Mvt. III *(continued)*

THE FINAL SCENE

Let's put all of this new knowledge into context by looking at two moments in cinematic history that are both compelling and uplifting. Few would disagree that without the addition of the music, the scene would be as riveting.

The Shawshank Redemption (1994) tells the story of Andy, a young man who was imprisoned for the murder of his wife. After the warden learns of Andy's expertise in financial matters, Andy is able to work toward building a library at the prison. One of the first records to be donated to the library is Mozart's *The Marriage of Figaro.* Andy is so mesmerized by the music that he plays it over the prison yard speakers. For one brief minute, the inmates are transported to another place. However, this act of defiance lands Andy in solitary confinement. He never says it, but he probably thinks it was totally worth it.

WEBSITE

VIDEO TRACK 6

Follow along with the excerpt as you watch the film clip. How does the director's choice of song fit so well with what these prisoners need to hear? Why was this one of the most compelling sections of the entire film?

Several pitches and other important rhythmic elements have been marked in the score. Pay careful attention to the beaming, which clearly identifies the main unit of beat. A new musical notation called a tie is present in this excerpt. A **tie** connects two noteheads of the same pitch. Tied pitches are held for the duration of both pitches, but only the first pitch is struck.

Mozart, "Sull'aria" from *Le Nozze di Figaro*

Titanic (1997) was one of the most expensive movies ever made in the 20th century, grossing nearly $659 million dollars. The main score of the film was composed by James Horner, but there is one scene from the movie that includes the hymn "Nearer My God to Thee."

Why was this hymn chosen? It has been said that the musicians in the *Titanic* band decided to stay on the ship until the very end, playing upbeat classical music to help calm the nerves

VIDEO TRACK 7

as passengers entered the lifeboats. Many passengers have stated to media outlets that the final song was "Nearer My God to Thee." James Cameron, the director of *Titanic*, chose to include this moment in the 1997 film. Follow along with the transcription as each member of the string quartet enters into the piece. The time signature of this particular excerpt is $\frac{4}{4}$, which is often abbreviated a capital C, for common time. Each measure contains four beats, and the quarter note receives one beat. Several musical elements have been marked in the score for you.

Sarah Flower Adams, "Nearer My God to Thee"

Reviewing Chapter Objectives

- Identify pitches when given treble, bass, and C clefs (pages 3–4).
- Define and recognize all accidentals (page 5).
- Notate and recognize whole and half steps (page 6).
- Identify note and rest values (page 8).
- Insert barlines in order to show correct meter (pages 9–10).

EXERCISES

I. Identify the following pitches using both pitch name and octave identification. Pay careful attention to the changing clefs.

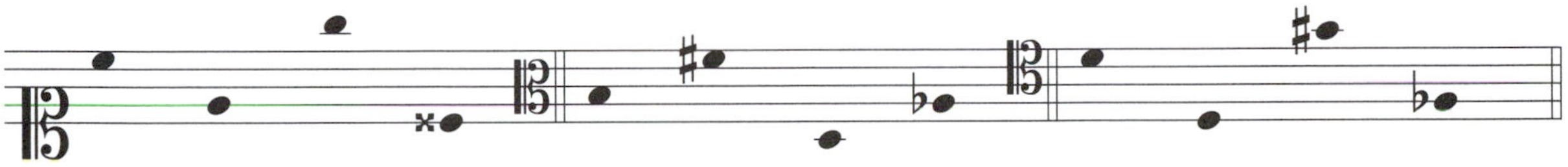

II. Notate the following pitches on the staff when given the pitch name and octave identification.

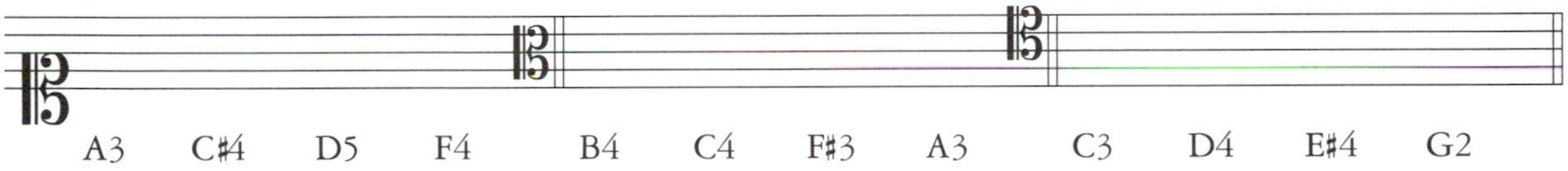

III. Notate the following whole and half steps above or below the given pitch. Use the keyboard in this chapter for reference as needed.

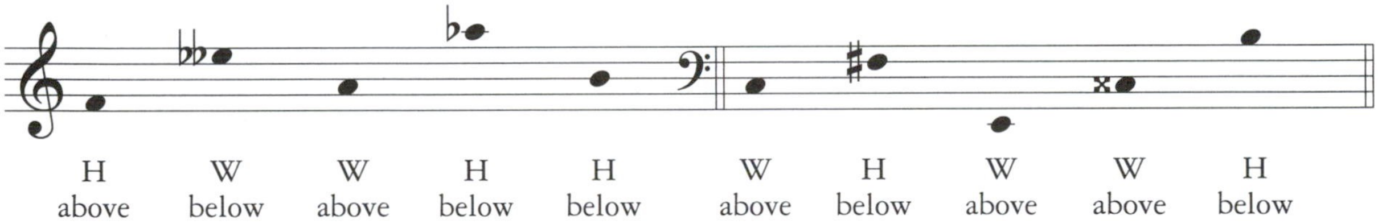

IV. Given the keyboard and pitches, draw lines from the pitches to their correct placement on the keyboard.

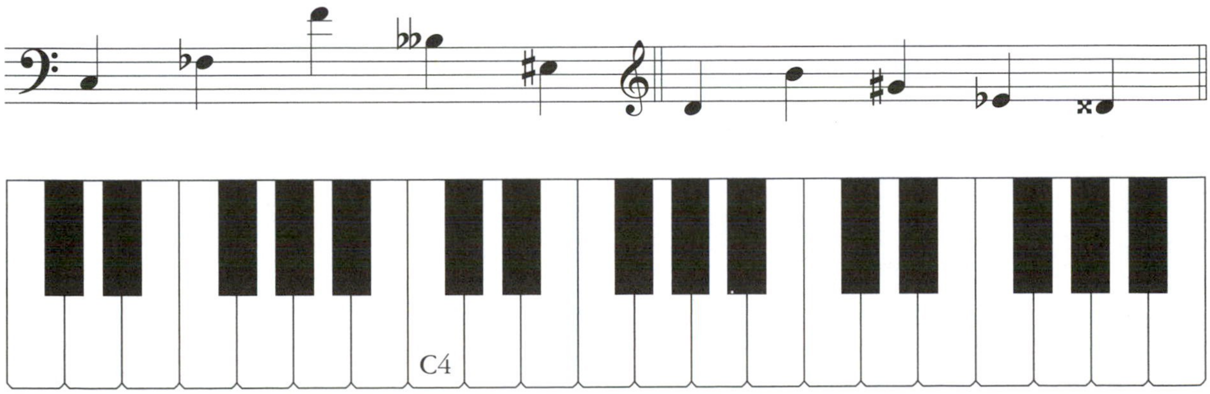

V. A variety of time signatures are given below. Identify the time signature as simple or compound and the meter (duple, triple, quadruple). Identify the number of beats per measure, and identify what note value is equal to one beat.

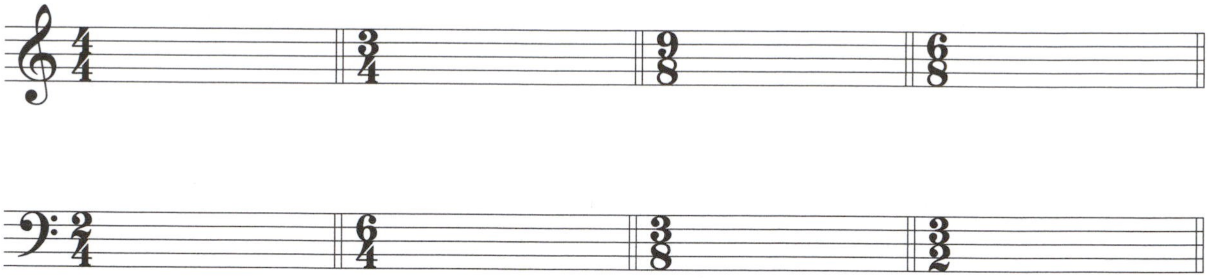

VI. Insert barlines in order to show correct meter. Be sure to include a double barline at the end of the line in order to complete the final measure.

ANALYSIS

Study the following pieces from two award-winning films. After you watch the YouTube excerpts, answer the questions that follow each example.

Chopin, "Ballade No. 1 in G Minor" from *The Pianist*

1. What is the difference between the first and second time signature (m. 6 and m. 8)? Be specific.
2. How many beats total is the pitch B♭ in measures 7 and 8?
3. Identify all of the pitches in measure 8 (pitch name and octave identification).
4. What is the definition of the tempo marking moderato?
5. What rests are used in measure 8?
6. Identify all of the pitches in measure 16 (pitch name and octave identification).
7. What is so compelling about this particular song in terms of its placement in the film scene?[1]

WEBSITE

VIDEO TRACK 8

[1]A full video clip of the scene is available at http://vimeo.com/27375584.

Johann Strauss, *The Blue Danube* from *2001: A Space Odyssey*

1. What is the time signature of the excerpt? Give the number of beats per measure and the note value that receives the beat.
2. How long (in total beats) will the pitches G4 and A4 be sustained in measures 50–52?
3. Identify all of the pitches in measure 46 (pitch name and octave identification).
4. Identify all of the pitches in measure 71 (pitch name and octave identification).
5. Identify all of the pitches in measure 75 (pitch name and octave identification).
6. Is this the composition you would have selected for the opening credits? Why or why not?

WEBSITE

VIDEO TRACK 9

AURAL SKILLS CONDITIONING 1

In 2009, an international open call was sent out to young symphony musicians encouraging them to upload an audition video to YouTube for the chance to perform with the YouTube Symphony. The YouTube community voted on the finalists one month later, and winners were invited to perform together at Carnegie Hall in New York City. In 2011, the process was repeated and the live stream of the YouTube Symphony's Grand Finale concert at the Sydney Opera House was the largest live stream YouTube ever produced. Amazing! Countless articles and books have been written about the power of YouTube since its inception in 2005. What are your thoughts on the power of YouTube in regard to the musician and artist?

Listen to the 2011 YouTube Symphony playing Benjamin Britten's *The Young Person's Guide to the Orchestra*. We will focus on the finale for this exercise, starting at 13:53. Beginning with the piccolo, each section of the orchestra enters with the featured melody line in quick succession. Keep the chart handy as you listen to the finale, listening carefully to the timbre, or the quality of musical sound, of each new instrument as it enters.

WEBSITE

VIDEO TRACK 10

Time	Featured Instrument
13:53	Piccolo
13:58	Flute
14:07	Oboe
14:14	Clarinet
14:23	Bassoon
14:35	Violin
14:42	Viola
14:49	Cellos
14:54	Bass
15:05	Harp
15:18	French horn
15:23	Trumpet
15:31	Trombone/tuba
15:38	Percussion
15:47–end	Tutti

Now, go back and listen to the entire piece from the beginning.

1. Make note of any times when the music surprised you. Describe what you hear that sticks out.
2. 00:29—The character of the music changes here. Describe the differences you hear between this and the opening theme. Do all of the same instruments continue to play? What about dynamic contrast? How would you describe the change in character or mood? How is this achieved?
3. 00:57—Which instrument is featured here? How does this instrument provide a contrast to previous music?
4. 01:37—Britten introduces the percussion section. Which important orchestral instrument is shown at 01:37? How many players of this instrument are included in a typical orchestra?
5. 02:20—What instrument is featured here? Compare the sound and appearance of this instrument to the one featured at 02:45. Which instrument is this? How is

the music played by the first set of instruments different in style from the music played at 02:45?

6. 08:35—The harp is often thought of as having an angelic sound. Do you agree with that description? How is this special sound used in today's popular music?
7. 10:23—This lively instrument brings the music out of a calm slumber. What other types of music of the 20th and 21st centuries feature this instrument?
8. 13:53—Does the finale of Britten's piece successfully bring closure to the music? Why or why not? What do you like or dislike about it?

Introduction to Reading Rhythm

Rhythm is a driving force in all music, from Bach to Beyoncé. We hear and feel the rhythm as we listen or dance to music. So why do we need to read or notate rhythm, anyway? Communication between musicians, engineers, and producers is an important aspect of the music business. It is important that anyone involved in the industry is able to speak and understand the same language. While there are different systems of counting rhythm, the Takadimi system is quickly gaining respect in both the education and recording worlds. Below is a chart of rhythmic values in simple and compound meter and their corresponding syllables in Takadimi.

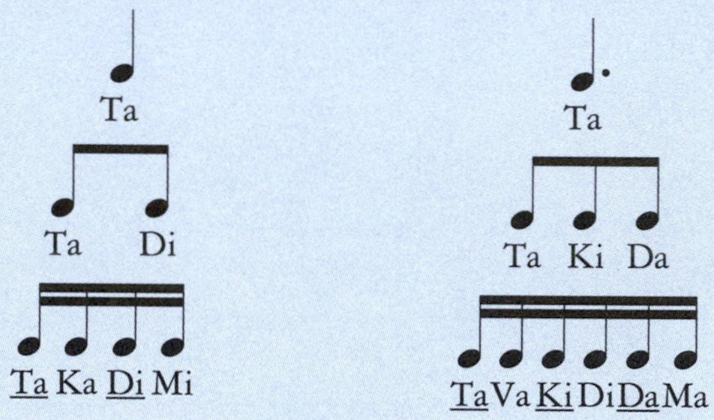

As a class, say the following syllables out loud as you follow along with the notation. Notice the difference between simple and compound meter. For a real challenge, try to conduct the strong beats as you perform!

Simple Meter

Compound Meter

Below are several more rhythmic examples. However, the Takadimi is not written out for you. Challenge yourself to perform these examples on Takadimi, writing in the syllables below the staff as needed.

1. 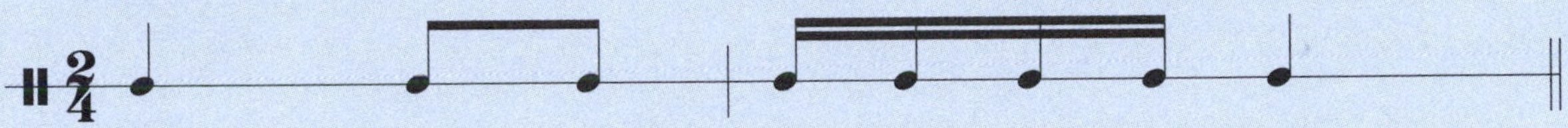

2. 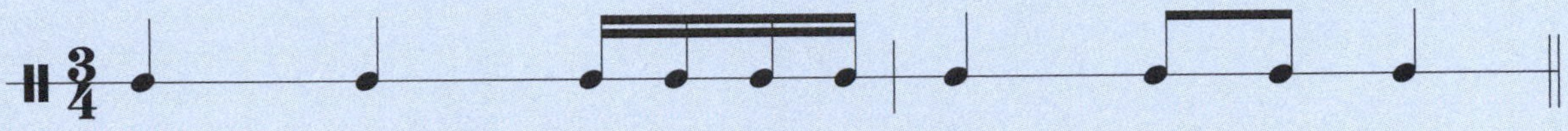

3. 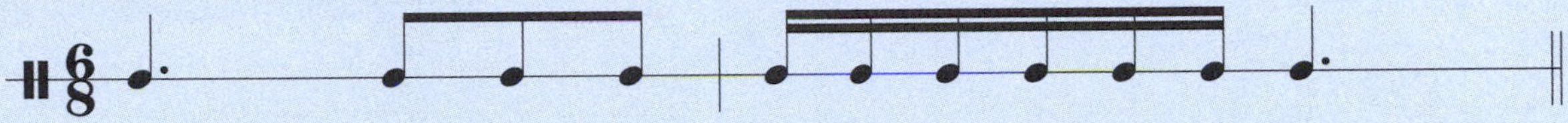

4. 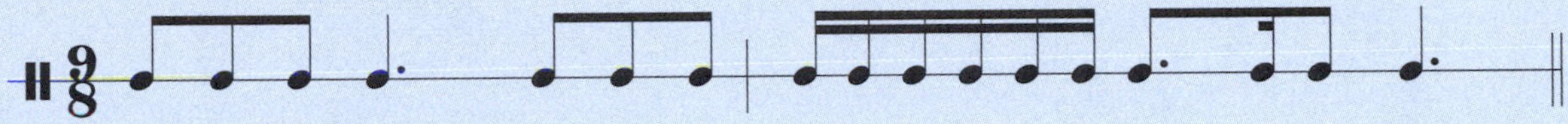

More Practice with Takadimi

To explore the fun of Takadimi, get in groups of two to four students. Each of you will compose two measures of unique rhythms that will become part of the larger group composition. First, pick a time signature that everyone will use. Write your two measures in that time signature on a scratch sheet of paper. Now, everyone will give their two measures to the student to their right. The goal here is to practice saying the syllables aloud in rhythm. One person will begin by performing the Takadimi that their classmate composed, and the rest of the group will perform their Takadimi in succession. Make sure you are counting beats as you wait for your turn, so you come in at the right time. The final product will be a four-, six-, or eight-measure phrase of Takadimi performed seamlessly.

Rhythmic Dictation

Mastering the skill of dictation requires a great deal of practice. There are many popular methods to help the student correctly transcribe a rhythm; however, one of the most effective involves chunking. Think of the rhythms presented in this chapter as patterns. Each beat contains a unique pattern with some beats containing two notes, some three, and some four.

Based on this, we can visualize all of the common beats in simple and compound time in the following manner:

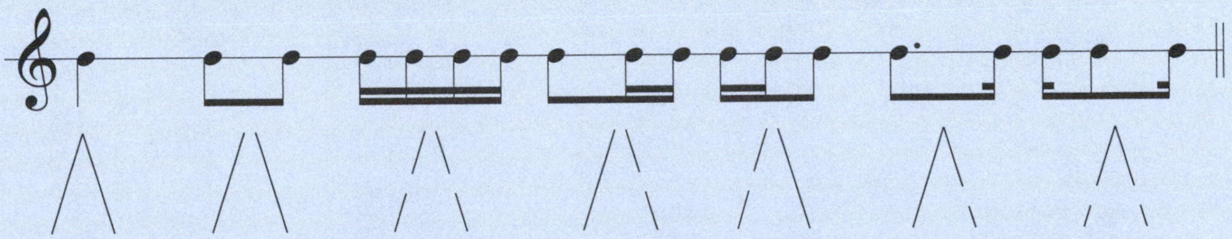

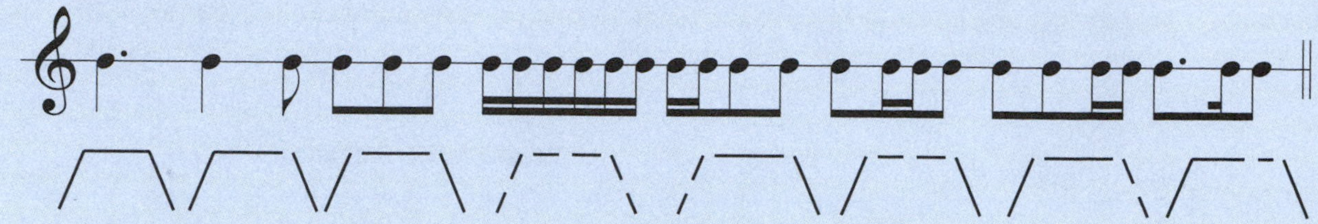

As you listen to a piece of music or a rhythmic line, practice sketching the beats using the shorthand shown above.

A simple meter dictation example might look like this.

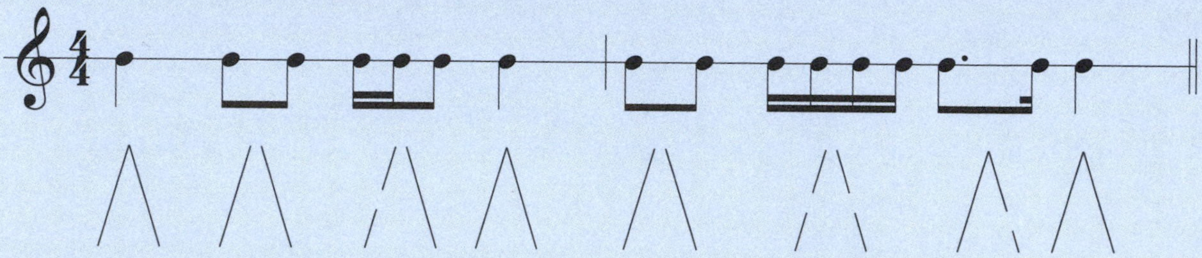

A compound meter dictation example might look like this.

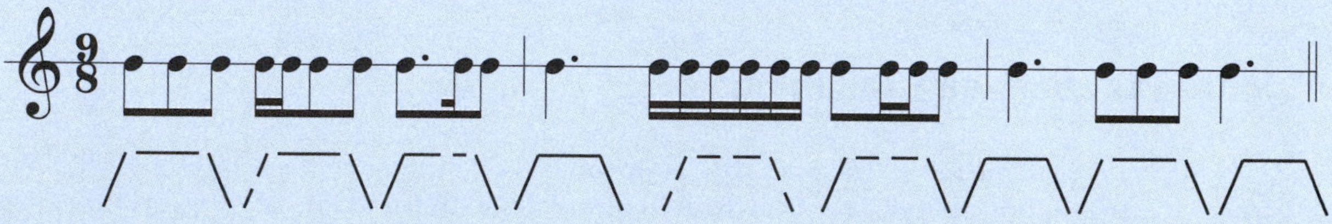

AUDIO TRACKS CH.1 RHYTHMIC DICTATION 1–4

You will hear two-measure examples performed by your instructor or played from the course website. Try quietly tapping along while listening to the melody to make sure you know where the beats are before beginning your sketch. You could even try conducting as you listen! Then, correctly notate the rhythm on the staff.

1. 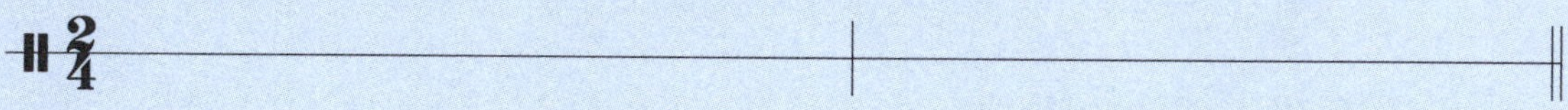

2. 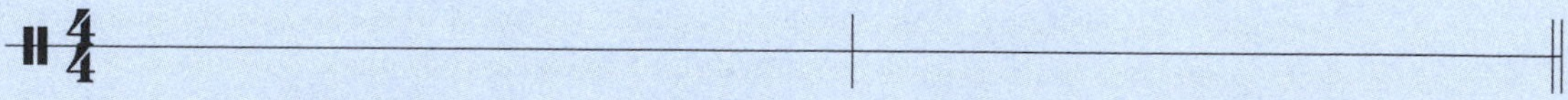

3. 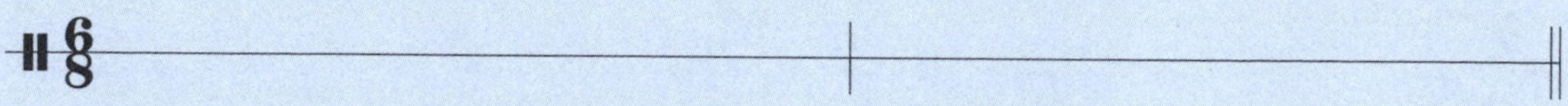

4. 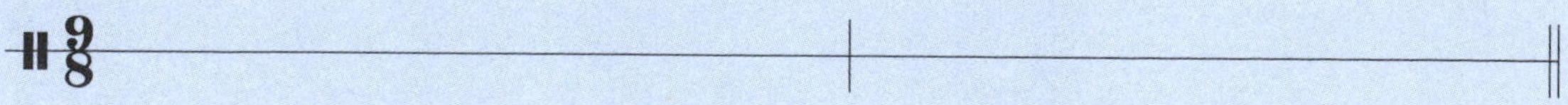

THE FINAL NOTE: REAL-WORLD PERSPECTIVE

Sharon Corbitt-House

STUDIO MANAGER OF GRAND VICTOR SOUND AND CO-MANAGER OF BEN FOLDS

Educational Background

I had one semester of college at a local community college in Arkansas and had a scholarship offer to Delta State University. The college professor talked me into quitting to move to Nashville to pursue music. He told me I could always come back, but I didn't. It is one of my biggest regrets actually. I started singing professionally when I was 13, cut my first album when I was 18. I started working in the music industry at the age of 19, and this next year will be my 30th year. I've been very fortunate to always have a job, whether that be in the management side or recording capacity.

Has the study of music theory and musicianship helped you in your career? If so, how?

I was the senior band president and first chair flutist, so I studied theory in high school, but I could always speak the language. I'm not a musician in the traditional sense, but I know what sounds good. I've always been able to hear when something is off. I've always had an ear for that kind of thing.

Was music always your intended career plan?

This was always my career plan. I know it sounds crazy, but I really knew at the age of three. I remember singing and dancing while my grandmother would play the organ. I would try to play the organ like she did or the guitar like my grandfather did. I just knew. This is my chosen path. I didn't choose it, it chose me. This career path is a beautiful, broken road. You don't choose a path in music, it chooses you.

How did your previous work at other studios in Nashville, including Ocean Way, help to prepare you for this position?

When I first moved to Nashville, I was making $125 a week managing a small studio for Denny Music Group and singing with my own band on the weekends. Once I left the road, I started managing artists in the 90s. I ended up managing a band that recorded at a studio in Memphis called House of Blues. The owner of the House of Blues, Gary Belz, and I got connected. Gary happened to co-own Ocean Way, and when a job opened, he said to me, "I really need someone who has good relationships with people in the industry." At that point, I had been around for awhile and knew lots of people, so I became the PR person for Ocean Way. My management experience allowed me to really be hands on with people that came in to record. I was at Ocean Way for seven successful years. We did everything from *O Brother Where Art Thou?* to Sheryl Crow . . . a lot of records in the early 2000s . . . we were in some way involved with, it seemed like.

After a few years at Sound Kitchen, I got a call from Kris Wilkerson about Ben Folds opening up RCA Studio A, and that he needed someone to come in and get it up and running. I walked into the studio that March of 2009, and I was like "O my gosh, I am home." I was excited about being reconnected with why I got into this business in the first place. I remember reading liner notes of albums that were recorded here, and all I wanted to do was to be in this space with those people. It is the greatest gift ever.

Most significant learning experience of your career.

This business is a feel thing; it isn't anything that you can learn in a textbook. It's part psychology really. Getting people in the right head space, 'cause honestly, like with athletes, you can be the greatest athlete, but if you aren't in the right frame of mind, you aren't going to do well. Same thing with people who are creating. You got to get out of your own way. It's got to be about the greater collective. When I realized that I was one part of this greater collective . . . that's when my career happened.

I believe there is an opportunity for learning in all experiences and I am more aware of that now. You are always learning, evolving, and changing. If you don't continually adapt, you won't survive in this business. I'm learning every day. That is what keeps me excited and engaged. I'm trying to figure out what the next move will be.

Greatest moment of your career so far.

I've had some incredible ones. But I'm always waiting for the next one. I stood in the room when Allison Kraus did "Down to the River to Pray" for *O Brother Where Art Thou?* with a 100+-person choir from the Baptist church. I stood in the room when Ralph Stanley recorded "O Death." I had a moment with Jack Ingram. He did a song called "Goodnight Moon" in the studio at Ocean Way. It was 3 a.m., and we turned down all the lights while he recorded. I flash back and think about it and my hair still stands up. You could just feel the energy in the room. It was just magical. Every day is exciting because of moments like that. You get to stand at the point of creation and watch as this beautiful piece of music is born.

CHAPTER 2

MAJOR SCALES AND KEY SIGNATURES

Artists in Residence: Famous Collaborations

Chapter Objectives

- Notate major scales
- Identify scale degree names
- Identify and notate major key signatures
- Determine scale type used in musical context

It is often said that behind every great person is a bunch of other people. Henry Ford went even further: "Coming together is a beginning, staying together is progress, and working together is success." Think of some great musical collaborations throughout time: Run DMC and Aerosmith, Jimmy Buffet and the Zac Brown Band, Idina Menzel and Kristen Chenoweth in *Wicked*, Jay-Z and Kanye West—the list goes on and on and covers every genre from jazz to rap to classical. Through a quick YouTube search, you can even find Sheryl Crow singing opera with the late Luciano Pavarotti. It's worth a view and a discussion.

WEBSITE

VIDEO TRACK 11

By nature, music is a collaborative effort. Take a moment to watch the arrangement of "Stand by Me" by the group Playing For Change. The video has over seventy million hits and includes musicians and performers from around the world. One of the great things about this video is that it shows the "rawness" of music and how a simple chord progression and melody can be performed by people of different cultures to create something quite unique. In most cases, musicians work with engineers, who work with producers, who work with songwriters, who learned from teachers, who learned from instructors who taught them the basics of music. Music fundamentals, including note and rhythm identification, scales, key signatures, and triads, form the basis for all the vocabulary in musical conversations, whether that be in the orchestra pit or in the recording studio. You *need* to master these skills to find a job in the field. As one professional musician stated, "It is not okay to suck at scales." Okay, point taken. Let's learn and let's master this material.

THE MAJOR SCALE

VIDEO TRACK 12

If you have ever taken any private lessons, you probably have spent a great deal of the lesson focusing on warm-ups. Tedious? Necessary? Yes and yes. For vocalists, this might consist of vowel sounds up and down the scale, while the pianist spends hours perfecting the fingering for each scale. Marie and Berlioz were especially focused on their practice in the film *The Aristocats.* Watch the short excerpt on the YouTube channel. As the cartoon kitties acknowledge, "Every truly cultured music student knows you must learn your scales and your arpeggios."

What is a **scale** anyways? A scale can basically be defined as an arrangement of pitches into a series of half and whole steps.

If we arrange the pitches in half steps within an octave, the **chromatic scale** is formed. Segments of this scale are used throughout jazz and musical theater and many times are found in extended cadenzas in classical music. Sharps are used on the ascent, and flats are used on the descent.

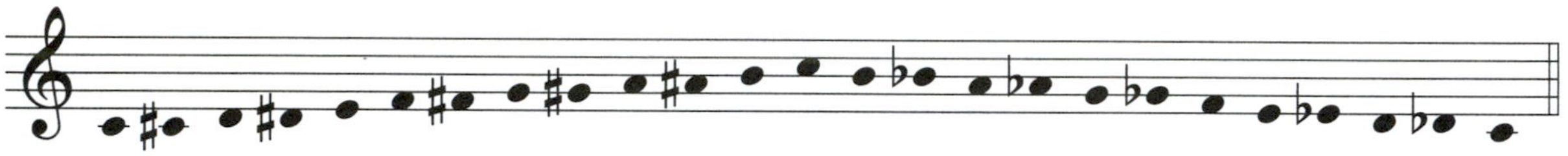

The most common scale types used in both classical and popular music are the major and minor scales. What is so amazing about these scales is that they serve as the basis for every pitch used in the song or composition. Any pitch that is taken from the scale on which the piece is based is called **diatonic**. Pitches used outside of the scale in a particular song or piece are called **chromatic**.

The **major scale** consists of seven different pitches and a repeated pitch at the octave. The half steps lie between the third and fourth scale degrees and the seventh and eighth scale degrees. The F major scale and D major scale are shown below. Notice that the pitches are continuous, meaning that a letter name is never repeated. This is the reason that we can't spell the B♭ as an A♯. Play through these scales on your keyboard or instrument. Pay careful attention to the placements of the half steps.

F Major Scale

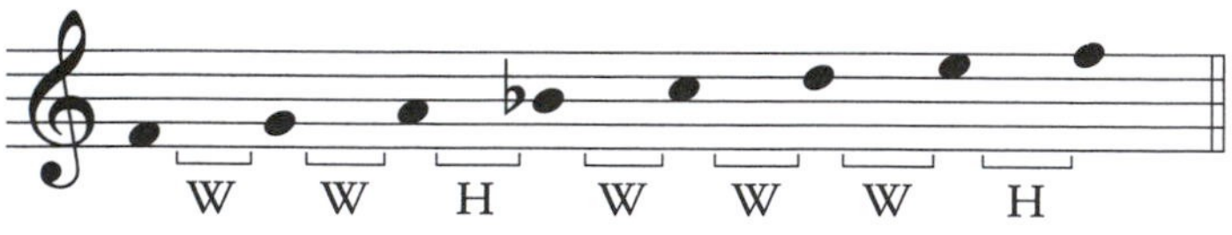

D Major Scale

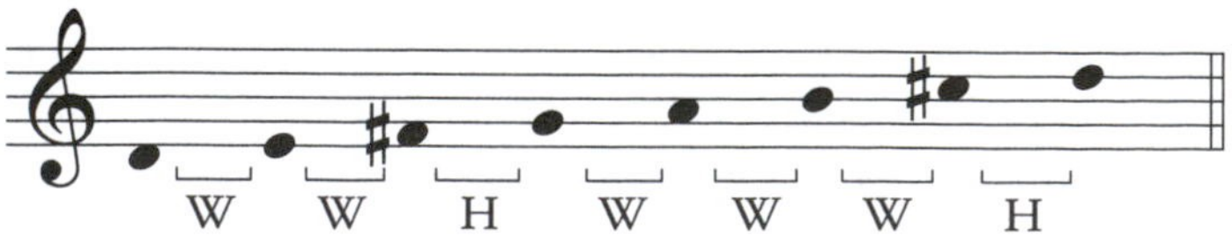

Each pitch in the scale is referred to as a **scale degree**. Most of the time, musicians use the caret symbol (^) to notate these scale degrees. Musicians go even further to give each scale degree a specific name. The first scale degree is called tonic because it is the basis for the entire scale. The leading tone is so named because of its tendency to lead to the tonic. These names will become even more essential when we learn about chords and functional harmony in Chapter 8.

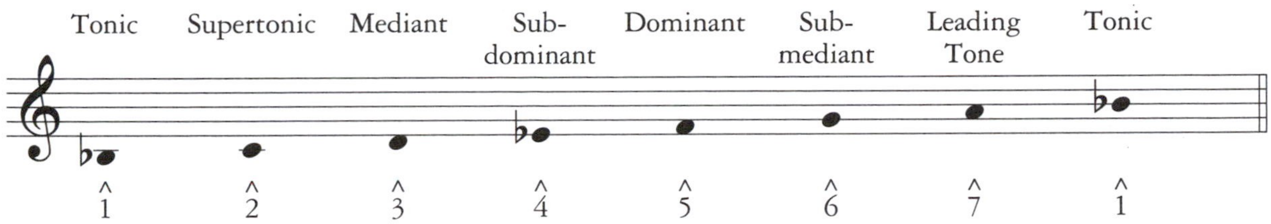

NOTATING MAJOR SCALES USING THE WWHWWWH METHOD

By understanding where the whole and half steps reside within the octave, it is relatively easy to construct a major scale. For example, say you are asked to notate an E major scale. First, notate all of the pitches consecutively between E and E as shown below.

The interval between $\hat{1}$ and $\hat{2}$ is a half step, so we must add a sharp in order to raise the F to an F♯. The interval between 2 and 3 is now a half step, but the pattern demands a whole step. Raise the G to a G♯. By following this pattern and adding the appropriate accidentals, the final major scale beginning on E will contain four sharps: F♯, G♯, C♯, and D♯.

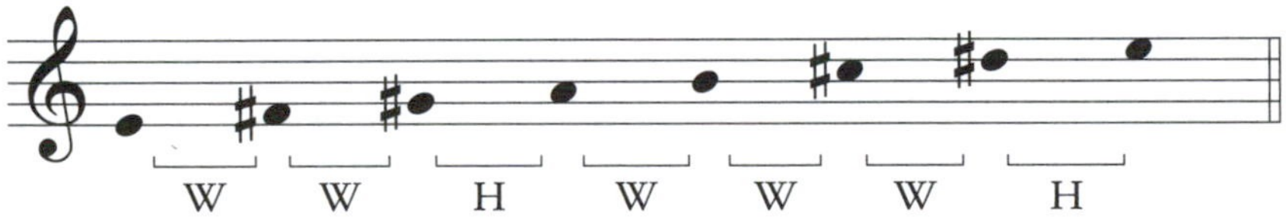

MAJOR KEY SIGNATURES

A **key signature** is a symbol given at the beginning of any tonal piece. It tells the performer what scale the piece is based on and also what accidentals to use. Why use key signatures? What is their purpose? Look at the following short melody. The first example uses *no* key signature. How confusing! Many pianists would run screaming from this type of arrangement. By setting the key signature, as in the second example, the pianist knows exactly what accidentals to play throughout the melody. In this case, every time the performer plays a B, E, A, D, or G, the pitch will need to be lowered a half step. Accidentals in the key signature are always in effect unless the pitch is cancelled with another accidental, including a natural. Because of the accidentals presented in this particular key signature, the performer would know that the short example is based on the D♭ major scale. Want to check? Arrange all of the pitches in consecutive order starting on D♭. You will be able to identify the WWHWWWH pattern.

D♭ Major Scale

IDENTIFICATION OF MAJOR KEY SIGNATURES

Memorization is the key here! No pun intended—well, kind of intended. You just need to memorize them. Speed and accuracy are important when it comes to key signatures. However, there are several tricks to identifying major key signatures while you work on your memorization.

In sharp keys, the last sharp is the leading tone to the tonic of the scale. That means if you simply think up a half step from the last sharp, you will be on the tonic, or the key. Let's take E major for example. The last sharp is D♯. A diatonic half step up from D♯ is E. B♯ is the last sharp in the key signature of C♯ major. Think up a half step from B♯, and you will arrive on C♯.

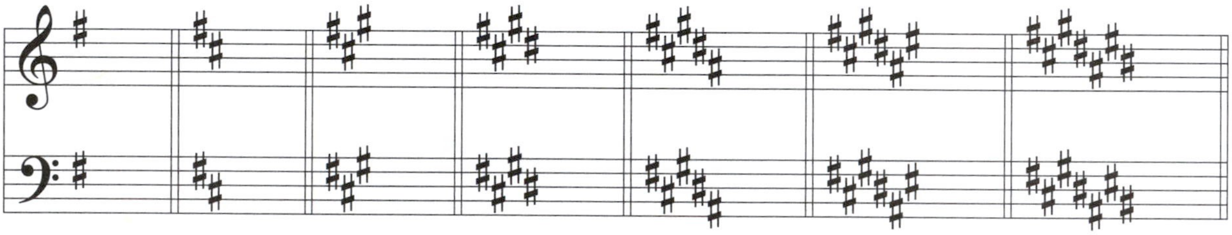

G D A E B F♯ C♯

Key signatures with flats are even easier to recognize. The second to last flat is the key name or tonic. Let's look at A♭. The second to last flat in the key signature *is* A♭. The only problem with this method is the key of F major. There is no second to last flat. This is one you just have to memorize. You also should note that F major is the only key that uses flats that does not have a flat in its key name.

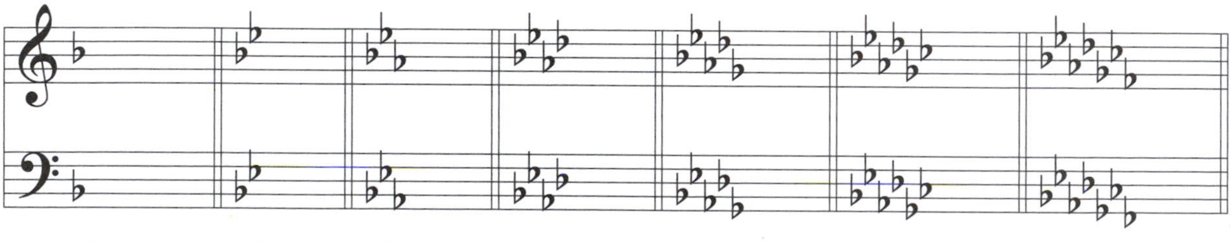

F B♭ E♭ A♭ D♭ G♭ C♭

NOTATING MAJOR KEY SIGNATURES

Placement is important, and the way that key signatures have been written on the staff goes back for hundreds of years. You may have observed that the sharps and flats seem to be in a particular order. If a key signature has sharps, it will always start with F♯. If a key signature uses flats, it will always start with a B♭.

Order of sharps: F♯, C♯, G♯, D♯, A♯, E♯, B♯
Order of flats: B♭, E♭, A♭, D♭, G♭, C♭, F♭

You will get to the point where you know exactly how many sharps are in each key, so when your concertmaster shouts out "B major," you know you are going to use five sharps and know exactly what those sharps would be. Until then, here's a shortcut to writing key signatures on the staff.

Notating keys that use sharps when given the tonic: Think down a half step from the tonic, and start writing the order of sharps to that point. Say you are asked to notate the key of E major. A half step down from E is D♯, so you would notate F♯, C♯, G♯, D♯.

Notating keys that use flats when given the tonic: Start writing the order of flats, and go one past the key name. Say you are asked to notate the key signature of D♭ major. You would notate the first four flats and go one beyond D♭ to create a key signature of five flats.

ARTISTS IN RESIDENCE

Collaboration 1: Norah Jones and Willie Nelson

It seems strange to even group these names together. What would a jazz singer have in common with a tax-evading country music legend? The daughter of famed Indian sitar player Ravi Shankar, Norah Jones was a jazz piano major at the University of North Texas, where no doubt she spent countless hours in the theory classroom. (She probably knows a thing or two about scales and key signatures.) Her first album, *Come Away with Me*, was released in 2002. The record earned her five Grammy Awards, including Best New Artist, Record of the Year, and Album of the Year. Jones was only 22 at the time.

Willie Nelson has a much different story. He dropped out of college to focus on his music, playing bars and clubs in Texas all throughout his early 20s. With no formal musical training and very little money, Nelson moved to Nashville in pursuit of a dream, but the dream came slowly. He released his first album in 1964 with RCA/Victor, but it wasn't until he signed with Columbia Records that Nelson was given creative rights over his music and thus became the poster child for outlaw country. In his 40s and 50s, Nelson reached his peak, winning ten Grammy Awards and nine Country Music Awards. He seems to love to collaborate with musicians, and four of his Grammys were awarded for collaborative projects with artists such as Lee Ann Womack, Ray Price, and Waylon Jennings.

In 2009, Nelson released the album *American Classic*, featuring jazz standards such as "Fly Me to the Moon" and "Come Rain or Shine." This was quite a switch from his earlier hits such as "On the Road Again" and "Crazy"! Paired with the vocal style of Norah Jones, the song "Baby It's Cold Outside" found its way to the Billboard charts in 2010 and was one of the most successful songs from *American Classic*. Listen to the duet on the YouTube channel, and discuss how these two artists from very different backgrounds blend in this particular collaboration.

VIDEO TRACK 13

What is the major key signature for "Baby It's Cold Outside?" The key signature has one flat, so the key must be F major. Circle any pitches in the excerpt that are *not* found within the F major scale. Write the pitches found in the F major scale at the top of the musical excerpt.

Willie Nelson and Norah Jones, "Baby It's Cold Outside." Composer: Frank Loesser

7
8
9
10
This eve - ning has been so ve - ry nice.
The wel - come has been so nice and warm.
out - side! Been hop - ing that you'd drop in! I'll hold your hands;
out - side! How luck - y that you dropped in! Look out the win -
11
12
13
14
My moth - er will start to wor - ry And Fa - ther will be pac - ing the
My sis - ter will be sus - pi - cious; My broth - er will be there at the
they're just like ice. Beau - ti - ful, what's your hur - ry?
- dow at the storm! Gosh, your lips look de - li - cious
15
16
floor, So real - ly, I'd bet - ter
door. My maid - en aunt's mind is
Lis - ten to the fi - re - place roar!
Waves up - on a trop - i - cal shore!

ARTISTS IN RESIDENCE

Collaboration 2: Appalachia Waltz Trio

Imagine this: an award-winning fiddle player, composer and former studio musician; a classical composer and bass player; and a world-renowned cellist, all in the same studio. These three great men of music, Mark O'Connor, Edgar Meyer, and Yo-Yo Ma, make up the group called Appalachia Waltz Trio, a collaborative effort to blend Appalachian music with classical, bluegrass, and American Roots music. O'Connor is no stranger to the studio: his playing can be heard on over 500 albums. Meyer is a classically trained bass player, but his repertoire spans genres and includes recordings of Bach and contemporary composers. Yo-Yo Ma is best known for his performances of Beethoven; however, it is his ability to play tango and bluegrass that sets him apart from other cellists. The trio's first album, *Appalachia Waltz*, peaked at number 1 on the Top Classical Charts in 1996–1997. It was met with great reviews, and *Bass Player* magazine even named it one of the top 30 essential bass recordings "based" only on Meyer's performance. The follow-up album, *Appalachian Journey*, was awarded the 2001 Grammy for the Best Classical Crossover Album. For more on Mark O'Connor and his current activities in the musical world, see *Final Note: Real-World Perspective* later in this chapter.

VIDEO TRACK 14

Listen to the song "Emily's Reel" from *Appalachian Journey.* Do you hear both a classical influence and a nod to traditional Appalachian music? An excerpt from "Emily's Reel" is shown below. Notice the key signature. What major key has two sharps? D major. Within the violin part in measure 109–110, there is a scale. Is it the outline of a G major scale? Why or why not? Circle the G scale, and try to write out WWHWWWH under the intervals.

Mark O'Connor, "Emily's Reel"

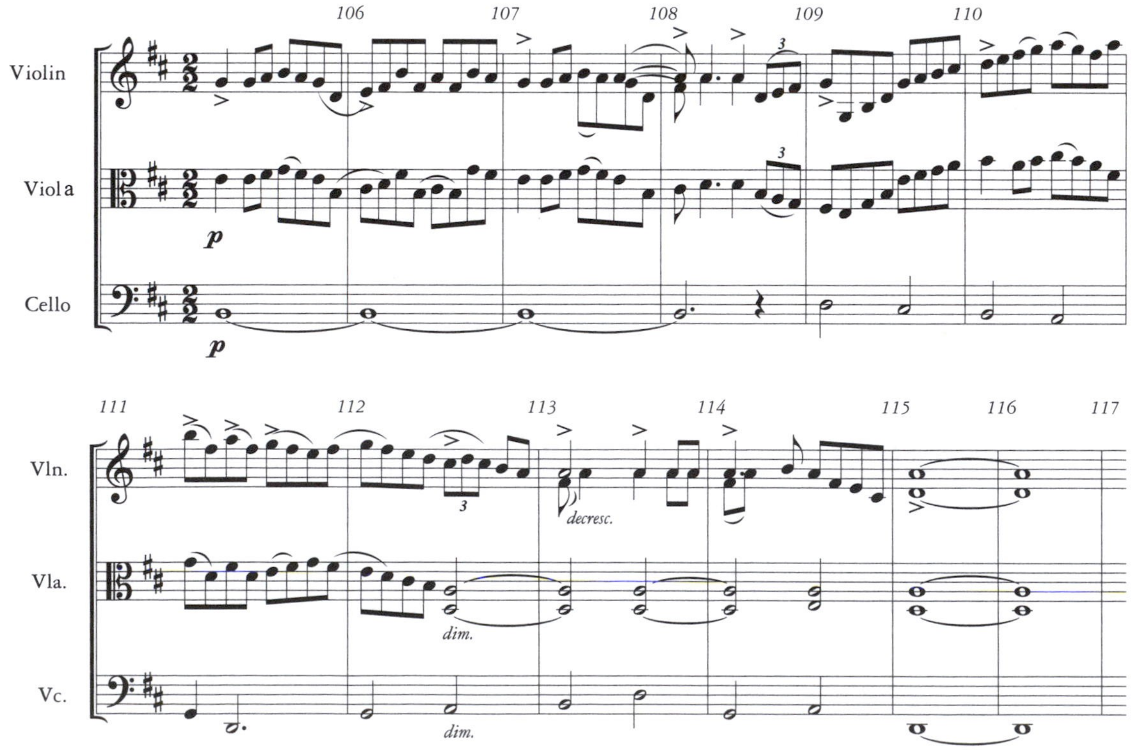

THE CIRCLE OF FIFTHS

A standard for any musician, the circle of fifths is a way of understanding the relationships between keys. It is also a great tool to help memorize key signatures and the order of flats and sharps. The sharp keys are on the right, and the flat keys are on the left. As an interval of a fifth is added, whether that be ascending or descending, another accidental is also added.

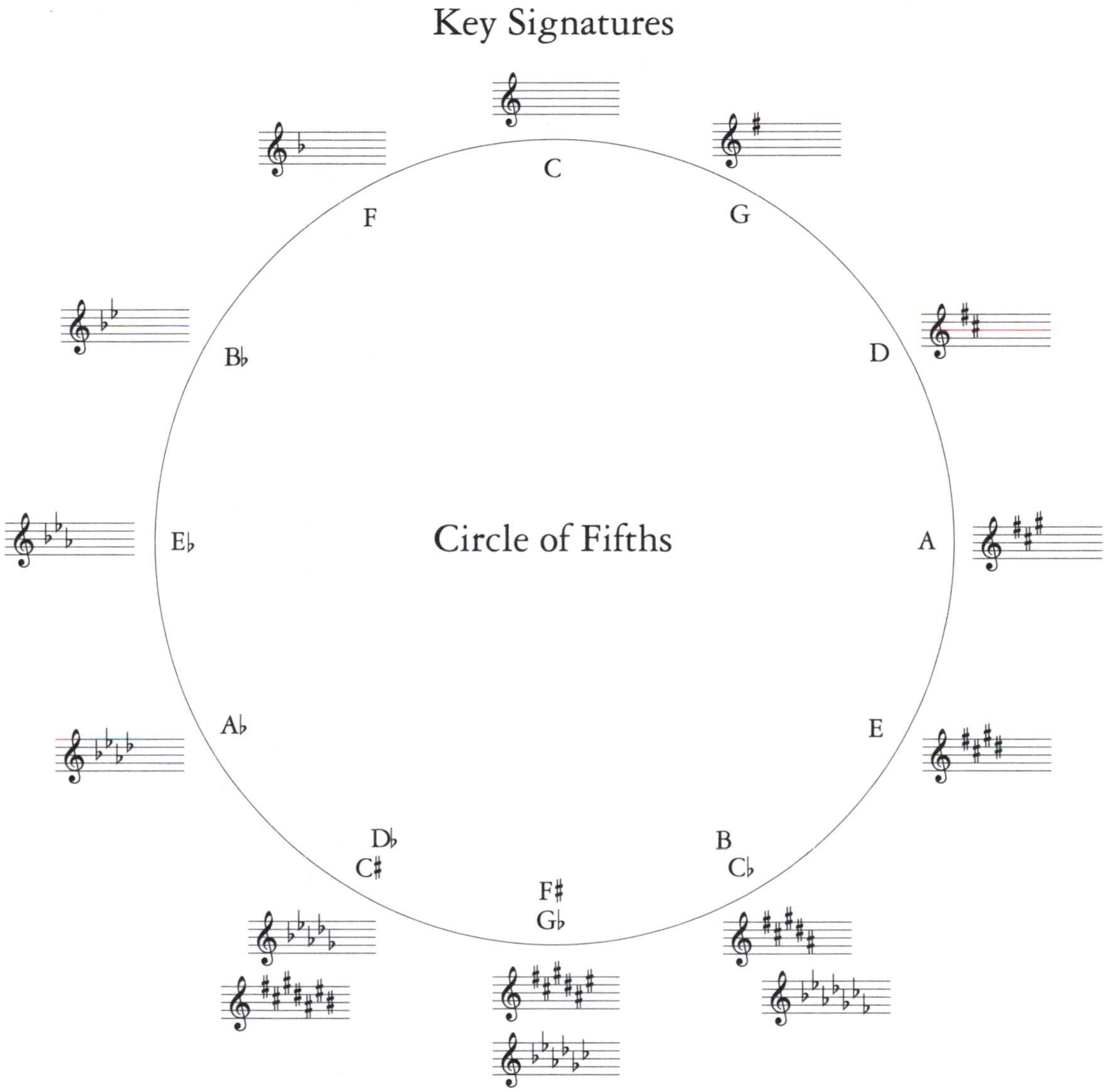

ARTISTS IN RESIDENCE

Collaboration 3: "We Are the World" Various Artists (1985)

Perhaps the most compelling of all collaborations in popular music is "We Are the World." The famine in Africa was big news in the mid 1980s, and one could hardly turn the TV on without hearing about children dying of hunger in Ethiopia. Along with producers Harry Belafonte and Quincy Jones, forty of the best-known musicians in popular music recorded

"We Are the World" in order to raise money for the charity USA for Africa. Although the lyrics and music were written by Lionel Richie and Michael Jackson, there is great speculation about how much Richie really contributed to the work. Many of the great artists weren't excited about the music per se, but they were dedicated to the cause. In an article from *Rolling Stone*, Billy Joel says, "Most of us who were there didn't like the song, but nobody would say so. I think Cyndi Lauper leaned over to me and said, 'It sounds like a Pepsi commercial.' And I didn't disagree." The public didn't seem to care, however, and in 1986, "We Are the World" won four Grammy awards, including Record of the Year, Song of the Year, and Best Music Video, not to mention the $60 million that was raised in charity funds.

VIDEO TRACK 15

Watching the video of "We Are the World" is like watching a short documentary of the biggest pop stars during the mid-1980s. Everyone who contributed to this collaborative effort—including those involved with the editing, sound recording, and final graphics—worked without pay. The famed producer Jones even posted a sign to the entrance of the session room: "Check your egos at the door."

VIDEO TRACK 16

Fast-forward 25 years. In 2010, a devastating earthquake hit the country of Haiti, and "We Are the World 25 for Haiti" was released, produced again by Quincy Jones and Lionel Richie. The song is similar to the 1985 version, but includes a rap verse and auto-tuned solos by T-Pain and Akon. The song was a commercial success, but only for a few months. Perhaps the American public had found other ways to send relief or was unhappy with the remake of a classic. Either way, National Public Radio put it best: "Collaboration is now commonplace. These days, 80 pop stars in one room isn't a milestone, it's a Kanye West album."

Artists Featured in "We Are the World," 1985 (in order of appearance on music video)		
Lionel Richie	Dionne Warwick	Steve Perry
Stevie Wonder	Willie Nelson	Daryl Hall
James Ingram	Al Jarreau	Huey Lewis
Tina Turner	Bruce Springsteen	Cyndi Lauper
Billy Joel	Paul Simon	Kim Carnes
Michael Jackson	Kenny Rogers	Bob Dylan
Diana Ross	Kenny Loggins	Ray Charles
Artists Featured in "We Are the World 25 for Haiti," 2010 (in order of appearance on music video)		
Justin Bieber	Janet Jackson	Adam Levine
Nicole Scherzinger	Barbara Streisand	Pink
Jennifer Hudson	Nick Jonas	BeBe Winans
Jennifer Nettles	Kanye West	Usher
Josh Groban	Miley Cyrus	Celine Dion
Tony Bennett	Enrique Iglesias	Fergie
Mary J. Blige	Jamie Foxx	Snoop Dogg
Michael Jackson	Wyclef Jean	

One of the most interesting facts about the original recording session is that the song was recorded immediately after the 1985 American Music Awards, probably in the wee hours of the morning considering the session lasted about 12 hours. Producers decided that everyone was already in town for the awards celebration, so it seemed an ideal time for the recording session. In 2010, the same approach was used, only this time all of the artists were in town for the Grammy Awards.

Take a moment to view both renditions on the YouTube Channel. Which do you prefer? Why do you think the original version was so well received while the 2010 version peaked as quickly as it fell off the charts?

The opening verse to "We Are the World" is written in the key of E major. Note that the key signature includes four sharps.

VIDEO TRACK 15

Michael Jackson and Lionel Ritchie, "We Are the World"

The main chorus of "We Are the World" is written in the key of E major as well. Look at the bass line. It includes the pitches A, B, and E, or $\hat{1}$, $\hat{4}$, $\hat{5}$.

Michael Jackson and Lionel Ritchie, "We Are the World" *(continued)*

Something interesting happens in measure 47. The key signature changes from four sharps to one flat. The new key is now F major which tells us two things. First, the scale that the song is based on is now F major, and second, the pitches F, C, G, and D are all natural, while the pitch B is now flat. This change in key signature affects every pitch until the end of the song.

Michael Jackson and Lionel Ritchie, "We Are the World"

ARTISTS IN RESIDENCE

Collaboration 4: The Three Tenors

To say that this was a collaboration of classical superstars is an understatement. Take, for instance, their debut concert in 1990. It drew an international television audience of over one billion. Yes, one billion. Luciana Pavarotti, Plácido Domingo, and José Carreras recorded only a few albums together through the late 1990s, but their success was far reaching. The songs on the albums included everything from famous arias to operatic renditions of Christmas songs.

So what brought these opera superstars together? In 1987, Carreras was diagnosed with leukemia and, following a hospital visit, Pavarotti and Domingo met and became fast friends. After Carreras recovered, they decided to perform a benefit concert for a leukemia foundation at the World Cup soccer competition. The album from the concert sold over ten million copies and holds the Guinness World Record for the best-selling classical album of all time. They knew they were on to something when they sold out Dodger Stadium in 1994. The initial album, *Three Tenors in Concert*, peaked at number 1 on the European and Australian charts. The album sold over three million copies in the United States alone. That's big news for the opera world. As you might expect, the 1990 album was a shoo-in for the Grammy Award for Best Classical Performance.

Tragically, the opera world lost Pavarotti to pancreatic cancer in 2007. His last performance was "Nessun Dorma" at the opening ceremony of the Winter Olympics in 2006. In his obituary, his friends and colleagues remembered him for his talent and his wit.

"I always admired the God-given glory of his voice—that unmistakable special timbre from the bottom up to the very top of the tenor range," Domingo said. "I also loved his wonderful sense of humor," he continued, "and on several occasions of our concerts with Jose Carreras—the so-called Three Tenors concerts—we had trouble remembering that we were giving a concert before a paying audience, because we had so much fun between ourselves."

VIDEO TRACK 17

Listen to the well-known aria "Nessun Dorma" from Puccini's opera *Turandot*. Although the song has been sung by the Three Tenors at various venues, listen to the original 1990 version on the YouTube Channel. The key signature has one sharp, so you would be inclined to say G major is the key. In the first five measures, there are lots of accidentals that would lead you to think in another key, but they are *not* consistent. However, trust your ears. When Carreras completes the line at measure 6, you do feel that you have arrived at the tonic. Check what pitch you see at measure 6: G! So we *are* in G major. Not for long. Look at measures 7–14. What accidental do you see that is consistent? The C is always sharped in these measures, so therefore the scale on which this section is based is one that has both an F♯ and a C♯. D major has both of these accidentals, and when Pavarotti finishes the line at measure 14, the new tonic is solidified as D. This is a little advanced, and we will learn more about this in Chapter 15. However, it is important for you to realize that accidentals must be consistent in order for a key to be determined.

Three Tenors, "Nessun Dorma" from Puccini's *Turandot*

BACKSTAGE PASS

When Collaborations Go Wrong, Very Very Wrong

Back in the late 1980s, it was fairly common for popular artists to lip-sync on award shows and public appearances. Many fans can probably remember sitting through concerts saying, "Wow, they sound *just* like my record." Amazingly enough, it sounded like the record because it *was* the record! Audiences were plenty happy to be in the presence of the popular icon, not caring too much about the sound quality: they wanted a show!

Milli Vanilli, fronted by Fab Morvan and Rob Pilatus, provided the entertainment factor the public so desired. They could dance, were easy on the eyes, and sang in a style that had teenagers singing along at the top of their lungs during the summer of 1989. Their first album, *All of Nothing*, released in 1988, was certified gold in their native Germany. Their second album, *Girl You Know It's True*, was number 1 in both the United States and Canada and was certified six times platinum. Hits from this album included "Girl You Know It's True," "Blame It on the Rain," and "Girl I'm Gonna Miss You," all of which peaked at the top of the U.S. charts.

That all changed during a live performance on MTV. They were dancing away to their hit "Girl You Know It's True" when the record jammed and began to skip, repeating the line over and over and over. The two lead "singers" continued to perform until they realized the record was not being fixed and quickly ran offstage. People in the music industry began to wonder whether Fab and Rob were really singing at all. Their accents during interviews were so strong, but no accent seemed to be present in the recordings. It turns out, that industry insiders were correct: one of the vocalists for the recordings, Charles Shaw, admitted that he was the main vocalist on the album. Twenty-seven lawsuits were filed under fraud protection against Morvan, Pilatus, and Arista Records. Eventually a settlement was reached and fans were reimbursed for concert tickets and recordings. Morvan and Pilatus were required to give back all of their awards, including the 1990 Grammy for the Best New Artist and three American Music Awards. Tragically, Pilatus committed suicide in 1998, just before he was set to go out on a new promotional tour for an album in which he actually sang.

Since the scandal of Milli Vanilli, very few artists have been allowed to lip-sync on an award show, which sometimes leaves fans questioning, how is *that* person's voice the same as what I hear on the radio? Is honesty always better? Today's popular artists continue to lip-sync. You need only do a quick search for Ashley Simpson's appearance on *Saturday Night Live* or Beyoncé's rendition of the national anthem at the 2012 Inauguration. However, unlike Milli Vanilli, both performers have proven themselves. Morvan and Pilatus of Milli Vanilli never sang a note.

Reviewing Chapter Objectives

- Notate major scales (page 27).
- Identify scale degree names (page 27).
- Identify and notate major key signatures (pages 28–29).
- Determine scale type used in musical context (pages 32, 35–39).

EXERCISES

I. Given the tonic and scale type, notate the correct pitches on the staff. Do not use key signatures.

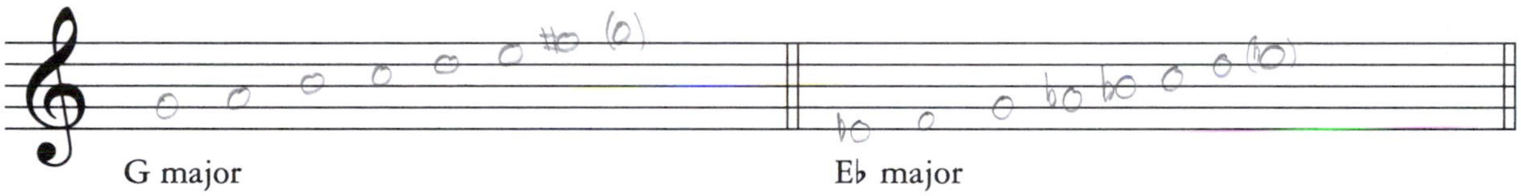

G major — E♭ major

B major — E major

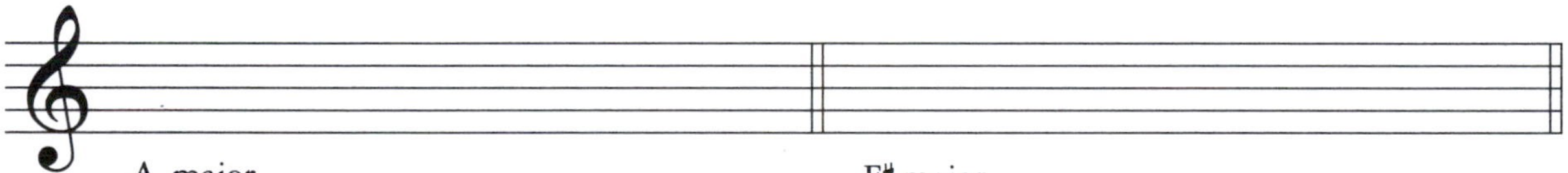

A major — F♯ major

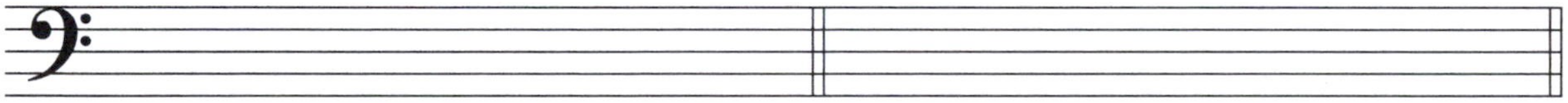

C major — B♭ major

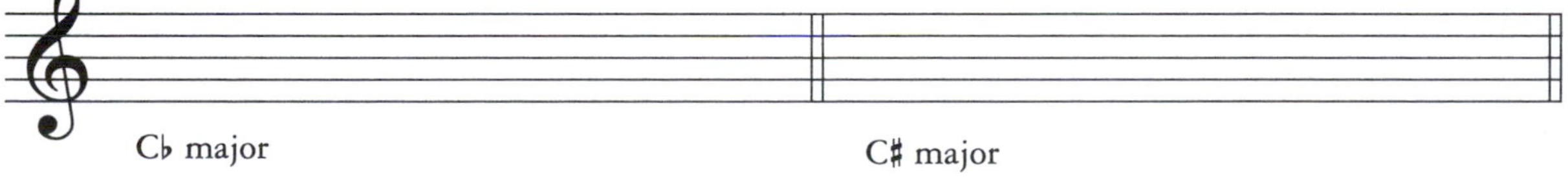

C♭ major — C♯ major

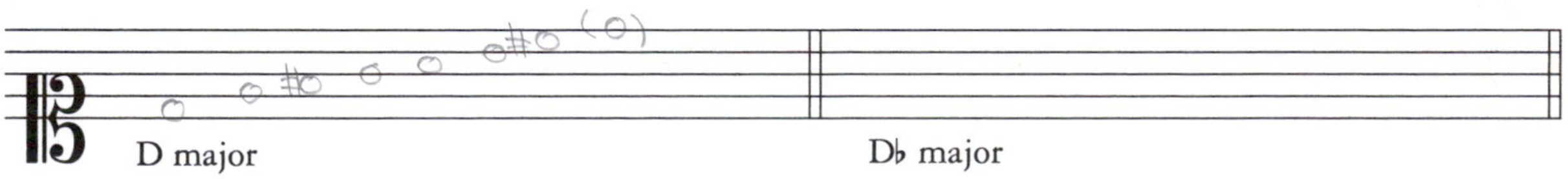

D major — D♭ major

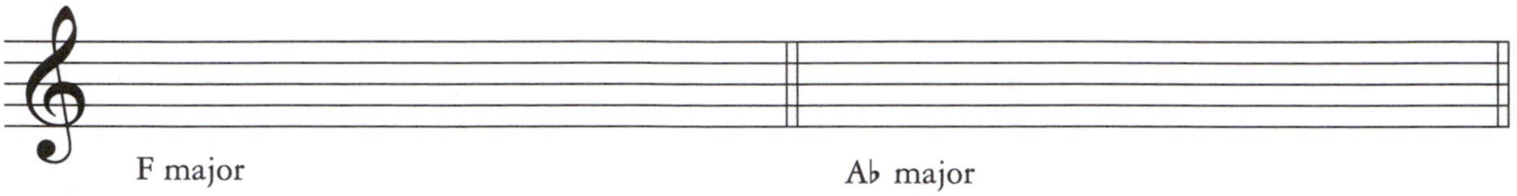

F major

A♭ major

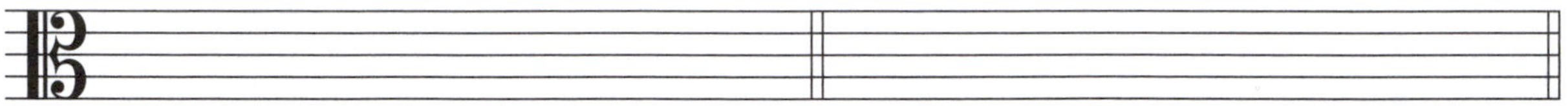

G major

B♭ major

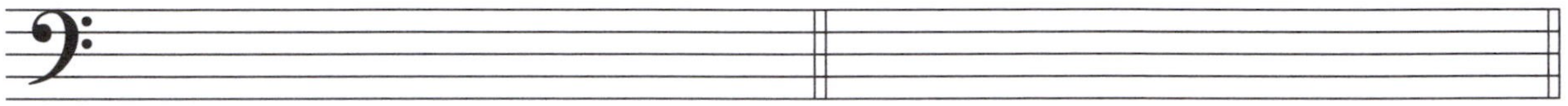

D major

G♭ major

II. Given the scale degree name, notate the correct scale *after* you have located the correct tonic. Use correct key signatures.

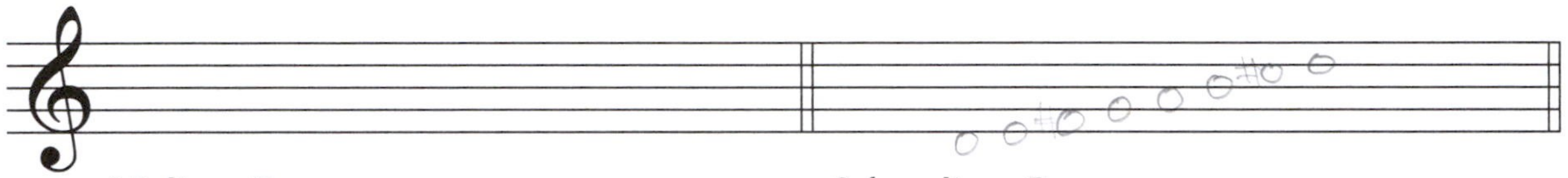

Mediant: F

Submediant: B

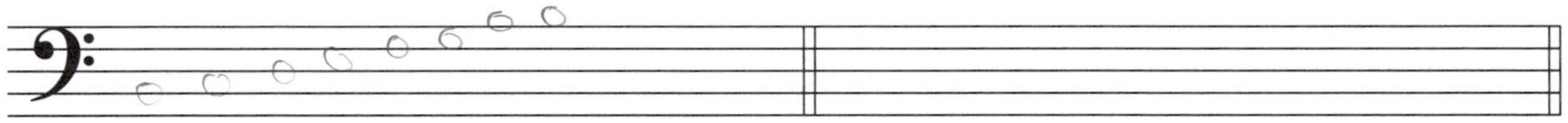

Leading tone: A

Supertonic: B♭

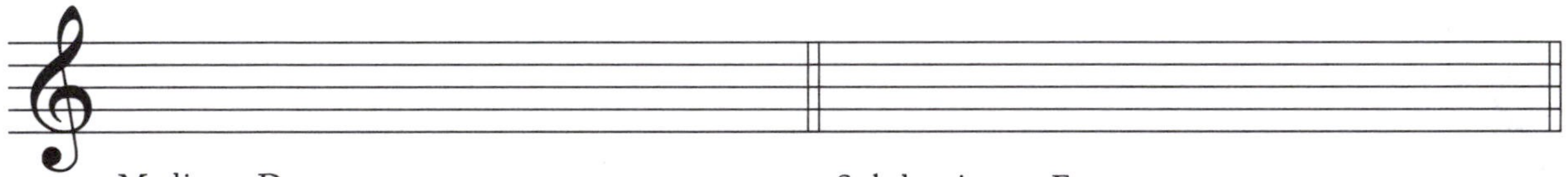

Mediant: D

Subdominant: F

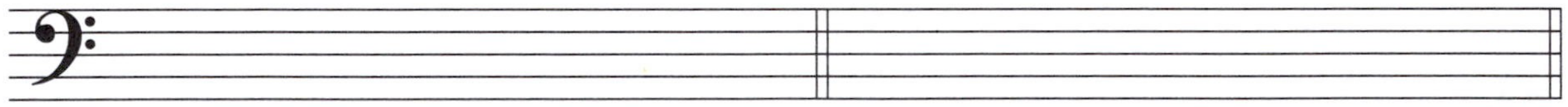

Dominant: D

Leading tone: A

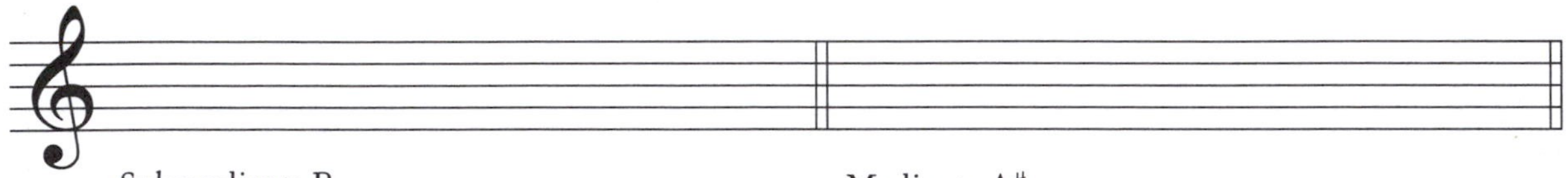

Submediant: B

Mediant: A♯

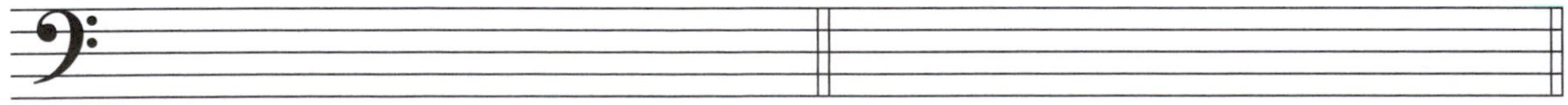

Dominant: B

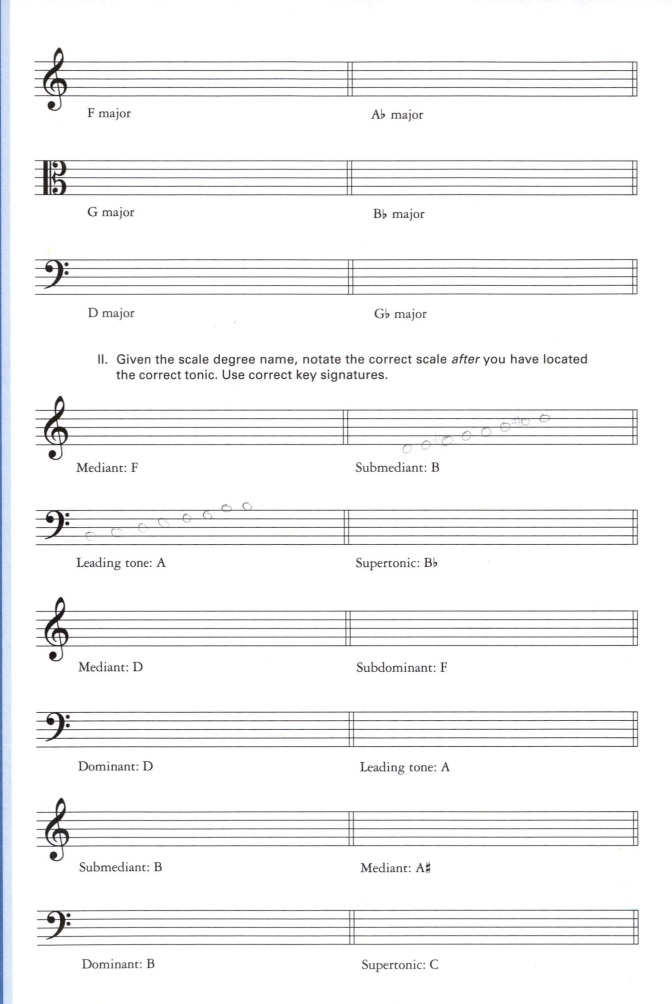

Supertonic: C

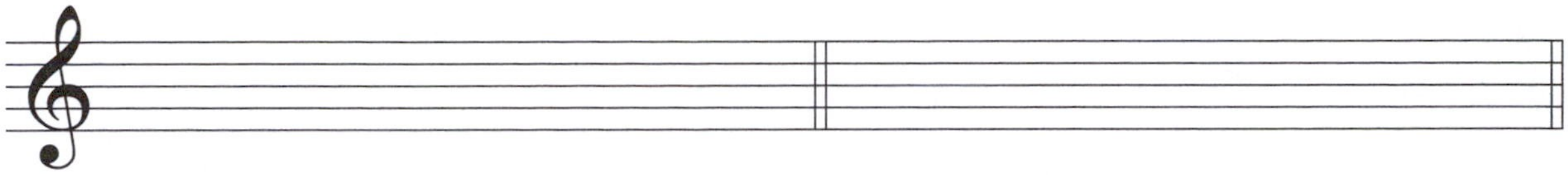

Subdominant: E

Leading tone: B ♯

III. Identify the major key signature.

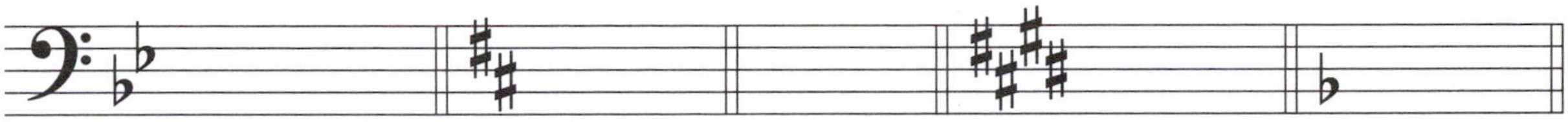

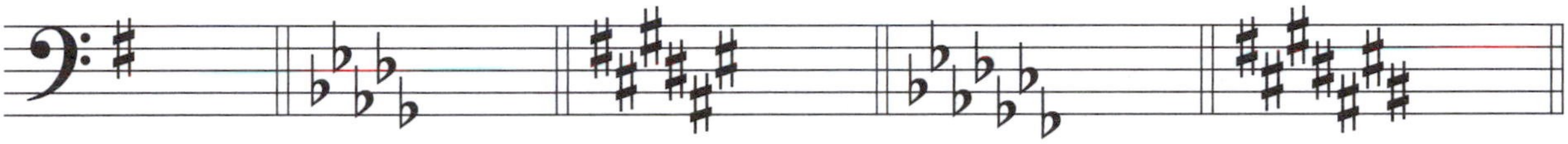

IV. Notate the following key signatures on the staff. Be sure to follow correct placement.*

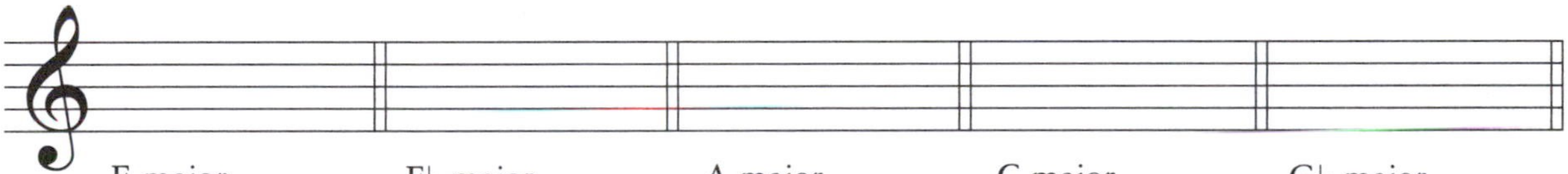

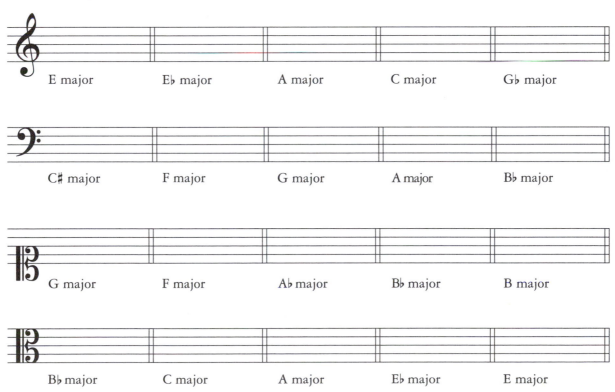

E major | E♭ major | A major | C major | G♭ major

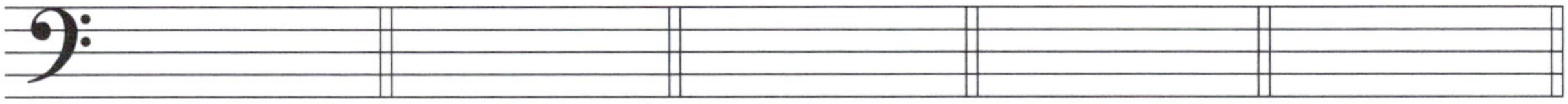

C♯ major | F major | G major | A major | B♭ major

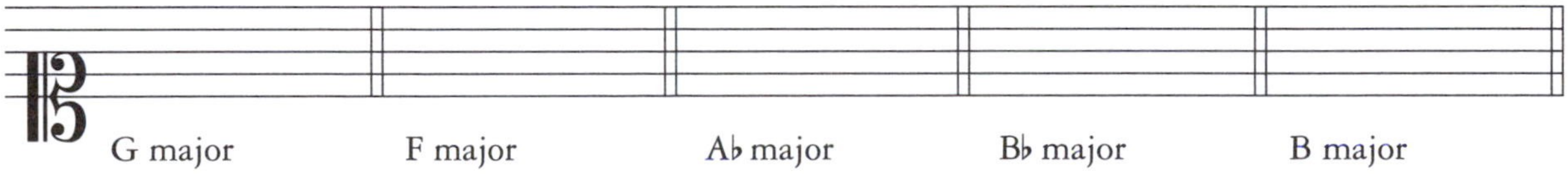

G major | F major | A♭ major | B♭ major | B major

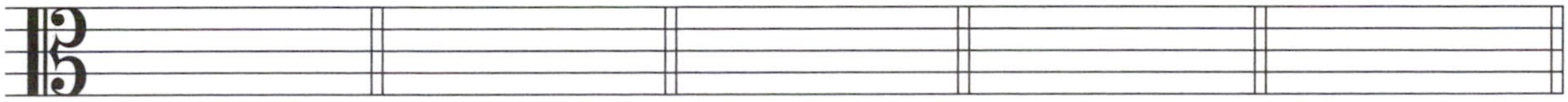

B♭ major | C major | A major | E♭ major | E major

*Placement for key signatures in C Clefs are explained in online resource.

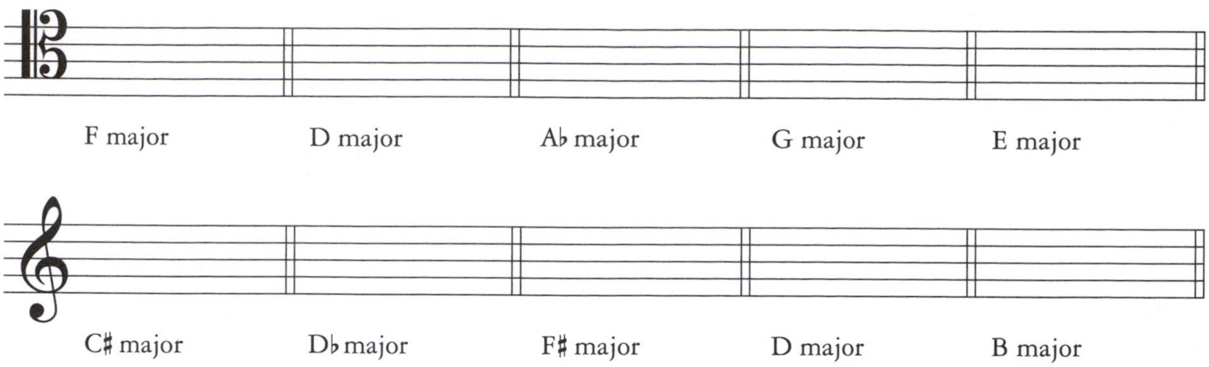

AURAL SKILLS CONDITIONING 2

Introduction to Solfège

Remember sitting in front of the TV watching Maria and the von Trapp children sing in the hills of Austria? What in the world were they singing about? And how is this helpful to learning music? Your 4-year-old self probably didn't ponder this, but the budding musician you are today needs to care and know about this phenomenon. In the scene, Julie Andrews's character Maria uses song to teach the von Trapp children the basics of solfège. **Solfège** refers to the syllables assigned to the scale degrees of major and minor keys. The D major scale is pictured below, with scale degree numbers and solfège syllables written beneath each note.

With your classmates, sing a major scale ascending and descending. Then, try singing the syllables in the following pattern:

do! do–re–do! do–re–mi–re–do! do–re–mi–fa–mi–re–do . . .

And descending:

do! do–ti–do! do–ti–la–ti–do! do–ti–la–sol–la–ti–do . . .

What other patterns for singing the scale can you come up with?

Sight Singing: Melodies That Move by Step

Ten melodies follow. First, identify the key. Try speaking the solfège syllables in rhythm. Then, sing the melodies on solfège in the correct rhythm.

1.

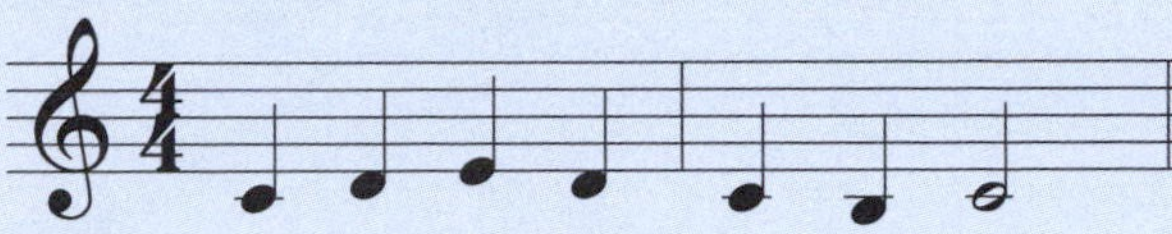

2.

3.

4.

5.

6.

7.

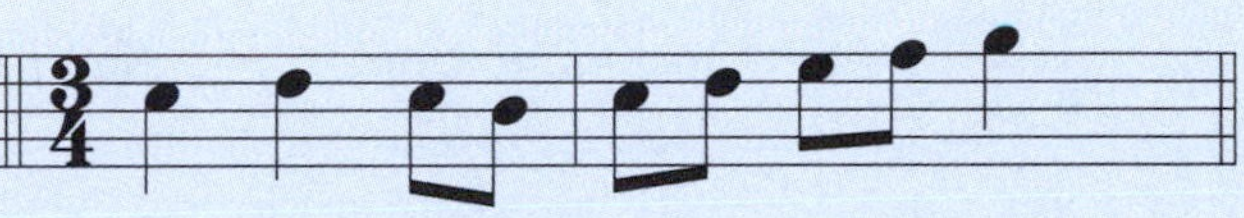

8.

9.

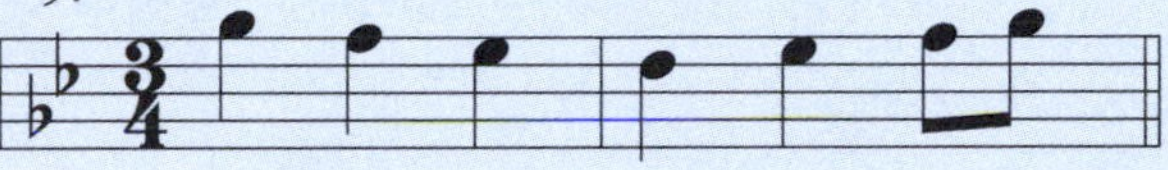

10.

You will hear your instructor perform part of a major scale and stop on a scale degree. This is also available for listening on the course website. Write down the solfège syllable for the scale degree that you hear.

1. ______ 2. ______ 3. ______ 4. ______ 5. ______ 6. ______

Now, you will hear the entire scale performed (ascending and descending), and then one scale degree will be played. Write down the solfège syllable that you hear.

7. ______ 8. ______ 9. ______ 10. ______ 11. ______ 12. ______

REPLAY

AUDIO TRACKS CH. 2 SCALE DEGREE 1–12

THE FINAL NOTE: REAL-WORLD PERSPECTIVE

Mark O'Connor

COMPOSER, EDUCATOR, AND MUSICIAN

There are many fiddle players in the world, but few can match the true musicianship of Mark O'Connor. His credits in both composition and performance are extensive, but it is perhaps his violin method that has received the most attention in recent years. The method offers a technical foundation using the repertoire found in traditional American string playing. O'Connor truly believes that "the modern classical violin student who develops a working knowledge of folk fiddling, jazz music and world music styles can enjoy a lifetime of music-making, and be more successful in the new music environment."

In his "20 Points of Creativity" from *O'Connor Method Book One*, O'Connor recognizes the importance of understanding the basics of music theory, including conditioning the ear:

> Learning how to read music and "find the music" aurally at the same time is paramount to nurturing creativity. Learning the "math" of what constitutes a whole note is important to be sure. However, of no less importance is learning what this sound—the sound of a single pitch sustained over four pulses—means in the context of ensemble playing. Putting some basic theory into context immediately in an ensemble is putting our best foot forward. Theory without a way or means to apply it, and therefore musically hear and feel it in a group class, ensemble or orchestra, is academic and can be boring and considered "not relevant" by young students.

This is the essence of true musicianship: to be able to understand the why and the how, using both our eyes and ears, all while producing and owning this understanding within our performance.

What inspired you to pursue music?

I felt that pursuing music was a calling since I was 12 years old. I had a lot of reasons for pursuing music and for being inspired to do so. Coming from a very poor household was incentive enough to get out there in the world and try to make it a better place through your own chosen art form, if you felt like you had something to offer. I could put a smile on people's face as a young prodigy performing on the road, right from the beginning. My music teachers for the most part loved me. I could sense the pride they felt in my progress. I could make some money from music as a kid; that always helps the inspiration a tad! My dad was blown away that I could come back from winning a major fiddle competition against adult competitors with an amount of money in my pocket for a weekend's effort that equaled his take-home pay for 2 months from his lumberyard job. I was expected to help the household. The sense of responsibility to one's talent kicked in very early on. My parents knew I was musically gifted and allowed me to travel by myself on airplanes, even as a 12-year-old, in order to perform concerts or enter music competitions. They could not afford to accompany me in most cases, and by the time I was 14, my mother was too sick from cancer to travel. She died when I was 19.

My most significant teacher, the iconic fiddler Benny Thomasson, didn't just teach me hour-long lessons, but sometimes up to 15 hours every other weekend. He also taught me while asking for no payment in return. He turned down many a paid customer to teach me for free. To this day, it is hard to imagine that kind of dedication in what he did for me and what he was wishing to accomplish for his own legacy I suppose. But the most powerful inspiration in the end for me was the fact that I could create music, invent new ideas on my instrument, change something that people thought couldn't be changed, to improvise, to develop a new style and approach in music and to show other musicians my own music along the way. The gift of sharing was inspirational. When my final teacher, the legendary Stephane Grappelli, mentored me, he simply allowed me to be the individual I already was at age 17. He showed me what he could and shared with me the secrets to his jazz violin success.

How has the study of music theory/musicianship helped in your compositional process? Helped in performance?

I had the kind of theory lessons throughout my childhood and my music training that helped make me a creative musician as well as a composer. It was a wonderful combination and the right combination for a player-composer. Learning every last thing about counterpoint or musical form as a young music student while ignoring basic ear training in how to identify chord sequences and rhythm so one could improvise on a simple bluegrass or rock & roll song, is not the right formula for learning to be musically creative in the 21st century. When you don't get proper balance as a student is when things begin to go wrong for that student, and to a larger degree the music culture is affected with less and less creative musicians. You could make a case there are more creative rappers than creative violinists. But the violinists get all of the music education by comparison. What have been the effects of this imbalance? Fewer player-composers in classical music in the last 50 years than in every 50-year period block since before J. S. Bach, who himself, was a player-composer. It is imperative for more musicians to be composers again, and more composers to be musicians again, certainly in academia. The separation of these two tracks was a bad idea.

What were some of the greatest challenges in your musical career? What did you learn along the way?

One of the greatest challenges in my music career was to resist and challenge the constant drumbeat from the top of the profession that everyone beneath them has to conform to prefabricated status quo approaches. By daring the dyed-in-the-wool conventions, I have gotten to be on the forefront of many new trends in professional music. Here is a list that we compiled from a new biography that is being written about my life in music.

> Mark O'Connor . . . helped to shape modern contest fiddling and perhaps saved the genre for a new generation, was on the forefront of developing the newgrass music style with Strength In Numbers as its shining capitulation, was one of the few musicians to usher in the "New Traditionalist" movement in Nashville's recording scene in the early 1980s, broke through as a contemporary violinist/composer combining classical, folk and jazz styles in a contemporary band setting with albums like *On the Mark*, created a new model for a string camp featuring what he calls the four pillars of string playing (classical, jazz, folk, world), the first to bring in American fiddling into classical music with his string quartets, The *Fiddle Concerto* and *Appalachia Waltz* with Yo-Yo Ma and Edgar Meyer, was the first composer of violin music that returned to tonal compositions for the concert stage in the late 1980s, released the O'Connor Method that demonstrates a student can learn more about good classical violin playing from a method using all American music and styles than from the Suzuki Method using all Baroque music, composed the very first improvised violin concerto two years ago.

What I have learned from all of these unique, breakout achievements is that there was always a chorus of people shouting from the rooftops along the way: *No Mark, no you can't—you are wasting your time, nothing is going to change, and you are just hurting yourself by believing you could change or develop anything. They are not going to care, just go back to doing what you were before. . . .* Yes looking back, it did make the very few people who initially supported me in each of these individual journeys seem like angels! It sure does!

Greatest moment of your career so far.

When I played the premiere of my composition "The Improvised Violin Concerto" at Boston Symphony Hall with conductor Federico Cortese and the Boston Youth Symphony Orchestras in 2010. At age 50, I had this fulfillment that there was something still left in the tank of creativity that no one had thought of pulling off yet for the violin. As I took the curtain calls at the world premiere, my entire career of highlights was passing before my eyes. I had just improvised for 40 minutes in a much-anticipated violin concerto that had string players flying in from out of state to witness. It was the first of its kind with symphony orchestra. The eruption from the audience at the conclusion still resonates. It was perfect. After all I had accomplished in my music career, to pull this out for my ninth concerto can be easily described as the greatest moment!

CHAPTER 3

MINOR SCALES AND KEY SIGNATURES

Artist in Residence: Lang Lang

Chapter Objectives

- Notate minor scales (natural, harmonic, and melodic)
- Identify scale degree names in context of a minor scale
- Identify and notate minor key signatures
- Determine scale type used in musical context

PARALLEL KEY RELATIONSHIPS

How are minor and major keys different? Well for one, each scale follows a completely different pattern in terms of whole and half steps. Let's look at a comparison between the E major and E natural minor scale. Have someone play through these two scales for you and pay careful attention to how the $\hat{3}$, $\hat{6}$, and $\hat{7}$ are lowered in the minor scale. This creates the pattern of WHWWHWW.

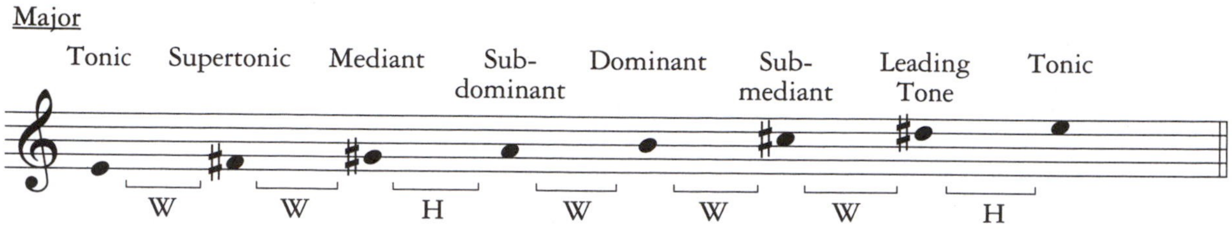

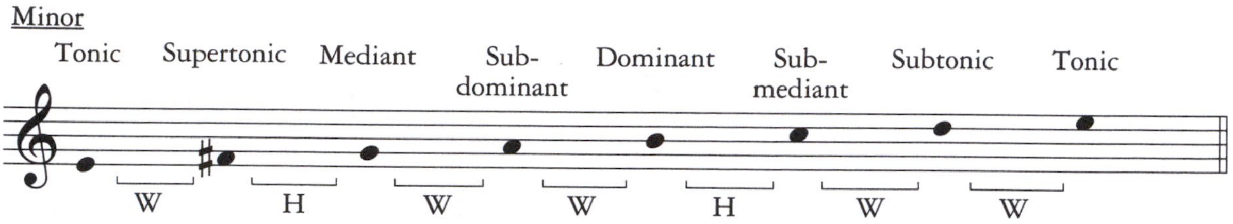

This relationship, called **parallel keys**, means that the two scales share the same tonic, but use different key signatures. When comparing the two, the natural minor scale includes a lowered $\hat{3}$, $\hat{6}$, and $\hat{7}$. The $\hat{7}$ is not called the leading tone in the natural minor scale. Why do you think this is?

NOTATING MINOR SCALES

We can use the exact same process that we learned for notating major scales when notating minor scales. Begin with the tonic, and notate all of the pitches in order on the staff. Using the pattern WHWWHWW, add in the necessary accidentals in order to duplicate the minor scale pattern.

Notate the F natural minor scale:

1. Write pitches in consecutive order on the staff.

2. Follow the pattern WHWWHWW to insert the appropriate accidentals.

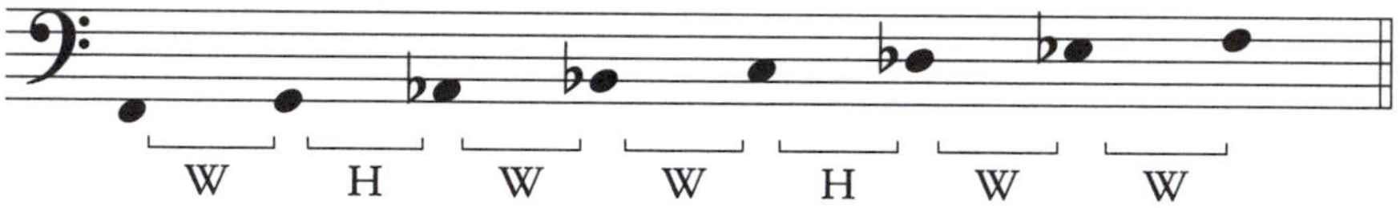

By studying the accidentals used to create the F minor scale, we can determine that the key of F minor has four flats.

RELATIVE KEY RELATIONSHIPS

Relative keys share the same key signature but have different tonics. Study the two scales shown. The G major scale has a key signature of one sharp, F♯, while the E minor scale also uses one sharp, F♯. G major and E minor are relative keys. In order to find the relative minor of any major key, you just need to count down three half steps. If it is easier for you, go up to the sixth scale degree of any major key. That pitch is the tonic of the relative minor key.

G major

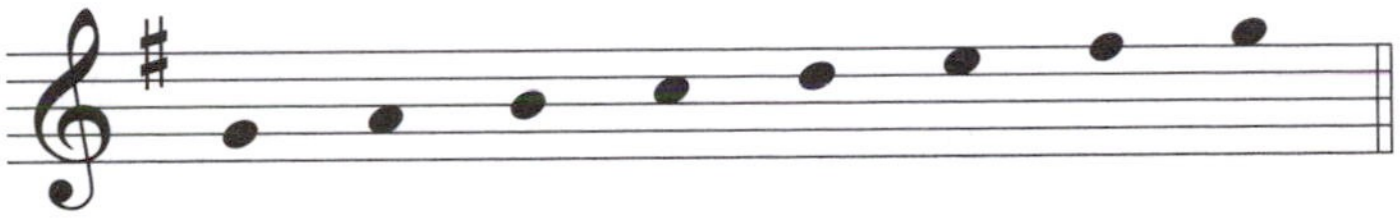

E minor

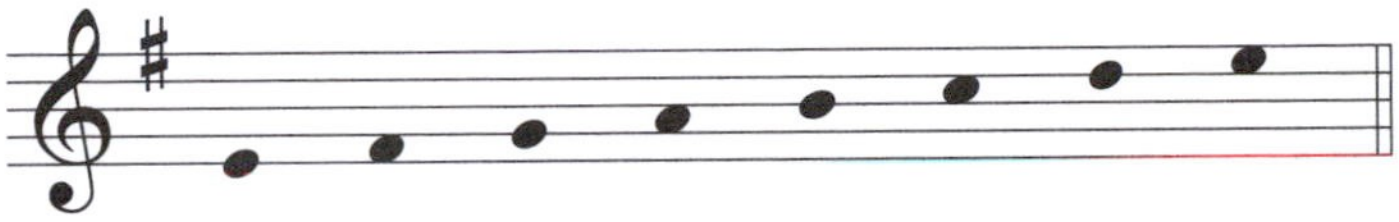

IDENTIFICATION OF MINOR KEY SIGNATURES

By this point, you should pretty much have mastered the major key signatures. Of course, you will want to memorize the minor key signatures, but as long as you can find the relative major key, you should be able to recognize and notate minor key signatures without too much trouble. The order of sharps and flats and their placement on the staff are exactly the same as major key signatures.

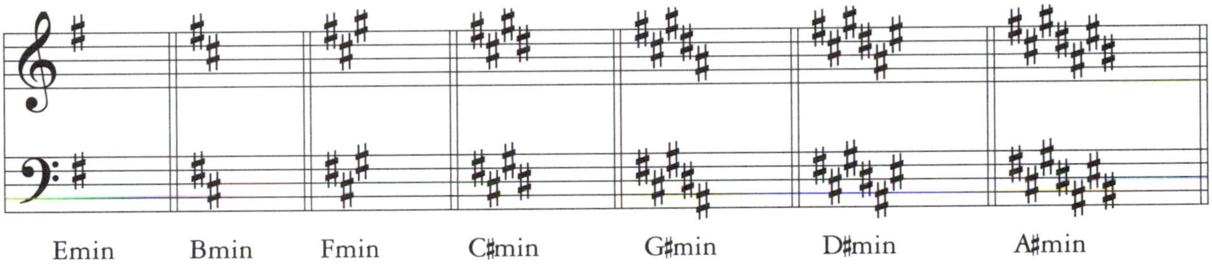

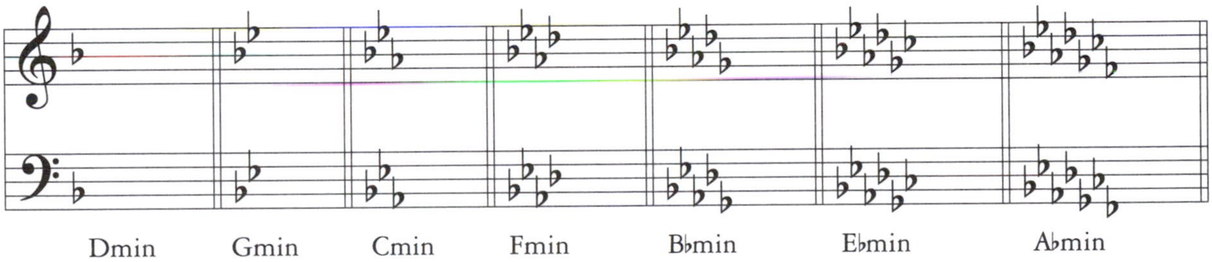

When asked to identify the minor key signature, determine the major key and count down three half steps (or count up to the 6th scale degree). For instance, you see a key signature of five sharps. Immediately, you know it is the key of B major. Count down three half steps to G♯, and there is your relative key! A key signature with five sharps represents the key of B major or G♯ minor. You would need to listen to the piece in order to determine whether the song was written in a major or minor mode.

NOTATING MINOR KEY SIGNATURES

Notating the minor key signatures on the staff also requires that you either have your minor keys memorized or can quickly determine relative keys. If you are asked to notate the key signature for D minor, you could count up three half steps to the pitch F and write the key signature for F major. After all, F major and D minor are relative keys and share the same key signature. If you were asked to notate the key signature of G minor, you could count up three half steps to B♭ and notate the key signature for B♭ major, the relative key of G minor. Notice that we don't use A♯ here. First of all, who would want to think in A♯ major!? But more important, when counting half steps, the relative relationship between the two keys needs to be a third apart, meaning there is a pitch letter in between the two keys. Think of it this way, you have the major and want the minor, count down (recognizing key signatures). You have the minor and want the major, count up (notating key signatures).

CIRCLE OF FIFTHS

As shown in the previous chapter, the circle of fifths can be used as an aid to memorize key signatures and the order of flats and sharps. The sharp keys are on the right, and the flat keys are on the left. As an interval of a fifth is added, whether that be ascending or descending, another accidental is also added. Major keys are found on the outside of the circle and minor keys on the inside. This circle makes it extremely easy to see the relationship between relative keys.

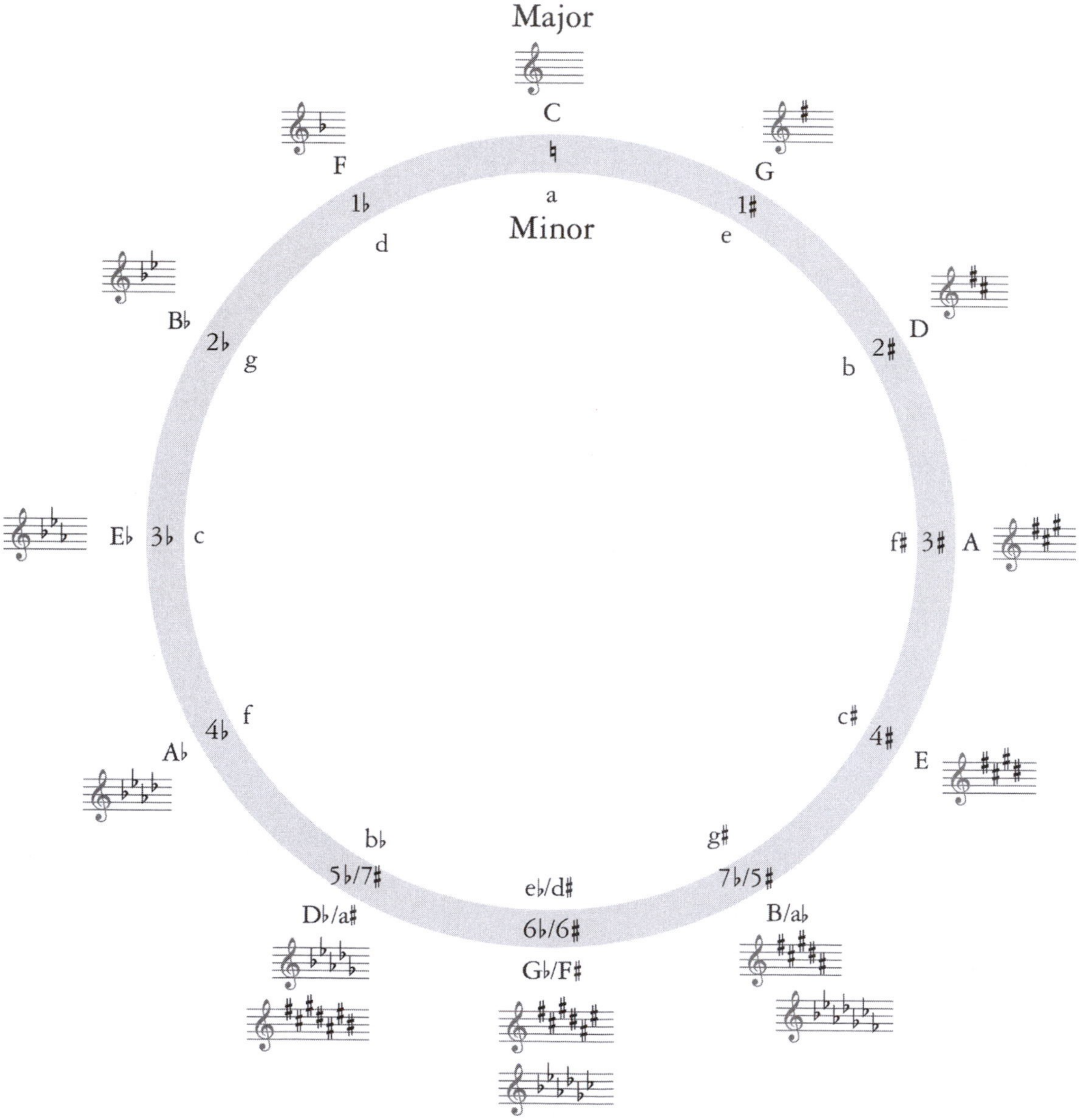

ARTIST IN RESIDENCE

An Overnight Rise to Stardom

As musicians, we all must embrace the opportunities that come our way. That moment happened for Lang Lang at the age of 17 when he was asked at the last minute to substitute for the famed pianist André Watts. This was not any typical performance: the piece to be played was the Tchaikovsky First Piano Concerto, and the accompanying ensemble was the Chicago Symphony Orchestra. In a *Chicago Tribune* article titled "17-Year-Old Sub Steals the Show at Ravinia Gala," the reviewer describes Lang Lang's performance:

> The fabulous technique, the absolute control (even at hell-bent tempos), the flexible rhythm, the firmly centered, infinitely colored tone that can switch on a dime from tornado-like intensity to supple delicacy, the risk-taking temperament—all these things are already there in his pianism. He is a phenomenal talent.

Ever since this performance in 1999, the music industry has been knocking, or more like pounding, on his door. Lang Lang has since played in concert halls and stadiums across the world, including performances at the 2007 and 2009 Nobel Peace Prize concerts, the revolutionary YouTube Symphony in 2008, the opening ceremonies of the 2008 Beijing Olympics, and the Queen's Jubilee Concert in 2012. In just the past 10 years, Lang Lang has been able to bring classical music to the masses. His playing can be heard on soundtracks of films such as *The Painted Veil* and *The Banquet*, and video games such as *Gran Turismo*, and his recordings are consistently on the top of the classical Billboard charts. But perhaps his biggest cross section of listeners became evident during the broadcast of the 2014 Grammy Awards.

Rolling Stone describes the unique collaboration on Metallica's hit "One" in the following account:

> Frontman James Hetfield played the song's iconic intro and Lang Lang played some expressive runs. Then, as the frontman sang about feeling disabled in war, Lang Lang stuck to his guns and played emotively along with the melody—then things got heavy. Just before the group was to launch into the track's jackhammer thrash riff, Lang Lang played classical trills and worked his way down to the lower notes on his piano, readying himself for the death rattle to come.

Take a few minutes to watch the Grammy performance on the YouTube channel. What effect does Lang Lang's opening have on the song as a whole?

WEBSITE
VIDEO TRACK 18

VIDEO TRACK 19

Listen and watch Lang Lang's performance of Rachmaninoff's *Preludes, Op. 23, No. 5,* as you follow along with the score. The key signature includes two flats, B♭ and E♭, which carries two possibilities in terms of keys and tonic, B♭ major or G minor. In order to determine which pitch is the tonic, B♭ or G, we must trust our eyes and ears. The eyes tell us that G is a very important pitch (it is continually repeated in the bass line for the first three measures), and the ear tells us that the pitch G is the true tonic and basis for the scale.

Rachmaninoff, *Preludes, Op. 23, No. 5*

G Minor Scale

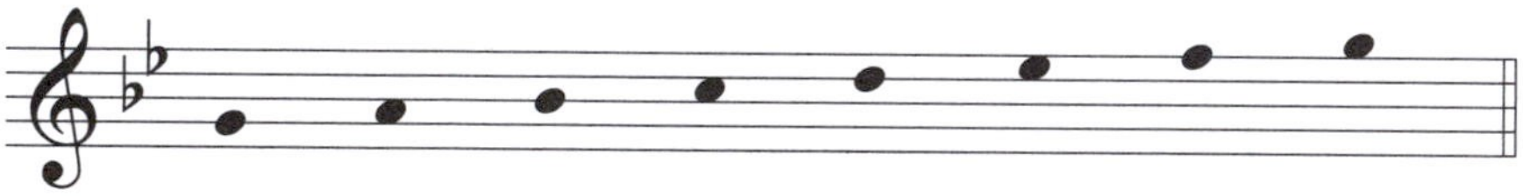

So, your question might be, where do the E♮ and F♯ come from? How is that explained in the key of G minor? Read on.

NATURAL MINOR SCALE

The first of three different minor scales, the **natural minor scale**, follows the key signature. Once the key signature is notated on the staff, the pitches follow in consecutive order up the octave. The intervallic makeup is WHWWHWW. Play through the natural minor scale.

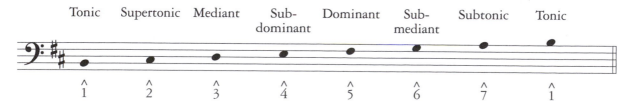

Tonic	Supertonic	Mediant	Subdominant	Dominant	Submediant	Subtonic	Tonic

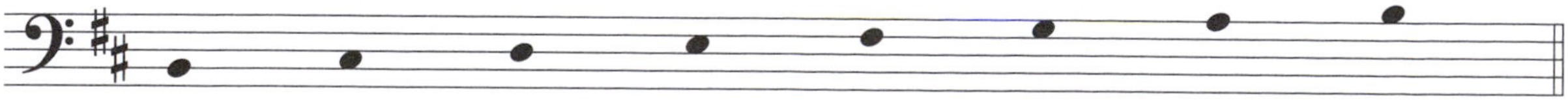

$\hat{1}$	$\hat{2}$	$\hat{3}$	$\hat{4}$	$\hat{5}$	$\hat{6}$	$\hat{7}$	$\hat{1}$

HARMONIC MINOR SCALE

We love the leading tone. There is something about that pull to the tonic that inspires songwriters to use it both harmonically in chords and within a melody. The **harmonic minor scale** does just that. The $\hat{7}$ is raised by one half step in order to create the half step relationship between the leading tone and the tonic. Play through the harmonic minor scale.

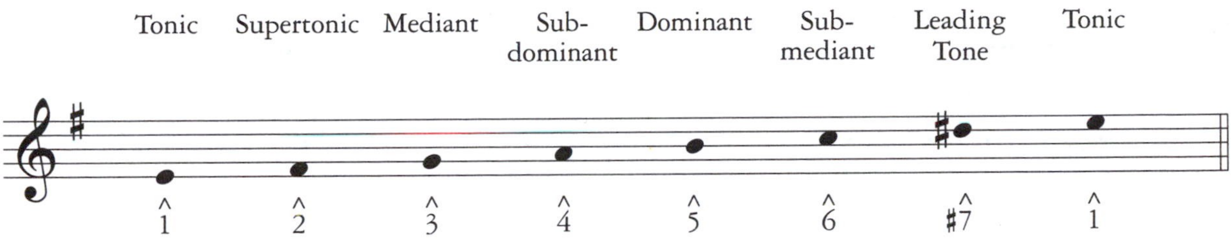

Look at the following example. The first line is in its original form, written in E major. The second and third examples are written using the E natural minor scale and the E harmonic minor scale. Even though it is subtle, the inclusion of the leading tone rather than the subtonic creates a completely different sound. Be sure to play through each example.

Rossini, Overture to *William Tell*

Franz Schubert's *Fantasy in F minor*, D. 940, is a constant conversation between two players. Written for four hands, the piece is played by two pianists who alternate the melody between the registers. In the YouTube video that accompanies this excerpt, Lang Lang plays through the composition with a young piano student.

Study the scores below. The key signature has four flats which signals that the piece is either based on the A♭ major or F minor scale. The opening six measures of the bass line highlight the pitch F. The E♮, notated in both scores, signals that the composer is using the F harmonic minor scale.

WEBSITE
VIDEO TRACK 20

Schubert, *Fantasy in F Minor*, D. 940

F Harmonic Minor Scale

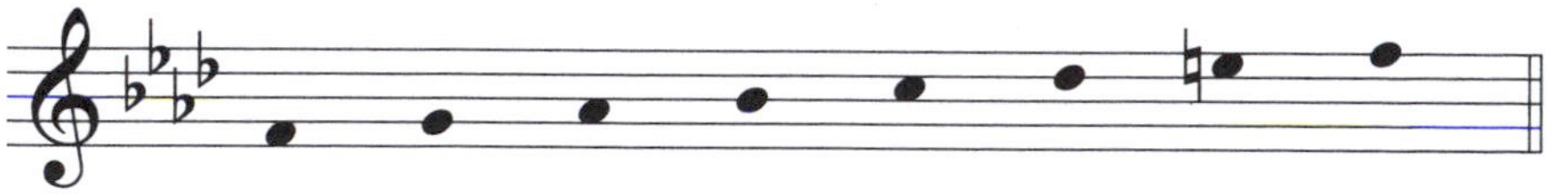

MELODIC MINOR SCALE

Although not a commonly accepted reason for the evolution of melodic minor, perhaps it is the singer that we blame for having to learn yet another form of the minor scale. The interval between the $\hat{6}$ and $\hat{7}$ of the harmonic scale is made up of three half steps, creating an interval that is very difficult to sing in tune when written as a second. Because of this, the $\hat{6}$ was raised on the ascent of the harmonic minor scale and the descent reverted back to the natural minor scale. A **melodic minor scale** is a natural minor scale with a raised $\hat{6}$ and $\hat{7}$ on the ascent. The $\hat{6}$ and $\hat{7}$ are lowered to the original natural minor scale on the descent. Play through the following scale.

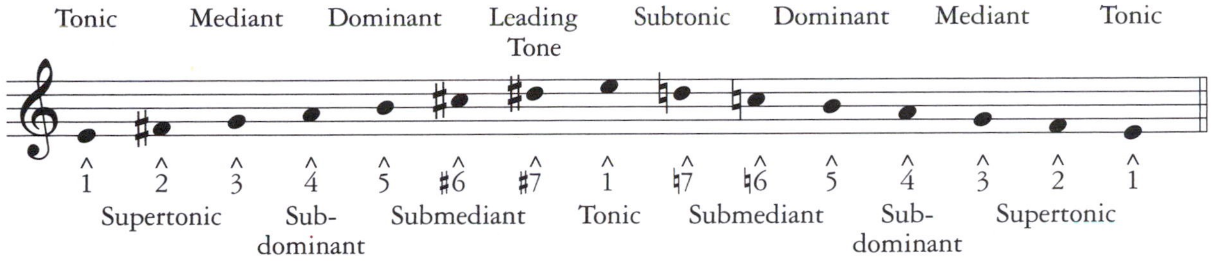

Watch Lang Lang's performance of "La Campanella" from *Grandes etudes de Paganini.* (Notice the audience reaction as Lang Lang takes the stage.) The key signature of this piece includes five sharps, and by using our eyes alone we might conclude that the piece is in B major. However, the addition of the F𝄪 and the pull to the G♯ firmly establish the key of G♯ minor. The E♯ and F𝄪 that are used through the opening section are the raised $\hat{6}$ and $\hat{7}$. Remember that in order to raise a F♯ a half a step Liszt would have to notate a F𝄪. The composition is in the key of G♯ minor and Liszt uses the pitches from the melodic minor scale.

VIDEO TRACK 21

Liszt, "La Campanella" from *Grandes etudes de Paganini*

Liszt, "La Campanella" from *Grandes etudes de Paganini (continued)*

G♯ Melodic Minor Scale

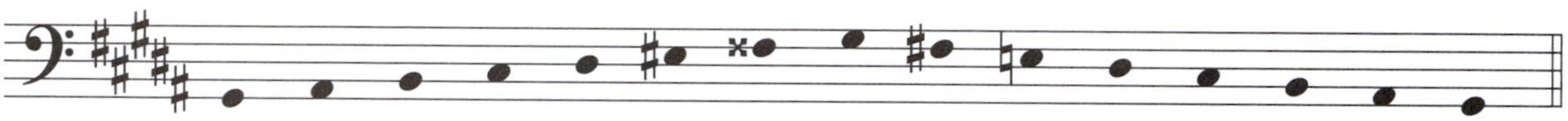

The Rachmaninoff example from *Preludes, Op. 23, No. 5* (page 54), is also based on the melodic minor scale. The E♮ and F♯ circled in the score below are merely the raised $\hat{6}$ and $\hat{7}$ of the G melodic minor scale.

WEBSITE

VIDEO
TRACK 19

Rachmaninoff, *Preludes, Op. 23, No. 5*

G Melodic Minor Scale

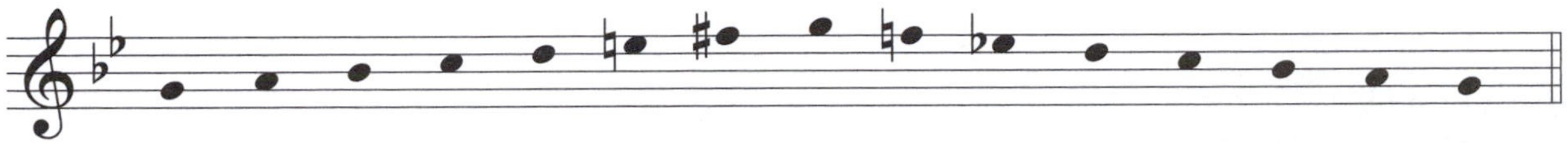

ARTIST IN RESIDENCE

Practice Makes Perfect

Before most 3-year-olds are able to sit still for 5 minutes, 3-year-old Lang Lang began taking piano lessons in Shenyang, China. Lang Lang was only 9 when his father and piano teacher decided it would be best for Lang Lang to study in Beijing to have a better chance of entering the Central Conservatory of Music. It was not a good time in Lang Lang's life. His father was extremely hard on Lang Lang and pushed him to extremes to perform and practice. The climax of this difficult relationship occurred shortly after Lang Lang moved to Beijing. Lang Lang recounts the events in an interview with *The Guardian* magazine:

> "One afternoon she [Lang Lang's piano teacher] said that I had no talent, that I shouldn't play the piano and I should go home. She basically fired me before I could even get into the conservatory!"
>
> Unbelievably, when Lang Lang's father heard the news, he demanded that the boy take his own life. "It's really hard to talk about. My father went totally nuts," says Lang Lang quietly. "He said: 'You shouldn't live any more—everything is destroyed.'" The father handed his son a bottle saying, "Take these pills!" When Lang Lang ran out onto the balcony to get away from him, his father screamed: "Then jump off and die."
>
> "I got totally crazy too," says Lang Lang. "I was beating the wall, trying to prevent myself from being a pianist by destroying my hands. I hated everything: my father, the piano, myself. I went nuts too. And then somehow, we just stopped. My father went out or I ran out—I can't remember, but somehow we stopped."

For 3 months after this altercation, Lang Lang did not touch the piano. He eventually rekindled his love for the instrument when a group of classmates highly encouraged him to resume playing. Lang Lang was admitted to the conservatory in Shanghai and has since made peace with his father, who now manages his career from China.

So what brought on that tense moment between father and son? Lang Lang's father has been quoted as saying, "Pressure always turns into motivation. Lang Lang is well aware that if he fails to be outstanding at playing the piano, he has nothing."

ARTIST IN RESIDENCE

Giving Back

In the midst of an extensive touring and recording schedule, Lang Lang finds the time to give back, especially to children. He was appointed the International Goodwill Ambassador for the United Nation's Children's Fund (UNICEF) in 2004 and serves on the advisory board of Carnegie Hall's educational program. In 2008, he launched the Lang Lang Foundation (www.langlangfoundation.org). The purpose of the foundation is "to inspire and motivate the next generation of classical music lovers and performers and to encourage music performance at all levels as a means of social development for youth, building self confidence and a drive for excellence." Through funding from both private and corporate sponsors, such as MasterCard and Sony, the foundation is able to offer musical experiences including the young scholars program, junior music camp, and "101 Pianists," a collaborative performance/master class experience that includes 100 young pianists and Lang Lang.

Reviewing Chapter Objectives

- Notate all three minor scales (pages 50, 55, 57)
- Identify scale degree names in context of the minor scale (pages 50, 55, 57)
- Identify and notate minor key signatures (pages 51–52)
- Determine scale type used in musical context (pages 55–58)

EXERCISES

I. Given the tonic and scale type, notate both the key signature and pitches on the staff. For melodic minor scales, notate both the ascending and descening line.

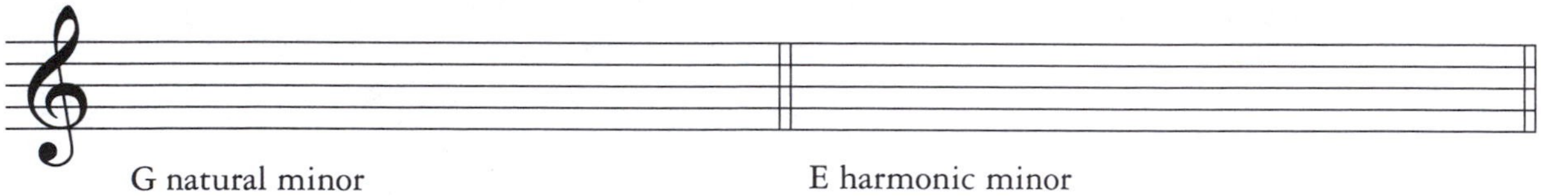

G natural minor E harmonic minor

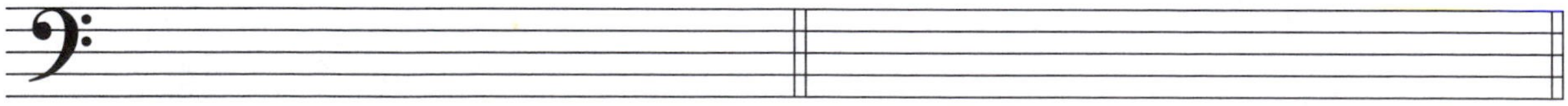

B harmonic minor A♭ natural minor

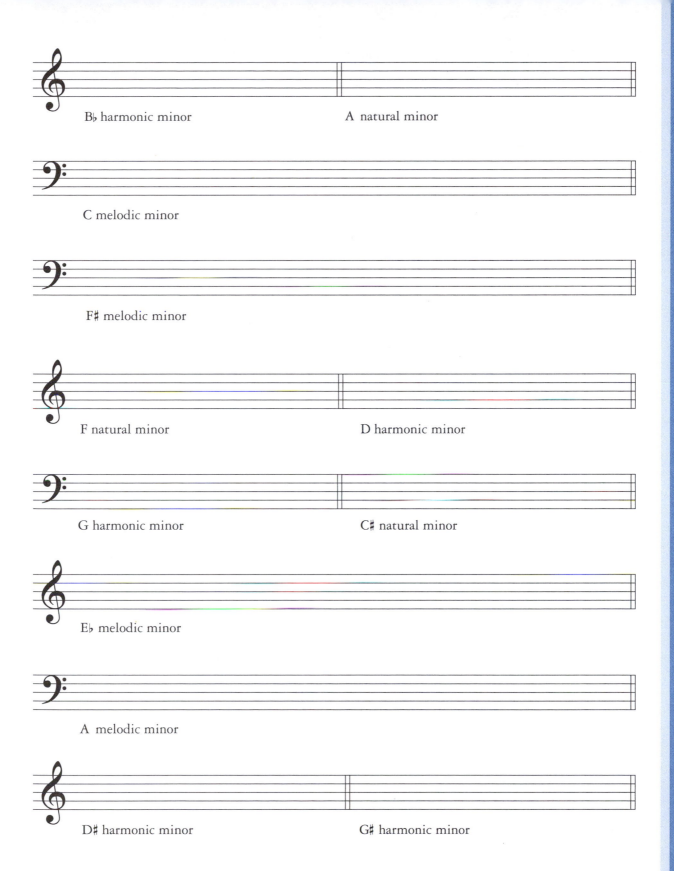

B♭ harmonic minor

A natural minor

C melodic minor

F♯ melodic minor

F natural minor

D harmonic minor

G harmonic minor

C♯ natural minor

E♭ melodic minor

A melodic minor

D♯ harmonic minor

G♯ harmonic minor

II. Given the scale type and scale degree name, notate the appropriate scale AFTER you have located the correct tonic. Use correct key signatures. For melodic minor scales, notate both the ascending and descening line.

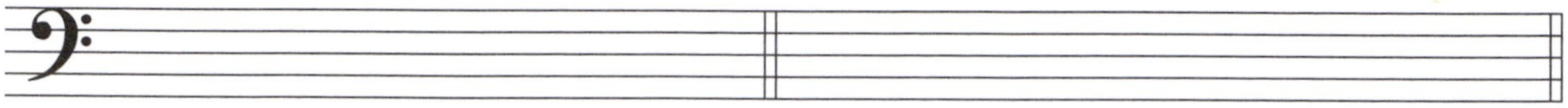

Harmonic minor, Leading tone: G♯

Natural minor, Submediant: C

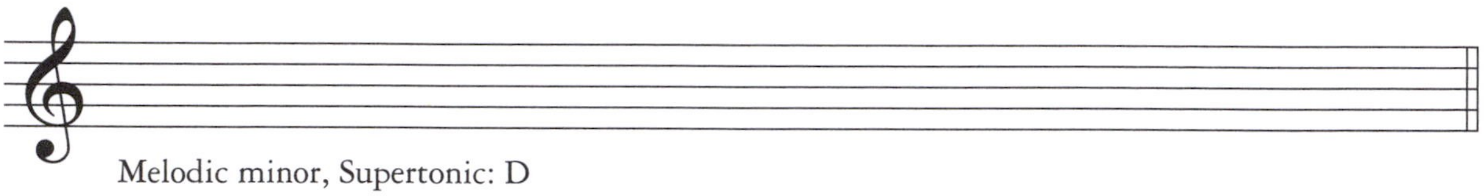

Melodic minor, Supertonic: D

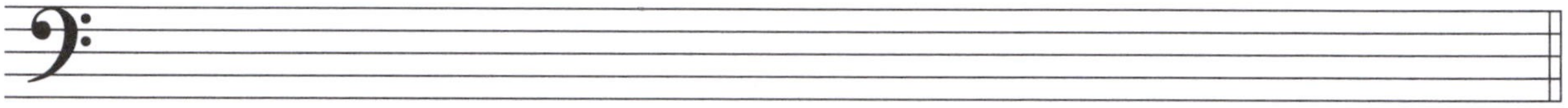

Melodic minor, Subdominant: E

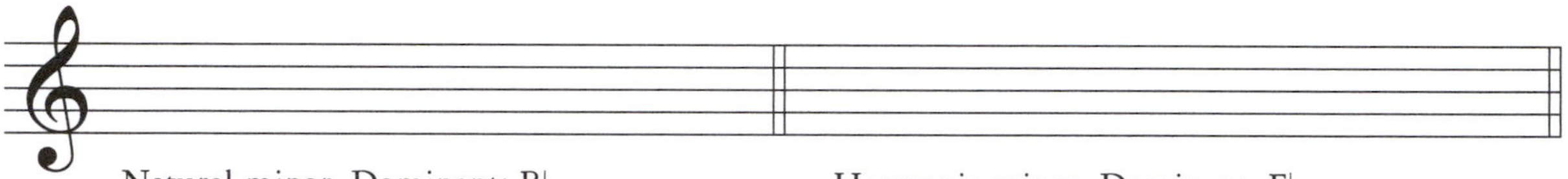

Natural minor, Dominant: B♭

Harmonic minor, Dominant: E♭

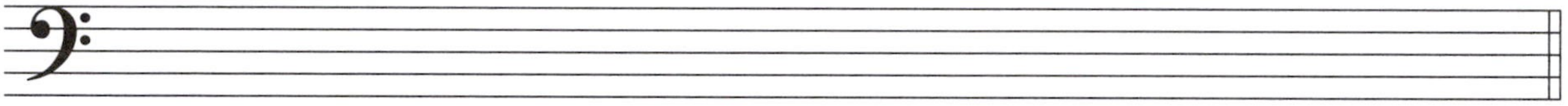

Melodic minor, Supertonic: B

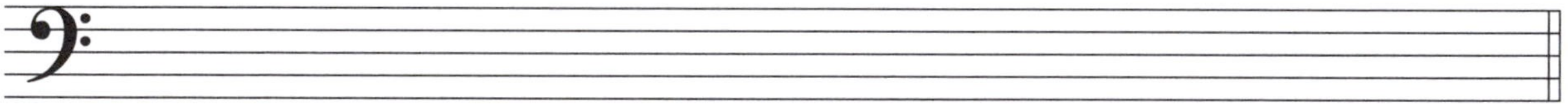

Harmonic minor, Supertonic: G♯

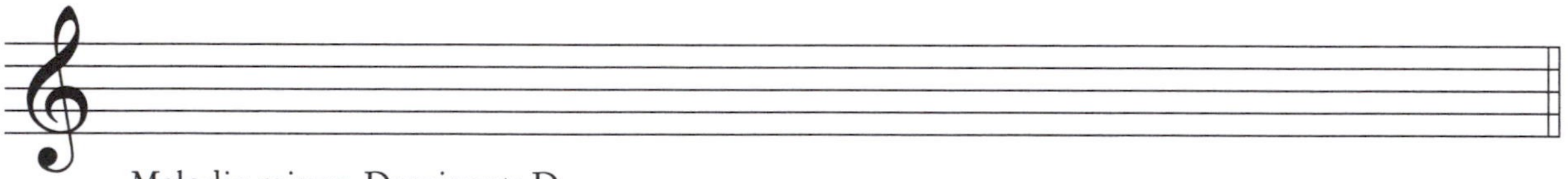

Melodic minor, Dominant: D

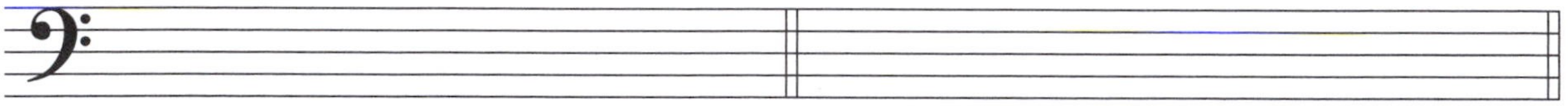

Harmonic minor, Subdominant: F

Natural minor, Subtonic: F

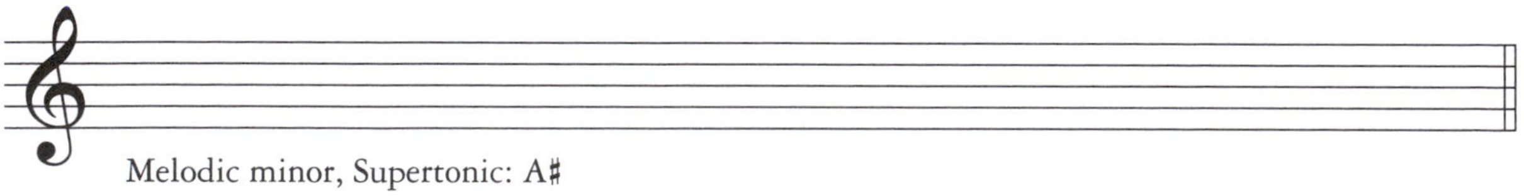

Melodic minor, Supertonic: A♯

III. Identify the minor key signatures.*

IV. Notate the following minor key signatures on the staff. Be sure to follow correct placement.

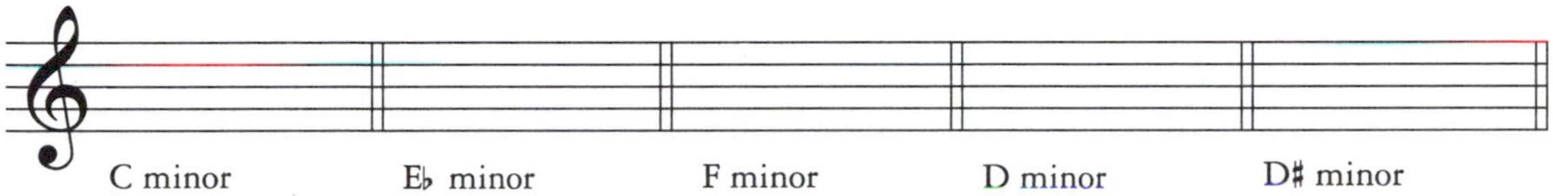

C minor | E♭ minor | F minor | D minor | D♯ minor

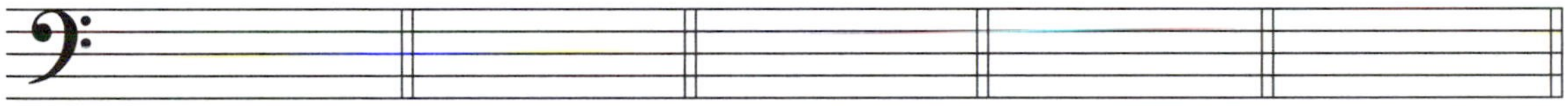

C♯ minor | B minor | F♯ minor | A minor | B♭ minor

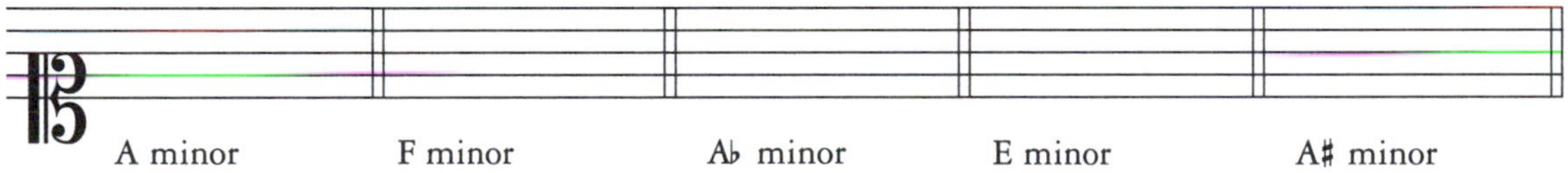

A minor | F minor | A♭ minor | E minor | A♯ minor

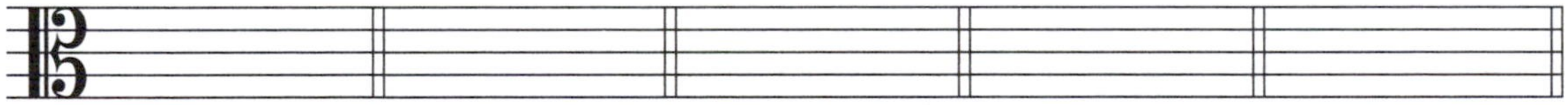

B♭ minor | C minor | F♯ minor | E♭ minor | D minor

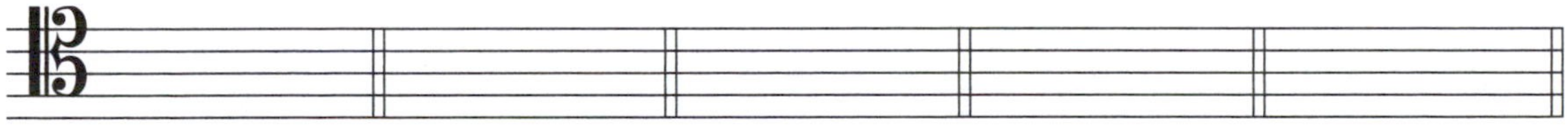

F minor | G♯ minor | B minor | G minor | E minor

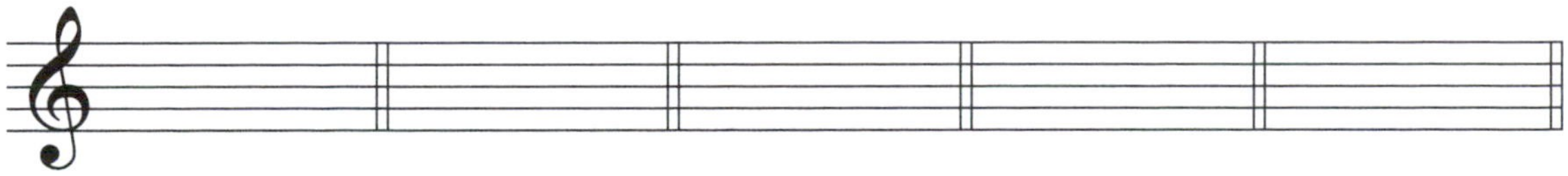

C♯ minor | E minor | A♭ minor | G minor | B minor

*Placement for key signatures in C Clefs are explained in online resource.

V. Play through the following melodies. Determine which scale the melody is based on by looking at the key signature. If the melody is based on a minor scale, correctly identify the minor scale type (natural, harmonic, or melodic).

VI. Analysis from Vivaldi's *The Four Seasons*

WEBSITE
VIDEO TRACKS 22 AND 23

The movements from *The Four Seasons* have been used in countless movies and television commercials. Brief excerpts for each of the four seasons are notated below. Using your ears and your knowledge of major and minor keys, determine the key of each excerpt. If the excerpt is in minor, determine the scale type used (natural, harmonic, or melodic).

Vivaldi, *The Four Seasons*

Summer
Allegro non molto
Vln. Solo
Vln. I
Vln. II
Vla.
Vc. and Bass
pp
7
6

Autumn

Winter
22
Vln. Solo
Vln. I
Vln. II
Vla.
Vc. and Bass
24
Vln. Solo
Vln. I
Vln. II
Vla.
Vc. and Bass

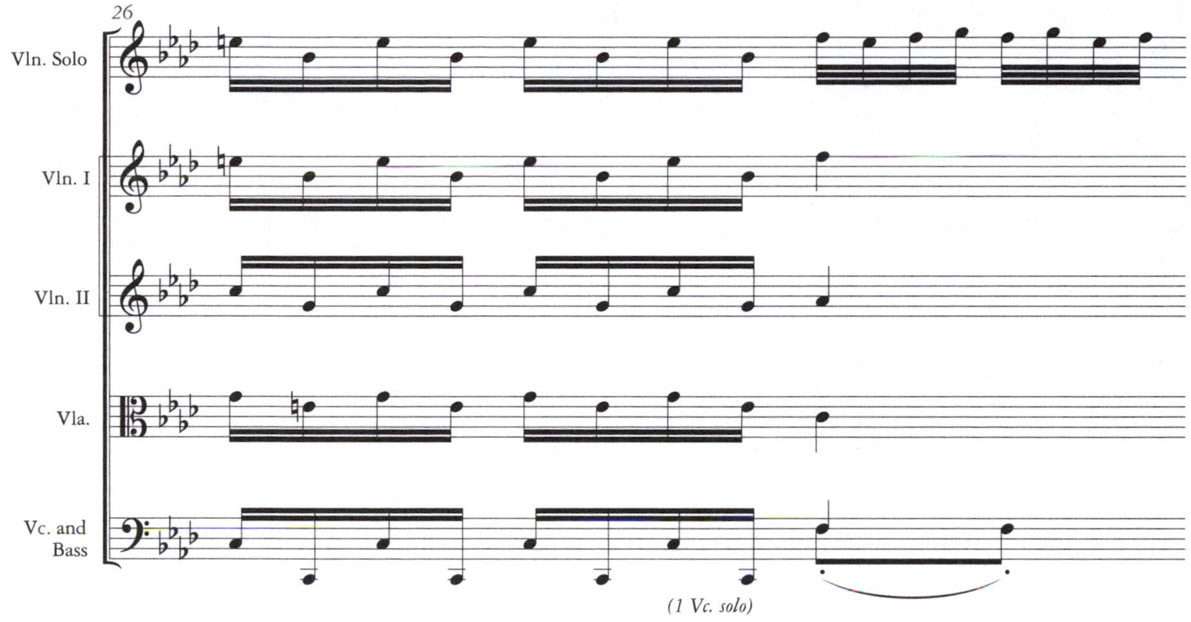

AURAL SKILLS CONDITIONING 3

Solfège is used for both major and minor scales. The B harmonic minor scale is shown below with solfège and scale degrees. In "moveable do" solfège, the syllable "do" is assigned to the tonic of any major or minor key.

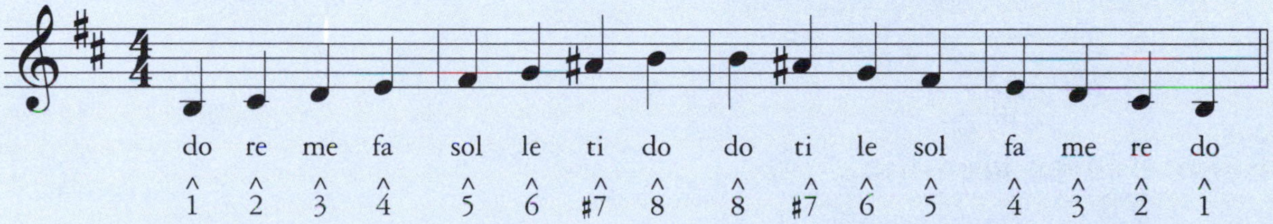

With your classmates, sing a harmonic minor scale ascending and descending. Then, try singing the syllables in the following pattern:

do! do–re–do! do–re–me–re–do! do–re–me–fa–me–re–do . . .

And descending:

do! do–ti–do! do–ti–le–ti–do! do–ti–le–sol–le–ti–do . . .

What other patterns for singing the scale can you come up with?

Sight Singing: Melodies That Move by Step

There are ten melodies following. First, identify the key. Try speaking the solfège syllables in rhythm. Then, sing the melodies on solfège in the correct rhythm.

1.

2.

3.

4.

5.

6.

7.

8.

9.

10.

Scale Degree Identification

AUDIO TRACKS CH. 3 SCALE DEGREE 1–12

You will hear your instructor perform part of a major or minor scale and stop on a scale degree. This is also available for listening on the course website. Write down the solfège syllable for the scale degree that you hear.

1. ______ 2. ______ 3. ______ 4. ______ 5. ______ 6. ______

Now, you will hear the entire scale performed (ascending and descending) and then one scale degree will be played. Write down the solfège syllable that you hear.

7. ______ 8. ______ 9. ______ 10. ______ 11. ______ 12. ______

CHAPTER 4

INTERVALS

Artist in Residence: Adele

Chapter Objectives

- Identify melodic and harmonic intervals both in quality and size
- Notate specified intervals
- Recognize intervals within a musical score
- Understand transposing instruments in terms of interval of transposition
- Transpose a musical line for use with various instruments

Imagine singing along to "Let It Go" from *Frozen* without the leap up on to the phrase "I don't care what they're going to say." Or if the opening of Goyte's "Somebody That I Used to Know" consisted only of the opening verses and not the large leap to the chorus with "She didn't have to cut me off." If you aren't familiar with these songs, just take a quick listen. Music would be pretty monotonous if the notes were made up of only half and whole steps. For that reason, we are grateful to take on the study of **intervals**, the distance between two pitches. **Melodic intervals** occur when two pitches sound in succession, and **harmonic intervals** occur when the pitches sound simultaneously.

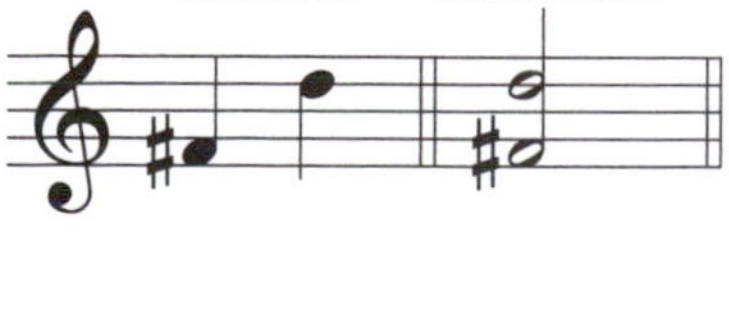

The **interval number**, or size, can be determined by counting the letters between the two pitches. The figure below shows several intervals and their corresponding interval number. The first example is a fourth, because the number of letters in between C and F, including the C and F is four (C, D, E, and F). The second example is a sixth, because the number of letters in between E and C♯ is 6 (E, F, G, A, B, C).

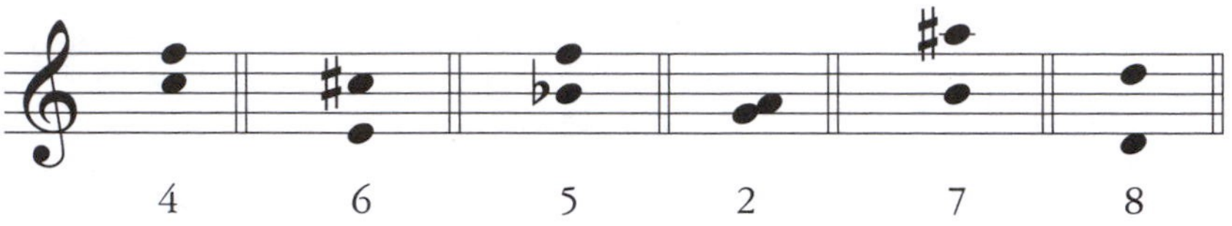

Play the following intervals on your keyboard or guitar.

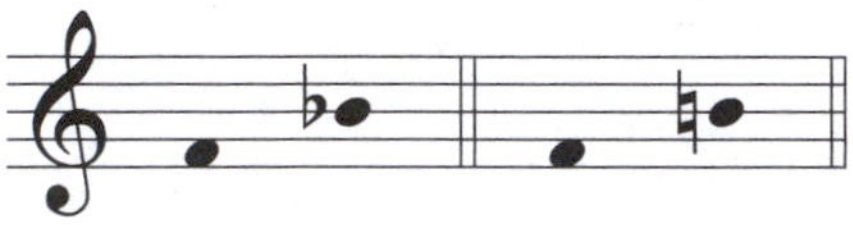

The distance between F and B is a fourth, so the interval size is the same, but they certainly sound different. That is because intervals are identified by both interval size and interval quality.

INTERVAL QUALITY: THE MAJOR SCALE METHOD (1, 4, 5, 8)

The intervals of the 1, 4, 5, and 8 are unique in many regards and are sometimes called the **perfect intervals**. Look at where these intervals naturally lie in the major scale in relationship to the tonic.

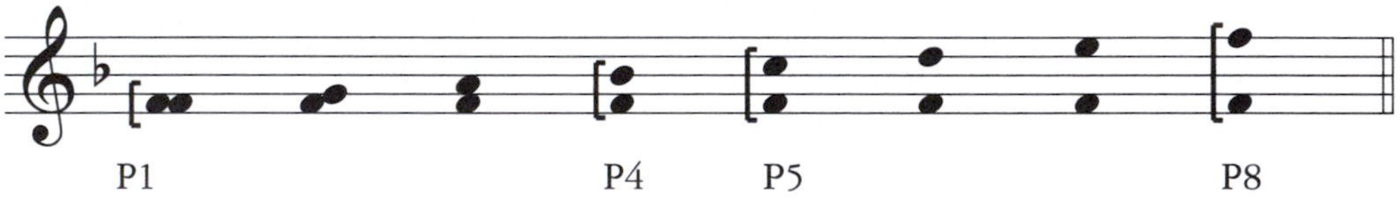

The perfect intervals are on the tonic, subdominant, and dominant. Listen to these intervals. When you play them, they should sound fairly consonant, especially historically speaking. More on why they are called perfect later (page 73)!

The smallest interval is that of the unison, sometimes called **prime**. The pitch F to the same pitch F is an example of this. The **octave** is formed when the pitch is repeated in a different register, such as F4 to F5.

If the upper pitch of a 1, 4, 5, or 8 is diatonic in the major scale of the lower pitch, the interval quality is always perfect.

But what if the interval uses a pitch outside of the major scale? This happens often, and for that reason, we need to have an excellent understanding of the major key signatures.

In order to identify the correct quality of the interval, determine whether the upper pitch is found within the major key of the bottom pitch. If the top pitch is found diatonically within the key, the interval is perfect. If the upper pitch is raised a half step, the interval is labeled augmented (+) because the interval is made larger. If the upper pitch is a half step lower, the interval is labeled as diminished (°) because the interval is made smaller. Let's put this into a specific context.

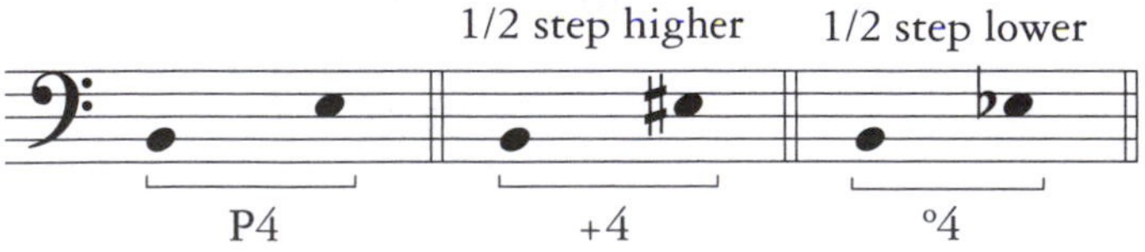

All three of the intervals are fourths. By thinking in the key of B major (the lowest pitch of the interval), you know that E is found diatonically in the key, so the first interval is a perfect fourth. The second interval uses E♯ and is a half a step above what you expect it to be—there's the augmented fourth. The E♭ is not found diatonically within the key of B major and is a half step below the expected E♮. The interval is labeled as a diminished fourth. The following chart may help you a bit!

Interval size 1, 4, 5, 8		
½ step below ⟵	Top pitch fits into key	⟶ ½ step above
Diminished	**Perfect**	**Augmented**

Study the example below to determine whether each upper pitch is diatonic.

The only interval that is perfect is the last interval.

INVERSION OF INTERVALS

You may be asking, "But, what if I can't think in the key of the bottom note? Who wants to think in the key of F♭, or even worse, G♯?" That's where inversion comes in and will fully answer the question about why 1, 4, 5, and 8 are called the perfect intervals.

An **inverted interval** is just that: the original lower pitch becomes the upper pitch and vice versa. When a perfect interval is inverted, it *stays* perfect. The pitches F up to B♭ create a perfect fourth (the B♭ is diatonic in the key of F). By flipping the interval and placing the B♭ as the lowest pitch, the interval is now identified as a perfect fifth (B♭–F). In the same manner, a diminished interval will invert to an augmented interval and an augmented interval will invert to a diminished interval.

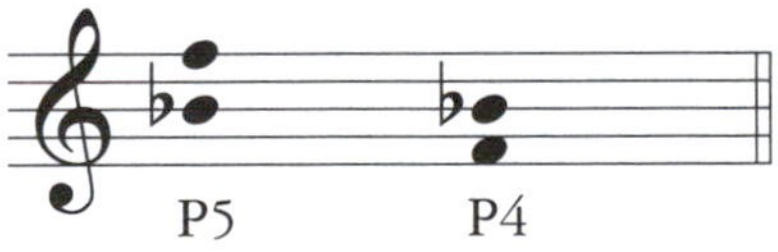

Inverting intervals is a helpful practice when you can't seem to think in the key of the bottom note. Study the interval below. No one wants to think in the key of F♭, so flip the interval. The B♭ is now on the bottom and we can easily determine that the interval is a diminished fifth. By default, the inversion of the diminished fifth is an augmented fourth.

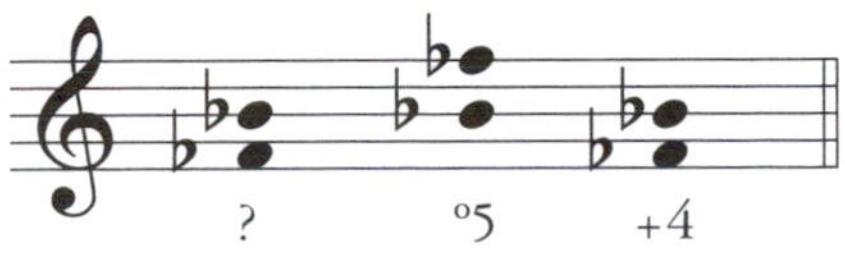

Perfect inverts to perfect.
Diminished inverts to augmented.
Augmented inverts to diminished.

BACKSTAGE PASS

Rolling in the Deep

WEBSITE

VIDEO TRACK 24

In early 2011, the then 23-year-old British singer Adele found herself at the top of the charts with two singles and two albums. That was no small task considering the only other group to reach this milestone was the Beatles back in 1964. You could hardly turn on the radio in 2011 without hearing "Rolling in the Deep" at least once every hour. The song spent 7 weeks at number 1 on the Billboard Hot 100 and is still one of the biggest-selling digital downloads of all time. The album *21* was number 1 in twenty-six countries and sold 352,000 copies in its first week. Unbelievable! By the time the 2012 Grammys came around, it was basically a given that Adele would sweep all the categories. No one was surprised when she left the auditorium with Record of the Year, Album of the Year, Song of the Year, Best Pop Solo Performance, Best Pop Vocal Album, and Best Music Video.

Born in London in 1988, Adele Laurie Blue Adkins was enthralled by music, including the vocals of Etta James, Ella Fitzgerald, the Spice Girls, Destiny's Child, and even Pink. In an interview with *Spinner* magazine, Adele describes watching a performance of Pink at Brixton Academy: "I had never heard, being in the room, someone sing like that live. I remember sort of feeling like I was in a wind tunnel, her voice just hitting me. It was incredible." Adele was only 13 years old.

21 wasn't her first album and it certainly wasn't her first success. Her debut album, *19*, entered the British charts at number 1. Adele credits her success in the United States with her October 2008 appearance on *Saturday Night Live*. During the taping of the show, *19* was ranked number 40 on iTunes. Less than 24 hours later, it had climbed to number 1. That's the power of late night television!

WEBSITE

VIDEO TRACK 25

Written by Adele and Ryan Tedder, the song "Rumour Has It" is the only single released from *21* to not reach the number 1 spot on Billboard's Hot 100. It peaked at number 16, but interestingly enough, the mash-up version heard on the television series *Glee* outranked the single by ascending to the number 11 spot in December of 2011. (Interestingly enough, it did take the top spot in both Israel and South Korea!) The jazz influences, along with the driving percussion motive, are the main players in this particular song.

Listen to "Rumour Has It" on the YouTube channel. How would you describe the overall sound, especially the sudden change at 2:20? Adele herself even called it a "bluesy, pop stomping song."

The middle eleven measures are strikingly different from the rest of the song. Study the following excerpt from "Rumor Has It." The perfect fourth and fifth and diminished fourths and fifths are marked for you in the score. Practice identifying other intervals throughout the score.

Adele, "Rumour Has It." Songwriters: Adele and Ryan Tedder

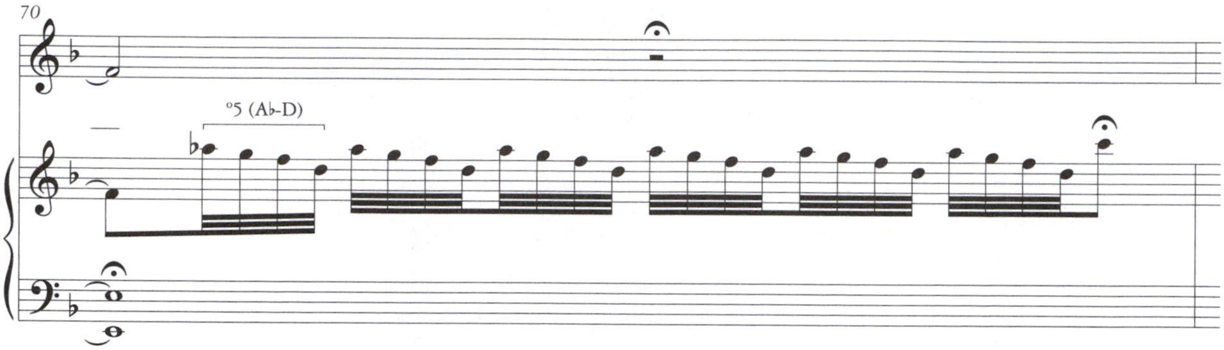

INTERVAL QUALITY: THE MAJOR SCALE METHOD (2, 3, 6, 7)

So, what about the remaining intervals found in the major scale? Well, as you might have figured out by now in terms of their relationship to tonic, they must be named something other than perfect. Listen to the following intervals as you play them on your piano or guitar.

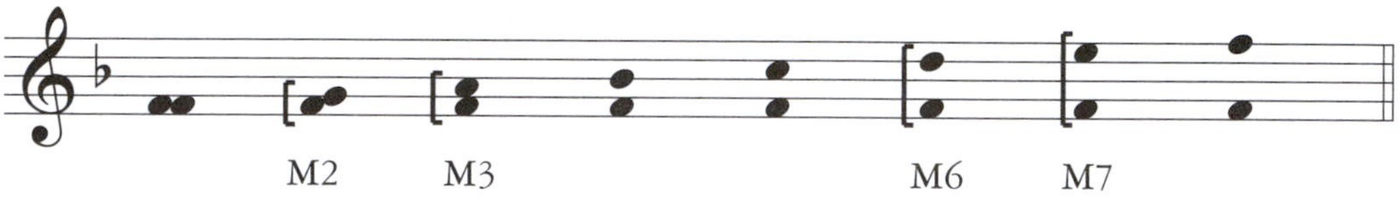

Just like intervals of the 1, 4, 5, and 8, we can determine quality by relating the top pitch of the interval to the lower pitch. If the top pitch is found diatonically within the key, the interval is major. If the upper pitch is raised a half a step, the interval is labeled augmented because the interval is made larger. Here's where it differs: if the upper pitch is a half step below, the interval is labeled as minor; if the upper pitch is a whole step below, the interval is labeled as diminished.

Interval size 2, 3, 6, 7			
½ step below ←	½ step below ←	Top pitch fits into key →	½ step above
Diminished	**Minor**	**Major**	**Augmented**

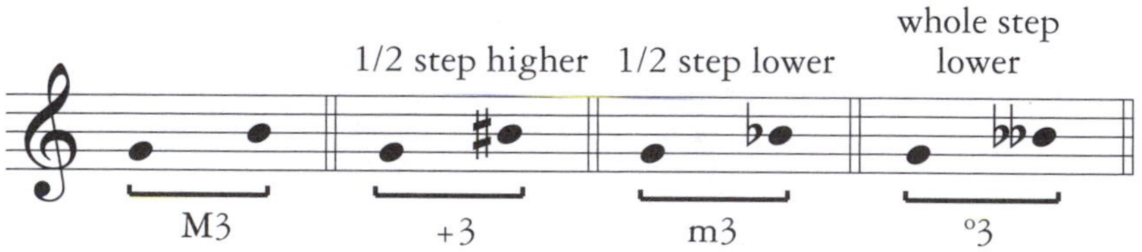

The key signature of G includes one sharp, F♯, so the B is diatonic in the key. That's why we would label the first interval above as a major third. Use the interval quality chart above to better understand the identification of the other intervals.

But again, what about if you don't want to think in the key of the bottom note? Let's look at F𝄪–D. It sounds horrifyingly difficult, right?

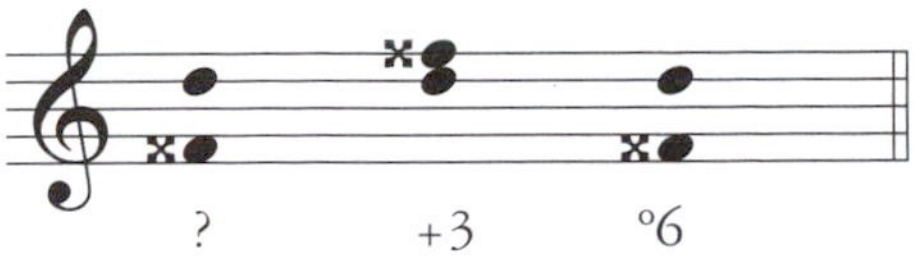

Not really. All you need to do is invert the intervals so that the F𝄪 is now the top pitch. By understanding that the D–F𝄪 is an augmented third, we can assume that the F𝄪–D is a diminished sixth.

Perfect inverts to perfect.
Minor inverts to major.
Major inverts to minor.
Diminished inverts to augmented.
Augmented inverts to diminished.

COMPOUND INTERVALS

What if an interval goes beyond the octave? In a **compound interval**, the interval spans a space larger than an octave. We label these intervals with the correct interval size, but interval quality is the same as its reduced version within the octave.

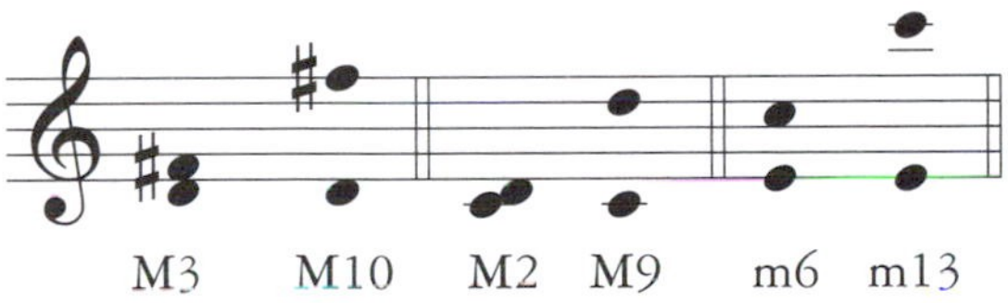

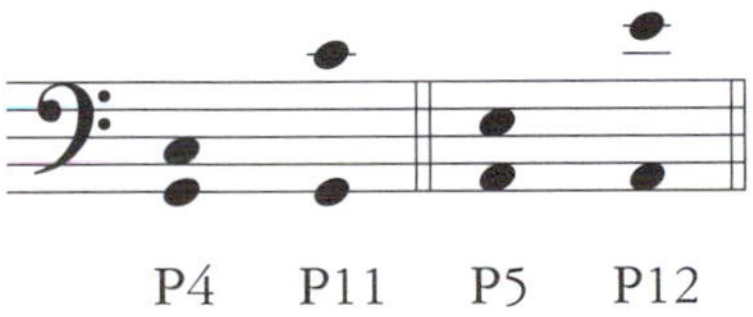

Released as the third single from *21*, "Set Fire to the Rain" quickly climbed to the top of the charts in eight different countries. How is this song different in both style and performance from "Rumour Has It"?

Study the intervals marked in the following score. All intervals sizes are included in the analysis, including several compound intervals.

WEBSITE
VIDEO TRACK 26

Adele, "Set Fire to the Rain." Songwriters: Adele and Fraser T. Smith

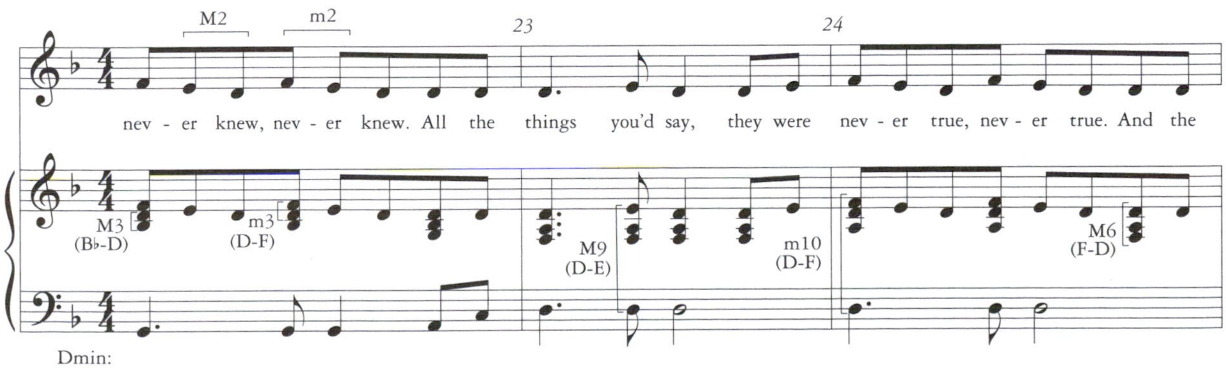

Adele, "Set Fire to the Rain." Songwriters: Adele and Fraser T. Smith *(continued)*

What if both pitches of the interval make it impossible for you to use the major scale method? Look at the following example.

No matter what you do or how you flip the pitches, you are not able to think in the key of G♯ major or even worse E♯ major. If both pitches are affected by the same accidental, the accidentals can be ignored. The distance between G♯–E♯ is exactly the same as G–E. Think in the key of the bottom note G. G has one sharp, F♯, so the pitch E should look exactly like this in G major. This is then a major sixth. Still a skeptic. Count the half steps.

THE HALF STEP METHOD

While the major scale method is the preferred method, some students find the half step method to be helpful when identifying interval qualities. Once you have mastered key signatures, you will no longer need to count half steps for interval identification. Here is the complete table of half steps:

Interval	Half Steps	Interval	Half Steps
P1	0	A4/d5	6
m2	1	P5	7
M2	2	m6	8
m3	3	M6	9
M3	4	m7	10
P4	5	M7	11

BACKSTAGE PASS

Time for Something a Little Different and a Little More Real

Adele's voice and performances are so different from what was popular in 2011. If you take a look at the other top hits of 2011, you will see the LMFAO's "Party Rock Anthem" and Katy Perry's "Fireworks" were the other songs topping the charts. What makes Adele so unique?

Perhaps the public was in the mood for a shift. We had already seen the large stage set, the crowd of backup dancers, and sophisticated laser shows. The biggest musical event of the year was not a large spectacle: it was a 23-year-old Londoner in a nice black dress and heels. She simply opened her mouth and sang, letting her voice speak for itself.

WRITING INTERVALS ON THE STAFF

Many times you will hear a conductor or session leader say something to the effect of, "Give me a perfect fourth above F or play a minor third above that D♭." In order to do this quickly, you will have to count letter names and then determine quality.

Say that you are asked to play a perfect fourth above F. Count up four letters from F, and you land on B. Determine whether the pitch B is diatonic in the key of F. It isn't, so in order for the pitch to be perfect and "fit" into the key, we need to add a B♭. The same process works for the minor third above D♭. Count up three, and you find the pitch F. F is diatonic in the key of D♭, but we want a minor third. Lower the F by a half step by inserting the flat.

A similar process should be used carefully to write an interval below a given pitch. You will have to count down on letter names, which always leaves a margin for error.

Let's say you are asked to write a minor sixth below the pitch G♯. Notate the given letter name, and count down to B. You know that the interval has to start with some sort of B—but whether it will be a B, B♯, or B♭ has yet to be determined. What interval is created when you insert the B? A major sixth, but we want a minor sixth. What do you have to do to make the interval smaller? Raise the B. Do not be deceived into thinking that sharps always indicate larger size. If the sharp is on the bottom, it is actually making the interval smaller.

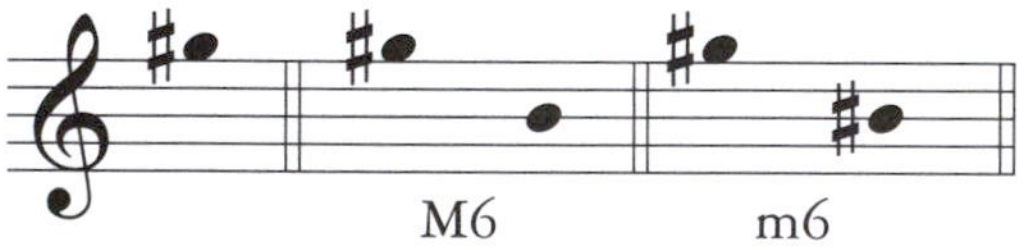

"Someone Like You" is one of those songs that everyone knows, whether you are a classical music buff or a bluegrass junkie. It is one of the most downloaded songs of all time in the United Kingdom and topped the charts in twenty-one countries. What is it about this song that makes it so compelling? Is it the fact that we all have been there? It is no secret that Adele wrote this, and the entire album *21*, about an ex-boyfriend. Her performance at the BRIT Awards shows how raw she still was from the entire experience. She later reflected on her feelings that night:

> "I was really emotional by the end because I'm quite overwhelmed by everything anyway, and then I had a vision of my ex, of him watching me at home and he's going to be laughing at me because he knows I'm crying because of him, with him thinking, 'Yep, she's still wrapped around my finger.' Then everyone stood up, so I was overwhelmed."

VIDEO TRACK 27

Study the intervals marked in the excerpt from "Someone Like You" while you listen to the song on the YouTube channel.

Adele, "Someone Like You." Songwriters: Adele and Dan Wilson

BACKSTAGE PASS

The Dangers of the Rock-Star Lifestyle

In late 2011, Adele was flying high on the success of *21*. But that all stopped abruptly when she suffered a hemorrhaged polyp on her vocal cords. She was ordered to go on vocal rest immediately to avoid permanent damage. All performances, including her sold-out tour, were canceled. This is not a unique phenomenon: other famous singers including Julie Andrews, Steven Tyler, and John Mayer have suffered vocal damage and gone through vocal surgery. In an interview with MTV, a doctor weighed in on Adele's vocal situation: "Given that it's a hemorrhage, that means it's blood, it's actual blood that's weighing the larynx down." It is virtually impossible to sing during a bout of laryngitis, so Adele rested and prepped for surgery. Everyone was concerned about whether she would sound the same after the surgery. After all, some singers have not come out on the other side of vocal surgery successfully, including the famed Julie Andrews. To make things even more dramatic, her comeback performance was scheduled for the Grammy broadcast. Watch the performance on the YouTube channel, and judge for yourself the success of her comeback.

WEBSITE
VIDEO TRACK 28

TRANSPOSITION OF INSTRUMENTS

When a clarinet player sees a D on the staff, the sound, or concert pitch, played is actually a C. What? Wait a second. So, the pitch on the staff isn't necessarily the same as the sound that the instrument plays? Exactly. For those who have played a transposing instrument for the past 10 years, this is a no-brainer. For others who have played piano or sung in choirs, this is mind-blowing.

But why are some instruments tuned differently, resulting in this need for transposition? Well, there are several reasons for this, including some pretty complicated historical background in terms of tuning and valves as well as factors involving flexibility of performance with instruments in a family. For instance, the clarinet family has five main clarinets (soprano E♭ clarinet, B♭ clarinet, clarinet in A, alto E♭ clarinet, and B♭ bass clarinet). All of these clarinets are designed to suit a particular range of sound. To make it easier for the performer to switch between all of these clarinets, all clarinet music is written so that the fingering for each instrument is the same. Musicians must understand transpositions in order to conduct, arrange, or compose. The following chart shows frequently used instruments and their transpositions.

Instrument Name	Transposition (sounds: when looking at score)	Transposition (written: when composing on staff)
Piccolo	Up a P8	Down a P8
English horn	Down a P5	Up a P5
Soprano clarinet in E♭	Up a m3	Down a m3
Clarinet in B♭	Down a M2	Up a M2

Instrument Name	Transposition (sounds: when looking at score)	Transposition (written: when composing on staff)
Alto clarinet	Down a M6	Up a M6
Bass clarinet	Down a M2 + P8	Up a M2 + P8
Soprano sax (B♭)	Down a M2	Up a M2
Alto sax (E♭)	Down a M6	Up a M6
Tenor sax (B♭)	Down a M2 +P8	Up a M2 +P8
Baritone sax (E♭)	Down a M6 + P8	Up a M6 + P8
Trumpet in B♭	Down a M2	Up a M2
Horn in F	Down a P5	Up a P5
Guitar	Down a P8	Up a P8
Double bass	Down a P8	Up a P8

When looking at a musical score:

Use the chart above to determine the interval of transposition. When the performer "plays" the note as written on the page, it will "sound" above or below the note based upon the interval of transposition. Be sure to transpose the key signature as well.

Look at the following arrangement of the chorus line of "Set Fire to the Rain" set for flute, B♭ trumpet, alto clarinet, and horn in F. The only instrument that does not transpose is the flute. Notice how the key signatures have also changed. Using the chart above, transpose the pitches and key signature with the given interval.

The melodic lines for all four instruments are exactly the same and are played in unison.

When writing music on the staff:

Use the chart to determine the interval of transposition.
Determine your key and transpose all key signatures.
Transpose all pitches before labeling on staff.

Let's say you were asked to write the final tag from "Someone Like You" for alto saxophone. Well, first you would have to look at the interval of transposition. An alto sax transposes down a major sixth. That means that in order to get the exact concert pitches of the melody below, you will have to write the key signature and melody *up* a major sixth. The concert pitch key is A major, so we need to include the key signature of F♯ major, a major sixth above A. The pitches are all notated a major sixth above the original. Have an alto saxophone player play the bottom line while you play the upper line on the guitar or keyboard in order to better understand this concept.

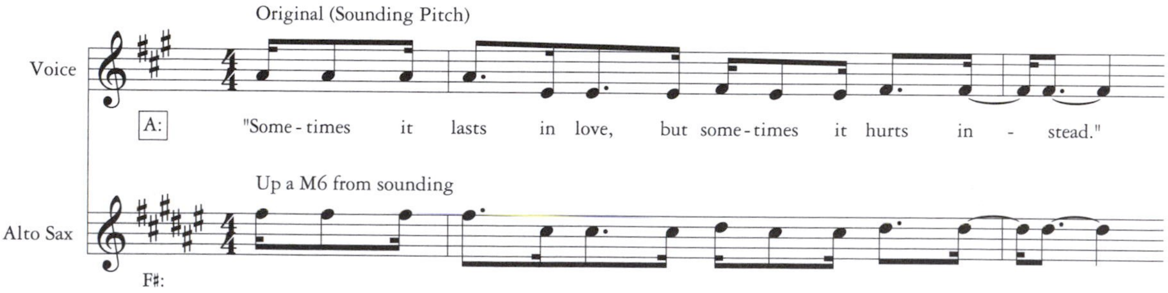

Study the arrangement taken from the middle eleven measures of "Rumour Has It." All of the instrument and vocal lines will sound in unison; however, they are all written with different key signatures and different pitches.

Original (Sounding Pitch)
Voice
Dmin:
All of these words whis - pered in my ear
Down a m3 from sounding
Soprano Clarinet in E♭
Bmin:
Up M2 from sounding
Clarinet in B♭
Emin:
Up M6 from sounding
Alto Sax
Bmin:
Up P5 from sounding
Horn in F
Amin:
V.
tell a sto - ry that I can - not bear to hear.
A. Sax.
B♭ Cl.
A. Sax.
Hn.

Reviewing Chapter Objectives

- Identify melodic and harmonic intervals both in quality and size (pages 72, 76)
- Notate specified intervals (page 80)
- Recognize intervals within a musical score (pages 75, 77–78, 81)
- Understand transposing instruments in terms of interval of transposition (pages 82–84)
- Transpose a musical line for use with various instruments (pages 84–85)

EXERCISES

I. Identify the following intervals by interval size and quality.

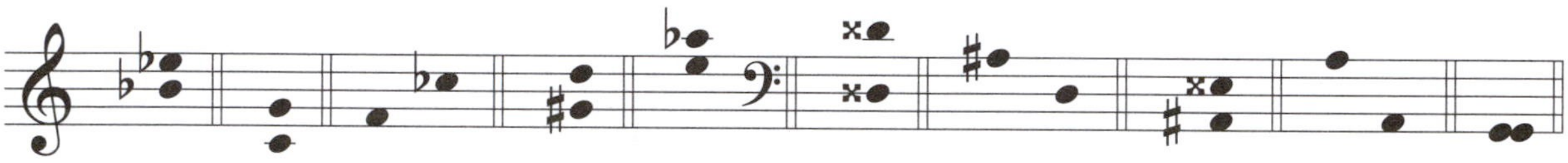

II. Identify the following intervals by interval size and quality.

III. Identify the following intervals by interval size and quality.

IV. Notate the interval *below* the given pitch.

M3 °4 m7 M6 m2 P5 P8 m6 +5 M2

V. Provide inversions of the given interval with the proper notation. Identify both the original interval and its inversion.

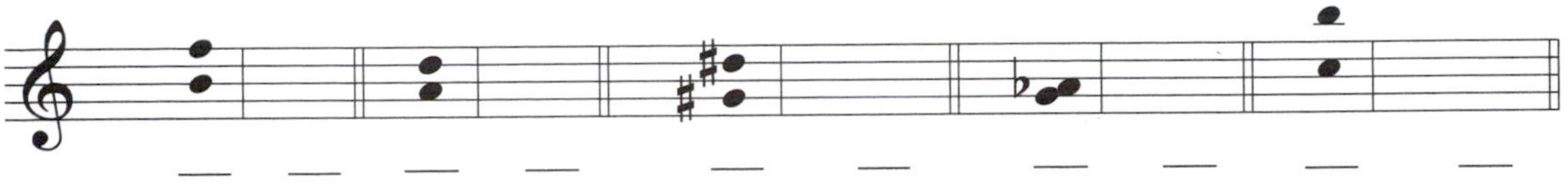

VI. Transpose the following melody for the given instruments. Be sure to notate the correct key signatures and pitches. Circle and label all of the melodic intervals in the given melody.

ANALYSIS

Identify all of the intervals circled in the score by filling in the correct interval number and quality in the blanks provided.

VIDEO TRACK 29

Taylor Swift, "You Belong with Me." Songwriters: Swift and Liz Rose

Taylor Swift, "You Belong with Me." Songwriters: Swift and Liz Rose *(continued)*

VIDEO TRACK 30

Rodgers and Hammerstein, "You'll Never Walk Alone"

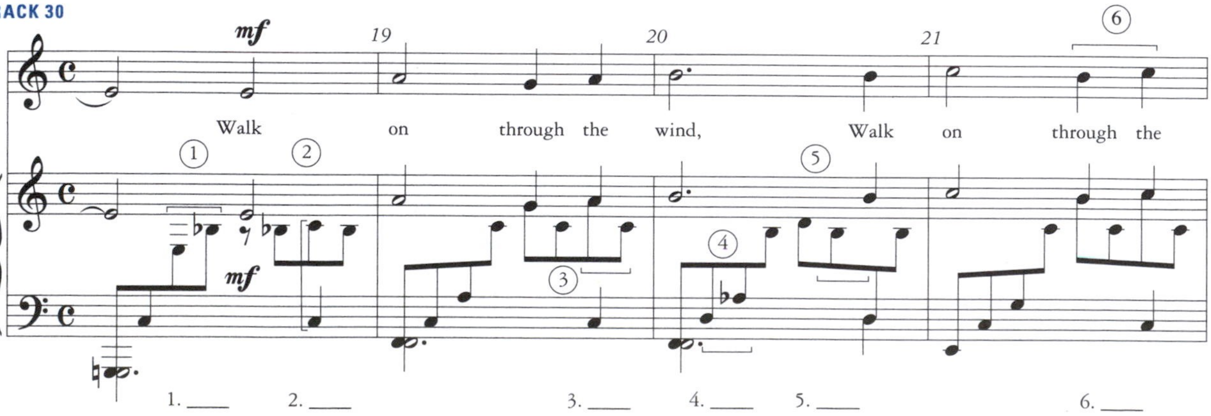

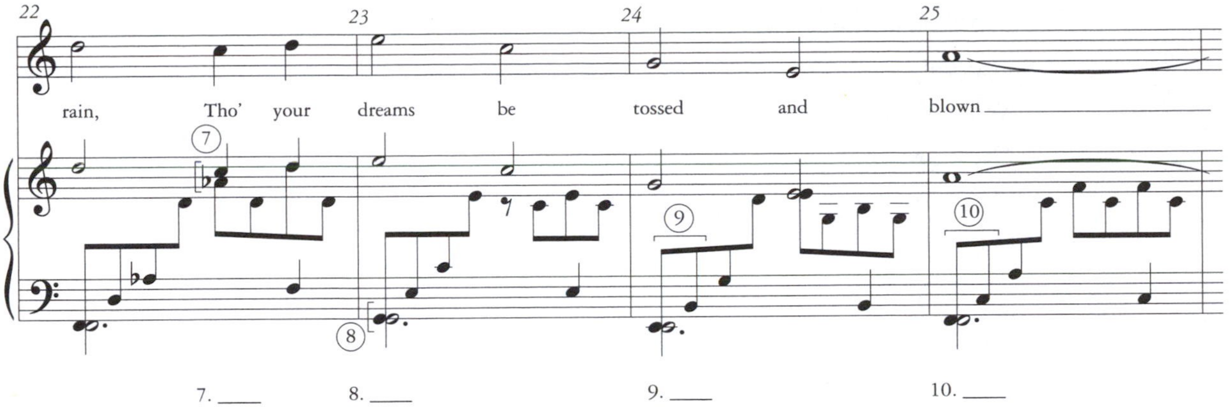

AURAL SKILLS CONDITIONING 4

Hearing Seconds and Thirds

Listen to the opening of Adele's "Rumour Has It." A few bars after the drum solo, the first vocal track enters with repetitive "oohs." The interval sung here is an ascending minor third. It is repeated so many times in this song it is almost as if Adele is trying to help drill this interval into your head!

WEBSITE VIDEO TRACK 25

The melody simplifies when we get to the chorus. The opening minor third motive is continuous, but now Adele belts out the title of the song with a descending major second. Sing the minor third along with the Adele track, and then sing the major second along with the chorus. The interval of a minor third should feel just a little wider than the major second when you're singing along.

Listen to "Summertime" from George Gershwin's *Porgy and Bess.* That famous opening line includes an example of a major third. Another popular example is the melody from "Swing Low, Sweet Chariot." Perhaps the easiest way to hear a major third is as the lowest third of a major chord, which can be heard arpeggiated in the beginning piano accompaniment of Adele's "Someone Like You."

WEBSITE VIDEO TRACK 31

The famous motive from Steven Spielberg's *Jaws* (1975) is the iconic example of a minor second. Be sure to listen to this simple yet concrete example of the interval.

WEBSITE VIDEO TRACK 32

Singing Seconds and Thirds

Sing the opening "oohs" of "Rumour Has It." Now, start on the same pitch but sing a major third instead of a minor third by raising the pitch of the second note by a half step. Try the same thing with the major second using the chorus line in "Rumour Has It." Raise the second pitch ("Has-it") so the result is a minor second below the first pitch ("Rumour"). Can you hear how changing the intervals slightly in "Rumour Has It" changes the character of each line? Practice singing the solfège syllables for each interval after establishing the tonic.

Common solfège for seconds and thirds based on the major scale:	
Interval	**Common Solfège**
Minor second	ti–do, mi–fa
Major second	do–re, fa–sol, sol–la
Minor third	re–fa, mi–sol
Major third	do–mi, fa–la, sol–ti

Interval Identification: Seconds and Thirds

AUDIO TRACKS CH. 4 INTERVAL ID 1–8

Your teacher will play eight intervals (m2, M2, m3, or M3). Write the interval performed in the spaces provided.

1. ______ 2. ______ 3. ______ 4. ______ 5. ______ 6. ______

7. ______ 8. ______

Hearing and Singing Perfect Fourths and Fifths

VIDEO TRACK 33

Another award-winning song written and performed by Adele is "Skyfall." Listen to the perfect fifth ("Let the sky fall") in the opening line of the chorus. Compare that to the pitches in the verse of "Set Fire to the Rain," which opens up with a perfect fourth ("I let it fall"), ("It was dark"), ("My hands"). If you are unsure about whether you're hearing a perfect fourth or a perfect fifth, try to hear a middle note (like the third of a major chord). If the interval is too small for that, it is a perfect fourth. Practice singing the solfège syllables for each interval after establishing the tonic.

Common solfège for fourths and fifths:	
Interval	**Common Solfège**
Perfect fourth	sol–do, do–fa
Perfect fifth	do–sol, sol–re

Interval Identification: Fourths and Fifths

AUDIO TRACKS CH. 4 INTERVAL ID2 1–4

Now, you will hear four intervals performed by your instructor or on the course website. Write the interval performed in the spaces provided.

1. ______ 2. ______ 3. ______ 4. ______

Mixed Intervals

AUDIO TRACKS CH. 4 MIXED INTERVALS 1–12

You will hear twelve intervals performed (m2, M2, m3, M3, P4, or P5). Write the interval performed in the spaces provided.

1. ______ 2. ______ 3. ______ 4. ______ 5. ______ 6. ______

7. ______ 8. ______ 9. ______ 10. ______ 11. ______ 12. ______

Sight Singing: Melodies with Leaps

The melodies below contain leaps of the third, fourth, and fifth. Using correct solfège, sing through the melodies.

1. 

2. 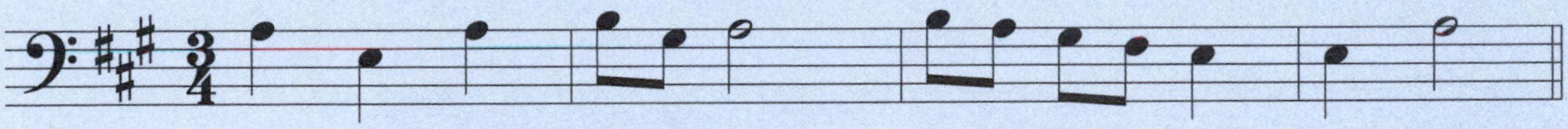

3. 

4. 

5. 

Melodic Dictation

You will hear a series of five pitches performed by your instructor or on the course website. Determine the solfège of the five pitches, and write the correct syllable in the spaces provided.

1. ______ ______ ______ ______ ______

2. ______ ______ ______ ______ ______

3. ______ ______ ______ ______ ______

4. ______ ______ ______ ______ ______

5. ______ ______ ______ ______ ______

REPLAY

AUDIO TRACKS CH. 4 MELODIC DICTATION 1–5

CHAPTER 5

TRIADS

Artist in Residence: The *American Idol* Phenomenon

Chapter Objectives

- Identify triads by root name and quality
- Notate triads when given root name and quality
- Notate and identify triads in inversion
- Identify triads within the context of a musical score

AMERICA HAS THE POWER

In the early years of this century, America became obsessed with reality TV. Families were glued to their television sets to watch the final episodes of *Survivor* and *Big Brother.* Viewers felt that they knew these reality stars personally, and they were passionate about which ones they wanted to see "left standing" at the end of the season. America was invested.

Television executives decided to tap into this new craze and create shows that were based on musical talent. Produced by 19 Entertainment, *American Idol* premiered during the summer of 2002 and was billed as a reality singing competition. Unlike other reality shows, the at-home audience became involved by texting or calling in their votes. America held an individual's dream in its hands, and this new power was exhilarating to the population. In 2012, *American Idol* broke all of its previous records with 132 million votes for the final show. Let's put that into perspective by saying that the U.S. population is somewhere around 320 million. It probably comes as no surprise that *American Idol* topped the ratings for 6 consecutive years.

Other shows have followed suit, including *America's Got Talent* and *The Voice.* But how many of the winners or finalists actually go on to do something with their newfound fame?

Listen to 2013 *American Idol* winner Candice Glover's final performance of "I Who Have Nothing." How would you describe her overall performance? Does she have what it takes to become a superstar recording artist? Why or why not?

WEBSITE

VIDEO TRACK 34

As you listen, pay careful attention to the musical line. Glover starts the song a capella, but at 0:40 a minor triad is introduced on the downbeat. The same triad is played over and over at the conclusion of the performance (1:58–2:02). What effect does the shift from a capella to single chord accompaniment have on the performance?

TRIADS

What exactly is a triad? Well, put in its most simple terms, a **triad** is made up of three pitches. Most common for our purposes is the tertian triad. When we stack two thirds on top of each other, the result is a root position triad, meaning that the pitches are superimposed on top of each other. The pitches of a tertian triad are called the root, third, and fifth.

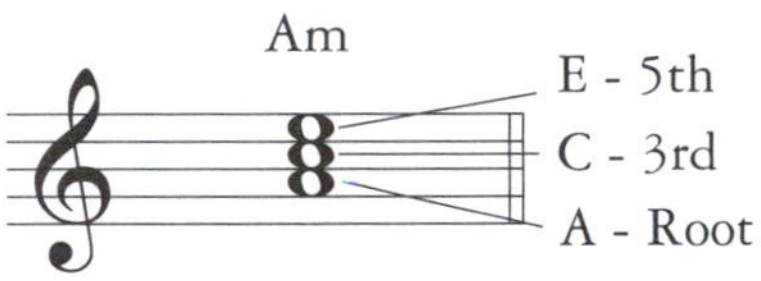

In Western popular and classical music we tend to use four basic triad qualities for all harmonies: major, minor, diminished, and augmented. The quality of the triad is determined by the quality of the intervals that make up the triad.

Triad Quality	Interval from Root to Third	Interval from Third to Fifth	Triad
Major	Major third	Minor third	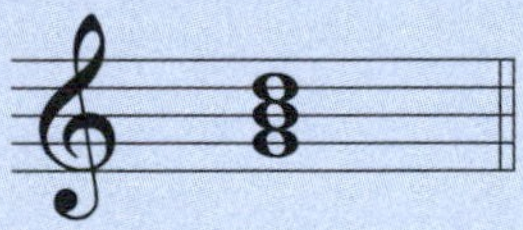
Minor	Minor third	Major third	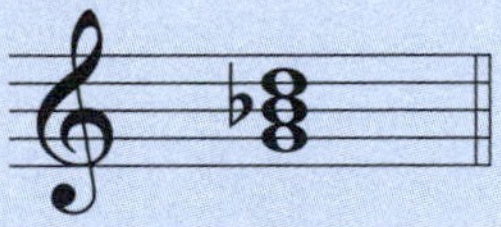
Diminished	Minor third	Minor third	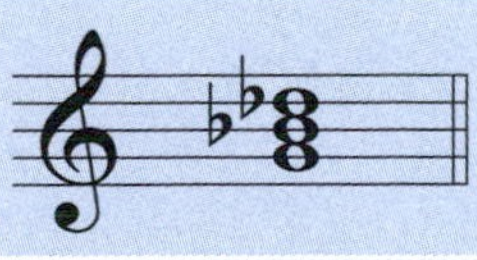
Augmented	Major third	Major third	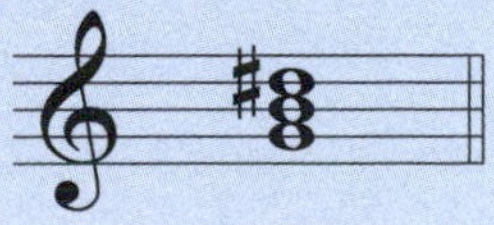

Let's look at two examples to determine the quality. In the first example, the distance from the root to the third is a major third and the distance from the third to the fifth is a major third. This first triad is augmented in quality. In the second example, the distance from the root to the third is a minor third followed by a major third. The second triad is minor.

Augmented Triad

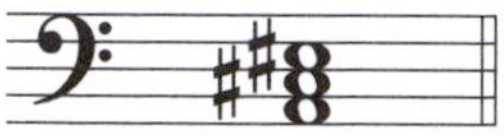

Minor Triad

We can also determine the quality of a triad based on the key signature of the root pitch. If the third and fifth of the triad are diatonic in the major key of the root pitch, the triad is major. Based on this rule, we can determine the other qualities:

If the third is lowered by a half step, the triad is *minor.*
If the third and fifth are lowered by a half step, the triad is *diminished.*
If the fifth is raised, the triad is *augmented.*

Let's look at the same two examples.

The root pitch of the first triad is A and the key of A major has three sharps: F♯, C♯, G♯. The notated triad should be A, C♯, E, but the fifth is raised to an E♯. This triad is augmented.

The second triad has F♯ as its root. The pitches of a F♯ major triad would be F♯, A♯, C♯ because of the accidentals found in the key of F♯ major. However, the A♯ is lowered a half step, so the triad is minor in quality.

CLOSED AND OPEN POSITION

Triads can be written in two ways in terms of spacing: open and closed. **Closed position** means that the three pitches are as close together as possible, or within the span of an octave. If the pitches of a triad span a space larger than an octave, we say that the triad is notated in **open position**.

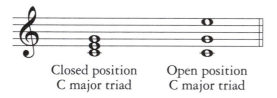

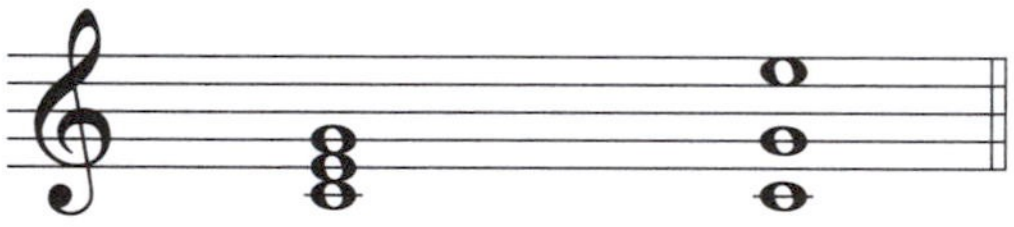

Closed position
C major triad

Open position
C major triad

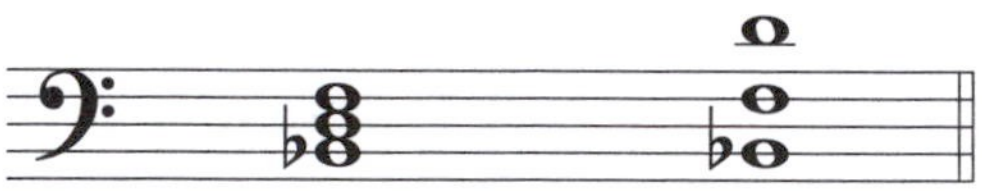

Closed position
B♭ major triad

Open position
B♭ major triad

TRIADS WITHIN CONTEXT

American Idol season 1 winner, Kelly Clarkson, has achieved great success following her debut performance on the *Idol* stage. Her song "Because of You" from *Breakaway* (2004) reached the top of the pop charts in three countries, including the United States. Listen to

Clarkson's performance while you study the triads highlighted below in the score. Can you find other triads within the excerpt? Remember, a triad is made up of three pitches, but any of the three pitches *can* be repeated in another octave.

WEBSITE
VIDEO TRACK 35

Kelly Clarkson, "Because of You." Songwriters: Kelly Clarkson, Ben Moody, and David Hodges

WEBSITE
VIDEO TRACK 36

Season 5 *American Idol* finalist Chris Daughtry found great success following the competition, including a hit with "What About Now" that peaked at number 3 on the Top 40 tracks during the summer of 2008. Assuming that each measure of the accompaniment represents a change in the triad used, what triads can be identified? Several have been labeled for you. Are there measures that include something other than a triad?

Daughtry, "What About Now." Songwriters: Josh Hartzler, David Hodges, and Ben Moody

BACKSTAGE PASS

Winners and Losers: Where Are They Now?

To say that shows such as *American Idol* launched the careers of many is an understatement. We can't even begin to speculate how these artists would have been heard or discovered without the reality shows that made each of them household names. The following is a list of winners from the first thirteen seasons of *American Idol* and what they have done in terms of the entertainment industry. A quick search on the web will give you even more details as to each artist's current position in the charts or who is on the touring circuit.

Season	Winner	After *American Idol*
1	Kelly Clarkson	Twenty million albums sold; three Grammy Awards
2	Ruben Studdard	Five albums released
3	Fantasia Barrino	Three million albums sold; Broadway
4	Carrie Underwood	Six Grammy Awards; inducted in Grand Ole Opry
5	Taylor Hicks	Broadway; show in Las Vegas
6	Jordin Sparks	Platinum debut album; acting; Broadway
7	David Cook	Platinum debut album; departed from RCA/19
8	Kris Allen	Platinum debut album; departed from RCA/19
9	Lee DeWyze	On tour playing smaller clubs
10	Scotty McCreery	Platinum debut album; ACM Best New Artist
11	Phillip Phillips	Gold debut album; top 10 hit with "Home"
12	Candice Glover	Album released in 2013
13	Caleb Johnson	Album released in summer of 2014

Interestingly, sometimes it pays to be a runner-up. Several contestants have gone on to successful careers both on Broadway and in the recording industry. Take a few minutes to discuss the following contestants from the reality shows and their impact on the music industry:

Clay Aiken, season 2 of *American Idol* (second place)
Jennifer Hudson, season 3 of *American Idol* (seventh place)
Chris Daughtry, season 5 of *American Idol* (fourth place)
Katharine McPhee, season 5 of *American Idol* (second place)
Kellie Pickler, season 5 of *American Idol* (sixth place)
Adam Lambert, season 8 of *American Idol* (second place)
Hillary Scott, various seasons of *American Idol* (rejected after round 1)
Jackie Evancho, season 5 of *America's Got Talent* (second place)

INVERTED TRIAD

How monotonous would it be if triads were found only in root position? Play the following triads on your piano or guitar. Feel free to experiment with both arpeggiated and blocked versions of the triads. Can you hear how the placement of the pitches has an influence on how you hear the triad?

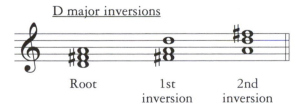

D major inversions

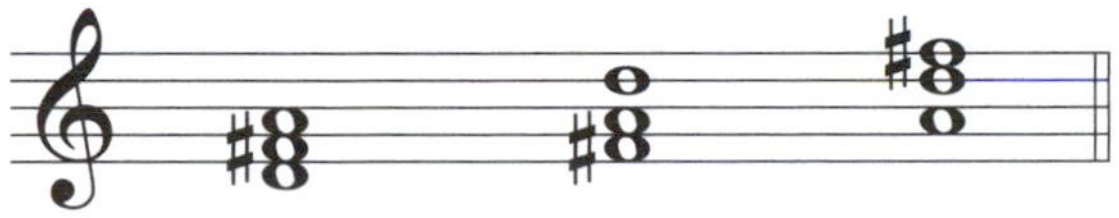

Root   1st inversion   2nd inversion

A triad is in **first inversion** if the third of the triad is the lowest sound pitch. A triad is in **second inversion** if the fifth of the triad is the lowest sounding pitch. The upper pitches can be placed in any octave, but the determining factor in terms of inversion identification is the triad pitch notated in the bass (or the lowest sounding pitch). It is also interesting to note that pitch doublings do not change how we determine the quality of the triad. Remember, a triad is just three notes!

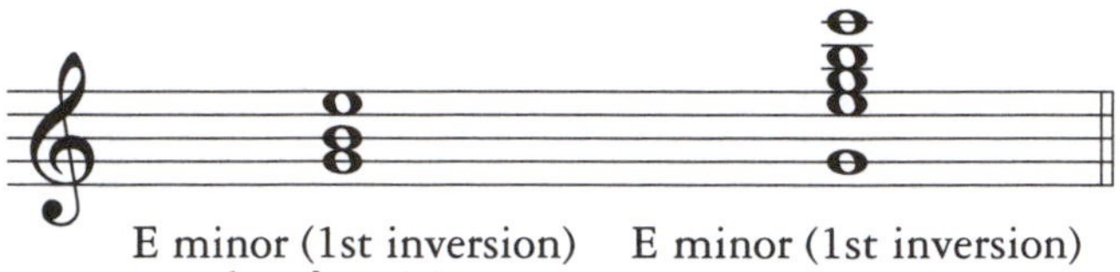

E minor (1st inversion) closed position — E minor (1st inversion) open position

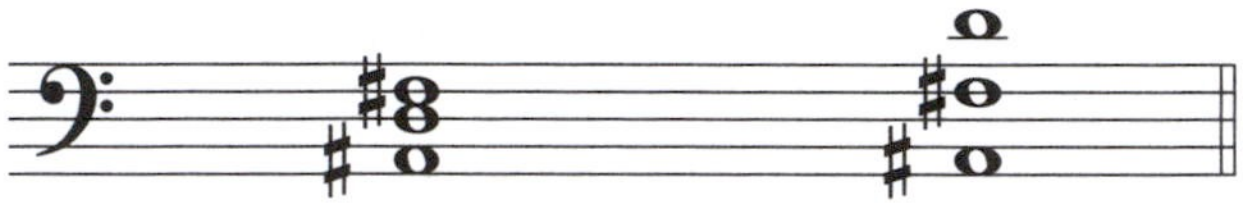

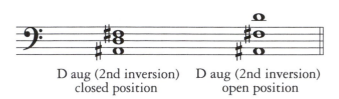

D aug (2nd inversion) closed position — D aug (2nd inversion) open position

So how do you determine the root if a triad is notated in an inversion? First, you need to stack the chord in thirds. Say you are given the following triad and asked to determine the root and quality.

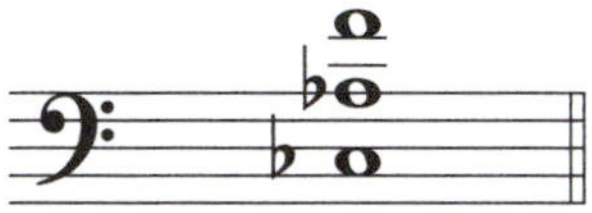

Before you are able to determine the root and the correct inversion, you *must* stack the pitches into thirds. This is such an important concept that it is worth repeating. Before you are able to determine the root and inversion, you *must* stack the pitches into thirds.

The pitches of the chord above are C♭–A♭–F. Are those pitches stacked in thirds? Nope. We need to figure out a way to arrange the letters so that there is always a letter in between. The result is F–A♭–C♭.

Now we can determine that the root is F and use the key signature method to determine the quality. The key signature of F major is one flat. This particular chord should be F–A–C in F major, but the third and fifth are lowered, so the triad is diminished. But wait—there's more! In what inversion is the triad? Well, once you have the pitches stacked in thirds, this is a simple question. What pitch is the lowest in the original example, the root, the third, or the fifth? The C♭ is the lowest, the fifth of the triad. The final answer is a F diminished triad in second inversion.

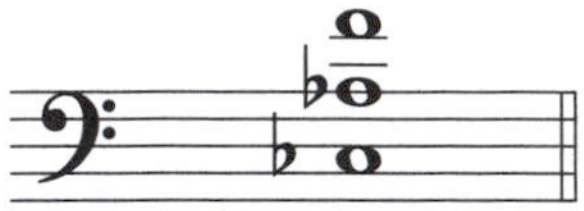

F dim (2nd inversion)
open position

VIDEO TRACK 37

Listen to *American Idol* season 12 winner Phillip Phillips's rendition of the famous song "We've Got Tonight" by Bob Seger. The piano introduction is quite simple and consists of triads on a vamping quarter note. Look at the first three chords in notation. Which of the triads are in inversion?

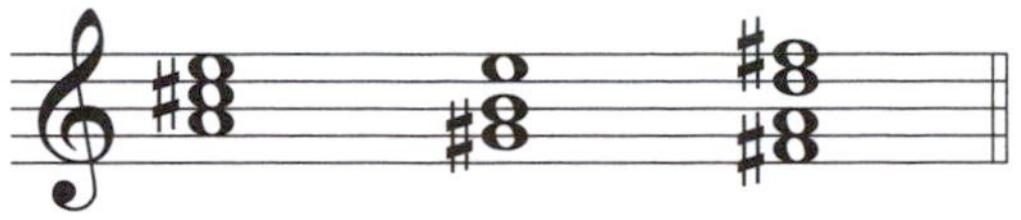

The first triad is in root position while the second two are in first inversion, meaning that the third of the chord is the lowest sounding pitch.

Study the following examples to understand the identification of the root, the quality, and the inversion. It may be helpful to write the pitches out before trying to stack into thirds.

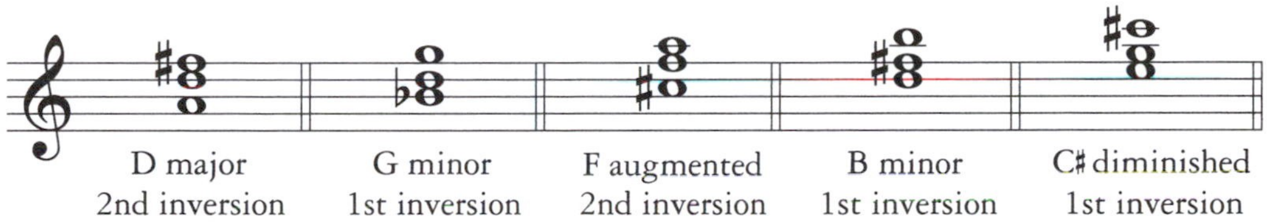

American Idol season 4 winner Carrie Underwood is one of the best-selling country artists of the past decade. All of her albums have reached number 1 and have been certified platinum. The song "Inside Your Heaven" from *Some Hearts* peaked at number 1 on Billboard's Hot 100 and was one of the top-selling country single of 2005. The opening ten measures consist of two alternating triads. As you study the score, ask yourself, is this accompanying pattern too simple or oddly effective?

WEBSITE

VIDEO TRACKS 38 AND 39

Carrie Underwood, "Inside Your Heaven."
Songwriters: Andreas Carlsson, Savan Kotecha, and Pelle Nylén

Carrie Underwood, "Inside Your Heaven."
Songwriters: Andreas Carlsson, Savan Kotecha, and Pelle Nylén *(continued)*

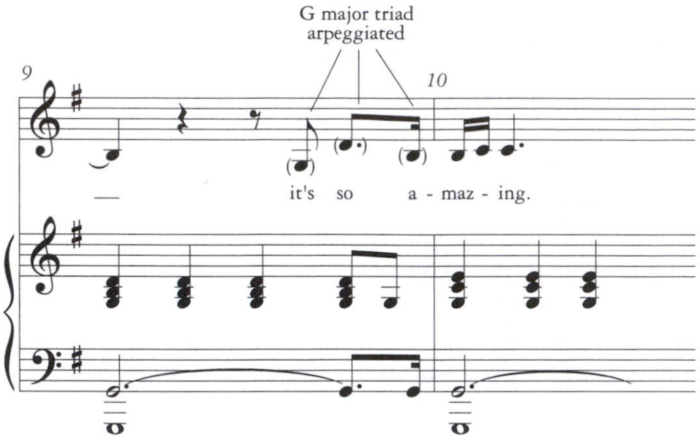

Sometimes songwriters compose a song that immediately resonates with the American public. The judges of *American Idol* knew that Phillip Phillips had a hit on his hands when he performed "Home" on the season finale. It was even used during the 2012 summer Olympic Games to highlight the U.S. women's gymnastics team. After one prime-time sampling during the games, the song leaped from the eighty-fourth spot to number 9 on the Hot 100 and was number 1 on iTunes the next morning. Eventually the song went on to hold the number 1 spot on several different Billboard charts, including the Top 40 and Digital Songs charts. Study the triads and qualities labeled in the score.

VIDEO TRACK 40

Phillip Phillips, "Home." Songwriters: Drew Pearson and Greg Holden

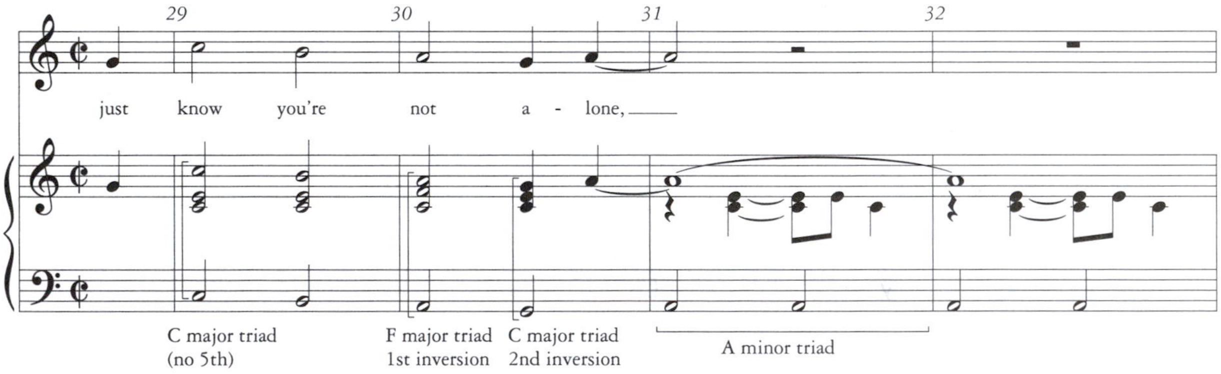

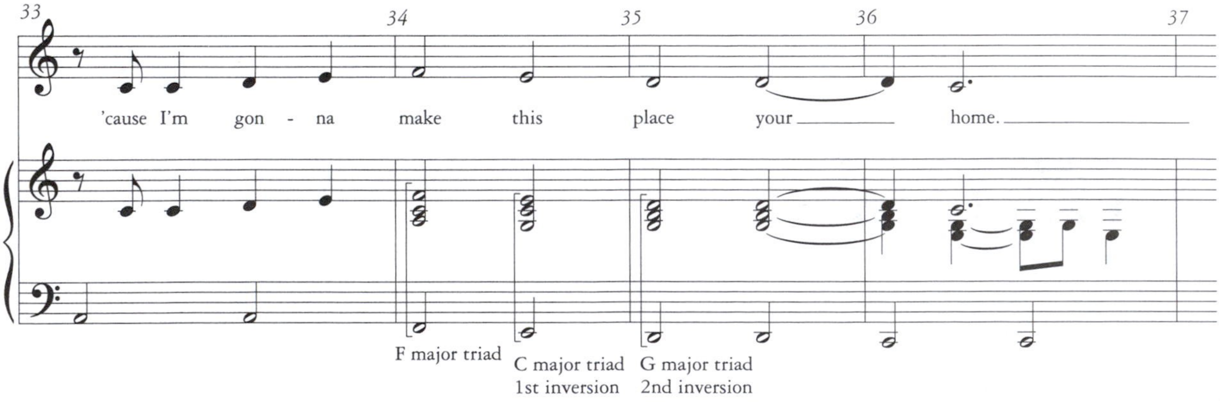

III. Notate triads in root position when given the root pitch and the quality.

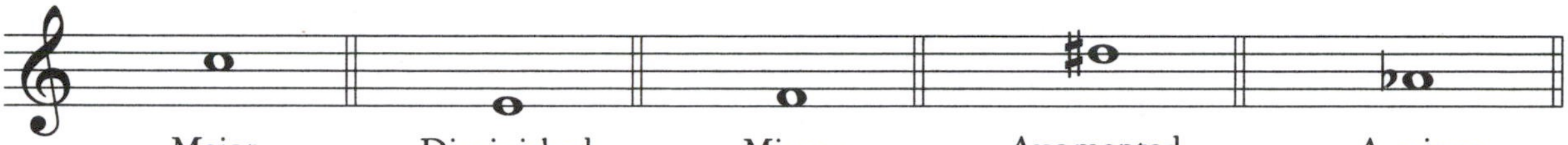

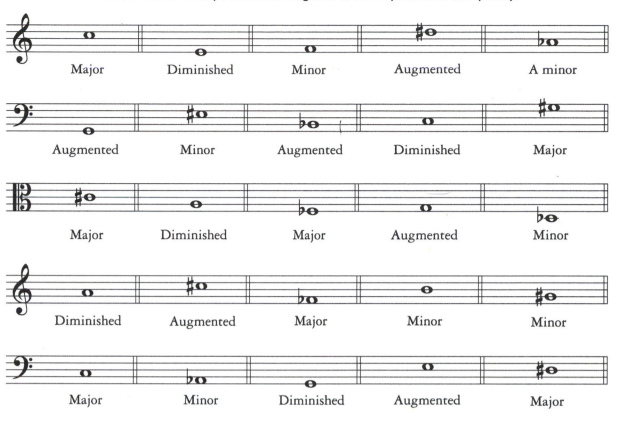

Major | Diminished | Minor | Augmented | A minor

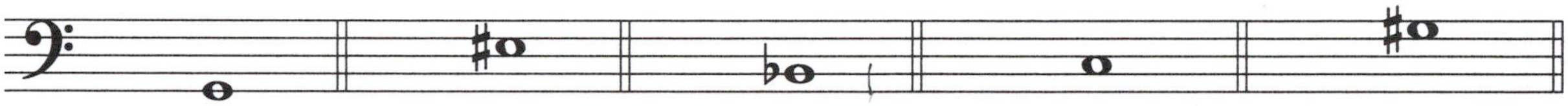

Augmented | Minor | Augmented | Diminished | Major

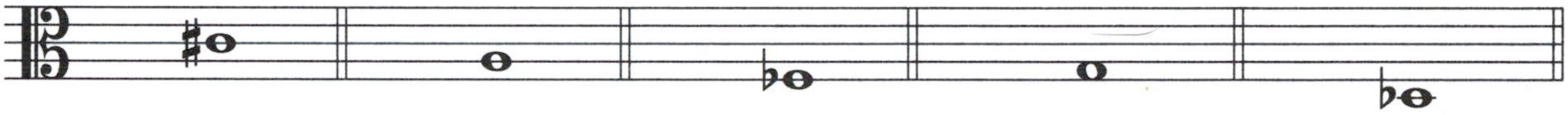

Major | Diminished | Major | Augmented | Minor

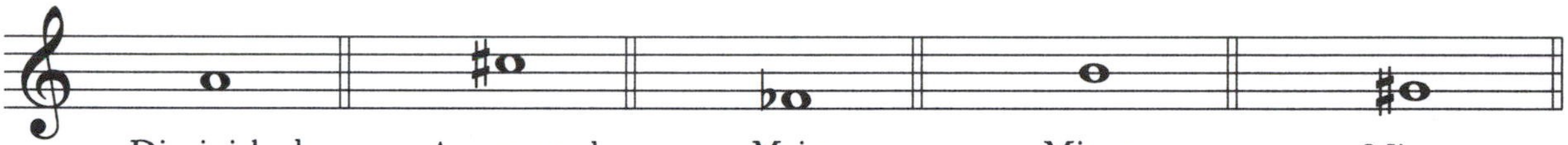

Diminished | Augmented | Major | Minor | Minor

Major | Minor | Diminished | Augmented | Major

IV. Given the root, third, or fifth of the triad and the quality, notate the correct triad on the staff.

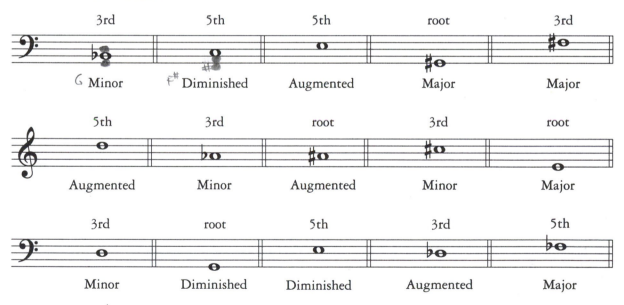

3rd | 5th | 5th | root | 3rd

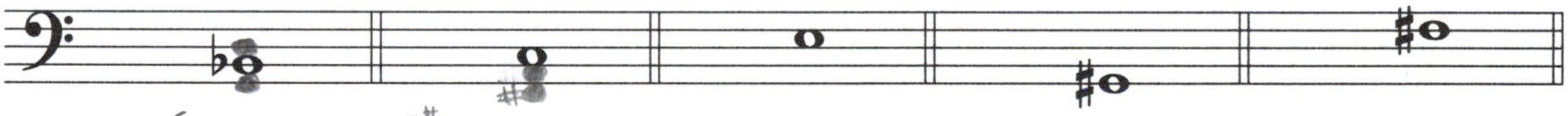

Minor | Diminished | Augmented | Major | Major

5th | 3rd | root | 3rd | root

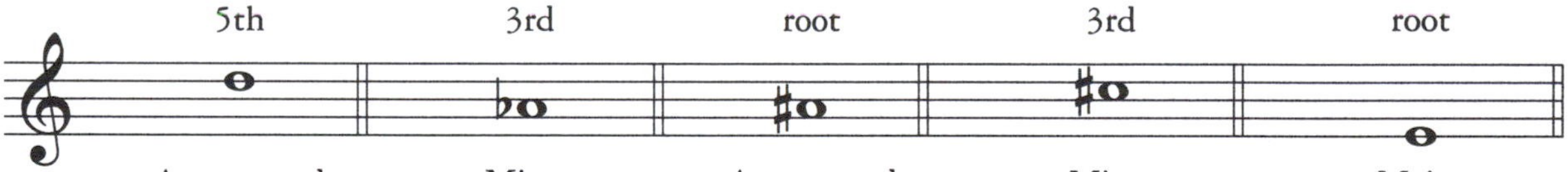

Augmented | Minor | Augmented | Minor | Major

3rd | root | 5th | 3rd | 5th

Minor | Diminished | Diminished | Augmented | Major

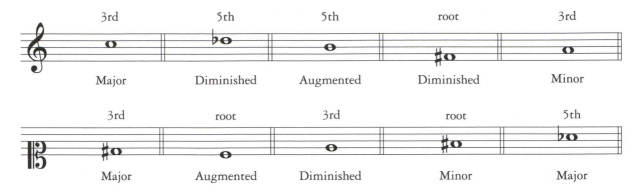

3rd	5th	5th	root	3rd

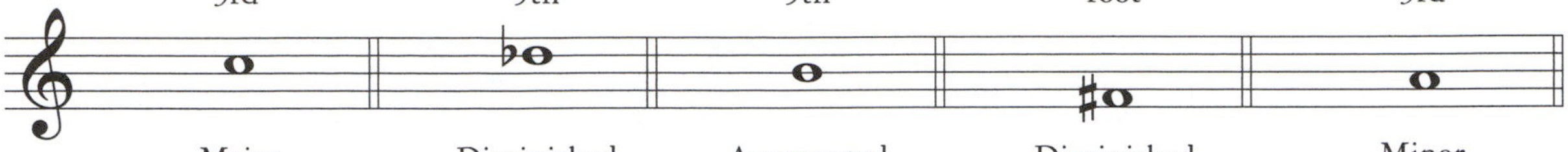

Major	Diminished	Augmented	Diminished	Minor

3rd	root	3rd	root	5th

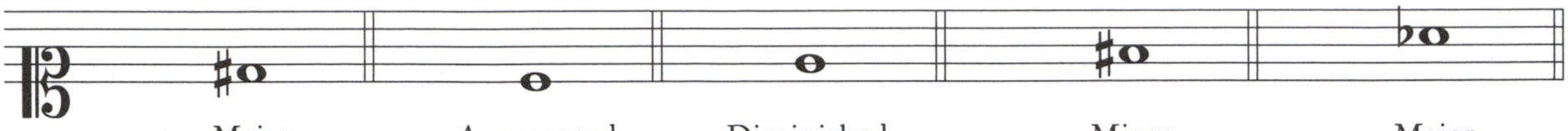

Major	Augmented	Diminished	Minor	Major

V. Identify the notated triads by root name, quality, and correct inversion.

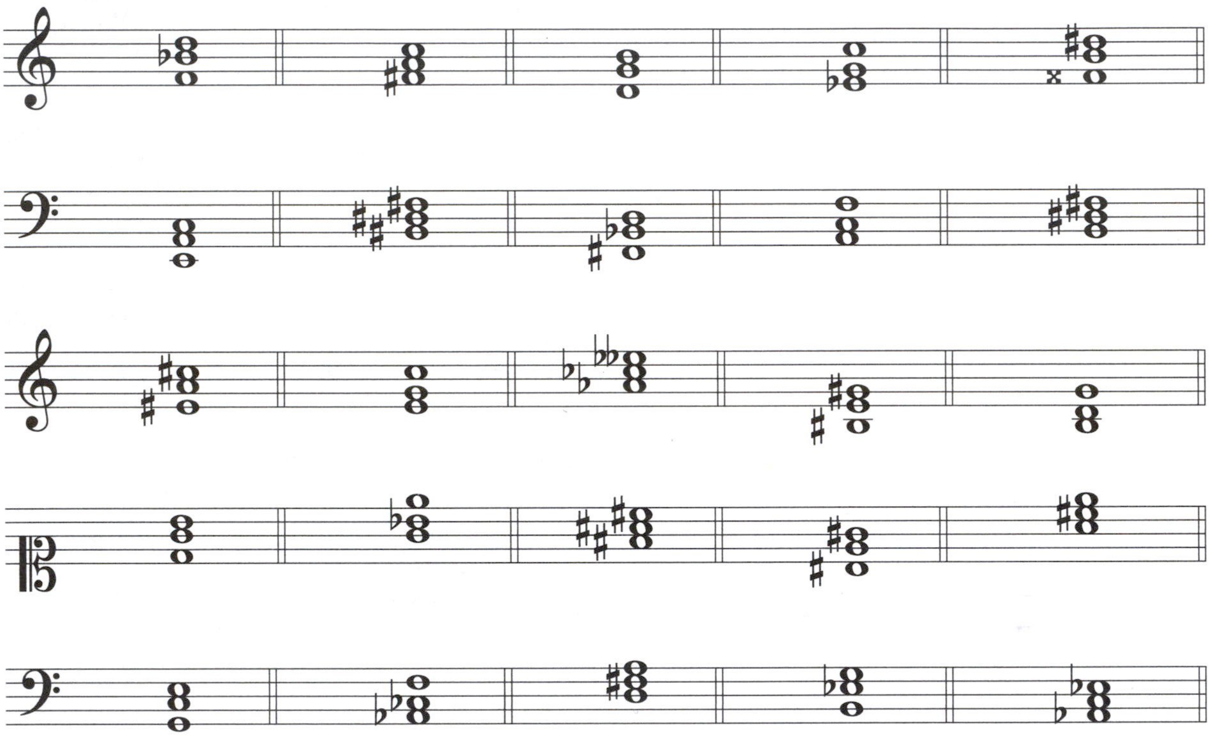

VI. Notate triads when given the root, quality, position, and inversion.

root position closed position	2nd inversion open position	1st inversion open position	2nd inversion closed position	root position open position

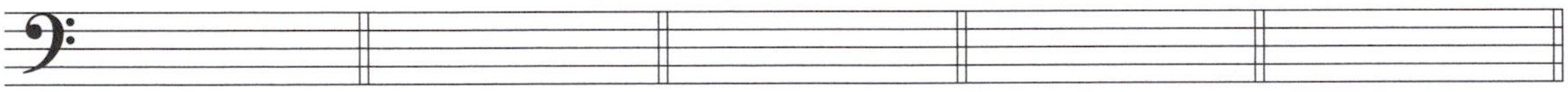

D major	E minor	F♯ diminished	G augmented	C♯ major

2nd inversion closed position	root position open position	root position closed position	1st inversion closed position	2nd inversion open position

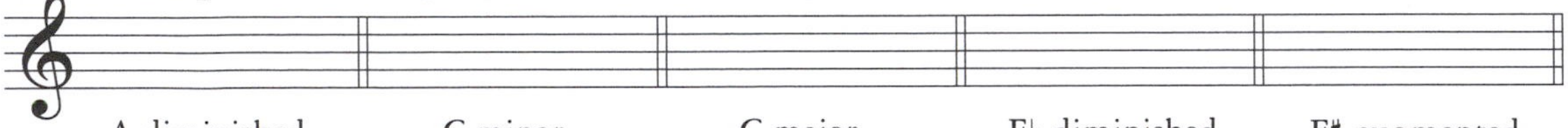

A diminished	C minor	C major	E♭ diminished	F♯ augmented

1st inversion closed position	root position closed position	root position open position	2nd inversion closed position	1st inversion open position

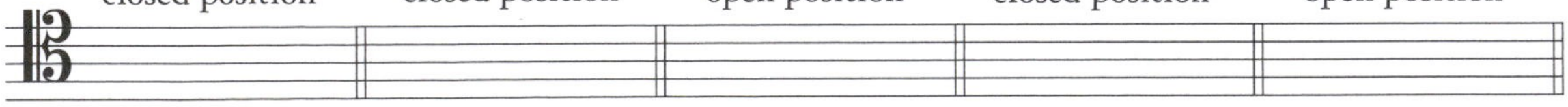

G♯ minor	A♭ minor	B major	B♭ augmented	C diminished

ANALYSIS

VIDEO TRACK 41

Kelly Clarkson's "Stronger" was released in 2011 and was immediately a hit on the Billboard Hot 100 and was a top 10 hit in over fifteen countries. As you listen to the song, continue to compare the vocal style here to Clarkson's earlier recordings. (Although the song was not written by Clarkson, one has to wonder whether she sang it while thinking of her dealings with Clive Davis and other members of 19.) Each measure, with the exception of measure 4, consists of one triad. Label the triads in terms of root, quality, and inversion. Do not include the pitches circled in your analysis.

Kelly Clarkson, "Stronger." Songwriters: Jörgen Elofsson, Ali Tamposi, and David Gamson

VIDEO TRACK 42

Jackie Evancho was 10 years old when she took second place in *America's Got Talent* in 2010, and she has achieved much success for someone so young. Her debut album, *Dream with Me*, spent 31 weeks on the Billboard chart, making her the youngest artist ever with a top 10 debut album. Listen to Evancho's performance of Gounod's "Ave Maria." Looking only at the accompaniment line, determine whether each measure consists of a triad. If there is a triad within the arpeggiation, label the root, quality, and inversion. If the arpeggiation is not a triad, mark the measure with an X.

Gounod, "Ave Maria" as sung by Jackie Evancho

AURAL SKILLS CONDITIONING 5

Hearing Triads

What do "Someone Like You" by Adele and "Inside Your Heaven" by Carrie Underwood have in common? For one, the introductions to both songs feature a solo piano playing triads. In "Someone Like You," the chords are arpeggiated, meaning each pitch in the triad is played one after the other. The opening chords in "Inside Your Heaven" are played as block chords, meaning each note in the triad is played at the same time.

WEBSITE

VIDEO TRACKS 27 AND 39

Listen to the beginning of "Inside Your Heaven." What quality triads do you hear? Write down the timings in which you hear a change in triad quality.

For more of a challenge, let's do the same thing with "Someone Like You." Try to figure out the quality of each arpeggiated triad in the beginning. Hint: not every triad is in root position!

Singing Triads

The following chart shows the common solfège syllables for triads based on the G major scale. Give yourself the tonic pitch and practice singing these triads on solfège. As a class, have several students hold a particular solfège syllable to form a harmonic triad.[1]

Quality	Solfège	Intervals	Lead Sheet Symbol
Major	Do-Mi-Sol Fa-La-Do Sol-Ti-Re	M3 + m3	G C D
Minor	Re-Fa-La	m3 + M3	A-
Diminished[1]	Re-Fa-Ti Ti-Re-Fa	m3 + m3	F♯o/A F♯o

The augmented triad is not found diatonically in a major key; however, it is used in pieces based on the harmonic minor scale. After singing the E harmonic minor scale, outline the augmented triad. Other triad qualities found in the harmonic minor scale are listed as well.

Quality	Solfège	Intervals	Lead Sheet Symbol
Augmented	Me-Sol-Ti	M3 + M3	G+
Minor	Do-Me-Sol Fa-Le-Do	m3 + M3	Em Am
Major	Sol-Ti-Re Le-Do-Me	M3 + m3	B C
Diminished	Re-Fa-Ti Ti-Re-Fa	m3 + m3	D♯o/F♯ D♯o

[1]The lead sheet symbol is given for reference. More information on how to read lead sheet symbols is given in Chapter 7.

Now that you have practiced singing the triads, listen to your teacher play all the triads on the piano. Can you hear the solfège syllables? Can you determine whether the lower third is major or minor? This takes practice, but soon you will be able to hear the differences without arpeggiating the chord.

Triad Identification

REPLAY

AUDIO TRACK CH. 5 TRIAD ID 1–8

Go to the course website or listen to your instructor play eight different triads. You will hear each triad arpeggiated and then played as a block chord. Write the quality of triad you hear in the spaces provided.

1. ______ 2. ______ 3. ______ 4. ______

5. ______ 6. ______ 7. ______ 8. ______

Review of Rhythmic Reading: The Addition of the Tie

Read through the following rhythmic exercises using Takadimi or other counting method. Be sure to correctly perform ties and dotted rhythms.

1. 

2. 

3. 

4. 

5. 

THE FINAL NOTE: REAL-WORLD PERSPECTIVE

Gregg Lohman

DRUMMER FOR KELLIE PICKLER AND SESSION MUSICIAN
ADJUNCT PROFESSOR, TENNESSEE STATE UNIVERSITY

Educational Background
B.M., Eastern Illinois University, Percussion Performance
M.M., University of Tennessee, Percussion Performance

Has the study of music theory and musicianship helped you in your career? If so, how?
With Kellie, I am the musical director as well, so just understanding chord structure really helps. As an instructor, it really helps in being able to explain concepts to my students. It goes hand in hand.

Was it in your original career plan to be a session musician? What experiences and opportunities led you to be on the road with Kellie Pickler?
That's exactly why I moved to Nashville. I would like to do more session work. I do some time in the studio, but my main job is to be on the road with Kellie.

It's all about who you know. I actually knew the guy that was putting the band together after Kellie appeared on *American Idol*. At first I was a little unsure. I had steady work playing with Aaron Tippin, whereas with a new act you never know how long it is going to last. Our first four gigs were all TV shows, *The View*, *The Tonight Show*, *Ellen*, and *The Today Show*. Seven years later, I am still working with Kellie.

You also teach applied percussion at Tennessee State University. Do you find it beneficial to continue to teach in the trenches while performing?
The playing really helps the teaching. I teach commercial music majors who really want to do what I do, so having gone through the school system prior to the road life, I am able to make this all more applicable to the students. Most of my training was in classical percussion, but I wish I had more of the contemporary styles presented in some of my earlier training.

How do you make yourself in public demand—in other words, how have you marketed yourself?

I'm not out there promoting myself too much. It is all about relationships. Keep building the relationships and keep in contact with others. The phone calls will come. It is about who you know. You may have to start by playing for little money and you will make the connections from those first gigs. Build those relationships. If you start by being arrogant, you will not get far.

As a session musician, have you ever found yourself uncomfortable playing a certain style, and how did you overcome it? Was there ever a genre (or setting) that you swore you would never play, but ended up taking the gig for monetary reasons?

I still do sometimes. If I know I am going on a gig with new music, I always practice well beforehand. It is all about keeping your skills up. When you are thrown into a situation like that, you can still play well and get through it. You are always improving yourself.

What are the challenges and advantages of joining a musician who has already gained a fan base due to reality talent competition?

Her crowds from the beginning were good. A lot of acts have to build the audience from the very beginning. She had immediate exposure and with her experience on *Dancing with the Stars* she even brought in a new crowd of fans. Her audience now ranges from 7 to 70. Kellie is just a good person and her fans relate to that.

Most significant learning experience of your career.

Before I had my first road gig, I was playing downtown . . . trying to make those connections I mentioned earlier. I was playing about eleven gigs a week in four-hour shifts. You don't really make any money, and one time I played an eight-hour shift and made less than $50. So, that was the point that I thought "What do I do?" I was playing to nobody, just trying to network. I'm really glad I did that. I grew musically, just by listening and playing with others. It ended up being a really good thing. It's crazy how it all works out, but you really need to focus on the progression, both musically and professionally.

Greatest moment of your career so far.

I was in a bad car accident last year, and coming back from that was an amazing thing. Kellie was supportive of me throughout the whole ordeal. She never said that they would replace me, just that I should take the time I needed to recover. She assured me that the job would be there for me when I came back. I was out of commission for a few months, so coming back after that and playing in an arena was an amazing moment. I ended up playing the last song in a neck brace on a concert to surprise Kellie. Great moment.

CHAPTER 6

SEVENTH CHORDS

Artist in Residence: Joshua Bell

Chapter Objectives

- Identify seventh chords by root name and quality
- Notate seventh chords when given root name and quality
- Notate and identify seventh chords in inversion
- Identify seventh chords within the context of a musical score

Look back at your analysis of the Gounod "Ave Maria" on page 106. Notice how for measures 2, 3, 6, 7, 10, 12, 13, and 14 you were not able to label a specific triad. Why was that? Well, for starters, those particular measures contained four different pitches instead of the three pitches required for the triad. Let's try stacking those pitches into thirds.

Measure 2	F–G–D–B♭ becomes G–B♭–D–F
Measure 3	E–G–C–B♭ becomes C–E–G–B♭
Measure 6	F–G–D–B♭ becomes G–B♭–D–F
Measure 7	E–G–C–B♭ becomes C–E–G–B♭
Measure 10	F–G–B–D becomes G–B–D–F
Measure 12	E–F–A–C becomes F–A–C–E

Measure 13	D–F–A–C is stacked in thirds
Measure 14	G–D–B–F is stacked in thirds

IDENTIFICATION OF SEVENTH CHORDS

All of these measures are made up of seventh chords. By **chord**, we mean any group of pitches sounding together. A **seventh chord** is a triad with the addition of another third, or the seventh above the root.

In order to make a triad a seventh chord, you just have to add another third to the top.

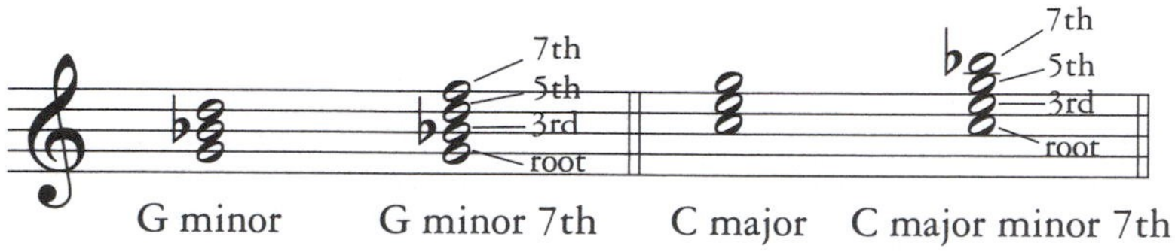

There are five qualities of seventh chords used extensively in music. The qualities are based on the same quality names as used for triads, including an additional qualifier to differentiate between the added seventh. Study the following chart to understand how these chords are identified in terms of quality.

Seventh Chord Quality	Lowest Triad	Interval from Root Seventh	Quality of Upper Third	Seventh Chord	Chord Name
Major-major	Major	Major seventh	Major third		Major seventh
Major-minor	Major	Minor seventh	Minor third		Dominant seventh or major-minor seventh[1]
Minor-minor	Minor	Minor seventh	Minor third	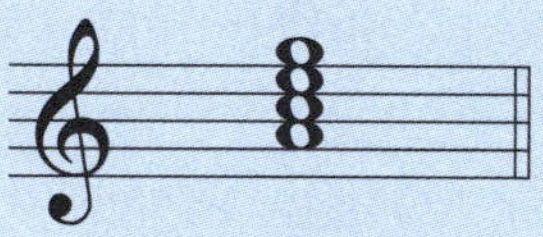	Minor seventh
Half diminished[2]	Diminished	Minor seventh	Major third		Minor seventh flat five
Fully diminished	Diminished	Diminished seventh	Minor third		Diminished seventh

[1]The dominant seventh chord is so named because the chord is typically built on the fifth scale degree. Most musicians in the popular and jazz sector refer to the major-minor seventh chord exclusively as the dominant seventh. We will use both chord names depending on the musical style being discussed.

[2]Some musicians prefer to identify the diminished seventh chords as diminished diminished and diminished minor.

Play through all of the seventh chords in the chart, and spend a few minutes building seventh chords on your own. To build a seventh chord, use the same process that you used to build a triad, but add the extra step of inserting a seventh to the top of the chord. For instance, let's say you want to build a fully diminished seventh chord on B. The key signature of B major has five sharps, so the major triad would consist of B–D♯–F♯; lower the third and fifth to form the diminished triad B–D–F. It might be easier to think of the quality of the top third rather than the seventh, so add a minor third to the top of your triad. A fully diminished seventh chord on B is B–D–F–A♭. As a class, practice spelling various qualities of seventh chords on different roots. Remember to always start with the lower triad and then add the seventh.

Can you now correctly identify the qualities of the seventh chords in the opening measures of the "Ave Maria"? The qualities are marked for you in the score. Note that the majority of the chords are inverted.

Gounod, "Ave Maria"

THE SOUND QUALITY OF THE SEVENTH CHORD

The sound quality of the seventh chord is very different from that of the triad. That is because, by nature, the interval of the seventh is very dissonant. By adding the seventh to a triad, you create a very dissonant sound that makes it a favorite in both popular and classical music. All you need to do is play a C major triad on the piano and then a C major-major seventh chord. It sounds like a completely different chord even though the root, third, and fifth are the same.

In his book *The Complete Musician*, Steve Laitz outlines the musical characteristics of seventh chords in the following manner. Be sure to play through each quality as you discuss each distinct sound.

Major-minor seventh chord (dominant seventh) is the most common seventh chord used in tonal music. It can be found regularly in music written from the early 17th century and is commonplace in popular music to this day. It regularly appears on the dominant scale degree, so much so that popular musicians often refer to the quality of this chord as the dominant seventh.

Major-major seventh chord (major seventh), with its major seventh, is more dissonant than the major-minor seventh chord. It appears more regularly in 20th-century popular music and jazz. You probably have heard this chord at the end of jazz pieces.

Minor-minor seventh chord (minor seventh) is a soft-sounding chord, because its minor seventh creates a less dissonant sound than that of the major seventh.

Half-diminished seventh chord (minor seventh flat five) is a mix of effect. The dissonance of the diminished triad is balanced with the less dissonant minor seventh.

Fully diminished seventh chord (diminished seventh) is the most dissonant of these seventh chords. It is found in classical music of the late baroque era and throughout the classical and romantic eras. It is also found in most popular music and jazz. It is the only seventh chord that contains all the same types of thirds and fifths: three minor thirds and two diminished fifths.

INVERSIONS OF SEVENTH CHORDS

We are grateful that the harmonies of the Western world are found not only in root position. The bass instruments and singers of the world are even more grateful. Just like triads can be inverted, seventh chords are also found in inversions.

Study the inversions of the F Major-major seventh chord. The only difference between inversions of a seventh chord and inversions of a triad is the possibility of third inversion when the seventh of the chord is the lowest sounding pitch.

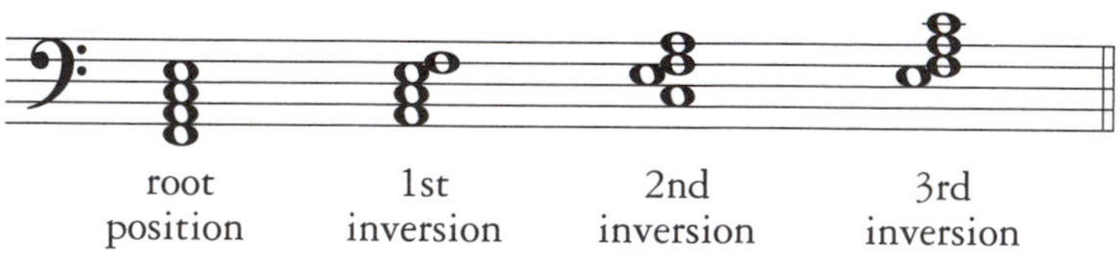

It is important to remember that you can have doublings of pitches and that the upper pitches can be placed in either closed or open position. The identification depends only on the root, the quality, and what chord member is the lowest sounding pitch. The following chord is still labeled as a G minor seventh in second inversion, regardless of position or doublings.

G minor minor 7th, 2nd inversion

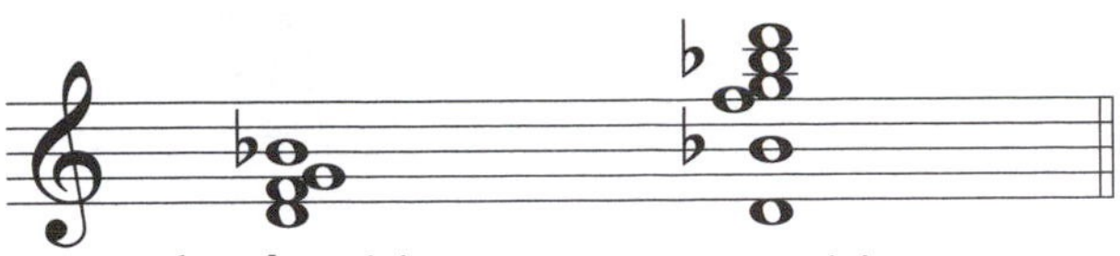

closed position open position

ARTIST IN RESIDENCE

The Poet of the Violin

In a 2012 *Newsweek* interview, Joshua Bell recalls his first violin competition at the age of 12. He compares the concerto he was playing, *Symphonie Espagnole,* to a triple axel in figure skating. Bell continues: "I began playing, and I messed it up worse than I ever could have imagined. . . . I turned to the audience and said, 'I'd really like to start over.'"

It's hard to believe that this virtuosic superstar ever made a mistake in his career. Bell began to study the violin at age 8, but was equally as serious about video games and athletics, winning a national tennis tournament when he was 10. However, in his teenage years, he traded tennis strings for violin strings and performed his breakout debut with the Philadelphia Orchestra. His first record with Decca came out when he was only 18 years old. Although he did graduate from Indiana University with an artist diploma in 1989, Bell was well on his was to superstardom before receiving any structured university training.

In the past several decades, Bell has performed with all of the leading orchestras, including the New York Philharmonic Orchestra and the Boston Symphony Orchestra, but he is equally as comfortable playing in small chamber settings. Bell also likes to "escape from the classical mould" from time to time and has recorded works of musical theater, bluegrass, and movie soundtracks, including the Oscar-winning soundtrack for *The Red Violin.*

So what impact has Joshua Bell had on the classical world? Perhaps the *Washington Post* said it best: "The American violinist with movie-star good looks has emerged as one of the finest musicians of his generation, whose interpretations can be seriously set beside and favorably compared to players twice his age. Dead players too."

And that competition where he asked to start over? He went on to play the best he had played in his life. He had nothing to lose. Bell actually ended up winning third place and taking the entire competition the next year. He says, "It taught me that when you take your mind off worrying about being perfect all the time, sometimes amazing things can happen. So much of performing is a mind game."

VIDEO TRACK 43

In 2009, Bell recorded the album *At Home with Friends* on the Decca label. The sixteen tracks include collaborations with artists such as Josh Groban, Regina Spektor, and Sting. Listen to the duet "O, Cease Thy Singing, Maiden Fair, Op. 4, no. 4" by Rachmaninoff. This performance, by Bell and Nathan Gunn, is highlighted by the intimacy of the performance venue. Several different seventh chords have been circled for you in the score. Can you also identify several triads?

Joshua Bell and Nathan Gunn, Rachmaninoff's "O, Cease Thy Singing, Maiden Fair, Op. 4, No. 4"

Most people have heard of Kristin Chenoweth for her role in the musical *Wicked*, but she was classically trained in opera. Watch the recording session of Chenoweth and Bell as they record the standard "My Funny Valentine." Why do you think the artists are videoed separately?

Study the excerpt taken from the original score. Several seventh chords are marked for you. Take a few minutes to stack other chords into thirds to determine quality. As you listen to the track, focus on the artistic liberties taken by the performers. Are the changes subtle? Chenoweth's performance begins at 2:28.

VIDEO TRACK 44

Joshua Bell and Kristin Chenoweth, Rodgers and Hart's "My Funny Valentine"

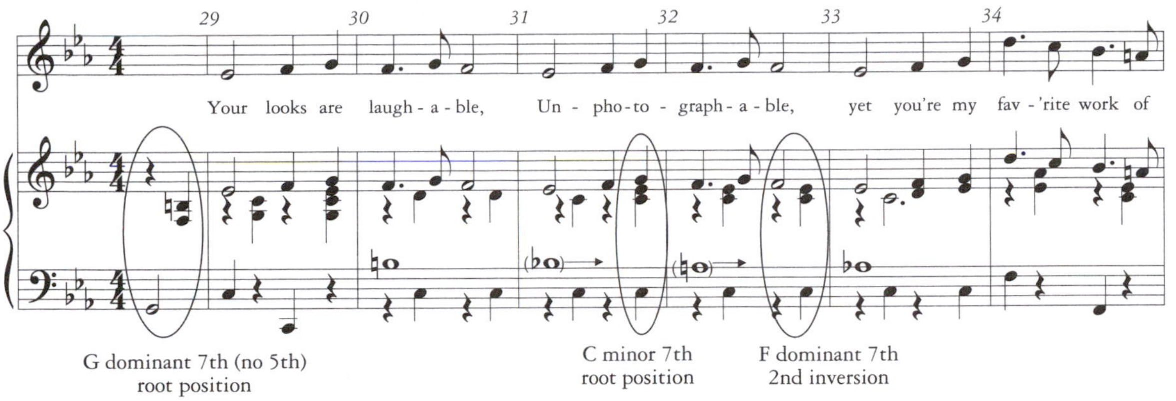

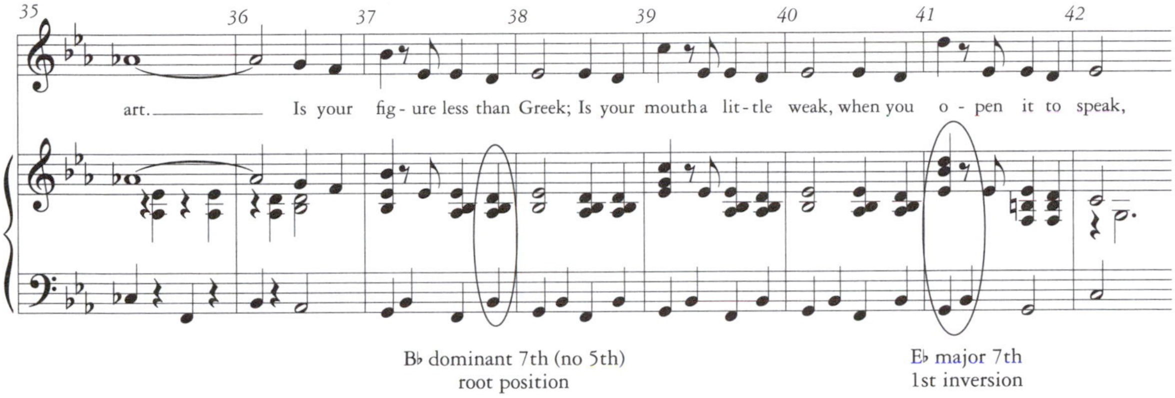

Study the reduction of Debussy's "La Fille aux Cheveux de Lin" while you listen to Bell's performance. Pay careful attention to the chords in measures 8 and 9. The pitches of the chords are F♭–G♭–B♭–D and G♭–A♭–C–E–B. Stack these two chords into thirds to determine the root. One is a seventh chord, and one is not. The quality of the true seventh chord is marked in the score.

WEBSITE
VIDEO TRACK 45

F♭–G♭–B♭–D♭ becomes G♭–B♭–D♭–F♭. The root is G♭.
G♭–A♭–C–E♭–B♭ becomes A♭–C–E♭–G♭–B♭. The root is A♭.

Joshua Bell, Debussy's "La Fille aux Cheveux de Lin"

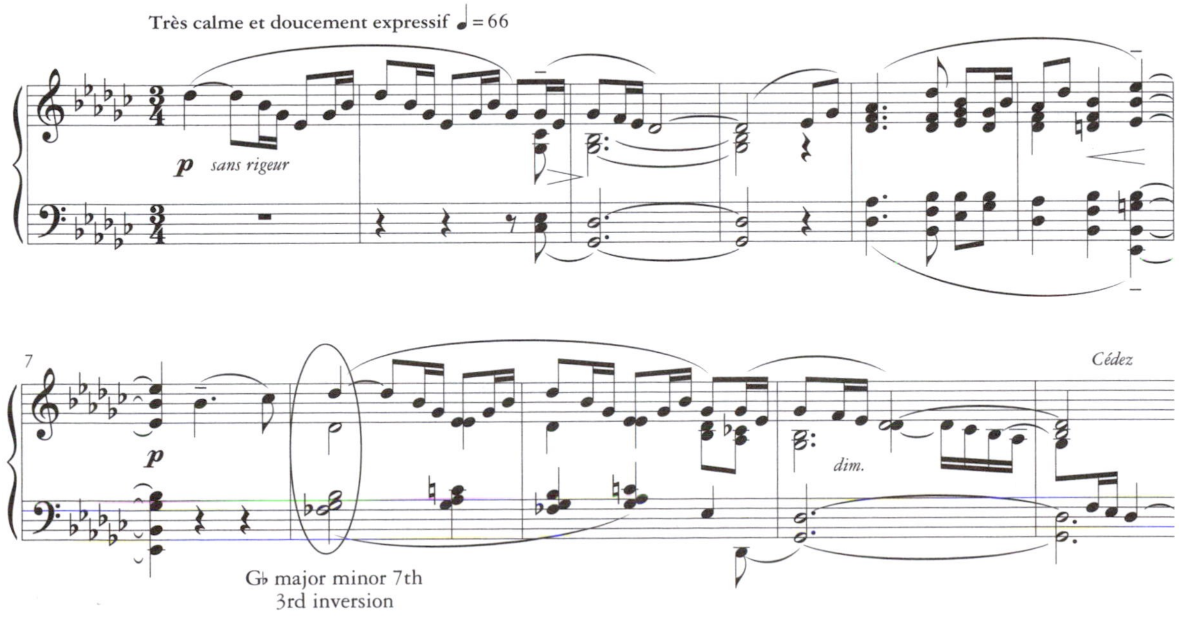

WEBSITE
VIDEO TRACK 46

In 2002, a director's cut of the film *Cinema Paradiso* was released in the United States to great public acclaim, although the film had already received the Oscar for Best Foreign Film in 1989. The love theme from the film, composed by Ennio Morricone, was rerecorded by Josh Groban and Joshua Bell for the album *At Home with Friends*. Listen to the performance as you analyze the seventh chords in the score.

Morricone, "Love Theme" from *Cinema Paradiso*

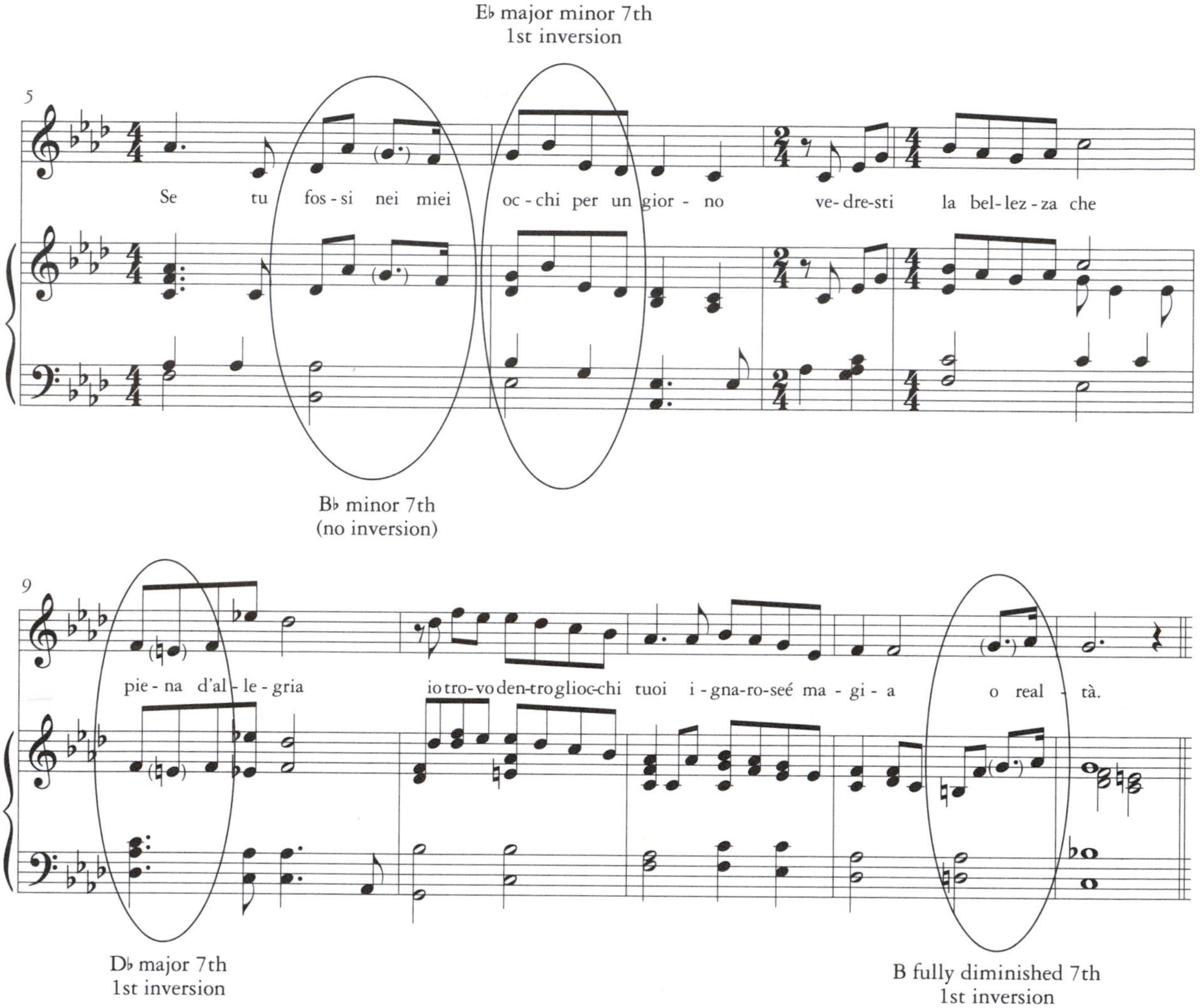

BACKSTAGE PASS

Playing for Pennies: The Subway Experiment

WEBSITE
VIDEO TRACK 47

Although he has performed in concert halls around the world, it is perhaps Joshua Bell's performance in the Washington D.C. subway that captured the most attention. On January 12, 2007, Josh Bell donned a baseball cap and a T-shirt and set up to play at the entrance to a busy metro stop. But here's the real kicker. This was no ordinary violin that Bell was playing. This was a 1713 Stradivarius violin worth about $4 million. Passersby barely paid any attention to the classical rock star, and it took 6 minutes of Bell's playing before one woman stopped to listen. It's also interesting to note that Bell began this performance with one of the most challenging pieces ever written for the violin, Bach's "Chaconne" from *Partita No. 2 in D Minor.*

After 45 minutes of playing, Bell had received about $32 in donations, and only seven commuters stopped to actually listen for more than a second. How compelling that Bell had played a concert several nights before where seats averaged $100 apiece. The full story of this experiment (Weingarten, 2007) is worth a read. In an interview with *Time* magazine, Bell reflects on the experience: "I have mixed feelings about it. It's the thing I get asked about most, and I don't want it on my tombstone. . . . But these are the audiences I want to reach. If someone claps at the wrong time at a concert, I'm like, 'Score!' "

What are your own thoughts of this experiment? Are there great acts lurking beneath the streets in major metropolitan cities? "If a great musician plays great music but no one hears . . . was he really any good?"

And as a postscript, Bell returned to the D.C. Metro in late September of 2014. Only this time, he was playing to a full crowd in Union Station. In response to the crowd of over 1,000, Bell is quoted as saying, "Wow, that's more like it!"

Reviewing Chapter Objectives

- Identify seventh chords by root name and quality (page 112)
- Notate seventh chords when given root name and quality (pages 112–113)
- Notate and identify seventh chords in inversion (page 114)
- Identify seventh chords within the context of a musical score (pages 116–118)

EXERCISES

I. Identify the seventh chord by root name and quality.

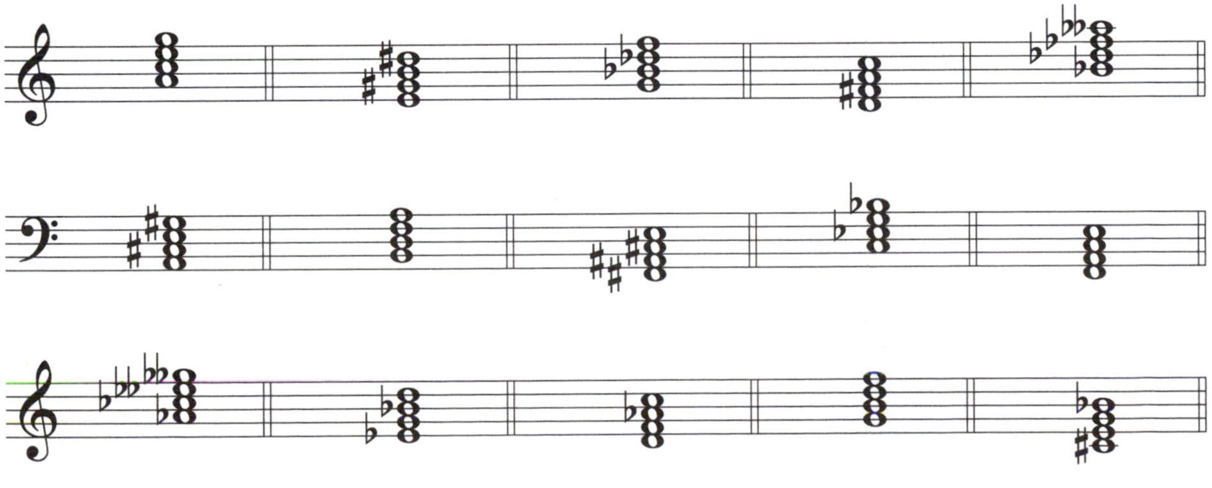

II. Given the root name and quality, correctly notate the following seventh chords.

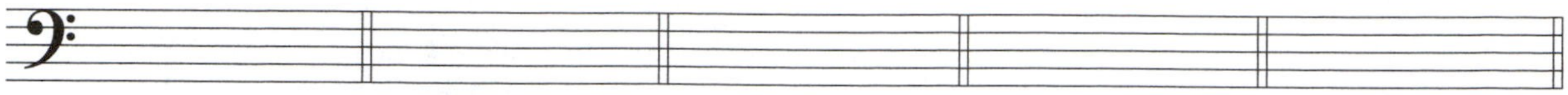

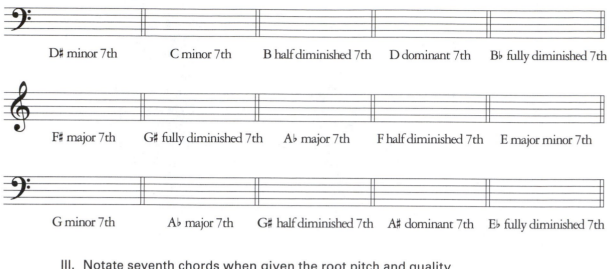

D♯ minor 7th | C minor 7th | B half diminished 7th | D dominant 7th | B♭ fully diminished 7th

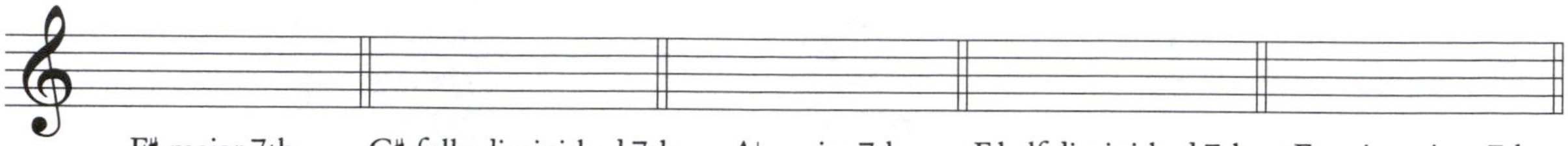

F♯ major 7th | G♯ fully diminished 7th | A♭ major 7th | F half diminished 7th | E major minor 7th

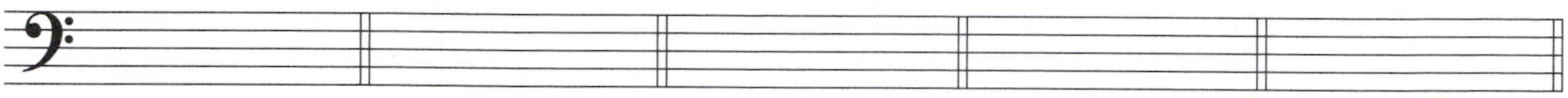

G minor 7th | A♭ major 7th | G♯ half diminished 7th | A♯ dominant 7th | E♭ fully diminished 7th

III. Notate seventh chords when given the root pitch and quality.

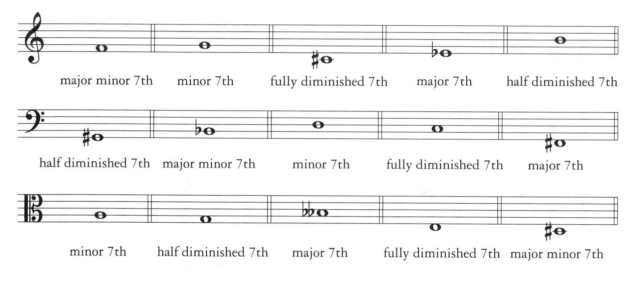

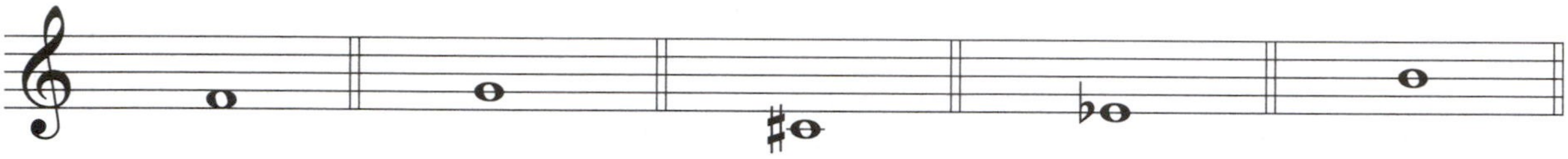

major minor 7th | minor 7th | fully diminished 7th | major 7th | half diminished 7th

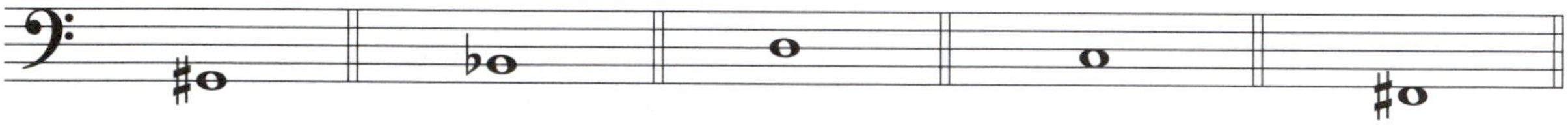

half diminished 7th | major minor 7th | minor 7th | fully diminished 7th | major 7th

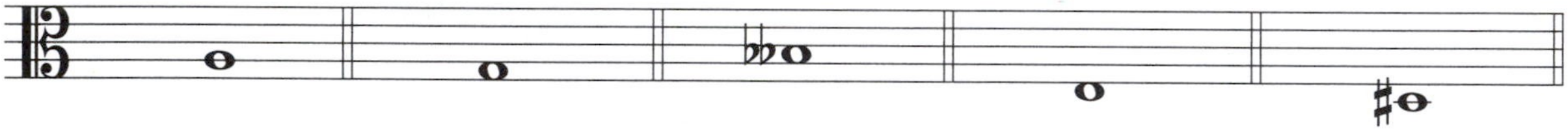

minor 7th | half diminished 7th | major 7th | fully diminished 7th | major minor 7th

IV. Given the root, third, fifth, or seventh of the seventh chord and the quality, notate the correct chord.

root | 7th | 3rd | 5th | 3rd

major minor 7th | major 7th | minor 7th | fully diminished 7th | half diminished 7th

5th | 7th | 3rd | 5th | 7th

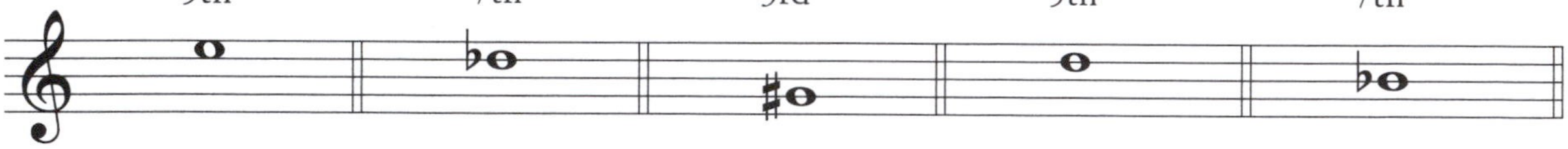

fully diminished 7th | half diminished 7th | minor 7th | major 7th | major minor 7th

7th | 5th | root | 3rd | root

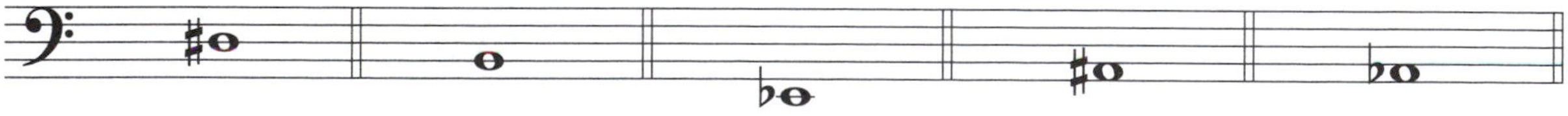

major 7th | half diminished 7th | fully diminished 7th | major minor 7th | minor 7th

V. Identify the notated seventh chord by root name, quality, and inversion.

VI. Notate seventh chords when given the root, quality, and inversion.

root position | 3rd inversion | 1st inversion | 2nd inversion | 1st inversion

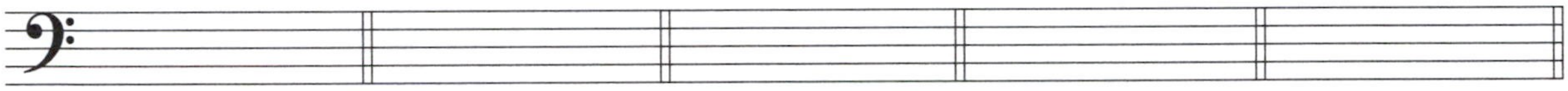

G dominant 7th | F♯ minor 7th | C half diminished 7th | G♯ fully diminished 7th | A major 7th

2nd inversion | 2nd inversion | root inversion | 1st inversion | 3rd inversion

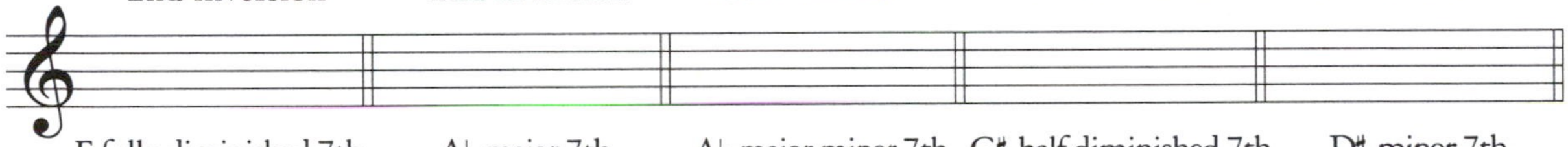

E fully diminished 7th | A♭ major 7th | A♭ major minor 7th | G♯ half diminished 7th | D♯ minor 7th

3rd inversion | 1st inversion | 3rd inversion | 2nd inversion | root position

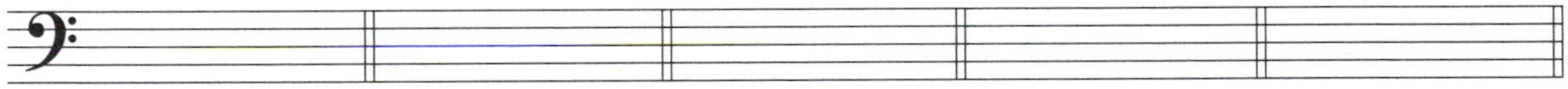

B♭ major 7th | F major minor 7th | D fully diminished 7th | C minor 7th | A half diminished 7th

ANALYSIS

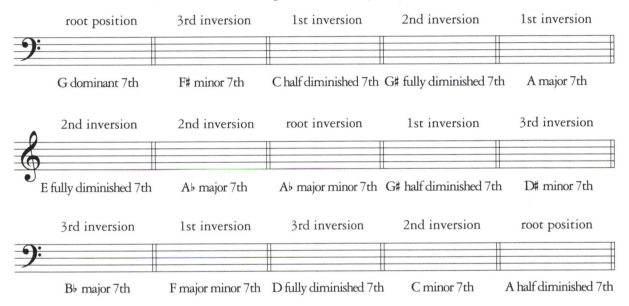

Gershwin's "I Loves You Porgy" from *Porgy and Bess* was arranged by Joshua Bell and Chris Gotti for inclusion on the *At Home with Friends* album. But take a moment to search on YouTube for other performances featuring vocalists, specifically Audra MacDonald and Norm Lewis. The performance begins at 2:40. Identify the qualities and inversions of the seventh chords labeled in the score.

WEBSITE

VIDEO TRACK 48

Gershwin, "I Loves You Porgy" from *Porgy and Bess*

5. ____

Camille Saint-Saëns's *Carnival of the Animals* was composed in 1886 and has been featured in the movie *Fantasia* and other films. The thirteenth movement, "Le Cygne," includes a variety of extended triads. There are three different types of chords used in this short excerpt, the triad, the seventh chord, and the extended harmony chord. Extended harmonies are discussed at length in the supplemental material online, but for now listen to Joshua Bell's performance and identify the qualities for the chords highlighted in the score.

WEBSITE
VIDEO TRACK 49

Saint-Saëns, "Le Cygne" from *Carnaval des Animaux*

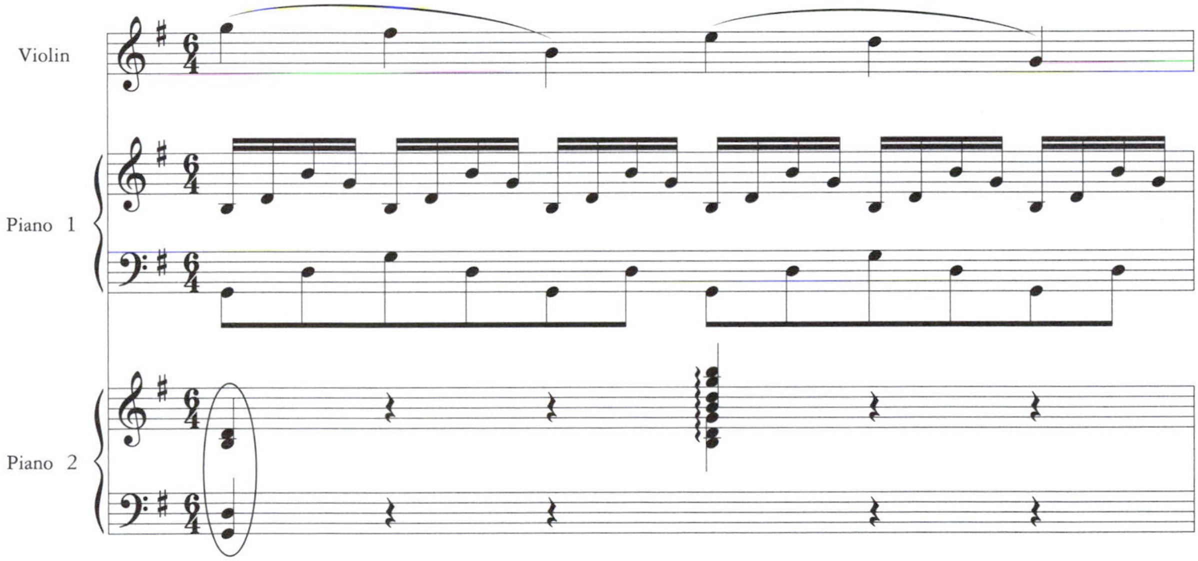

1. ____

Saint-Saëns, "Le Cygne" from *Carnaval des Animaux (continued)*

Topping the charts in 2013, "When I Was Your Man" features seventh chords in the introduction. Correctly identify the chords circled below, including root, quality, and inversion.

VIDEO TRACK 50

Bruno Mars, "When I Was Your Man."
Songwriters: Bruno Mars, Andrew Wyatt, Philip Lawrence, Ari Levine, and Moe Faisal

AURAL SKILLS CONDITIONING 6

Hearing and Singing Solfège: Joshua Bell

Listen to Joshua Bell's performance of "Somewhere" from Leonard Bernstein's *West Side Story*. The solfège for that famous melody is written below. Can you sing the solfège while Bell plays? After singing along a few times, can you hear the solfège syllables as you listen to Bell play? What is the opening interval (Sol → Fa), and what chord does it outline?

VIDEO TRACK 51

sol–fa–mi–do–la
la–sol–fa–mi–do–la
ti–do–re–mi–fa–sol–mi–do
la–fa–re
do–ti
sol . . .

VIDEO TRACK 52

Now, listen to Bell's performance of Tchaikovsky's *Violin Concerto, Canzonetta: Andante.* The solfège for the solo violin's open melody is written below. Listen to the first few minutes of the piece to get a feel for the rhythm of the melody. Can you sing the solfège along with this heart-wrenching tune? *Note: The solfège in parentheses are part of an ornament. Don't feel as if you have to sing every note, but make sure you get back on track with the rest of the syllables.

sol–do–re–me–fa–sol–sol–sol– (sol–le* fa sol te le) sol
sol–do–re–me–fa–sol–sol–sol
fa–me–re–me–re–do–ti–le–sol
sol–do–re–me–fa–sol–sol–sol– (sol–le* fa sol te le) sol

Sight Singing: Melodies That Outline Triads and Seventh Chords

The following melodies outline triads and seventh chords, just like the examples above. For any challenging interval, ask yourself the following questions: What chord am I outlining? Should the chord be major or minor?

Major Keys

1.

2.

3.

4.

5.

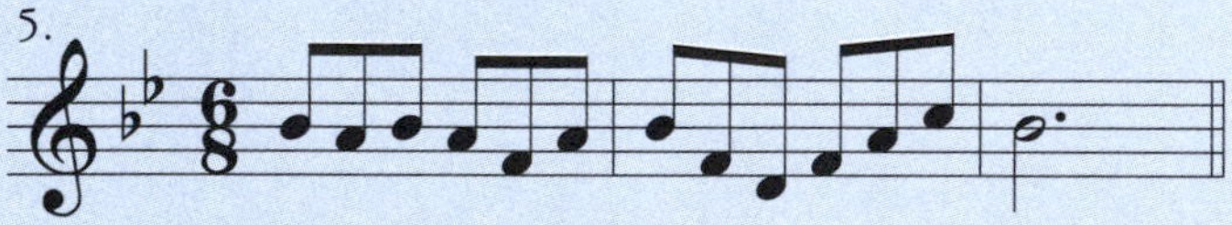

Minor Keys

1.

2.

3.

4.

5.

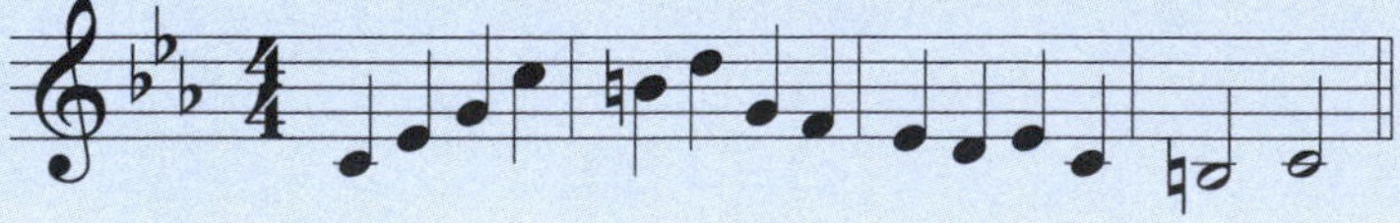

THE FINAL NOTE: REAL-WORLD PERSPECTIVE

Frank Babbitt

VIOLIST FOR CHICAGO SYMPHONY AND LYRIC OPERA OF CHICAGO

What course or courses did you take in college, other than lessons, that best prepared you for your career in performance? How so?

I'm convinced that the courses that best prepared or helped me on the path to becoming a complete musician were music composition and analysis related. I've always had a passion for learning about the life and times of the great composers as a means to gain a greater understanding of their music. Playing a Dvorak Quintet in Spillville, Iowa, in Dvorak's St. Wenceslas Church, for example, was an unforgettable experience partly because I had read so much about his life and experience in America. I could almost feel Dvorak's presence in the church and imagined his longing for his native Bohemia as he gazed out over the prairie. Indeed, there is longing and sadness in the music he composed during those months in Iowa, but how do we talk about those emotional qualities in real musical terms? With a knowledge of music analysis, harmonic and structural, it is possible to understand Dvorak's musical language on a deeper level. What are the elements that make a particular piece of music a "masterpiece"? This approach to understanding the elements of music is very important to me when I work on my own solo or chamber repertoire as well as with my students. As a teacher, it is not enough to point out that there exists tension or drama in the music without exploring how the composer creates and releases that tension. I believe that a performer's interpretative choices should be grounded in this knowledge. It opens up a universe of possibilities!

Has the study of music theory and ear training helped you in your career? If so, how?

It is not possible to be a complete musician without a thorough understanding of music theory and a well-trained ear. The study of these disciplines has helped me in every facet of my career as a musician, which has included work as a children's choir director, professional chorus member, session musician, private teacher, chamber musician, orchestra player, and many others. Even when I'm not working as a musician it helps me! When I appear as narrator on Stravinsky's "The Soldier's Tale" I am aided immeasurably by my knowledge of music theory and my trained ear; it allows me to function fully as a member of the musical ensemble.

Most significant learning experience of your career . . . or the "Aha" moment.

It was a sobering one. I was made aware of the fact that, despite my endless hours of perpetration, I was still unaware of the need to "leave no stone unturned" as I prepared for an opera orchestra audition. I had diligently prepared all the notes with the correct tempos and dynamics but, as my coach pointed out, it was simply not enough. It was not going to carry the day. I had not managed to capture the true feeling and style of the piece, the music "between the notes." The suggested remedy was to find and purchase a recording of the opera in question as well as a full score and then work to create a musical and emotional context for what I was playing. I studied the opera and played endlessly with the recording until it became almost second nature to me. What had been a weakness became a strength. I could now play the excerpt with confidence, passion and the sure knowledge that I was capturing the style and language of the composer.

If you could give one piece of advice to a young student interested in studying performance, what would that be?

Never stop learning! Always be progressing as a musician, and seek out those who possess the knowledge or skill you are interested in acquiring. Your work should be about engaging in a daily process rather than obsessing about the big "goal." Mentors seem to somehow appear when we identify an aspect of our musicianship or knowledge that we urgently need to strengthen. Embrace the weakest aspect of your playing and work ceaselessly to improve it! My own arduous audition-taking experience (I took more than twenty) was aided immeasurably by working with an older colleague whom I had approached about listening to my audition list. It was my desire to understand what made this successful musician "tick" that not only helped me with the short-term goal of winning a job but provided me with the tools to be a more successful performer and teacher. A life in music is a journey that we must work hard and prepare for, always leaving "no stone unturned"!

What, or who, inspired you to study music?

In looking back I was probably most inspired by my early experiences with live music. There was a small roadside tavern on the lake in northern Wisconsin where our family spent every summer running a small resort. The proprietor was a German immigrant named Max who was also a trained concert violinist. When I first knew him he had retired from professional music and spent his time presiding at his tavern and entertaining his guests by playing his violin to selections accompanied by the jukebox. It was here that I first heard the *Tales from the Vienna Woods*, *Clair de Lune*, and *Hungarian Dance #5*, along with many others. I was inspired, I think, not just by his considerable technical command of the instrument but also by his ability to speak directly to people's hearts and emotions when he played. He didn't so much play the violin, as he became the violin. Max was another unlikely mentor as we were separated by nearly 60 years in age. I'm now playing in the same opera house that he was working in during his career during the 1930s and 1940s!

CHAPTER 7

LEAD SHEET SYMBOLS

Artist in Residence: Elvis Presley

Chapter Objectives

- Translate traditional notation into lead sheet symbols
- Notate triads and chords when given lead sheet symbols
- Indicate inversions using lead sheet symbols
- Realize lead sheet notation when looking at musical excerpt

The year is 1956. It is a hot Sunday evening in early September. Millions of viewers—over fifty-five million viewers to be exact: 82 percent of all Americans—are tuned in to watch a young singer from Tupelo, Mississippi, perform live on *The Ed Sullivan Show.* Elvis Presley had been topping the charts for months with the songs "Heartbreak Hotel," "Don't Be Cruel," and "Hound Dog," so he was well known to the teenagers who listened to the pop radio stations. However, this particular performance would become a turning point in Elvis's career. The next morning, everyone in the country would know his name, but maybe not for his music. One review in the *New York Journal American* stated, "He can't sing a lick, makes up for vocal shortcomings with the weirdest and plainly planned, suggestive animation short of an aborigine's mating dance."

WEBSITE

VIDEO TRACKS 53 AND 54

Watch Elvis's performance on *The Ed Sullivan Show.* He starts off innocently enough with a rendition of "Don't Be Cruel" and "Love Me Tender." Perhaps the producers had been warned about his provocative dancing style because the video was shot from the waist up. That all changed during the second half when Elvis closed his second set with a sultrier version of "Hound Dog." The cameras were filming the entire physique of Mr. Presley, gyrations and all. (Watch Elvis's performance of "Hound Dog" on *The Milton Berle Show*. You can even hear the nervous chatter, shock, laughter, and screams from the in-studio audience.) Parents were outraged by the performance, and many banned their children from listening to Elvis. It didn't matter. The year was 1956. "Hound Dog" was on the charts for 23 straight weeks. And Elvis was at the top of his game.

Let's look at the chords and melody used in "Hound Dog." The entire song is based on three chords, B♭ major, E♭ dominant 7, and F dominant 7. Instead of the chords being written in the bass clef, the chord symbols are written above the staff. This type of shorthand is known as **lead sheet notation** (or **pop chord symbols**). What do you think the N.C. stands for?

Elvis Presley, "Hound Dog." Songwriters: Jerry Leiber and Mike Stoller

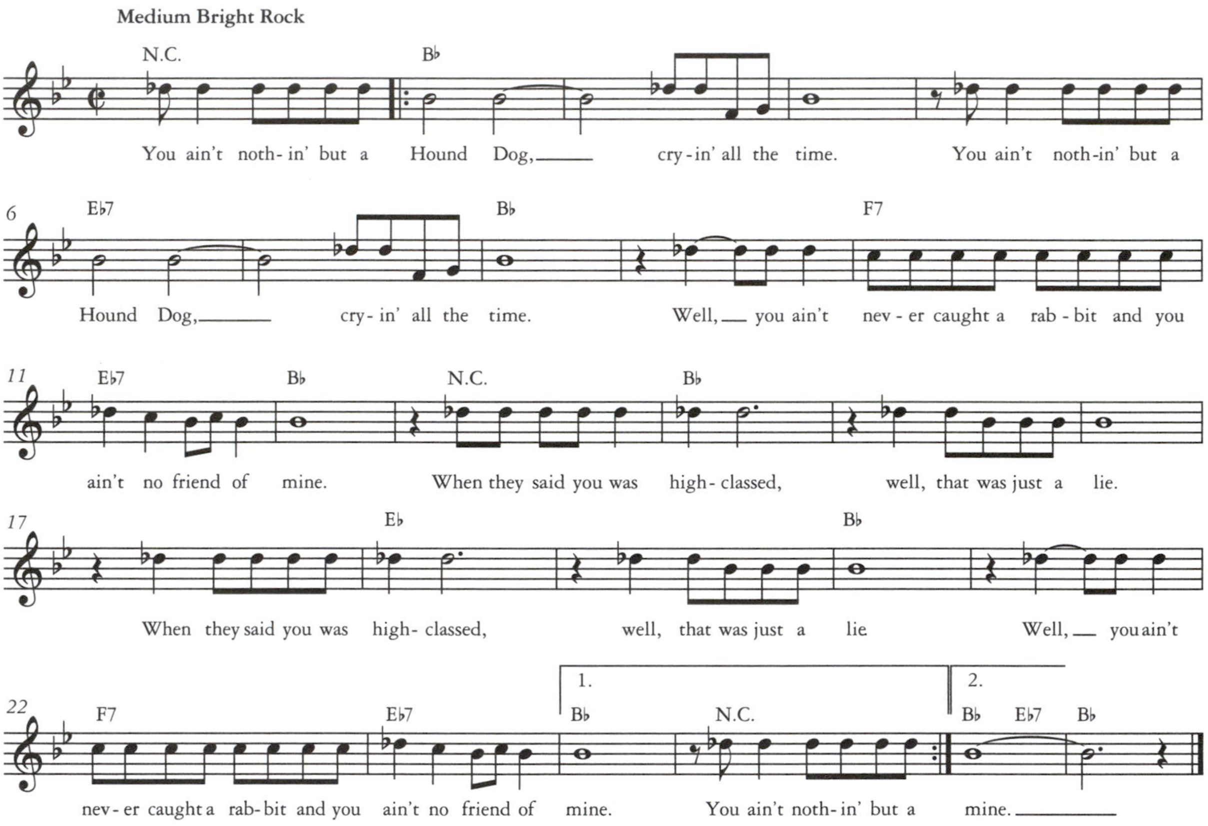

Popular and jazz musicians rely on lead sheets for both improvisation and performance. A lead sheet simply shows the lyrics, the basic chords, and sometimes, but not always, the vocal melody. Lead sheet symbols are basically shorthand for writing out triads and chords. Lead sheet symbols *always* indicate the root pitch with a capital letter. There are multiple ways to represent different chords, so the following charts include most, if not all, of lead sheet symbols used in music today.

Lead Sheet Symbols for Triads

Major Triad	G GMAJ	
Minor Triad	EM EMIN E-	
Augmented	D+ DAUG	
Diminished	F♯o/Ao	

Lead Sheet Symbols for Seventh Chords

Major Major	GΔ7 GMAJ7	
Major Minor	D7	
Minor Minor	EMIN7 E-7 EM7	
Half Diminished	F♯ø7 F♯MIN7(♭5) F♯MIN7(−5)	
Fully Diminished	F♯o7 F♯DIM7	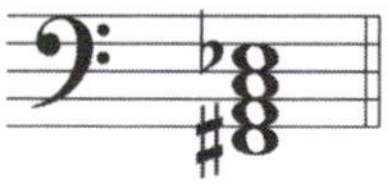

Lead sheet symbols indicate the root, the quality, and the inversion of every harmony. Inversions are specified with a slash after the chord symbol followed by a letter to indicate the lowest sounding pitch.

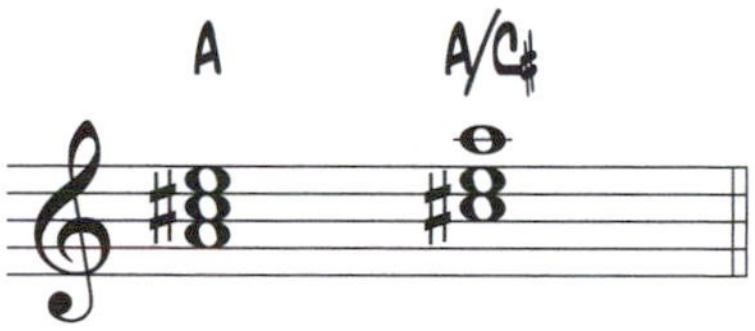

WEBSITE
VIDEO TRACK 55

Scandalous as it could be, "All Shook Up" (1957) spent 7 weeks at number 1 and 21 weeks on the chart. Play along with Elvis's performance while you realize[1] the lead sheet

[1]The term *realize* or *realization* refers to the translation of lead sheet symbols or Roman numerals into sounding pitches.

symbols on the guitar or keyboard. How do the chords used in this song resemble the chords used in "Hound Dog"? Do the changes in melody alter the sound of the piece even though the chords are the same?

Elvis Presley, "All Shook Up." Songwriters: Elvis Presley and Otis Blackwell

VIDEO
TRACK 56

"Love Me Tender" topped the charts in 1956 and is still one of Elvis's most performed songs. Study the lead sheet and the outline of the corresponding chords. Realize the chords as you follow along with the score.

Elvis Presley, "Love Me Tender." Songwriters: George Poulton, Elvis Presley, and Vera Matson

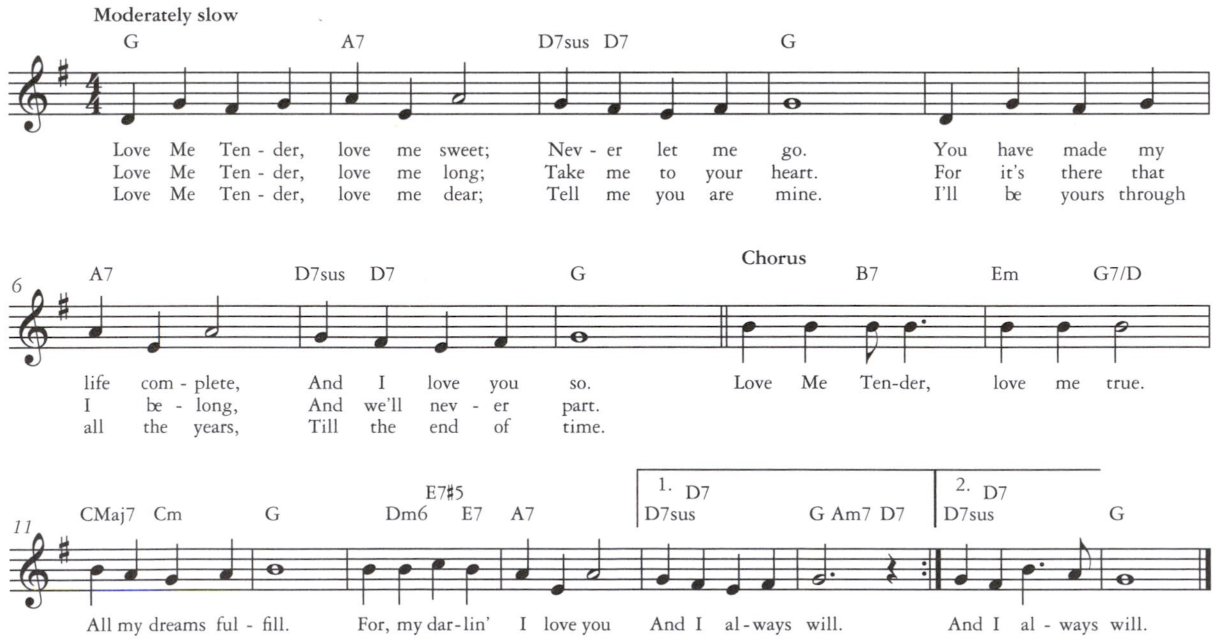

The chords used in "Love Me Tender" are all notated below. Three chords should jump out to you as different: the D^{7}sus, Dminor6, and the E$^{7\sharp5}$. The sus tells the performer to add a fourth above the root and omit the third. The fourth (G) will typically lead into the third (F♯) of the next chord. The addition of the number 6 by a chord simply means to add a sixth above the root: in this case, the D. The ♯5 tells the performer to raise the fifth above the root pitch. Play through all these chords on the piano or on your guitar. Do the chords seem to flow into the next? There's a reason for that. You will find more on that in Chapter 8!

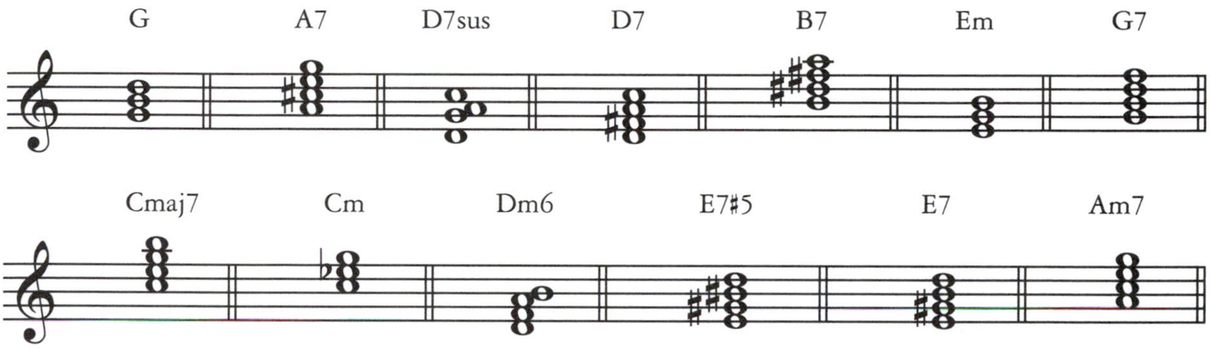

BACKSTAGE PASS

Play It Again, and Again, and Again

As you probably have gathered by now, Elvis Presley's music is not extremely complex in terms of melody or harmony. So what made this artist so popular?

First, his is a great story, and books upon books have been written about him. A young Elvis was inspired by the sound of the blues and gospel music that surrounded him in his youth. He graduated from high school, and on his lunch break from a local warehouse, he walked into Sun Recording Studio to record a few songs. It is not as if he had a record deal: anyone could make a record for $4 back in the 1950s. It's quite a deal, actually, considering the minimum wage at that time was $1 an hour. The recording engineer passed along the record to the famous Sam Phillips, and the rest is rock and roll history. How many musicians do you know of today who have paid less than a day's wages to record even a single song?

Second, Elvis had a completely new sound that was embraced by the radio industry. He wasn't the first singer to initiate this mixture of country and rhythm and blues, but he was one of the first white men to be embraced by the U.S. audience. Radio was the social mecca for American teenagers, and it is important to understand how radio could make or break a performance career. Teenagers would call in requests to the disc jockeys, and requests would determine amount of airplay. That's why when Elvis recorded the song "That's All Right" in 1954, the record was immediately sent to local DJs. It became so popular that one DJ actually played the song fourteen times in a row while fielding requests from the phone line. In a world of satellite and internet radio, Spotify, and iTunes, this is almost inconceivable.

For what other reasons, in terms of radio, marketing, environment, management, and musical style, do you think Elvis maintained his popularity well into the 1970s?

WEBSITE

VIDEO TRACK 57

Fast-forward a few years into the 1960s. Elvis has returned from the war, and America is happy and dancing. Listen to the 1962 hit "Return to Sender" while you study the lead sheet symbols below. How is the inclusion of N.C. (no chord) an effective moment in the song in terms of the text?

Elvis Presley, "Return to Sender." Songwriters: Winfield Scott and Otis Blackwell

BACKSTAGE PASS

King of Rock and Roll? Who Decides?

Some fans and scholars have disputed whether Elvis deserves to be called the "king of rock and roll," and, in fact, it is not clear who even came up with that title. Perhaps we can blame (or give credit to) RCA records. In 1955, RCA offered $35,000 to Sun Records for all rights to the Presley recordings. One year later, the marketing frenzy began and Elvis was everywhere. There were Elvis shoes, lipstick, clothing, jewelry, pencils, and even pajamas and lunchboxes for the younger kids. By December 1957, Elvis Presley products grossed about $55 million (equal to about $410 million today). But what about the music?

Elvis has had more top 40 hits than any artist to date. Take a look at his chart history to determine whether you think he is deserving of his royal title. (You will also understand why Elvis merits his own station on Sirius XM. These titles represent just the songs that topped the charts; plenty more were in the top 10.)

1956	"Heartbreak Hotel"
	"Hound Dog"
1957	"All Shook Up"
	"Teddy Bear"
1956	"Heartbreak Hotel"
	"Hound Dog"
1957	"All Shook Up"
	"Teddy Bear"
	"Party"
1958	"Jailhouse Rock"
	"Don't"
	"Wear My Ring Around Your Neck"
	"Hard Headed Woman"
	"King Creole"
1959	"One Night"
	"A Big Hunk O'Love"
	"A Fool Such as I"
1960	"Stuck on You"
	"A Mess of Blues"
	"It's Now or Never"
1961	"Are You Lonesome Tonight?"
	"Wooden Heart"
	"Surrender"
	"Wild in the Country"
	"Little Sister"
1962	"Can't Help Falling in Love"
	"Good Luck Charm"
	"She's Not You"
	"Return to Sender"
1963	"Devil in Disguise"
1965	"Crying in the Chapel"
1969	"In the Ghetto"
	"Suspicious Minds"
1970	"The Wonder of You"
1972	"Until It's Time for You to Go"
1977	"Way Down"

Reviewing Chapter Objectives

- Translate traditional notation into lead sheet symbols (page 131)
- Notate triads and chords when given lead sheet symbols (page 131)
- Indicate inversions using lead sheet symbols (page 131)
- Realize lead sheet notation when looking at musical excerpt (pages 132–133)

EXERCISES

I. Give the appropriate lead sheet symbols for the chords notated below. Be sure to indicate inversions with a slash.

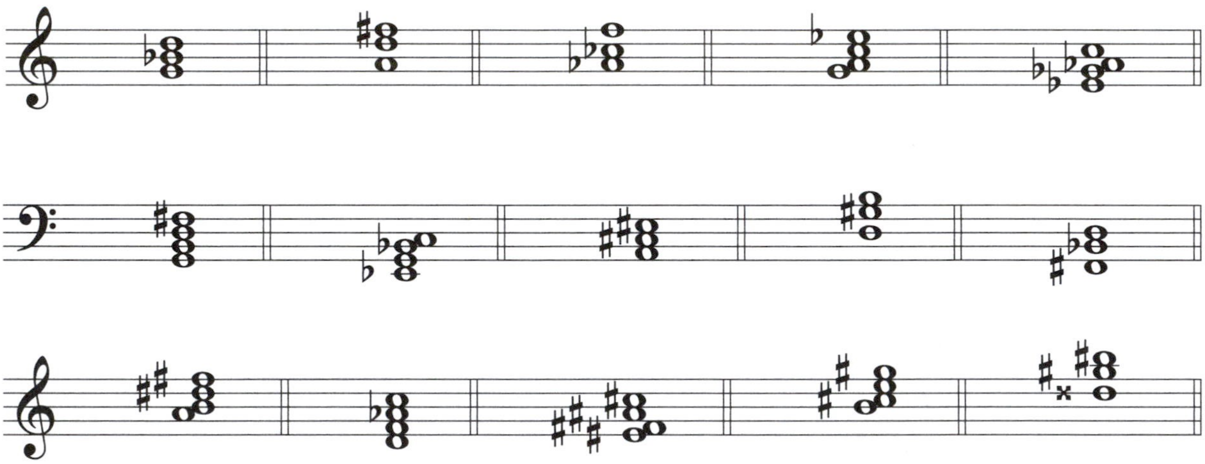

II. Notate the following chords when given the lead sheet symbols.

ANALYSIS

Fun.'s "We Are Young" was one of the power anthems of 2012. The following excerpt is from the lead-in to the chorus. Using the staff line provided, notate all of the chords used in the excerpt. Be sure to account for any chords not written in root position.

WEBSITE

VIDEO TRACK 58

Fun., "We Are Young." Songwriters: Jeff Bhasker, Jack Antonoff, Andrew Dost, and Nate Ruess

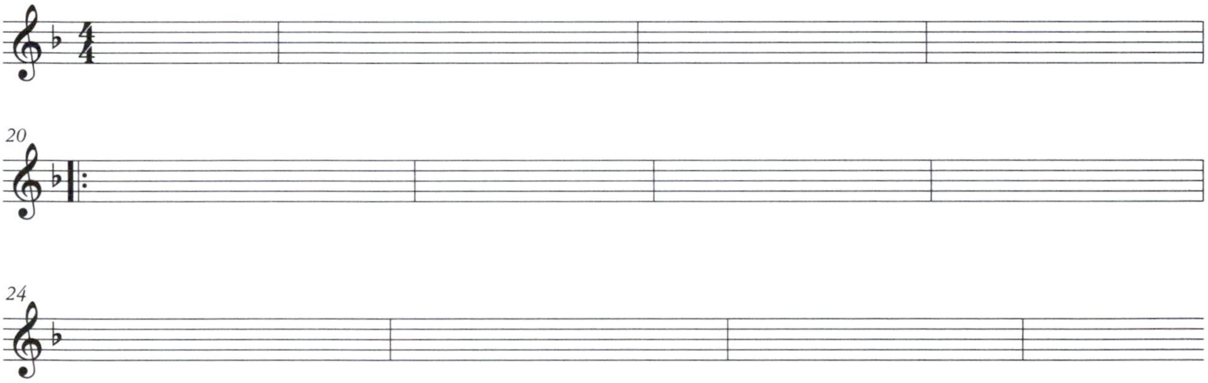

The opening of Fun.'s "Some Nights" is performed a capella and written in three parts. Before completing the following items, take a minute to study the chords and compare the score notation to the lead sheet symbols given in the arrangement.

WEBSITE

VIDEO TRACK 59

1. There is no indication of inversions given in the lead sheet; however, several of the chords do indicate inversion in the printed score. Add in the necessary lead sheet symbols to show the correct inversions.
2. How often (in terms of rhythm) do the chords tend to change?
3. What triad is notated on the grace note on the word "luck"?
4. Circle all of the pitches in the melody that are not part of the chord shown in the lead sheet.

Fun., "Some Nights." Songwriters: Jeff Bhasker, Jack Antonoff, Andrew Dost, and Nate Ruess

Sarah Hurst, a songwriter from Austin, Texas, recently released an album titled *Fine to Wait*. Study the lead sheet for the entire song while you listen to her performance on the YouTube channel. Write out the notation for every chord used in the song "To the Moon."

WEBSITE

VIDEO TRACK 60

Sarah Hurst, "To the Moon." Songwriter: Sarah Hurst

To the Moon (Key of F)

Verse 1

Cm B♭
The world's looking sad

F/A F/B♭
Hearts in need of mending

F/A F/B♭
Hearts in need of mending

C B♭
Does love ever last

F/A F/B♭
I always see it ending

F/A F/B♭
I always see it ending

Gm Am B♭ C
And people are grieving cause life's getting tough

Gm Am B♭ C
Cause people keep leaving the ones they claim to love

Chorus

Gm Am B♭ C
But no one can take away the love we have found

Gm Am B♭ C
Because deep in your heart is where my love abounds

Gm Am B♭ C
And I'm fine to wait for you here on the ground

Gm Am B♭
So fly to the moon

E♭ Am B♭ C
And to the moon my love will follow you

Verse 2

Cm Bb
Deep in your eyes

F/A F/Bb
I see years to come

F/A F/Bb
I foresee years to come

Cm Bb F/A F/Bb
I won't be surprised if we get to keep our love

F/A F/Bb
We can keep our love

Pre-Chorus

Gm Am
The dreams I was dreaming

Bb C
You worked your way in

Gm Am
And I won't be leaving

Bb C
My love has no end

Chorus

Gm Am Bb C
But no one can take away the love we have found

Gm Am Bb C
Because deep in your heart is where my love abounds

Gm Am Bb C
And I'm fine to wait for you here on the ground

Gm Am Bb
So fly to the moon

Eb Am Bb C
And to the moon my love will follow you

Bridge

Gm Am
Deep in the ocean

Bb C
There's still love to spare

Gm Am
Or climb all the mountains

Bb C
My love will find you there

Last Chorus

Gm Am Bb C
But no one can take away the love we have found

Gm Am Bb C
Because deep in your heart is where my love abounds

Gm Am Bb C
And I'm fine to wait for you here on the ground

Gm Am Bb C
So fly

Gm Am Bb C
Fly

Gm Am Bb
Darling, fly to the moon

Eb Am Bb C
And to the moon my love will follow

AURAL SKILLS CONDITIONING 7

Hearing and Singing Seventh Chords

In Chapter 6, you learned about six different qualities of seventh chords. For now, we will focus on singing only the most common seventh chords: major-minor (dominant seventh), fully diminished, and minor-minor. The following chart shows the solfège syllables for these chords. Give yourself the tonic pitch, and practice singing each chord on solfège.

Quality	Solfège	Intervals	Lead Sheet Symbol
Major-Minor/ Dominant 7th	Sol-Ti-Re-Fa	M3 + m3 + m3	A7
Fully Diminished	Ti-Re-Fa-La	m3 + m3 + m3	C♯o7
Minor-Minor	Do-Me-Sol-Te Re-Fa-La-Do	m3 + M3 +m3	D–7 E–7

Now that you have sung through these seventh chords, listen to your teacher play them for you on the piano or guitar. Can you hear the solfège syllables as the chords are being played? Listen to the quality of the intervals. For instance, a chord that has an M3 on the bottom can only be one quality right now—major!

Hearing and Singing Progressions: Elvis Presley, "Can't Help Falling in Love"

WEBSITE

VIDEO TRACK 61

"Can't Help Falling in Love" was number 1 on the Billboard Easy Listening chart for 6 consecutive weeks in 1961. Written by Hugo Peretti, Luigi Creatore, and George David Weiss, the melody is based on Jean-Paul-Égide Martini's famous "Plaisir d'Amour" (1784). The lead sheet symbols and their corresponding solfège syllables are shown below. Listen to the song on the YouTube channel. Can you hear the different qualities of the triads? Do the dominant seventh chords stand out to you?

D Do-Mi-Sol *Wise*	F♯– Mi-Sol-Ti *men*	B– La-Do-Mi *say only . . .*		
G Fa-La-Do	D Do-Mi-Sol	A7 Sol-Ti-Re-Fa		
G Fa-La-Do	A7 Sol-Ti-Re-Fa	B– La-Do-Mi	G Fa-La-Do	D/A Sol-Do-Mi
A7 Sol-Ti-Re-Fa	D Do-Mi-Sol			

Play the song again, and try singing along with the solfège for each chord. In class, have a group of students sing the solfège as accompaniment while another group of students sings along with the lyrics. Here is a model:

Group 1:	do–mi–sol–mi	mi–sol–ti–sol	la–do–mi–do–la–do–mi–do	
Group 2:	Wise	men	say	only

fa–la–do–la	do–mi–sol–mi	sol–ti–re–fa . . .
fools	rush	in . . .

Switch up the groups after you've done this a few times so each student has a chance to sing both lyrics and solfège.

Seventh Chord Identification

You will hear eight seventh chords played by your teacher or on the course website. Each chord will be played arpeggiated and as a block chord. Write the quality of seventh chord you hear in the spaces provided below.

AUDIO TRACK CH. 7 SEVENTH CHORD ID 1–8

1. ______ 2. ______ 3. ______ 4. ______

5. ______ 6. ______ 7. ______ 8. ______

Hearing Sixths and Sevenths

Listen to the Beatles' timeless song "Across the Universe" on the YouTube channel. Starting around 0:48, listen to the wide intervals on the lyrics "my world." John Lennon first sings a major sixth followed by a minor sixth on the same lyrics. Can you hear how the major sixth is just a bit wider than the minor sixth? Sing along with the recording a few times during this section. Then sing the melody in solfège:

VIDEO TRACK 62

re	re	re	re	do	re	fa
Nothing's		*gonna*		*change my*		*world*
do	do	do	do	ti	do	mi
Nothing's		*gonna*		*change my*		*world*

For another popular example of the minor sixth, listen to the opening of Scott Joplin's "The Entertainer." And if you've ever sung the famous carol "Jingle Bells," you've sung a major sixth without knowing it! Sing the first two notes of the melody starting with "Dashing through the snow" to practice this interval. For other examples of a major sixth, listen to the traditional Irish folk song "My Bonnie Lies over the Ocean" or the television channel NBC's network chime.

In Chapter 6, you heard and sang along with Joshua Bell's rendition of "Somewhere" from *West Side Story*. The melody begins with a minor seventh, sol → fa. Think of the solfège for a dominant seventh chord: sol–ti–re–fa. The minor seventh simply outlines the chord, making sol → fa an easy way to sing the interval. What are some other ways you can sing a minor seventh? Which way do you prefer?

In "Over the Rainbow" from *The Wizard of Oz*, Dorothy sings an octave (the first two notes, "Some-where") and then descends by a minor second (on the first syllable of "over"). The distance between this pitch and the first pitch is a major seventh. Think of the interval as wanting to resolve outward to become an octave. To practice singing a major seventh, sing the opening line to "Over the Rainbow" and stop on the third note. Then, sing the beginning note again. Practice this interval a few times.

Singing Sixths and Sevenths

The following chart shows common solfège for singing sixths and sevenths. Give yourself a tonic pitch and practice singing each interval. Figure out which solfège works best for you. For instance, is it easier to hear a minor sixth in the context of a minor key (do–le) or outlining a major chord (do–**mi**–sol–**do**)?

Minor sixth	do–le, mi–do
Major sixth	do–la, me–do
Minor seventh	do–te, sol–fa
Major seventh	do–ti

Interval Identification: Sixths and Sevenths

REPLAY

AUDIO TRACK CH. 7 INTERVAL ID 1–10

You will hear ten intervals (m6, M6, m7, and M7) performed. Write the interval you hear in the spaces provided.

1. ______ 2. ______ 3. ______ 4. ______ 5. ______

6. ______ 7. ______ 8. ______ 9. ______ 10. ______

THE FINAL NOTE: REAL-WORLD PERSPECTIVE

Laying Martine

2013 NASHVILLE SONGWRITERS HALL OF FAME INDUCTEE

Educational Background

I began my education at Denison University in Ohio, but I left after only 1 year. I then spent a year as a copyboy at *Time* before enrolling in Columbia University as a history major. We lived in Connecticut, and I was a day student commuting daily to Columbia on the train. Before my senior year of college, I wrote my first song. I immediately was addicted to songwriting, and I began taking my songs down to the New York music publishers between classes. My interest in school began to fade. There were certainly no classes in songwriting at that time. Finally, I hit a point where songwriting had consumed me, and I couldn't bear to go to class another day. I left Columbia with fifteen credits to go.

Can you describe your very first songwriting attempt? How old were you?

I was 20 years old and listened to my friends talk about their excitement in working in the corporate world after graduation. I thought, "Wow, I would die in one of those jobs. What do I love the way they love what they're doing?" There was a portable radio sitting in the gutter of the house I was painting that summer, and at one point the song "Abilene" by George Hamilton IV came on . . . and so did a light bulb in my head. I thought, "That's what I love . . . music. I wonder if I could write a song? Yes! I thought, I can, I can do that!" Over the next few days, I wrote a song called "Swagger." I sang it over and over again until I thought it was perfect. Since I played no instrument, I just made up a melody and sang it "in the air." Then, once it was finished, I wondered, what do I do with it?

I had to find out.

From reading all the music magazines, I knew of a musician's hangout in New York called the Turf bar. After pacing the sidewalk outside the door a few times over the course of several days, I finally got the courage to go inside where I met two songwriters. They said, "You need a demo" and told me where to go. I rented a studio and some musicians (I think the whole endeavor cost around $80) and sang the main melody to them. Since I was just singing a capella, the musicians listened and tried a few chords under my vocal. "That sound like what you're thinking?" the piano player said. I was astounded at how great it sounded . . . so much fuller and more exciting than I could have imagined. Next thing I knew I was at the microphone, and they were playing under me like they'd known the song since birth.

I took the demo, which I thought was a total smash, to Elvis's publisher, the name of which I'd gotten off Elvis's records and looked up in the New York phone book. The man at Elvis's publishing company listened, but he didn't like it as much as I did. "Well, I like it," he said, "but it isn't for us." Unwilling to give up easily, I said, "It could be a girl's song, like for The Angels" (who had just recorded the huge hit "My Boyfriend's Back"). He steered me to The Angels' producers right across the street. Those three guys and I hit it off, and I started bringing them my new songs. I was hooked . . . and thrilled when they told me they were going to pay me $10 a week to bring in my songs. You have to realize that lasagna in a restaurant across the street was 40 cents and a phenomenal jelly donut was a dime. The $10 totally changed my life.

How did the move to Nashville happen?

Linda (my wife) and I were living in Connecticut, and I'd been writing songs for awhile and taking them around New York. I got several recordings, including one by Bo Diddley, but nothing that could help me earn my living. I got it in my head that if only I could be associated with a guy named Ray Stevens, learn from him, be his gofer, whatever, that I might actually amount to something. Ray was in Nashville. He'd written number 1 pop songs, won a Grammy for his vocals, and produced huge hit records. One day I went to LaGuardia Airport, flew to Nashville, took a taxi to Ray's office, and told the secretary that I would like to play Ray a few songs. After waiting awhile, the secretary asked when I was leaving. "Well," I said, "I guess after I see Ray Stevens." By some miracle, Ray *did* see me and it was the start of a magical relationship. Ray became my publisher. He taught me most everything I know about songwriting. He introduced me to his friends, Chet Atkins, Owen Bradley, Bob Beckham . . . people who made Nashville go at the time.

Tell me about the song "Way Down" and how you finally got one of your songs into Elvis's hands.

Bob Beckham was a famous music publisher. He had a close relationship with Felton Jarvis, Elvis's producer. Bob knew I was always out pitching my songs, and one day he asked me if I had anything for Elvis. I had pitched Elvis at least twenty songs and heard nothing back. "Yes," I said, "I sure do." That afternoon I took two songs to Bob's office. Two weeks later, Felton called Ray Stevens and said, "Elvis is going to wig out over this 'Way Down' song." I was deliriously excited. But then weeks went by and we heard nothing.

Months later, I heard that Elvis was again looking for songs. I had another copy of "Way Down" made and dropped it off at Bob Beckham's office. Two hours later, I got a call from Bob's secretary saying, "Layng, Elvis has already recorded this song. It was recorded in the Jungle Room in Graceland in October."

A week later Felton Jarvis called. "Layng," he said, "I'm at Creative Workshop mixing 'Way Down.' Want to come over?" As I walked into the reception area of the studio I heard the thunder of the bass and drums bleeding out of the control room, and then . . . Elvis's voice came on singing my song. I stopped in my tracks. How is this possible, I thought? I opened the control room door and BOOM! The music's volume hit my face like a wall. Suddenly, the recording engineer hit the "Stop" button. Silence. "Hey, Layng," Felton said. "Your song is a smash. Sit down and listen." I settled into a chair, closed my eyes, and the music came on again. It was a feeling, a sense of accomplishment that I'll never be able to properly describe . . . even to myself.

"Way Down" was released as a single in June of 1977 and was at number 1 on the day that Elvis died.

Do you have any advice for anyone interested in pursuing music in Nashville?

As a songwriter, it is my responsibility to bring the record producers and artists a song they want, not their responsibility to like my songs.

Regarding whatever side of the music business you might set out to pursue, do not be afraid to change. Understand that within the music business, there are a lot of exciting jobs that are less obvious than singing, playing an instrument, songwriting, etc. Jobs like music publishing, record production, artist management, directing videos, graphic design, public relations, record promotion. If you see another facet of the business that interests you, try it. You might love it. People always say, "Follow your passion" . . . but it's unbelievable how passionate and excited you can get when you discover and pursue something you're really good at.

Again . . . and repeating myself . . . do not be afraid to alter your original plan if you feel an attraction or leaning toward an aspect of the music business different from the one you initially had in mind.

If you do think you're cut out for a career in the music business, go to a music center and jump into the "real river," the real music business . . . don't stay too long in the less-connected "river" of your hometown. Seek to play, sing, show your talent to the highest level people you can find, and . . . most likely . . . that will be in a music center like Nashville, LA, New York, Austin, etc.

As unrelated to the music business as it may sound, take an interest in all the practical parts of your life . . . not only the creative. Yes, the music business is fun . . . but surviving in it is your goal. Take the time to learn about mortgages, investments, insurance (health, life, cars, houses), and be prepared for the day you need to know about that stuff. It'll come.

And more than anything else, build a reputation as a responsible person. Be responsible to your family, your friends, to the people you work with, and toward everyone with whom you come in contact each day. Call if you're going to be late. Commit only if you're going to deliver. Show respect to everyone. You'll sleep better, and do . . . a lot better.

CHAPTER 8

ROMAN NUMERALS AND FIGURED BASS

Artist in Residence: Cecilia Bartoli

Chapter Objectives

- Identify chords within a given key using Roman numerals
- Define and apply harmonic function
- Analyze chord inversions using figured bass symbols
- Define and apply the uses of second inversion triads
- Understand the basics of part writing in SATB context
- Analyze chords using Roman numerals in the context of a musical score

While understanding the harmonic makeup of a popular song lies in the realization of chords in a lead sheet or chord chart, understanding the *function* of these harmonies lies in Roman numeral analysis. Study the following progression in the key of B major. Play along on your keyboard or guitar.

B	G♯MIN	E	C♯MIN	F♯7	B
I	vi	IV	ii	V^7	I

Roman numerals are assigned to chords based on their placement within the scale. The above progression is in B major, so the first chord would be labeled with the Roman numeral I because the chord is built on the first scale degree. The G♯ minor chord is built on the sixth scale degree, so the Roman numeral would be vi, and so on. The resulting progression is I, vi, IV, ii, V^7, I. It is important to notice that qualities are shown in the Roman numeral as well; uppercase for major, lowercase for minor, and the addition of the augmented and diminished symbol as needed.

When it comes to chord qualities in a major key, I, IV, and V are always major; ii, iii, and vi are always minor; and vii° is always diminished. Look at the B♭ major scale and the chords built on each scale degree. Be sure to play through the chords on your keyboard or guitar.

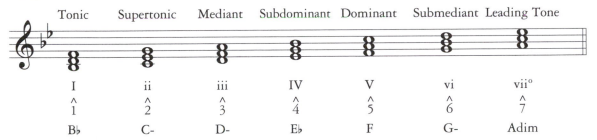

Major

Tonic	Supertonic	Mediant	Subdominant	Dominant	Submediant	Leading Tone

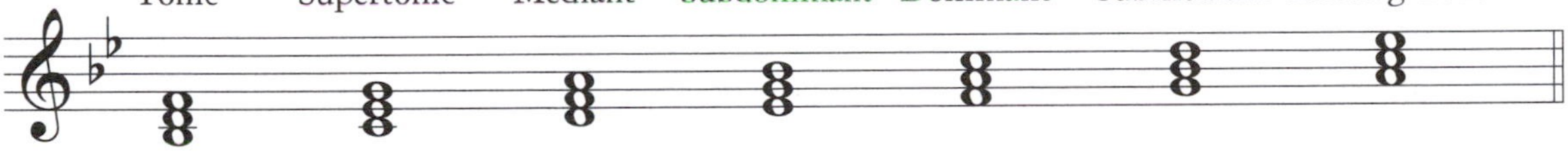

I	ii	iii	IV	V	vi	vii°
$\hat{1}$	$\hat{2}$	$\hat{3}$	$\hat{4}$	$\hat{5}$	$\hat{6}$	$\hat{7}$
B♭	C-	D-	E♭	F	G-	Adim

Analyzing chords in minor keys is a little bit trickier because we have three different forms of the minor scale. Although most music in a minor key tends to use the pitches of the harmonic minor scale, all the chords presented below are possibilities. Notice that the chord built on the seventh scale degree in the natural minor scale is called the subtonic; it does not contain the leading tone that creates the half step relationship and pull to the tonic.

Natural Minor

Tonic	Supertonic	Mediant	Subdominant	Dominant	Submediant	Subtonic

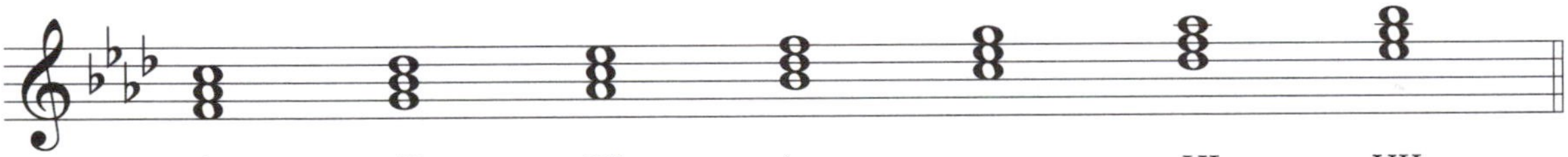

i	ii°	III	iv	v	VI	VII
$\hat{1}$	$\hat{2}$	$\hat{3}$	$\hat{4}$	$\hat{5}$	$\hat{6}$	$\hat{7}$
F-	G°	A♭	B♭-	C-	D♭	E♭

Harmonic Minor

Tonic	Supertonic	Mediant	Subdominant	Dominant	Submediant	Leading Tone

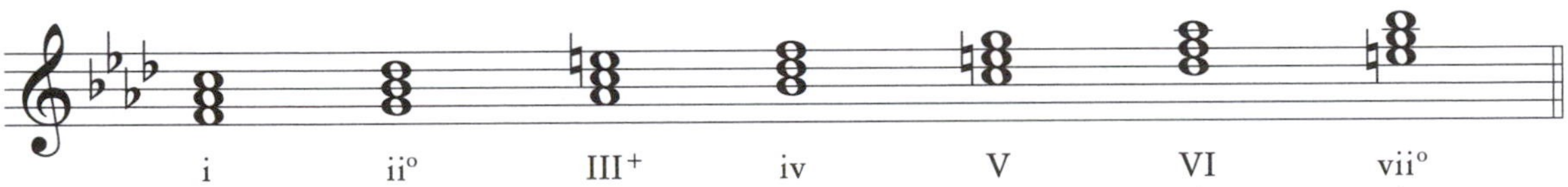

i	ii°	III+	iv	V	VI	vii°
$\hat{1}$	$\hat{2}$	$\hat{3}$	$\hat{4}$	$\hat{5}$	$\hat{6}$	♯$\hat{7}$
F-	G°	A♭+	B♭-	C	D♭	E°

Melodic Minor

Tonic	Supertonic	Mediant	Subdominant	Dominant	Submediant	Leading Tone

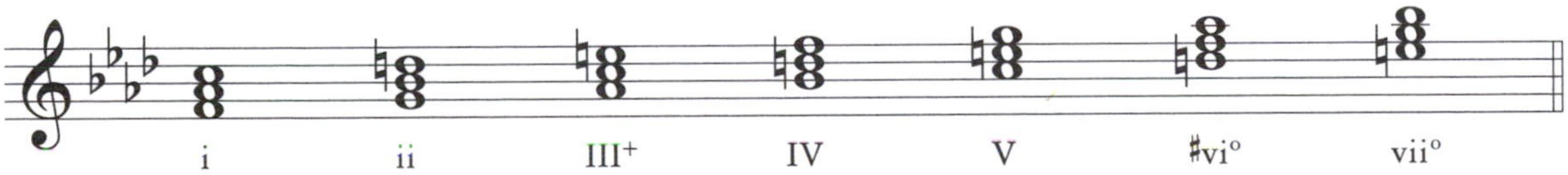

i	ii	III+	IV	V	♯vi°	vii°
$\hat{1}$	$\hat{2}$	$\hat{3}$	$\hat{4}$	$\hat{5}$	♯$\hat{6}$	♯$\hat{7}$
F-	G-	A♭+	B♭	C	D°	E°

Just like triads, Roman numerals assigned to seventh chords indicate the root and quality of the chord based on its location within the scale. However, there are a few symbols that must be included to indicate the quality of the seventh, in addition to the triad. Other possibilities exist, but the most common types of seventh chords are shown in both major and minor keys.

Major

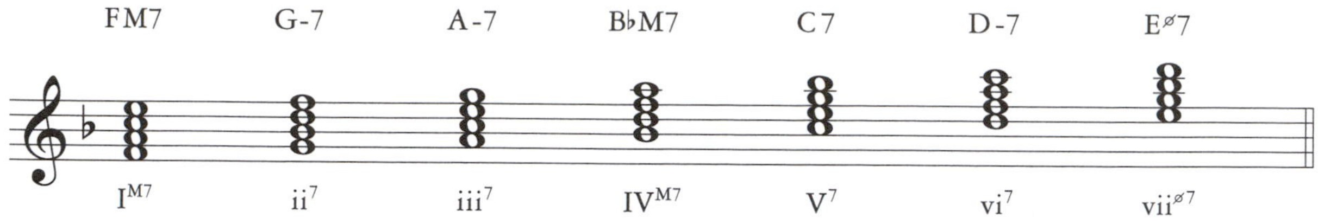

Minor

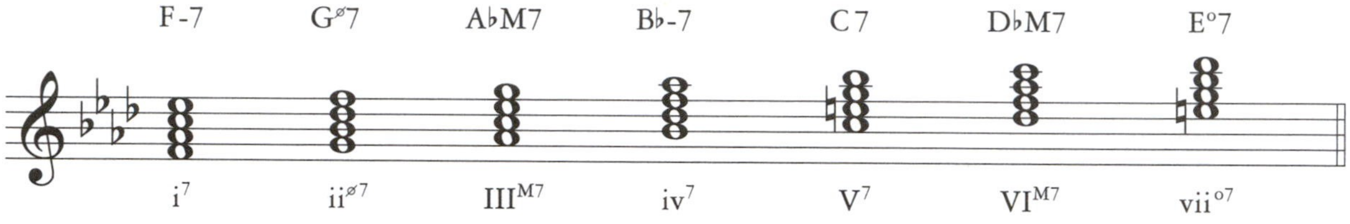

Let's try to realize Roman numerals in several keys. Say that your concertmaster tells the orchestra to play a subdominant seventh chord in the key of F minor. You nod enthusiastically because you know exactly what to do!

The subdominant in the key of F minor is the pitch B♭. Build a minor seventh chord on that B♭ (minor triad with a minor seventh). The resulting pitches would be B♭–D♭–F–A♭. You're on it.

You're in a session playing background acoustic with some of the biggest names in country music. The bandleader makes a quick change, telling you to play a subtonic chord instead of the leading chord in D minor. You don't even question it and play a C major instead of a C♯°. Miss this instruction and your phone may not ring for months.

So why do we even need Roman numerals? For one thing, it makes transposition extremely easy. The I-IV-ii-V progression found in so many popular and classical pieces can be adapted to any key. But more important, Roman numerals indicate function. Certain chords just love to go to certain other chords.

HARMONIC FUNCTION

Chords move in a specific way called **harmonic progression**. For hundreds of years, composers and songwriters have followed these so-called "rules" to create progressions that are pleasing to the ear and, in many ways, predictable. Consumers—whether of the 19th century or the 21st—like "predictable."

You probably are familiar with the song "Hallelujah" by Leonard Cohen. It has been recorded over 300 times by artists such as Jeff Buckley, Rufus Wainwright, and K.D. Lang. The song was even featured in the 2003 film *Shrek*. The second main phrase of the song includes the lyrics, "It goes like this, the fourth, the fifth, the minor fall, the major lift." You probably just sang along with the lyrics without even knowing that Cohen was talking about harmonic function.

"The fourth, the fifth"
Chord roots move up by fourth/down by fifth (I–IV, V–I, ii–V, vi–ii).

"The minor fall"[1]
Chord roots move down by third (I–vi, vi–IV, IV–ii).

"The major lift"
Chord roots move up by second (IV–V, V–vi, I–ii).

Chords are also grouped in three distinct categories: tonic, predominant, and dominant. The goal of any progression is typically to get back to the tonic. This could be a never-ending cycle until the composer wants it to end.

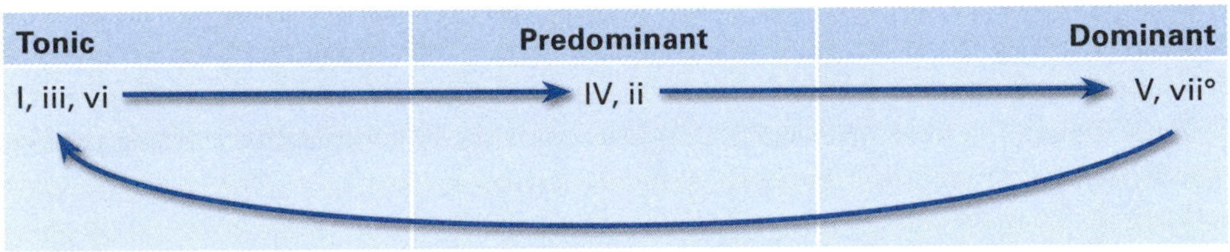

Take a few minutes to improvise on progressions. Start on the I chord. You can easily go to the IV, the vi, or even the ii. If you move to the ii, you can go *up a fourth* to V, *up a second* to iii, or *down a third* to the vii°. The choice is yours, so take some time to experiment with different progressions. For minor keys, the only difference is the quality of the chord, not the function of the chord. You can use all of the same rules in creating progressions regardless of key or mode. Use the chart on page 147 to review qualities.

FIGURED BASS

In lead sheet notation, inversions are shown with a slash that indicates the pitch to be played in the bass, such as D/A. With Roman numerals, we use a system called figured bass. **Figured bass** indicates the intervals of the notes above the bass pitch in order to show inversions. This all came about in the 17th century when keyboard players were asked to improvise the upper voices against a given bass line.

Study the chords below, paying careful attention to how the figured bass indicates the intervals above the lowest pitch.

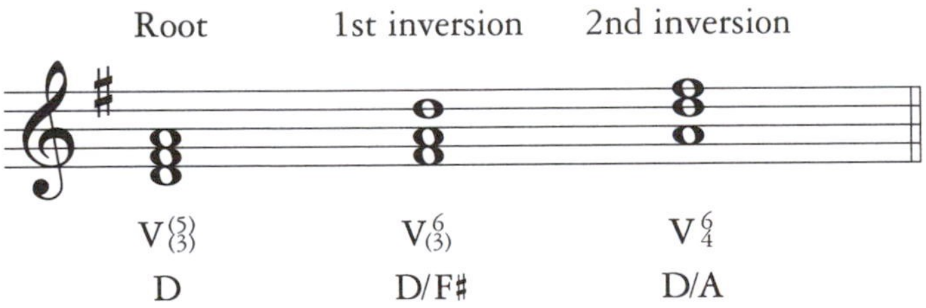

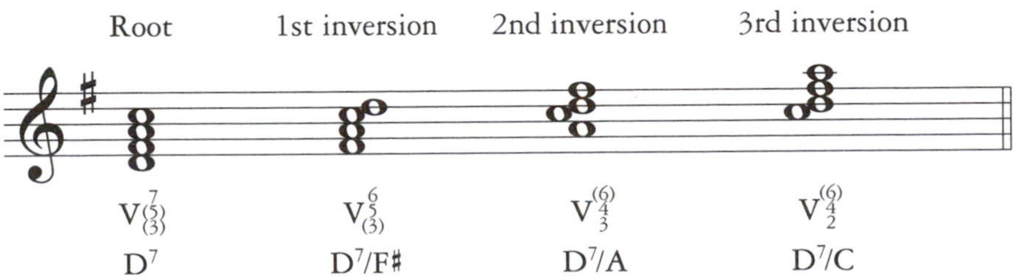

[1]The chords in "Hallelujah" are based around the tonic, so the minor fall moves to the vi chord and the major lift moves up to the IV chord, a substitution for a predominant harmony on the ii.

Over the past century, theorists have opted to not use the figured bass symbol $^5_3$ in Roman numeral analysis, and it is understood that any chord without a figured bass symbol is a triad in root position. In many musical scores and analysis, the $^6_3$ has been shortened to a superscript 6: (^{6}).[2]

THE UNIQUENESS OF THE SECOND INVERSION TRIAD

The second inversion triad is considered an unstable chord. This particular triad is sometimes referred to as the "six-four chord" because of its figured bass symbol. Play a D major triad in second inversion. Hint: the A should be the lowest sounding pitch. Do you hear how the pitches seem to want to move somewhere? For that very reason, there are three main types of second inversion triads. Although there are exceptions, triads in second inversion tend to fall into one of these categories:

Pedal six-four: The lowest pitch of the triad acts as a "pedal" common tone between two chords in root position. Most often the chord is a IV$^6_4$.

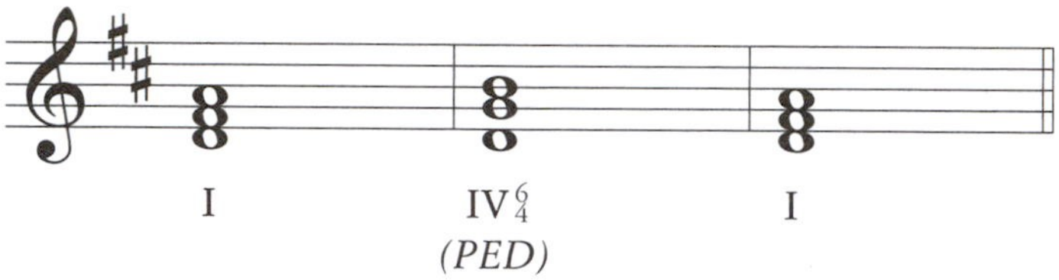

Passing six-four: The lowest pitch of the triad acts as a passing tone in order to move from a root position chord to a chord in first inversion.

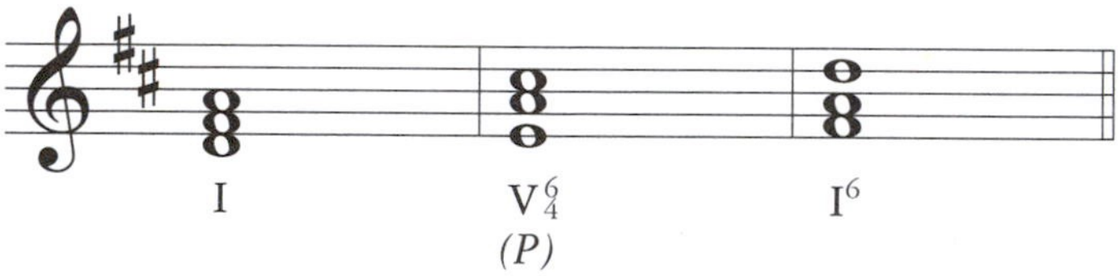

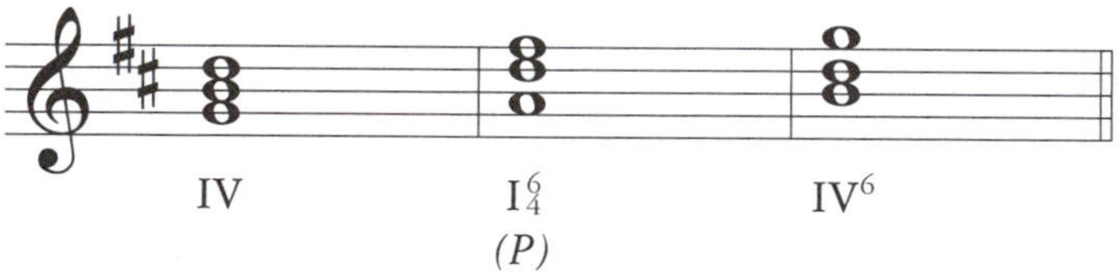

Cadential six-four: The triad in second inversion sets up the final cadence, through the connection that the second inversion chord leads directly into the root position dominant. The most important facet about this type of six-four is found in the voice leading. The sixth above the bass moves to the fifth above the bass. The fourth above the bass moves to the third above the bass. It is dominant in function, so even though it's built on the tonic, many theorists opt to label it with a V instead of a I. While this may seem confusing at first, don't forget that Roman numerals show function and this second inversion chord contains two pitches whose sole purpose is to lead directly to V. Try thinking about the ^{6} and the ^{4} as non-chord tones moving to the root position dominant. For that very reason, cadential six-four chords will be labeled as Cad$^6_4$.

[2]The first inversion figured bass symbol causes a great deal of confusion for some musicians who are schooled in both classical and popular music. For instance, a D^6 in popular music would be a D major chord with an added B. However, in classical music that same D^6 would be a D/F♯. That is why it is always important to know your context.

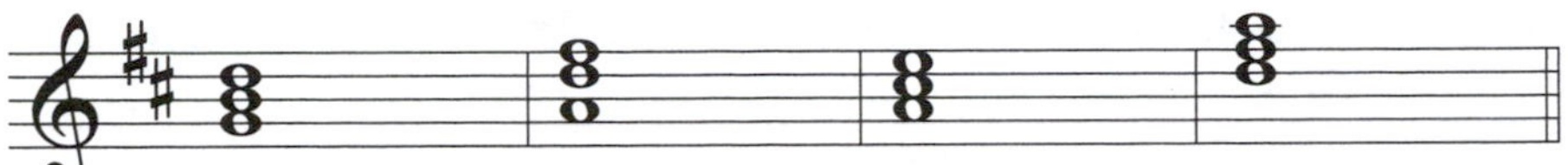

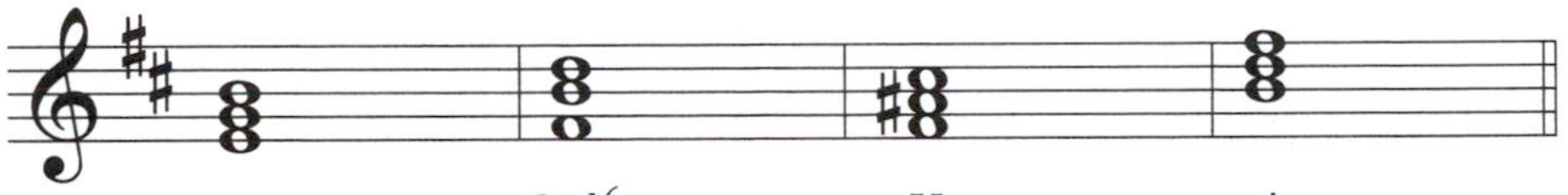

Let's take the progression found at the beginning of this chapter and add inversions as well as a seventh chord.

B G♯MIN/B E/B C♯MIN7/B F♯7/A♯ B

The resulting Roman numeral analysis, including figured bass, would be:

IMPORTANT THINGS TO REALIZE ABOUT REALIZATION

Look at the foregoing progression. Did you notice that the seventh of the chord resolves down and the seventh of the key resolves up? Well, those are just two of the important rules in the study of voice leading. While many musicians spend years studying the art of counterpoint, or how voices work together, only a few are highlighted here.

When realizing progressions on the staff,

1. Move each voice to the closest possible pitch to create smooth voice leading.
2. Keep a common tone whenever possible. If no common tone is present, move the upper voices in motion contrary to the bass voice.
3. In four-part writing (SATB), double the root in root position chords and the bass in second inversion chords. For chords found in first inversion, any pitch can be doubled that creates smooth voice leading. (See exception in item 4.)
4. Never double the leading tone or any altered pitch.
5. The seventh of the key (leading tone) resolves up.
6. The seventh of the chord resolves down.[3]

Realizing chords on the staff can be a truly creative process and is slightly addictive when you get the hang of it. Let's take the following progression and realize it for four voices.

[3]There are countless resources to help you master the art of part writing. This is merely a brief introduction and should not be considered an exhaustive list of all part-writing rules. For more information on available bibliographic resources, consult http://jmtp.ou.edu/resources-bibliographies.

1. Notate the bass line. By understanding what the figured bass symbols mean, you should be able to figure out what pitches need to be placed in the lowest voice.

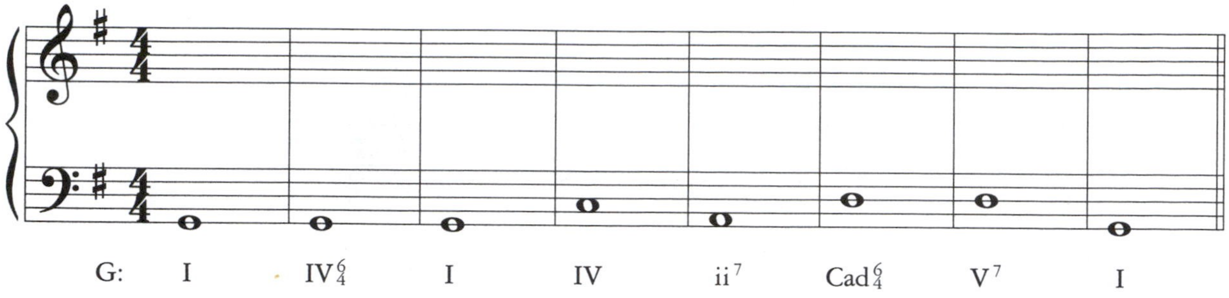

2. Now add the upper pitches chord by chord. It might be helpful for you to have all of the letter names written out below the staff and cross them off as you go. The first two chords have been completed for you. Remember that you need to double the bass on second inversion chords!

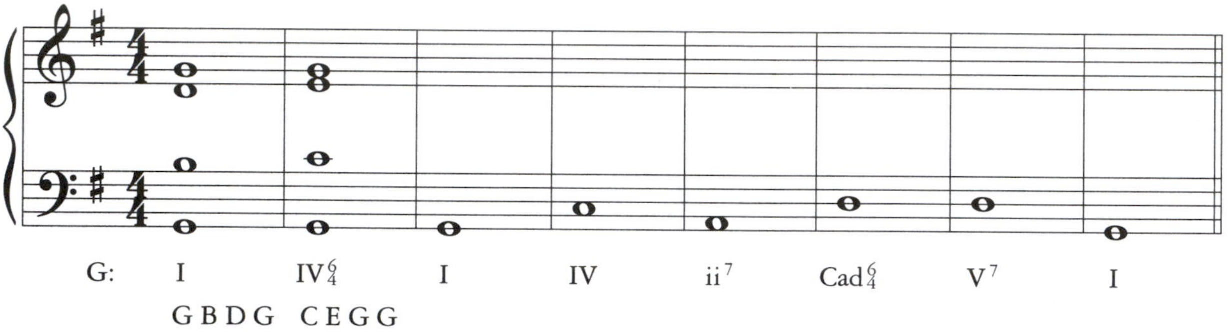

3. Continue to realize all of the chords, paying careful attention to create a smooth line in all the voices. The following realization is just a sample. There are several interpretations of this progression, so be sure to share your interpretation with the class.

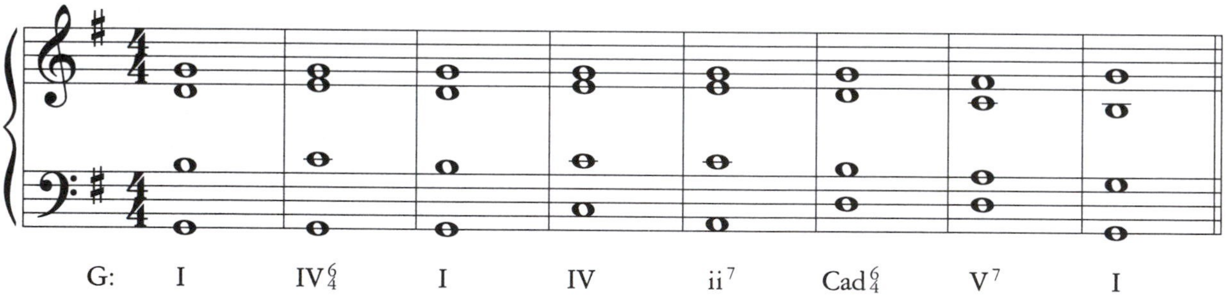

ARTIST IN RESIDENCE

Schooling Americans in Italian Art Song

Thousands of young singers in the last decade of the 20th century were immediately drawn to the vocal talents of Cecilia Bartoli. Her 1992 album, *If You Love Me/Si tu m'ami,* contained twelve songs from *Twenty-Four Italian Songs and Arias of the Seventeenth and Eighteenth Centuries*, a book well known to any singer beginning to study classical voice. Then editor of *Opera News*, Patrick J. Smith, reviewed the recording: "Bartoli's mezzo, fully capable of handling the artless simplicity of these eighteenth-century Italian love songs, has an easy sensuousness." The album remained at the top of the Billboard charts for an astounding 33 weeks. And thus began a new phenomenon in applied study. Singers began to learn pieces by listening to high-quality digital recordings rather than plunking out the pitches on the piano in a stuffy practice room. Who knows how many vocalists continue to use this same recording to learn the basics of Italian art song?

The title track from Bartoli's 1992 album is in the key of G minor and includes both triads and seventh chords. Non-chord tones, pitches that do not belong to the sounding harmony, are marked in parentheses—( )—and should not be considered in the analysis at this point. As you listen to Bartoli's performance, trace the function of the chords in this particular excerpt. Do the chords seem to follow traditional harmonic progression?

WEBSITE

VIDEO TRACK 63

Cecilia Bartoli, Pergolesi's "Se tu m'ami"

Cecilia Bartoli, Pergolesi's "Se tu m'ami" ***(continued)***

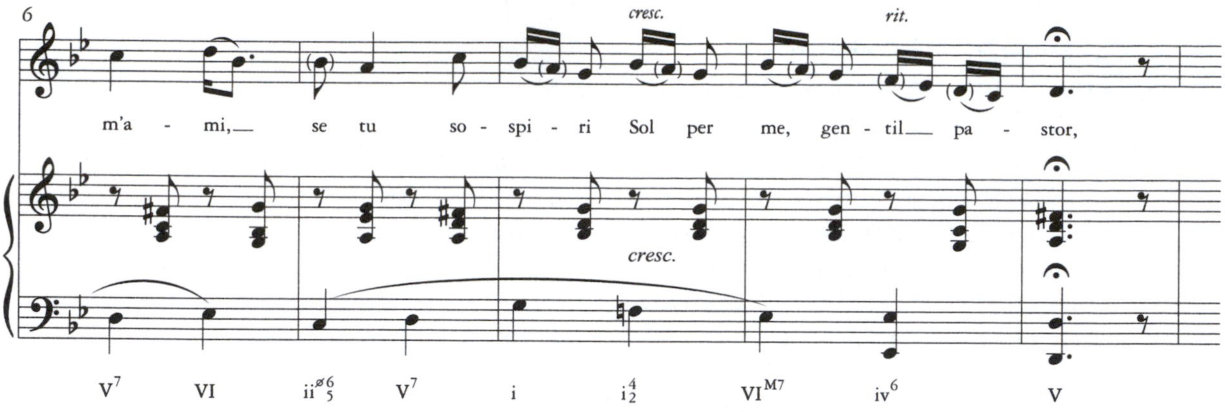

Translation: If you love me, if you sigh only for me, dear shepherd

VIDEO TRACK 64

Almost every high school and early college vocal student has sung "Caro mio ben." Its well-known melody and wide range make it a perfect teaching tool for the aspiring student. However, the harmonies are not so easily identified because of non-chord tones. (We will discuss NCTs further in Chapters 10 and 11.) Listen to Bartoli's performance on the YouTube channel. How would you describe the harmonic rhythm, or how fast the chords are moving? What Roman numerals appear the most in the excerpt? Do you see any patterns?

Cecilia Bartoli, Giordani's "Caro mio ben"

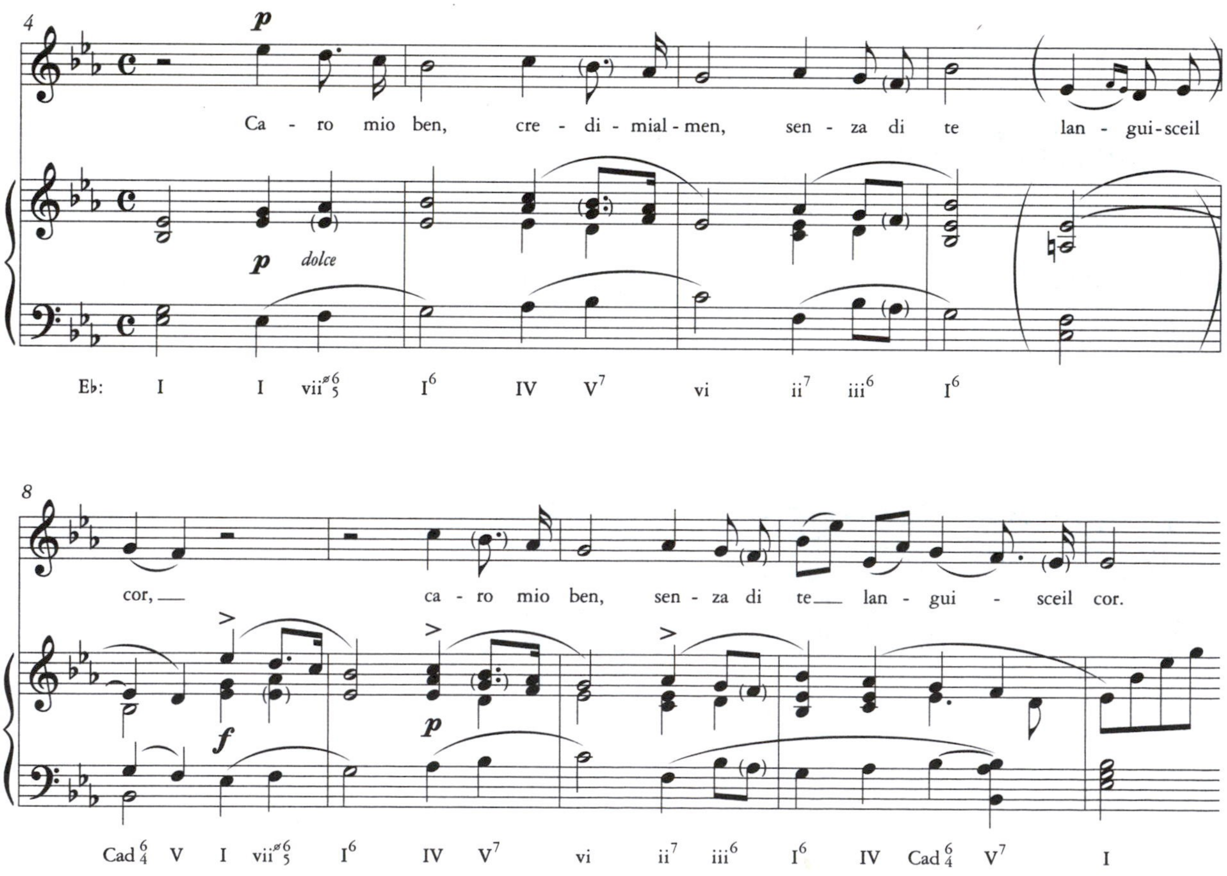

Translation: My dear beloved, believe me at least, without you my heart languishes.

ARTIST IN RESIDENCE

A Diva on the Stage: Bringing the 18th Century Back into Style

Cecilia Bartoli's parents were both talented singers, and she spent her early days in and around the opera houses of Italy. In a 1998 interview published in the book *Cinderella and Company*, her mother explains:

> "It was like this," she said. "When she was small, she liked to sing as much as talk. Always humming around the house imitating us. I thought she was musical and she had some piano lessons. When she was fifteen, I said: 'Cecilia, let's see if you have a voice.' We tried. There was a voice."

Unlike most professional classical singers, Bartoli found success in her early 20s with several debuts, including Cherubino in Mozart's *Le Nozze di Figaro* and Idamantes in Mozart's *Idomeneo.* But it was perhaps a chance appearance on a Maria Callas tribute show that pushed Bartoli toward the top. Several important conductors, including Daniel Barenboim, saw that performance, as well as her New York debut at the Mostly Mozart Festival in 1990 when she was 24. In the *New York Times* review of the concert, critic Donal Henahan was not exactly blown away: "Miss Bartoli herself seemed too concerned with the notes to delve into their expressive depths."

At age 29, she made her Metropolitan Opera debut in *Così fan tutte,* and she returned the next year to sing the title role of *La Cenerentola.* The review in the *New York Times* was again slightly critical, Bernard Holland writing, "Miss Bartoli's lovely voice and telling diction make their peace with this big house, but I doubt she possesses the power-charged sound to dominate it."

Fast-forward 20 years, and there are still mixed reviews on Bartoli's voice and its capability of filling a large hall. However, the exemplary marketing by Decca Records and Bartoli's expertise in performing the music of Mozart, Bellini, and Rossini are undisputed by critics. She has won five Grammy Awards for classical voice and is still performing in both recitals and opera productions throughout the world. A *New York Times* review of her 2013 performance in *Norma* states, "She produced a lovely legato in 'Casta diva,' introduced fresh, stylish ornamentation and sang coloratura with unfailing accuracy. Furthermore, she projected the emotional volatility that stems from Norma's consuming anxiety." It looks like Ms. Bartoli is finally winning the respect of critics and smiling all the way to the bank: she has sold over ten million records and videos, making her one of the best-selling classical artists of all time. Take that, critics.

Best known for her performances of Mozart, many of Bartoli's performances highlight the lyrical lines of classical composers. In the following scene, Zarlino is assuring her boyfriend, Masetto, of her faithfulness and love. With a quick search on YouTube, you should be able to find numerous performances of this famous work. As you listen to the performance, follow along with the Roman numerals. You will notice that although the inversions change, the focus of the entire eight measures is on the tonic and dominant chords. This is not a rare occurrence, and you might be surprised at the prominence of I and V in both classical and popular music.

Cecilia Bartoli, Mozart's "Batti, batti" from *Don Giovanni*

Translation: Beat me, dear Masetto, beat your poor Zerlina. I'll stand here as meek as a lamb and bear the blows you lay on me.

WEBSITE

VIDEO TRACK 65

"Voi Che Sapete" from Mozart's opera *Le Nozze di Figaro* tells the story of the pageboy Cherubino who is desperately in love with every woman he meets. With very few exceptions, the chords change every measure and are outlined in the arpeggiated piano line. The non-chord tones are in parentheses and are not considered in the analysis. Just like the previous Mozart example, this particular excerpt is also based around the tonic and dominant harmonies.

Cecilia Bartoli, Mozart's "Voi Che Sapete" from *Le Nozze di Figaro*

Translation: You who know what love is, Ladies, see if I have it in my heart.

Reviewing Chapter Objectives

- Identify chords within a given key using Roman numerals (page 147)
- Define and apply harmonic function (pages 148–149)
- Analyze chord inversions using figured bass symbols (page 149)
- Define and apply the uses of second inversion triads (pages 150–151)
- Understand the basics of part writing in SATB context (pages 151–152)
- Analyze chords using Roman numerals in the context of a musical score (pages 153–154, 156)

EXERCISES

I. Provide a Roman numeral analysis. Be to sure include figured bass symbols for chords in inversion.

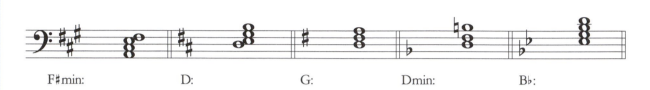

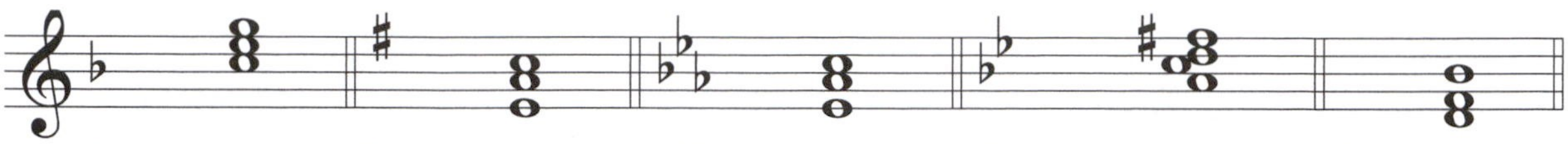

F: G: E♭: Gmin: C:

F♯min: D: G: Dmin: B♭:

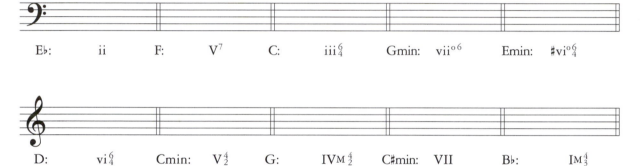

II. Notate the key signature on the staff and construct triads that correspond to the Roman numeral and figured bass.

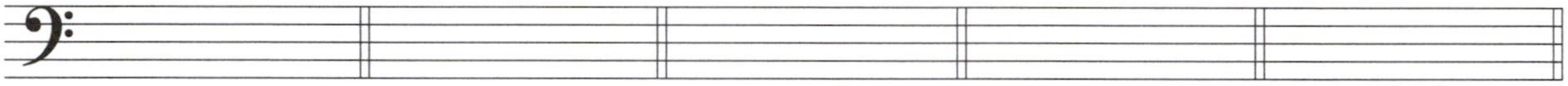

E♭: ii F: V^7 C: iii^6_4 Gmin: vii^{o6} Emin: $\sharp vi^{o6}_4$

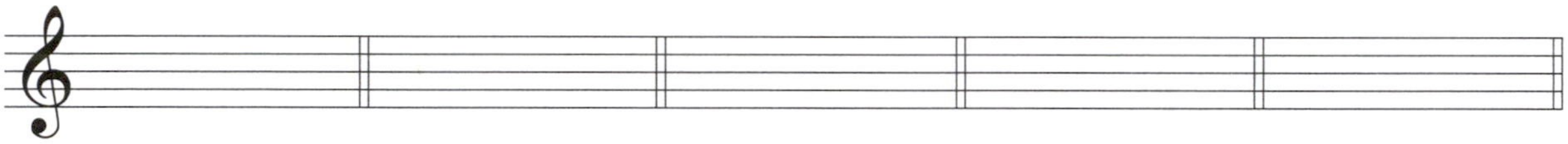

D: vi^6_4 Cmin: V^4_2 G: IVM^4_2 C♯min: VII B♭: IM^4_3

III. Construct the chords when given the lead sheet symbol. Give Roman numeral analysis for both the major and relative minor keys, including correct figured bass symbols.

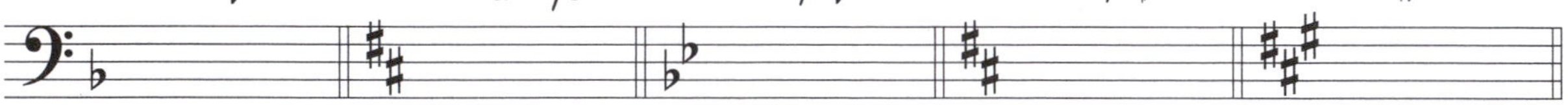

IV. Provide both a Roman numeral and lead sheet symbol for the chords notated on the staff. Be sure to indicate inversions.

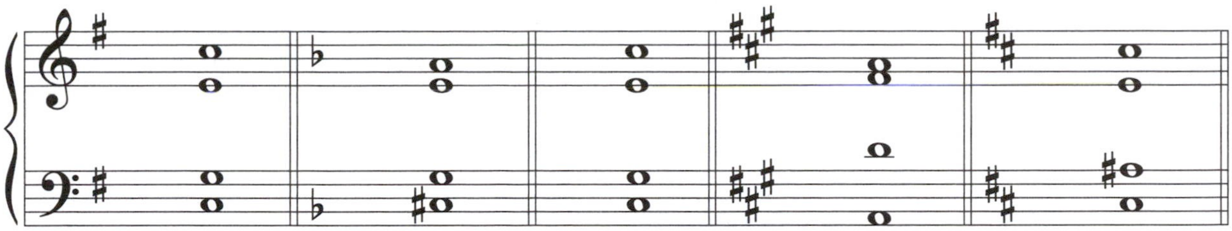

G: Dmin: C: A: Bmin:

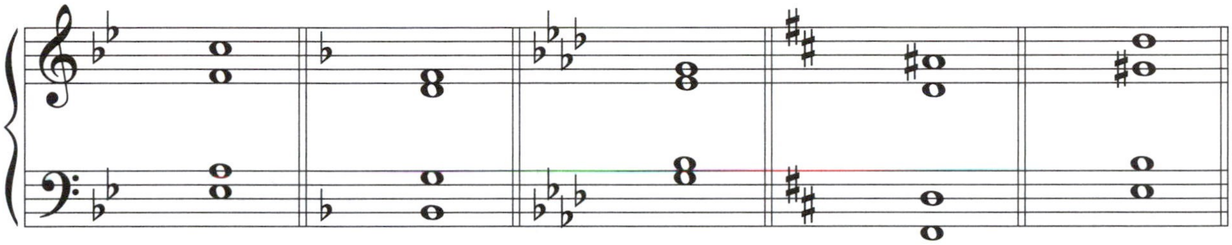

B♭: F: Fmin: Bmin: Amin:

V. Given the bass note and figured bass, notate the correct triad or seventh chord on the staff.

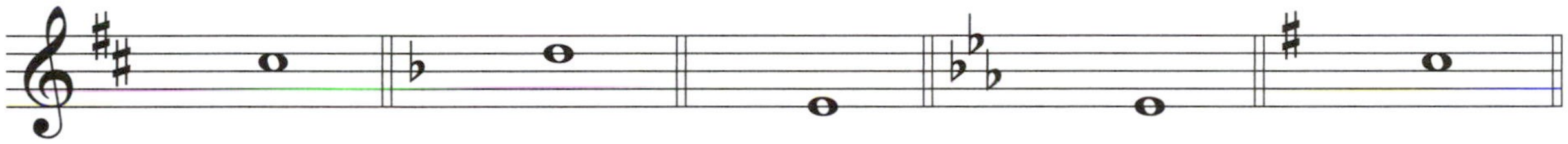

D: 6 F: $^{6}_{5}$ Amin: $^{6}_{4}$ E♭: 6 Emin: $^{4}_{3}$

E: $^{4}_{2}$ Amin: $^{5}_{3}$ C: 6 G: 7 Fmin: $^{6}_{4}$

VI. Given the Roman numerals and figured bass, realize the following progression for SATB. Be sure to follow the basic rules given on page 151.

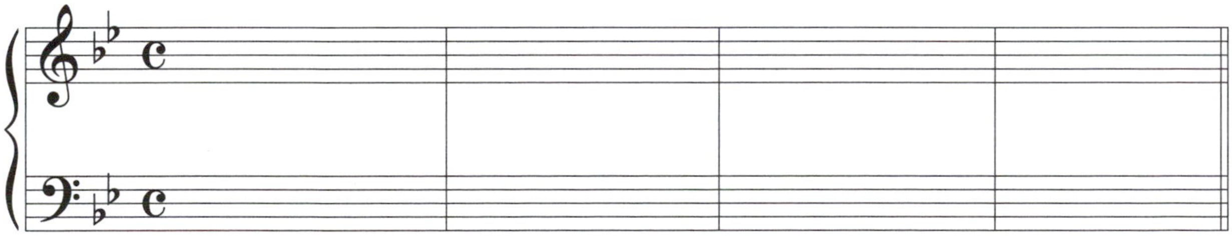

B♭: I V^{6}_{5} vi IV Cad $^{6}_{4}$ V^{7} I

ANALYSIS

Complete a Roman numeral analysis for the following excerpts. Be sure to indicate the inversion with the use of figured bass. Non-chord tones are in parentheses and are not to be considered in the analysis. Be sure to mark second inversion chords with Ped, P, or Cad$^6_4$. Focus only on the pitches of the accompaniment line when the excerpt includes both voice and accompaniment.

1. William Billings, "Here Is a Song, Which Doth Belong" (The melody is in the tenor voice.)

VIDEO
TRACK 66

2. Cecelia Bartoli, Bellini's "Vaga luna"

Translation: Lovely moon, you who shed silver light on these shores and on these flowers; and breathe the language of love to the elements

VIDEO
TRACK 67

3. Maria Callas, Puccini's "O mio babbino caro" from the Opera *Gianni Schicchi*

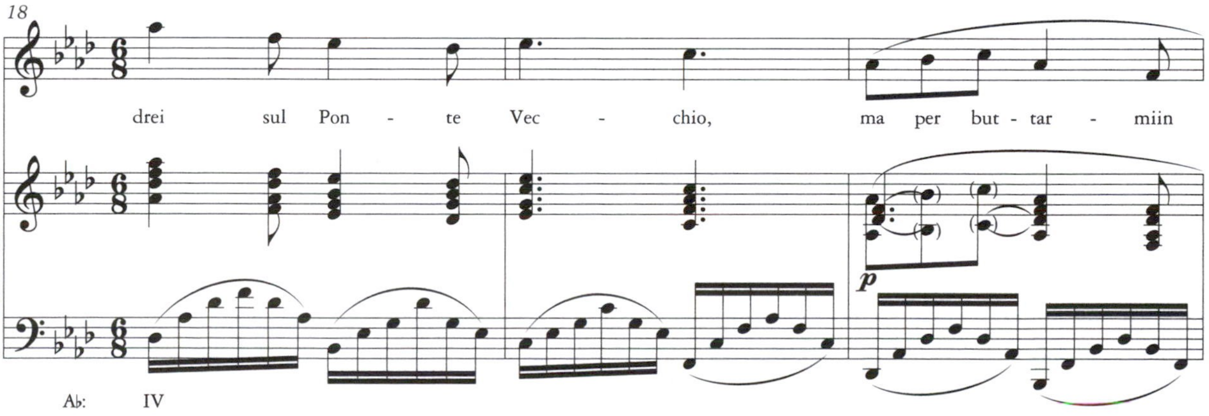

Maria Callas, Puccini's "O mio babbino caro" from the Opera *Gianni Schicch (continued)*

Translation: I would go to Ponte Vecchio and throw myself in the Arno! I am pining and I am tormented, Oh God! I would want to die!

WEBSITE

VIDEO TRACK 68

4. Cecilia Bartoli, Rossini's "Non piu mesta" from the Opera *La Cenerentola*. Although the entire excerpt from measures 56–89 is presented below, provide an analysis only for measures 56–63. How is the same progression used over and over throughout the excerpt?

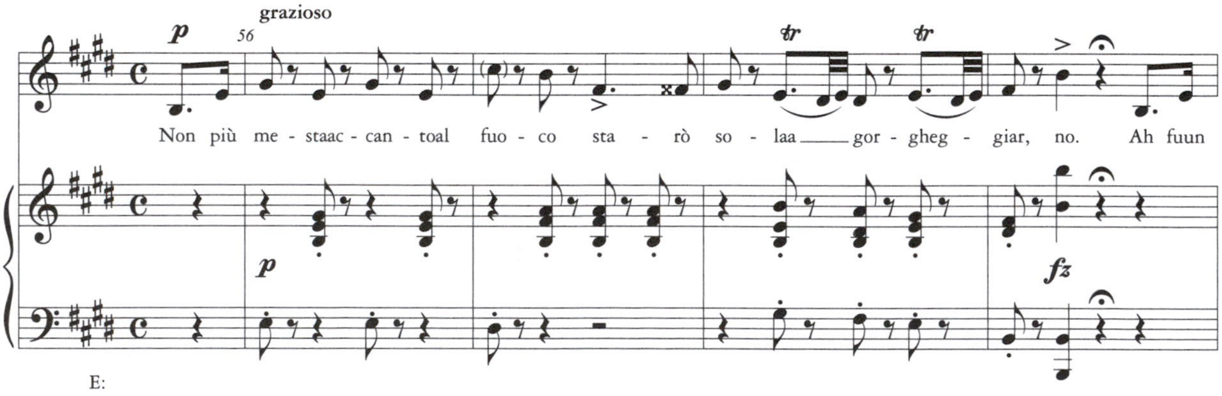

60
lam - po,un so - gno,un giuo - coil mi - o lun-go pal-pi - tar.
p
64
Non più me - sta ac-can - toal fuo - co, non più
68
me - staac-can - toal fuo - co sta - rò so - laa gor - gheg -
71
giar, no. Ah fuun lam - po,un so - gno,un giuo - co,il - mio
fz
p

74
lun-go pal-pi - tar. Non più me - sta
78
ac-can - toal fuo - co, non più me - sta ac-can - to al
81
fuo - co sta - rò so - laa gor - gheg - giar. Ah fuun
84
so - gno, un lam - po, un giuo - co il mio lun - go pal - pi -

Translation: No more sadness by the fire, To be warbling alone, no! Ah it was a flash, a dream, a game; My long life of fear {or "my long tremble"}

COMPOSITION PROJECT

Isn't harmonic function fascinating? Why exactly do certain chords like to go to certain chords? Take a few minutes to improvise on a variety of chord progressions using all of the rules of function mentioned in this chapter. Start with a tonic chord and then move through the cycle as shown on 149. Possibilities might include I, IV, ii, V; I, vi, IV, V; or I, IV, V, I. After you have discovered your own favorite progression, try to put it into a context of a musical composition. If this is the first time you have ever tried to write a composition, start simply by following the guidelines below.

The composition must meet the following requirements:

1. It must be at least eight measures long.
2. Its time signature will be $\frac{4}{4}$ or $\frac{6}{8}$ (your choice).
3. There must be two chords per measure; *however,*
   a. measure 4 should contain *only* the V or V^7 chord; and
   b. measure 8 should contain *only* the I chord (preceded by the V or V^7 chord).
4. The piece must be composed on a grand staff. The bass staff will contain block chords, while the treble staff will contain the melody. (*Note: you can compose the piece with different instruments if you like; just make sure that it still has the block chords in the bass and the melody in the treble.*)
5. The piece must be analyzed with both Roman numerals and lead sheet symbols.

In the end, your composition should look similar to this.

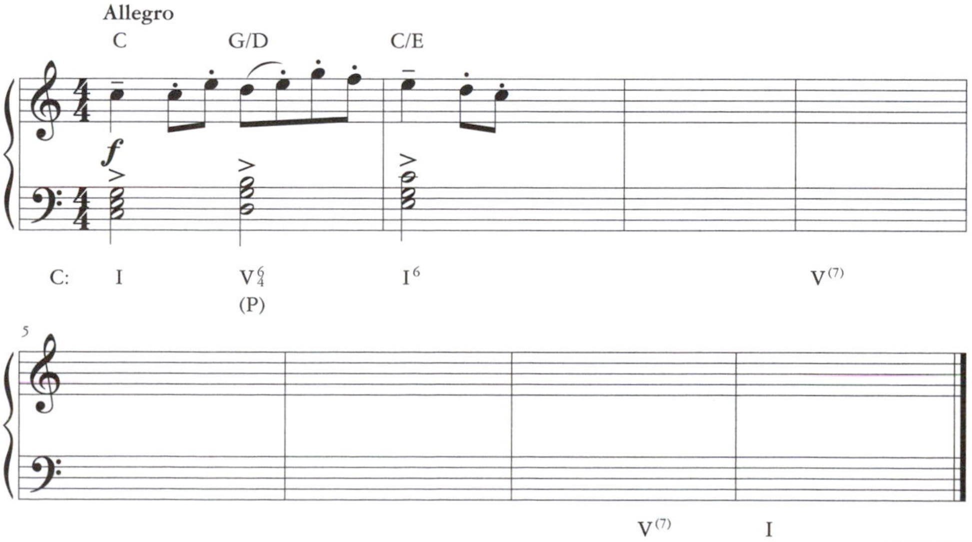

6. Once you compose the piece, you must transpose the melody for two other transposing instruments (different keys). You can either put the transposed melody on a separate staff or add the instruments to the grand staff you already have.

Creative Decisions

1. Make sure that the harmonic progression you compose is functional (i.e., it follows the rules presented in Chapter 8). The rules are the same for minor as they are for major.
2. You may compose the piece in major or minor. *Note:* if you choose to use minor, pay special attention to the leading tone. Always have your V chords contain the leading tone.
3. Be sure to resolve the sevenths of chords down by step and leading tones up by step (especially in the melody, since the harmonies are block chords).
4. Add in inversions to smooth out the bass line. If you use a $^6_4$ chord, be sure to specify the type.
5. The harmonies do not need to simply be half notes (or dotted half notes if you choose $^6_8$), but follow these rules if you want to make your harmonies more interesting:
   a. Do not use non-chord tones in the harmonies.
   b. Make sure that the harmony contains all of the tones of the chord.
   c. *Keep it simple!* Complicated rhythms and leaps in harmonies don't always work, so it may be best to stick with simple arpeggiated harmonies.
6. Compose the melody *after* you decide the harmonies. Make sure the melody is interesting and sing-able. Also, be careful with non-chord tones in the melody. Only use one non-chord tone before returning to a chord tone.
7. Use accents/phrase markings/dynamics/tempo markings at your own discretion to make your composition interesting.
8. Be creative! Compose the best piece you can with the criteria provided.

AURAL SKILLS CONDITIONING 8

Hearing Tritones

WEBSITE

VIDEO TRACK 69

In Leonard Bernstein's "Maria" from *West Side Story*, Tony expresses his new feelings for the beautiful woman he has just met. He sings the interval of a tritone when he first voices his beloved's name. Listen to the song on the YouTube channel. Can you hear the tritone on the word "Maria" in the melody? Does it sound as dissonant as you would expect? How does Bernstein resolve this dissonant interval?

Singing Tritones

As Tony demonstrates in the opening lines to "Maria," it *is* possible to sing a tritone despite its dissonant nature. Following are the most common solfège for singing a tritone. Practice singing the tritone on solfège. Be sure you give yourself the tonic before attempting this. How do you hear the interval resolving?

Interval	Solfège
Tritone	fa–ti (ti–fa), re–le (le–re)

Singing Intervals (All)

Practice singing the intervals below using the solfège of your choice. Refer to Chapters 4 and 7 for the solfège charts. Give yourself a starting pitch and sing the ascending intervals. After you've mastered this, go through and sing the descending intervals. This is tricky but possible if you really establish the tonic pitch and practice!

1. m6 2. M3 3. P5 4. M2 5. M7 6. m3

7. TT 8. M6 9. m2 10. P4 11. m7 12. M3

Identifying Intervals (All)

REPLAY

AUDIO TRACK CH. 8 INTERVAL ID 1–15

You will hear your teacher perform fifteen intervals, ascending and descending. The audio files are also available on the course website. All intervals covered up to this point are a possibility. Write the interval performed in the spaces provided.

1. ______ 2. ______ 3. ______ 4. ______ 5. ______ 6. ______

7. ______ 8. ______ 9. ______ 10. ______ 11. ______ 12. ______

13. ______ 14. ______ 15. ______

Singing Triads and Seventh Chords

Give yourself the tonic pitch and sing the following triads and seventh chords on solfège. Refer to the solfège charts in Chapters 5 and 7.

1. M 2. m 3. d 4. + 5. Mm^7

6. mm^7 7. °7 8. M 9. Mm^7 10. °7

Identification Chords

REPLAY

AUDIO TRACK CH. 8 CHORD ID 1–10

You will hear ten triads and seventh chords performed by your teacher or on the course website. All triads and seventh chords are possibilities. Write the quality of the chord performed in the spaces provided.

1. ______ 2. ______ 3. ______ 4. ______ 5. ______

6. ______ 7. ______ 8. ______ 9. ______ 10. ______

Singing Progressions: Mozart, "Voi Che Sapete"

In previous chapters, you practiced singing various qualities of triads and seventh chords. Singing harmonic progressions puts those skills in context. It may take some practice before you are able to sing progressions as easily as you can play or hear them. You will find after some practice that singing progressions enhances your ability to both hear and play the same progressions. The opening progression to Mozart's "Voi Che Sapete" is written below. Use your knowledge of solfège and understanding of harmonic function to sing through the progression.

I	V^6_5	I	ii^6_5	V	I
do-mi-sol	ti-re-fa-sol	do-mi-sol	fa-la-do-re	sol-ti-re	do-mi-sol

Why does V^6_5 lead so well into I? How does the inversion of the ii^7 chord add or detract from the voice leading?

For this next group activity, establish a key and sing the scale as a class. Write Mozart's progression from "Voi Che Sapete" on the board. Instead of arpeggiating the chords in unison, have each class member hold a note of the chord. Every note in the chord should be heard. Go to the next chord, but remember your voice-leading should move to the closest available pitch. If you picked *mi* in the I chord, it would be easier to sing *re* or *fa* in the V^6_5 than to leap down to *ti*. Make sure the quality of each chord sounds correct before moving on to the next chord. Do you prefer singing progressions this way (in harmony with your classmates) or arpeggiated in unison? Why?

Performing the Do–Ti Test

While we can rely on our knowledge of harmonic movement to help us correctly identify a progression, the Do–Ti test allows us to really understand the function. As a progression is played, try to sing the syllable *do* with each chord. If *do* doesn't seem to fit, try to sing *ti*. If *ti* doesn't fit, try to sing the syllable *re*.

Look at the following chart. If you can sing *do* with the chord being played, you really only have three options; I, IV, or vi. The tonic chord sounds so stable in the progression that eventually your ears will be able to tell the difference between the tonic and the subdominant. By figuring out the qualities right away, you can eliminate one or two of the chords easily, depending on if you hear a major or minor quality. The same can be said for the chords under the syllable *ti*. Your teacher will play through a few progressions while you sing along with the Do–Ti test in order to better understand its purpose.

Ti	Do	Re
V	I or i	ii or ii°
vii° or VII	IV or iv	
iii or III	vi or VI	

Finish the Progression

Following are four incompetent harmonic progressions. Using your knowledge of harmonic function, fill in the blanks with an appropriate chord.

1. I _______ V vi _______ I

2. _______ I IV _______ V _______

3. i vii°7 _______ VI _______ i

4. i _______ V i iv _______ _______ i

After filling in the missing chords, sing through each progression on solfège, arpeggiated and in harmony with your class. Which progressions sound the best? Why? Are there any chords that you particularly like singing?

Harmonizing Melodies

The following three melodies appear with a harmonic progression written beneath. Divide into two groups. Have one group sight-sing the melody on solfège while the other group sings the harmonies written beneath on solfège. (For the second group, each student will hold a note in the chord in harmony, like in the "singing progressions" activity earlier.) After going through each melody, switch groups so that each student gets the chance to perform both the melody and accompaniment.

1.

2.

3.

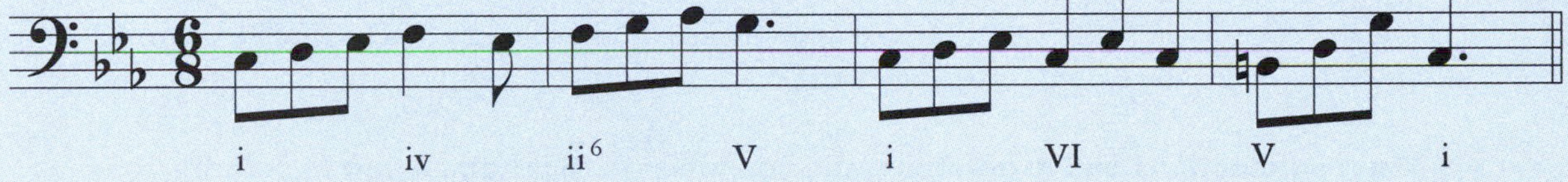

THE FINAL NOTE: REAL-WORLD PERSPECTIVE

Amy Bishop Greene

FORMER OPERATIONS COORDINATOR AT LYRIC OPERA OF CHICAGO

Educational Background

B.A. in English/Communications from Milligan College (small, private, liberal arts college). I took voice lessons during undergrad but no other academic music study. I studied voice and opera for 2 years at University of Tennessee, including introductory music theory/ear training, diction, and music history.

What inspired you to pursue this particular career path?

While I was studying voice and opera, it became clear to me that I wasn't cut out for a career as a singer. I didn't enjoy auditioning, I was a good but very average singer, and I really enjoy singing when I don't feel a lot of pressure. When I told my opera director how I was feeling, he suggested that I look into opera administration. In his words, "Someone's gotta run those places!" I love being a part of the artistic process, and I'm much better suited to work behind the scenes.

Has the study of music theory and musicianship helped you in your career? If so, how?

It has helped me! In order to have a career working with singers and instrumentalists, it's crucial to be able to speak their language. In fact, I wish I were more knowledgeable about theory! Knowing the operatic repertoire has been especially useful. Having studied singing and the voice, I can relate to singers and understand their concerns. The more I know about *their* jobs, the better I'm able to do mine.

What connections and experiences did you possess that helped you to acquire the position at the Lyric Opera?

My biggest connection and inspiration was Carroll Freeman, my opera director at University of Tennessee. He opened my eyes to the world of arts administration. He also ran the Opera in the Ozarks festival, and gave me a summer job there. I had previously worked for another not-for-profit organization, but it was that summer experience that I believe opened the door to my working full time at Lyric Opera. Studying opera and voice was also a big factor.

What responsibilities do you have and what role do you play in the company?

I work in the Rehearsal Department, which does all of the scheduling for the principal singers, chorus, orchestra, ballet, supernumeraries, actors, music staff, and stage managers. We also act as concierges for the principal artists. Most are from out of town, and many are from other countries, and we help them organize travel, find housing in Chicago, find a doctor or dentist if needed, arrange child care and pet sitting, and many other things! No matter what they may need while they're here, we help them get it. Our department also serves as the liaison between all the backstage staff and artists and the rest of the company. When people have questions about payment, taxes, benefits, interviews, tickets, or anything else, we help connect them to the department that can help. I also calculate payroll hours for the artists, manage the children's chorus, and work on the management team during union labor contract negotiations.

What advice would you give for students who are interested in pursuing a career in arts administration?

Definitely have a good working knowledge of an instrument as well as solid academic musical training. Pursue jobs at large companies—that's where the entry level jobs are! Use any connection you have. Use any connections your professors have! Internships are invaluable and often result in being hired on with the company. An advanced degree isn't necessary—work experience is often more valuable.

Most significant learning experience of your career.

I really learned a lot in a short amount of time working at Opera in the Ozarks. I got to participate in many aspects of putting an opera together, from the auditions through to opening night. I also learned about a lot of other things that go into producing a show: marketing, ticket sales, and fundraising are crucial parts of the process. This broad overview gave me a foot in the door for what has become a 15-year career.

CHAPTER 9

PHRASES AND CADENCES

Artist in Residence: Michael Jackson

Chapter Objectives

- Define key terms in relation to phrase structure
- Recognize and notate five types of cadences
- Create a phrase chart, including motivic material and phrase length
- Define and identify periodic structure
- Recognize phrase and periodic structure in classical and popular contexts

Say the following sentence out loud:

> Before I wrote "Beat It" I had been thinking I wanted to write the type of rock song that I would go out and buy, but also something totally different from the rock music I was hearing on Top 40 radio at the time.
>
> —Michael Jackson in *Moonwalk*

See the comma and the period? Those punctuation marks denote the endings of a phrase, or a "sequence of two or more words arranged in a grammatical construction and acting as a unit in a sentence." So how does the definition of a grammatical phrase transfer to the one for a musical phrase? Well, pretty easily. The two or more words are the pitches and/

or chords, and the grammatical construction is the phrase defined by the punctuation, or, in music, the cadence.

CADENCE TYPES

Cadences are the final two chords composed in a musical **phrase**, a complete musical thought using melodic and rhythmic motives. Phrases and cadences are intertwined in such a way to create a formal structure to most tonal pieces.

Authentic Cadence

The authentic cadence is a progression of the dominant functioning chord (V or vii°) to the tonic (I(i)). The cadence can be labeled in two different ways depending on the strength of the cadence itself. A **perfect authentic cadence (PAC)** includes a root position V and I chord, and in the tonic triad, the tonic must be present in the soprano voice. If the soprano voice is notated with a $\hat{3}$ or $\hat{5}$, the first chord is a vii°, or any chord is in inversion, the term **imperfect authentic cadence (IAC)** is used. Why do you think there are separate identifiers for these two types? Listening will help you to answer this question. Play the following chorales in order to better understand the differences.

The final cadence of the phrase is a perfect authentic cadence. Both the V and I are in root position, and the soprano voice in the final tonic chord is notated on $\hat{1}$.

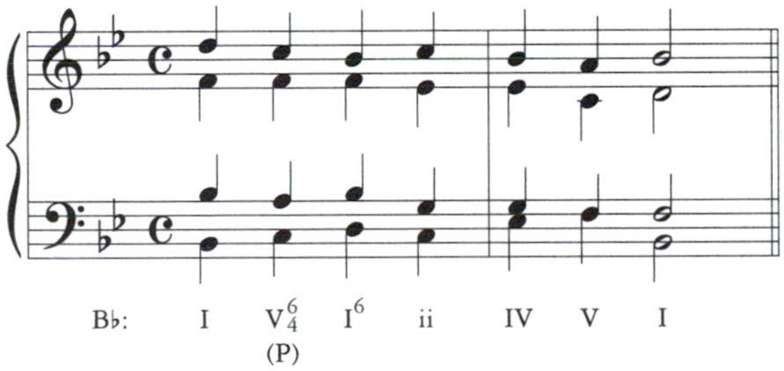

The imperfect authentic cadence also uses root position for the V and I, but the soprano voice in the final tonic chord is notated with $\hat{5}$.

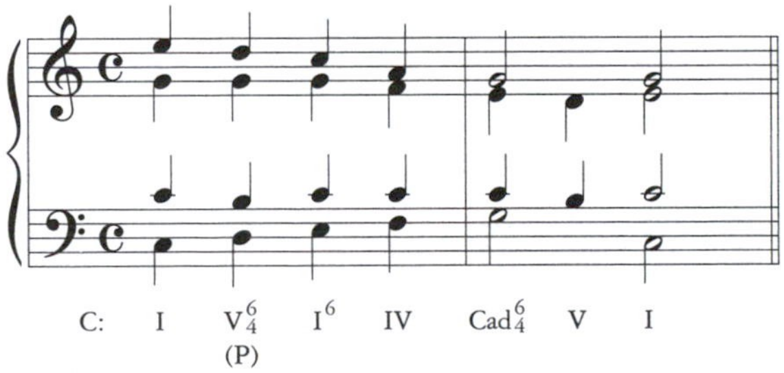

The final cadence includes a vii°–I, so the cadence type is imperfect authentic.

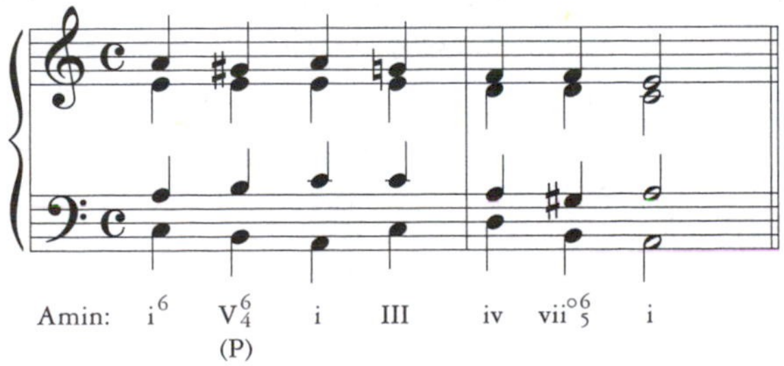

Deceptive Cadence

Ah, deception. There's nothing more compelling than taking your listener to a place that is unexpected. A **deceptive cadence (DC)** is just that: a dominant chord that you think will resolve to the tonic moves to something other than the I, most often the submediant.

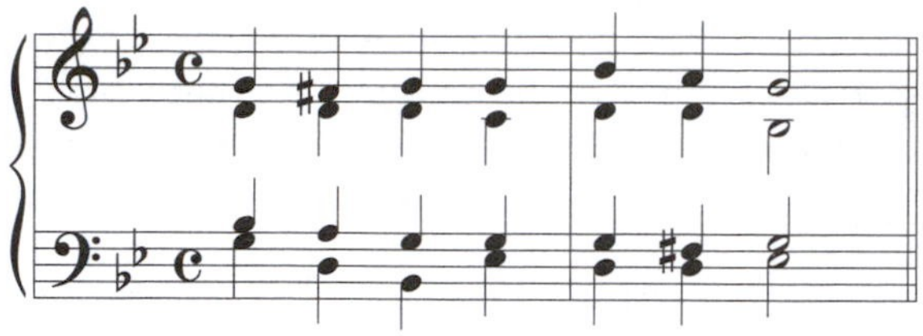

Gmin: i V i^6 iv^6 Cad$^6_4$ V VI

Half Cadence

Think back to the opening phrase of this chapter. Remember the comma? Well, typically, the "commas" in music are taken up by the **half cadence (HC)**, a cadence in which the phrase ends on the unstable dominant harmony. The dominant harmony can be approached by the ii, IV, or I.

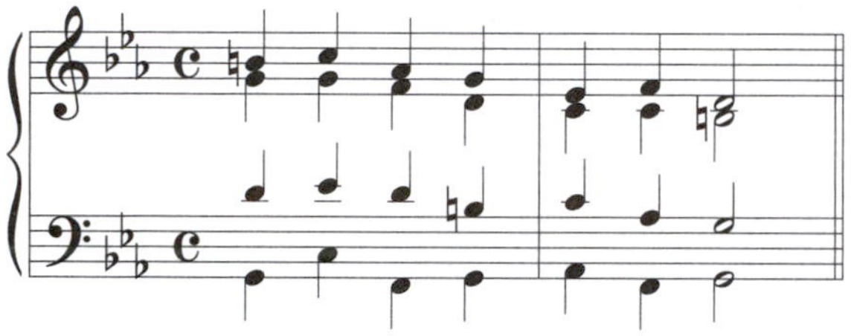

Cmin: V i $ii^{\circ 6}$ i VI iv V

Plagal Cadence

In a **plagal cadence (PC)**, the subdominant harmony moves directly to the tonic, bypassing the dominant all together.

C: I I^6 V I^6 IV I

PHRASES

Phrases are typically two, four, or eight measures long and must conclude with some type of cadence. Let's look at a few folk tunes before we start to analyze more popular literature.

The folk song "London Bridge" is made up of two phrases. Each phrase concludes with a type of cadence. Play through the melody with the chords. Can you see (and hear) the cadences marked in the score?

Traditional, "London Bridge"

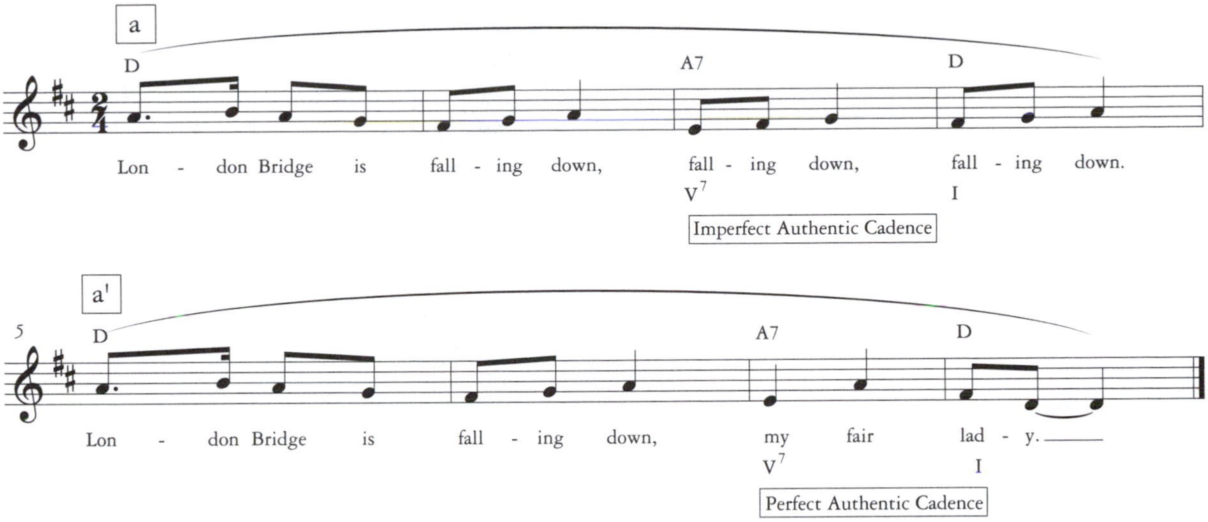

A phrase chart for "London Bridge" shows that the melodic or motivic makeup is similar for each phrase. The melodic content is indicated with lowercase letters. The superscript number indicates that the phrase is similar, but a bit different due to the cadence. We call this superscript number *prime*.

Study the phrase charts for "Frère Jacques" and "Greensleeves." Be sure to play the melody along with a realization of the chords as you study the phrase structure. Do the musical phrases tend to follow the text?

Traditional, "Frère Jacques"

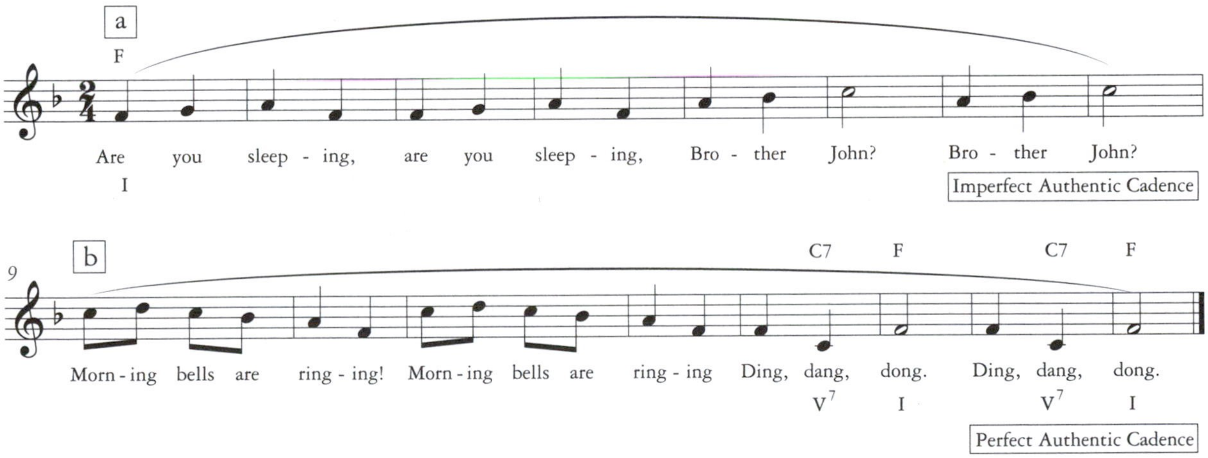

Traditional, "Greensleeves"

Traditional, "Greensleeves" *(continued)*

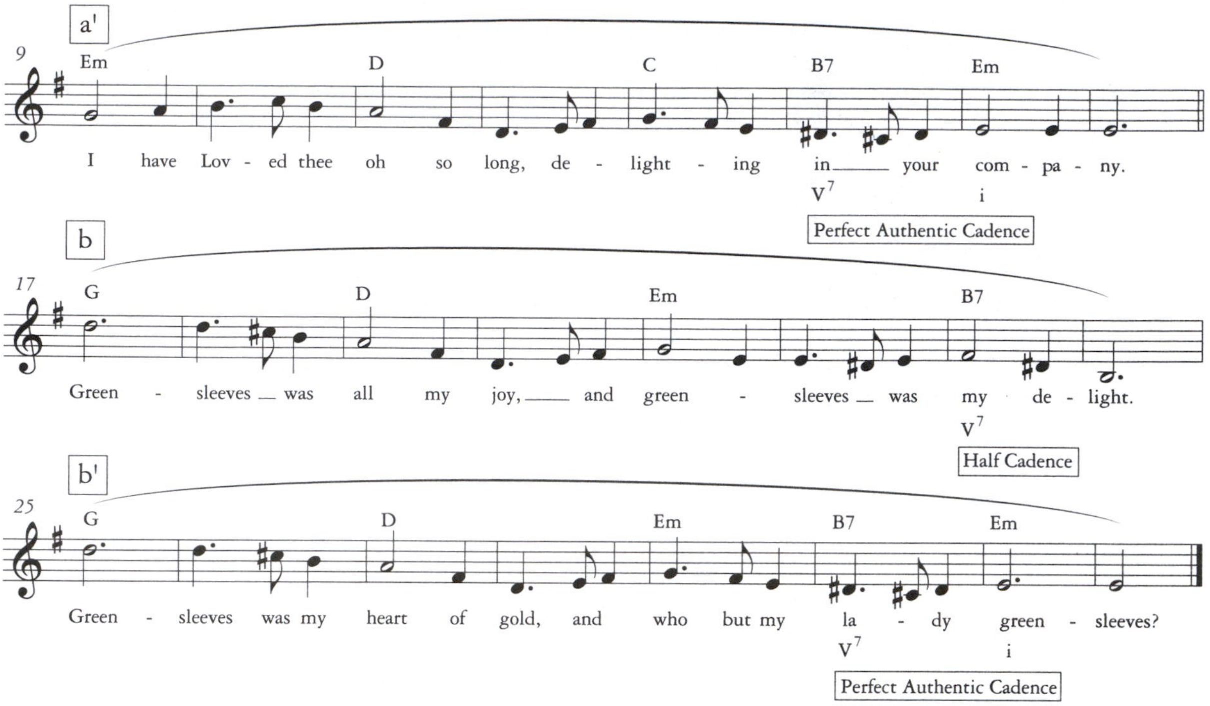

PERIODS

The **period** can best be defined as a combination of phrases into a larger structural unit, much like a written sentence. Often periods are made up of two phrases: the first phrase is called the antecedent, and the second phrase is called the consequent. The antecedent always concludes with a weaker cadence than the PAC that concludes the consequent.

There are two main identifiers for periodic structure:

Symmetrical versus asymmetrical: This has to do with the lengths of the phrases in terms of beats and/or measures. If the phrases are identical in terms of length, we call the period *symmetrical*. If the phrases contain different beats and/or measures, the period is labeled *asymmetrical*.

Parallel versus Contrasting: This has to do with the melodic content of the phrases. If the melodic material used in each phrase is the same, the term *parallel* is used. This can be tricky if only a few pitches are different, but always trust your ear. Does it sound different enough to call the phrase contrasting?

Look back at the phrase charts for the folk songs above, and compare them to the periodic structure given for each:

"London Bridge": symmetrical parallel period
"Frère Jacques": symmetrical contrasting period
"Greensleeves": two symmetrical parallel periods

ARTIST IN RESIDENCE

Child Star to Solo Superstar

WEBSITE
VIDEO TRACK 70

It's hard to imagine the career of a superstar beginning at the age of 5, but that's exactly what happened when Michael Jackson joined his four older brothers in the musical group the Jackson 5. Jackson sets the scene in his autobiography: "I was so little when we began to work on our music that I really don't remember much about it. Here's what I remember. I remember singing at the top of my voice and dancing with real joy and working too hard for a child." By the age of 10, Michael Jackson, along with the rest of the Jackson 5, were signed to Berry Gordy's Motown label. Their big break came when they were asked to appear on *The Hollywood Palace*, a TV variety show hosted by different people each week (Diana Ross was the host during the Jackson 5's debut).

The Jackson 5 closed their performance with "I Want You Back," and the song went to number 1 in 2 short months. Michael's vocals on this song have been described as follows: "[It's as] if his lungs are about to burst into flames any second." Listen to this performance. How would you describe Michael's sound? The Jackson 5 enjoyed a string of hits through the early 1970s, including a Saturday morning cartoon, but by 1972, the group was starting to butt heads with the folks at Motown. Gordy was not allowing the group to have any say in musical decisions, and the Jackson brothers wanted more control in their recordings. The group severed ties with Motown and signed with Epic Records.

However, there was a bigger storm brewing in the Jackson family. Michael was anxious to begin his solo career, and with the talented producer Quincy Jones, he released his first solo album, *Off the Wall*, in 1979. Quincy reflected on his work with Jackson: "Michael is the essence of what a performer and an artist are all about. He's got all you need emotionally, and he backs it up with discipline and pacing. He'll never burn himself out." Michael had ownership of the entire music process, from writing to producing to performing. *Off the Wall* produced four top 10 hits, and Jackson dominated the American Music Awards in 1981. But the best was yet to come.

WEBSITE
VIDEO TRACK 71

Let's check out the phrases and cadences used in one of Jackson's earliest number 1 solo songs, "Ben," from the movie of the same name. It's hard to believe when you listen to this song that Jackson is singing about a friendship with a rat!

This particular excerpt contains two phrases, the first ending with a half cadence and the second with a perfect authentic cadence. Does this make a period? Well, yes. By definition a period is the combination of phrases into a larger unit. The phrases are not symmetrical because the repetition of the melody in the second phrase actually extends the phrase by one measure. The periodic structure of this excerpt is an asymmetrical contrasting period.

Michael Jackson, "Ben." Songwriters: Walter Scharf and Don Black

ARTIST IN RESIDENCE

Breaking All the Records

Do a quick Google search for the best-selling record of all time. You will find lots of sites devoted to this search, and there is no disputing that Michael Jackson holds the number 1 spot for the album *Thriller.* The album, released in 1982, generated seven top 10 hits, eight Grammys, and eight American Music Awards; and held the number 1 album spot for 37 weeks. *Thriller* remained in the top 10 for 80 weeks. (that's over 1½ years!) Jackson also held the highest royalty-earning rate at $2 an album. Considering that *Thriller* sold an estimated sixty-five million copies, Jackson was a rich man indeed.

WEBSITE
VIDEO TRACKS 72 AND 73

So what makes this album so amazing? Well, there are probably many elements at play here. Quincy Jones was an Epic producer in both senses of the word. He put up a great deal of money ($750,000) for the production of the album, and he knew how to bring together some of the greatest songwriters and performers in the business, including guest performances by Eddie Van Halen, Toto, and Paul McCartney. But it was perhaps television that shot the tracks of *Thriller* straight to the top. "Billie Jean" premiered on MTV in late January 1983 and "launched *Thriller*'s sales into the stratosphere." The video for "Thriller" clocks in at 13 minutes and is more like a small feature film than a music video. You would think that this would become a bit mundane in comparison to the typical 3 minutes, but apparently not. The video sold over a million VHS copies back in the 1980s and has been viewed on YouTube well over 200 million times (and that's on the legal channel)!

But it was when Jackson performed his notorious moonwalk and created a fashion statement with the sequined glove on the television special *Motown 25* that a new standard was set for all pop artists in terms of live performances. *Rolling Stone*'s online biography of Jackson summarizes the monumental performance in this manner:

It was startlingly clear that he was not only one of the most thrilling live performers in pop music, but that he was perhaps more capable of inspiring an audience's imagination than any single pop artist since Elvis Presley. There are times when you know you are hearing or seeing something extraordinary, something that captures the hopes and dreams popular music might aspire to, and that might unite and inflame a new audience. That time came that night, on TV screens across the nation—the sight of a young man staking out his territory, and just starting to lay claim to his rightful pop legend.

Jackson was the complete package. He could sing, write, dance, and perform like no other and had the backing of a talented team to help him get to the top.

WEBSITE

VIDEO TRACK 74

Released in 1988, Jackson's album *Bad* generated five number 1 hits, including the introspective song "Man in the Mirror." Interestingly enough, after Jackson's death in 2009, this particular song reached the top of the charts again as one of the top downloaded song on iTunes during the month of September.

Study the two excerpts taken from "Man in the Mirror." The first includes a deceptive cadence. The dominant harmony is heard for two whole measures, but the cadence on the word "change" is not to the expected I, but a ♭II!! The one–beat rest before the cadence also extends the phrase to five measures. The sudden change, no pun intended, is shocking, but oh, so effective.

Michael Jackson, "Man in the Mirror." Songwriters: Siedah Garrett and Glen Ballard

Another excerpt from "Man in the Mirror" uses the same technique of extending the phrase. The phrases conclude with a plagal cadence and a perfect authentic cadence. This is a period structure because of the weaker plagal cadence, but the problem comes in measures 28–29. The pitches in the vocal line at 28 would suggest a PAC, but the harmony doesn't really change until 29. The phrase is extended by one beat, creating an asymmetrical, contrasting period.

Released in 1991, "Black or White" was the first single from the album *Dangerous.* It quickly rose to number 1 on the Hot 100 and spent 7 weeks at the top. The music video that accompanies the song was revolutionary due to its morphing of images during the final chorus.

WEBSITE

VIDEO TRACK 75

The musical phrases are marked in the score. While there could be a case made for longer phrases, the shorter phrase markings match up better with the text. The phrases are all irregular in terms of length, and Jackson chose to extend the phrases with chord *and* melodic repetition. The phrases all conclude with plagal cadences, and the conclusive feeling of the PAC is missing. Because the conclusive cadence is not present, this excerpt is an example of a phrase chain, or **phrase group**.

Michael Jackson, "Black or White." Songwriters: Michael Jackson and Bill Bottrell

Reviewing Chapter Objectives

- Define key terms in relation to phrase structure (page 176)
- Recognize and notate five types of cadences (pages 173–174)
- Create a phrase chart, including motivic material and phrase length (pages 175–176)
- Identify periodic structure (page 176)
- Recognize phrase and periodic structure in classical and popular contexts (pages 178, 180–182)

EXERCISES

I. Play through the following chorales and determine the final cadence at the end of the phrase. The Roman numerals have been given to you for the first two chorales. The pitches in parentheses are non-chord tones and are not included in the analysis of the chords.

Provide a Roman numeral analysis, including figured bass. Label the types of second inversion chords used, and identify the final cadence.

C:

II. Provide Roman numerals and correct notation that represent the cadences specified.

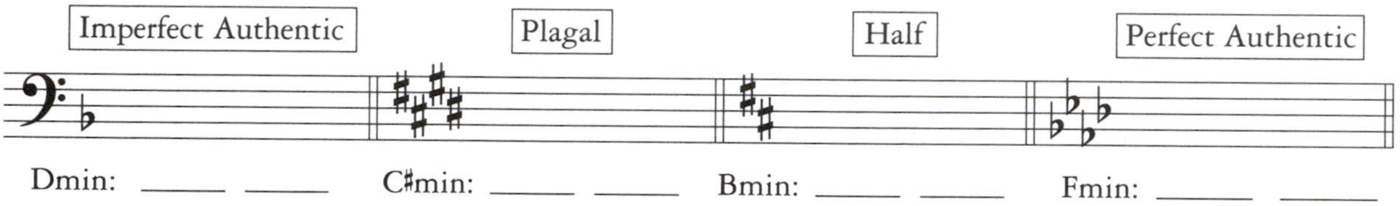

III. Create phrase charts for the following pieces representing both standards and popular music. Be sure to indicate cadences and melodic motives in your phrase chart. Try to determine the periodic structure.

Bates and Ward, "America the Beautiful." Hint: The cadence in measure 8 is a half cadence.

VIDEO TRACK 76

Taylor Swift, "Love Story." Songwriter: Taylor Swift

ANALYSIS

The opening two measures of this choral piece serve as an introduction. Begin analyzing the phrase structure in measure 3.

VIDEO TRACK 77

King's College, Mozart's "Ave Verum Corpus," K. 618

King's College, Mozart's "Ave Verum Corpus," K. 618 *(continued)*

VIDEO TRACK 78

This piece may be challenging in terms of seeing the phrase structure, but probably not so much in terms of listening for phrase structure. The key does change in the middle of the excerpt; however, use your ears to best determine the type of cadence at the end of the phrase. Which voice part has the melody? Use that as your guide in determining motives and cadence points.

Universitäts Chor Müchen, Mendelssohn's "Die Nachtigall," Op. 59, No. 4

AURAL SKILLS CONDITIONING 9

Listening for Cadences

The Beatles' famous song "Hey Jude" spent 9 weeks at number 1 on American charts. Listen to the song on the YouTube channel and mark the timings that correspond to the end of each phrase you hear. Make sure you listen to the whole song, but mark only the ends of phrases until about 1:30. Remember to use your musical instincts, and the text, to determine where the phrases begin and end. The first box is filled in for you.

WEBSITE
VIDEO TRACK 79

Time (end of phrase)	Cadence	Motive
0:12	Imperfect authentic	a

Identifying Cadence Types

REPLAY

AUDIO TRACK CH. 9 CADENCE ID 1–6

In this chapter, you learned about the four types of cadences (authentic, half, plagal, and deceptive). You will hear a four-chord progression performed by your instructor in the classroom or on the course website. Using your knowledge of the different types of cadences, circle the correct cadence below.

1. Authentic Half Plagal Deceptive
2. Authentic Half Plagal Deceptive
3. Authentic Half Plagal Deceptive
4. Authentic Half Plagal Deceptive
5. Authentic Half Plagal Deceptive
6. Authentic Half Plagal Deceptive

Hearing Phrases and Cadences Beyond the Four-Measure Phrase: Jackson 5, "I'll Be There"

WEBSITE

VIDEO TRACK 80

Michael Jackson's performing career began with the collaboration with his brothers in the Jackson 5. One of their most beloved songs, "I'll Be There," provides a great example to hear phrases and cadences that do not follow the typical four-measure phrase. Listen to the song in conjunction with the chart below, which lists timings and cadences for the first 2 minutes. The phrases are analyzed *after* the instrumental introduction.

Can you hear the end of a musical idea? Can you hear the harmonic closure at each authentic cadence? How does the cadence in the third phrase sound different from the others?

Time (end of phrase)	Cadence	Motive
0:34	Perfect authentic	a
0:54	Perfect authentic	a
1:08	Imperfect authentic	b
1:17	Perfect authentic	b
1:38	Perfect authentic	a′
1:58	Perfect authentic	a″

You might be tempted to mark the end of the first phrase on the words "salvation back" at the conclusion of the fourth measure. However, the harmony used here is a vi–iii. Would a phrase ever end on the iii chord? Anything is possible in music, but as we have learned about function, this would be a very weak move. You can't call it a deceptive cadence because there is no dominant chord. In this example, the iii chord does not signify the end of the phrase but rather lengthens the phrase until the final cadence. The phrases in "I'll Be There" are longer than most: they are eight measures long!

Other Examples for Individual Study

VIDEO TRACKS 81–85

1. "Lo, How a Rose E'er Blooming," Renée Fleming and the Mormon Tabernacle Choir

   Make a phrase chart, including cadences and motives through 0:42. Do you hear the first cadence at 0:08 or 0:19? Why? Either analysis is acceptable, and your analysis might differ depending on the performance of this famous German carol. How does Renée Fleming convey her interpretation of the phrase structure? Find another arrangement of this piece and compare it to Fleming and the Mormon Tabernacle Choir's interpretation. Is it faster or slower? Do cadences occur more frequently or less frequently?

2. "Still Fighting It," Ben Folds

   What type of cadence do you hear at 0:43? Does it resolve like you would expect it to? Why or why not? Hint: this type of progression is common in popular music but harder to find in classical music.

3. "Nimrod" from Elgar's *Enigma Variations*, Daniel Barenboim and the Chicago Symphony

   This famous movement from the *Enigma Variations* is one of Elgar's best-known works. Listen all the way through and mark the timings where you hear a cadence. Are there many or very few noticeable cadences in this slow piece? Do you think this piece is effective in invoking a deep emotional response in the listener? Why or why not?

4. "Disappear," The Gabe Dixon Band

   What type of cadence do you hear around 2:20?

5. "You're Gone," Diamond Rio

   Listen to the chorus, starting around 1:00. What type of cadence do you hear at the end of the chorus? Do the lyrics at this cadence ("And the bad news is, you're gone") have an influence on the progression in any way?

CHAPTER 10

NON-CHORD TONES I

Artist in Residence: Pink

Chapter Objectives

- Define passing tone, neighbor tone, anticipation, appoggiatura, escape tone, and neighbor group
- Identify non-chord tones within a context of a musical score
- Notate specified non-chord tones when given chord progression

Leonardo da Vinci is credited with saying, "Simplicity is the ultimate sophistication." Some of the more compelling musical lines are made up of just a few pitches. However, there's a time for simplicity and a time for complexity when dealing with melodic lines. Play through the following examples on the piano. The melodies in the first two examples include pitches found only in the chord indicated by the lead sheet symbol. In the first example, the pitches change only when the chord symbol changes. The melody in the second example is more varied and jumps around: pitches are found in each of the given chords. The rhythm is also a bit more interesting. The third melody is based on the second melody; however, new pitches are added as "links" between the chord tones. Which one is the most compelling in terms of the melodic content? There is no right answer here. It all depends on where you are in the compositional process and what you are trying to convey to your listener.

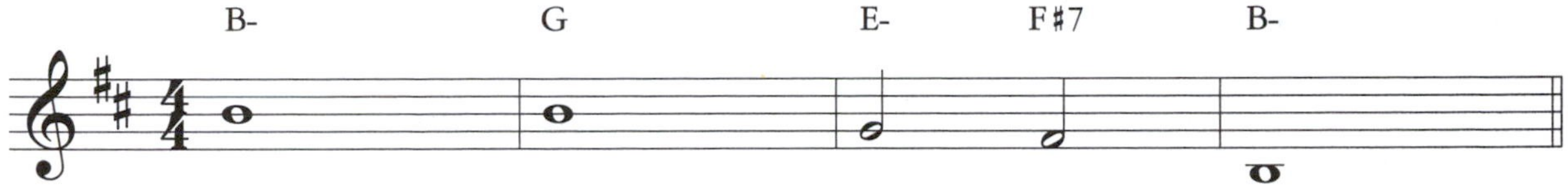

The pitches used in the third melody include notes that are not part of the given chord, creating an interesting (and singable) melodic line above the harmony. These pitches are called **non-chord tones** or **embellishing tones**. Non-chord tones can be either diatonic (pitch is found within the key) or chromatic (pitch is not diatonic in the key). Let's look at all of the non-chord tones found in the third melody.

NON-CHORD TONES

Passing Tone

A **passing tone (PT)** fills the interval between two chord tones. The C♯ in the first measure of the third melody is a passing tone.

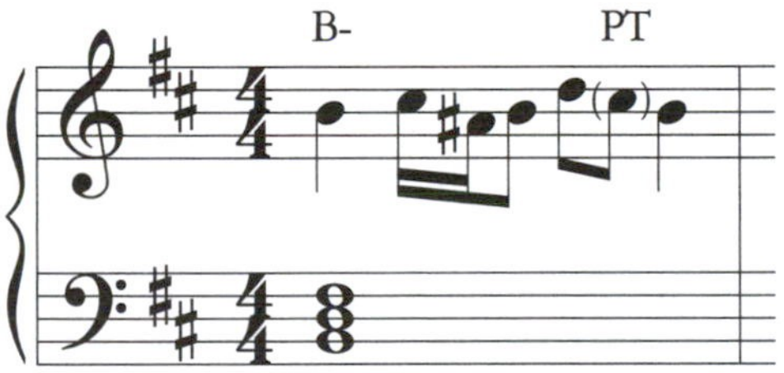

Neighbor Tone

A **neighbor tone (NT)** is used to embellish a single pitch. Think of it as what happens in a typical suburban neighborhood: the pitch goes next door to say "Hey" and comes right back home. The neighbor tone can be labeled as an upper neighbor (UN) or lower neighbor (LN) depending on the direction of the non-chord tone. The F♯ in the second measure is a lower neighbor tone.

Anticipation

It's like this non-chord tone is an overachiever. An **anticipation (ANT)** is a bit ahead of the game: it anticipates a pitch that fits in the next chord. Look at measures 3 and 4 of the melody. The D♮ at the end of measure 3 is not diatonic in the F♯^{7} chord; it is anticipating the D found in the next chord at measure 4.

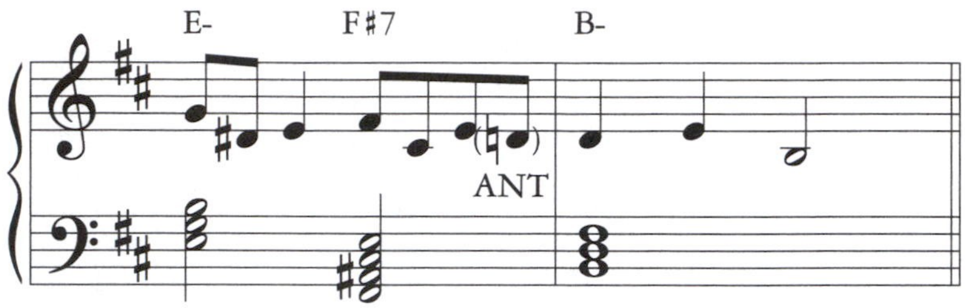

Appoggiatura

Isn't that just fun to say? In Italian, the term means "support" or "to lean on." An **appoggiatura (APP)** is approached by a leap and resolved by a step. Look at measure 3 of the melody. The D♯ does not fit into the chord of E minor. Look to the left of the D♯ (leap), and now look to the right (step). The D♯ is labeled as a chromatic appoggiatura. (The D♯ is not diatonic in the key of B minor.) See how it leans into the next chord tone, in this case the E? Very effective.

Escape Tone

The **escape tone (ET)** functions exactly like an appoggiatura except that the approach and resolution are switched. An escape tone is approached by step and resolves by leap. The final measure of the melody includes an escape tone on the pitch E.

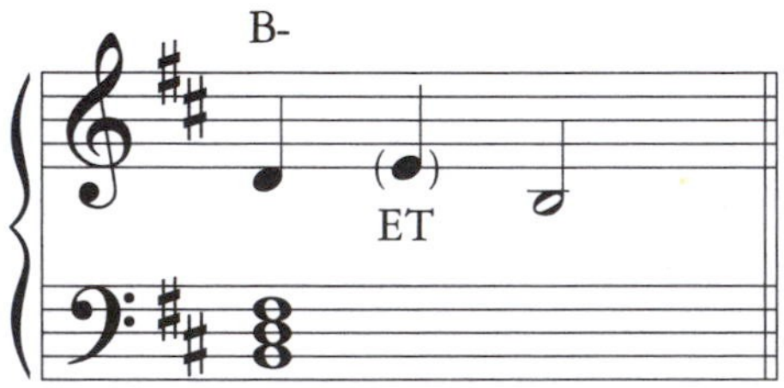

Neighbor Group

Sometimes called the double neighbor, the **neighbor group (NG)** embellishes a pitch as a lower *and* an upper neighbor. Look at the first measure. The inclusion of the pitch C♯ and A♯ wrapped around the chord tone B creates a neighbor group.

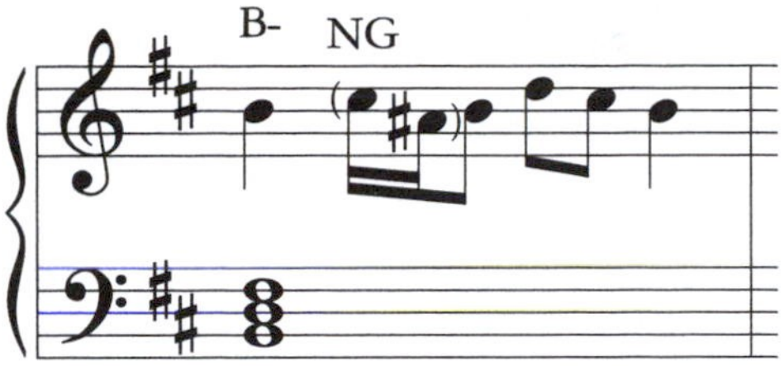

Now that you have a better idea of non-chord tones, study how each NCT is labeled in the melody from the opening of the chapter. Of course, the complexity of this melody is a little excessive in that six different non-chord tones are used within the span of four measures. This is not typical in "real" music literature, and many times a melody will contain only two or three of the non-chord tones presented here.

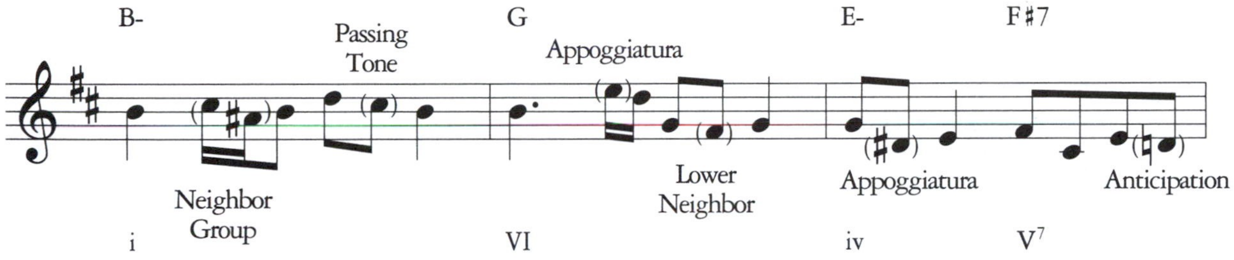

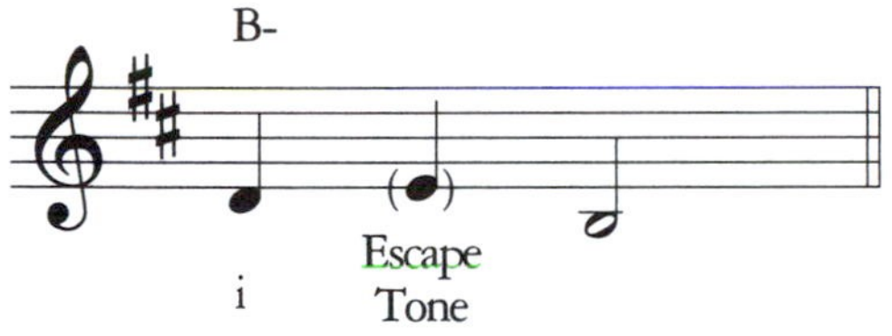

ARTIST IN RESIDENCE

Finding Her Voice among the Pop Princesses

The headline in a 2009 *Rolling Stone* article asks, "Why does Pink feel like she has so much to prove?" It seems that Pink, born Alecia Moore, has always been fighting for her place in the entertainment industry, constantly proving her talent and justifying her place on the top of the charts. She launched her solo career at the same time as Britney Spears and Christina Aguilera, but Pink's life experience was quite different from her peers'. After all, Pink was experimenting with acid and Ecstasy by the time she was 15. Spears and Aguilera were idols on the Mickey Mouse Club when they were in their early teens. Pink's first album, *Can't Take Me Home*, includes singles that sound similar to other pop groups of the time, including Destiny's Child, Spears, and Aguilera.

WEBSITE
VIDEO TRACKS 1–2

Listen to the rhythms and vocal style in the Pink song "There You Go" and compare it to any of the songs from Aguilera's debut album or "Bills, Bills, Bills" by Destiny's Child. The backbeats are the same, the vocal timbre is the same, and even the basic song topics are strikingly similar. When it was time to record her second album, Pink wanted to stand out from her competition and hired Linda Perry as her new collaborator. The 2009 article in *Rolling Stone* describes the collaboration: "The album they wrote together, 2001's *Missundaztood*, created a new template for pop music: slick dance-floor-ready drum

programming, crunchy rock guitars and unusually impassioned vocals with lyrics drawn directly from Pink's own life." The album went quadruple platinum, and Pink's reputation as a rocker was set. Since 2001, Pink has released four more albums including the 2012 *The Truth about Love* that has sold millions of copies both in the United States and abroad. Pink was even named 2013 Billboard Woman of the Year. And as for having to prove herself? "I'm the constant underdog in America," Pink says. "It's been this constant fight to prove I have some kind of talent. Every two years I hear, 'Oh, this new girl's going to knock you off your pedestal,' and two years later, she's a waitress again."

WEBSITE

VIDEO TRACK 3

"Get the Party Started" is considered by most fans to be the Pink anthem. The first single released from *Missundaztood*, it quickly rose to the top 10 of the Hot 100. The chord usage is at the height of simplicity, a constant repetition of the tonic with a brief movement to the minor dominant. All of the non-chord tones are labeled in the score. As you listen to the performance of the excerpt, focus on the appoggiatura and its effectiveness leading to the end of the phrase.

Pink, "Get the Party Started." Songwriter: Linda Perry

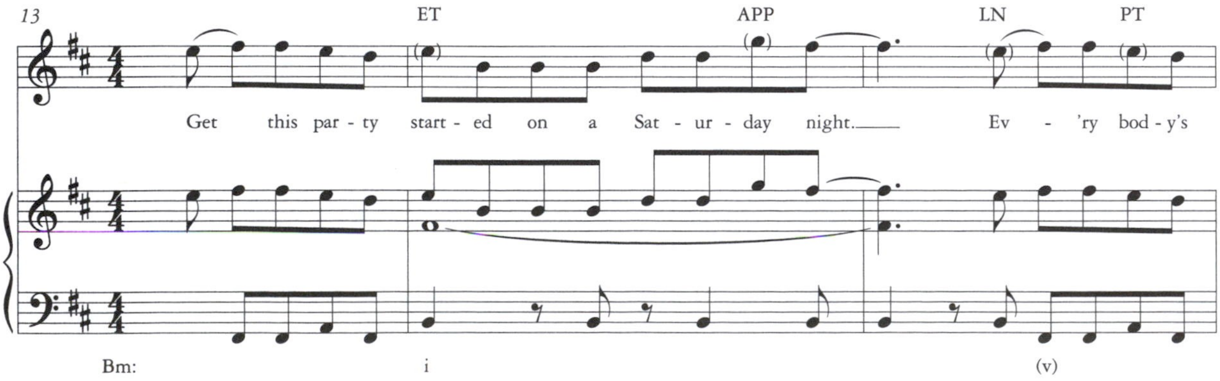

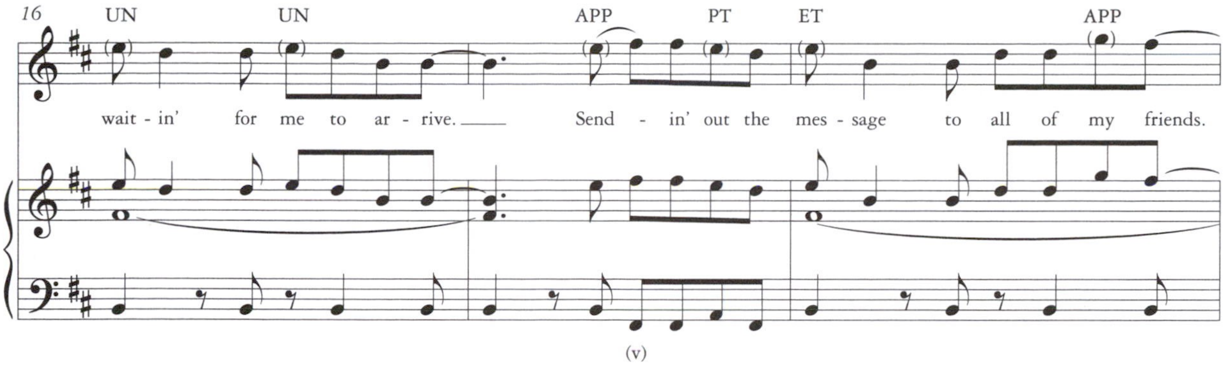

Released in 2010, "Glitter in the Air" was the sixth single released from *Funhouse*. It did well on several charts and received a great deal of airplay on top 40 stations. Study the chords and the non-chord tones. The passing bass line is very effective in the last line of this excerpt and includes two passing tones connecting the F and the C.

WEBSITE
VIDEO TRACK 4

Pink, "Glitter in the Air." Songwriters: Billy Mann and Alecia Moore

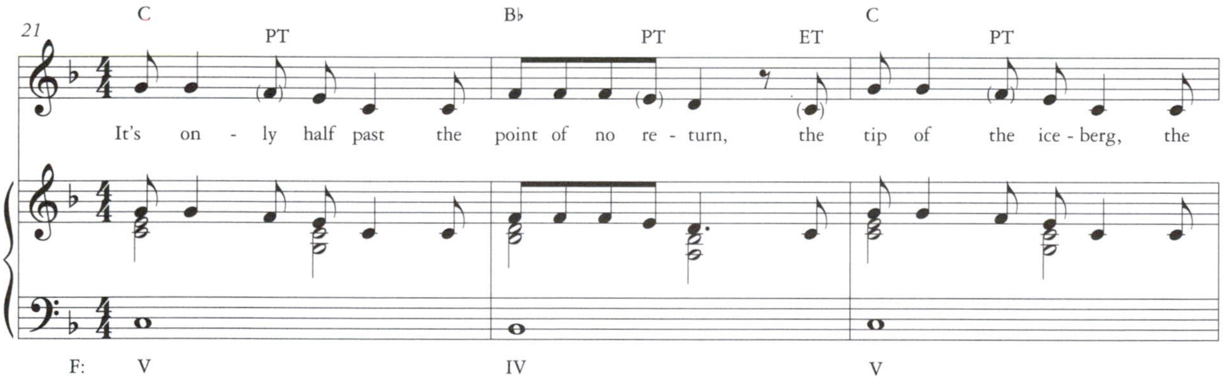

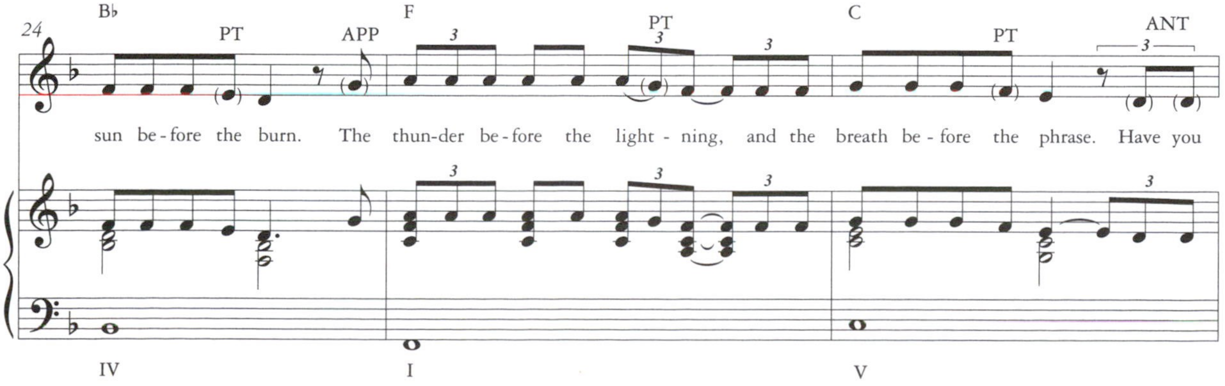

Pink, "Glitter in the Air." Songwriters: Billy Mann and Alecia Moore *(continued)*

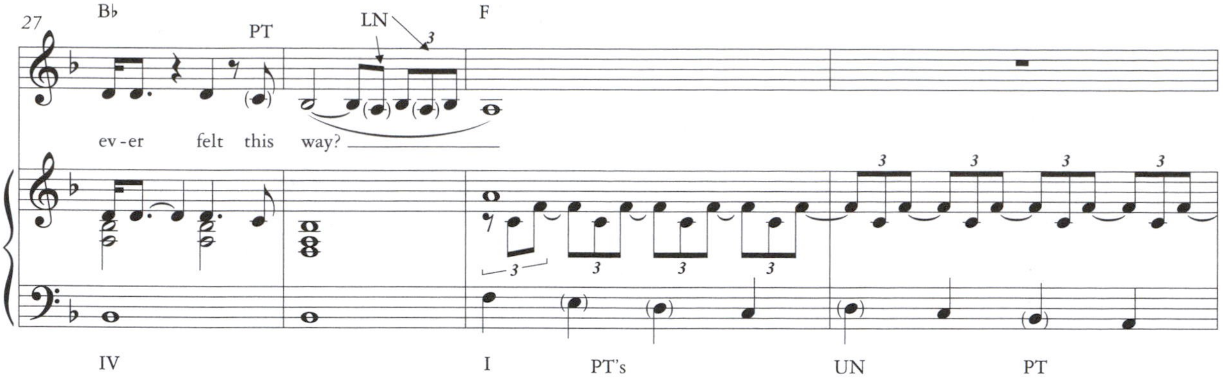

VIDEO TRACK 5

Written and performed by Pink and Nate Ruess of the group Fun., "Just Give Me a Reason" was released in the fall of 2012. Both Pink and Ruess were at the top of their game in 2012 with chart toppers such as "Blow Me (One Last Kiss)" and "Some Nights." Ruess talked with MTV News about the experience: "Writing the song was a whole different learning experience and was really fueled by the fact that Pink is so strong and independent and so very much herself. At the end of the day it's so hard to argue against her because what she does is always so great." The result of that songwriting experience was one of the most popular songs of Pink's career. Study the excerpt from "Just Give Me a Reason." The main non-chord tone used is the anticipation. How would the vocal line be changed if the anticipation were not included?

Pink and Nate Ruess, "Just Give Me a Reason." Songwriters: Alecia Moore, Nate Ruess, and Jeff Bhasker

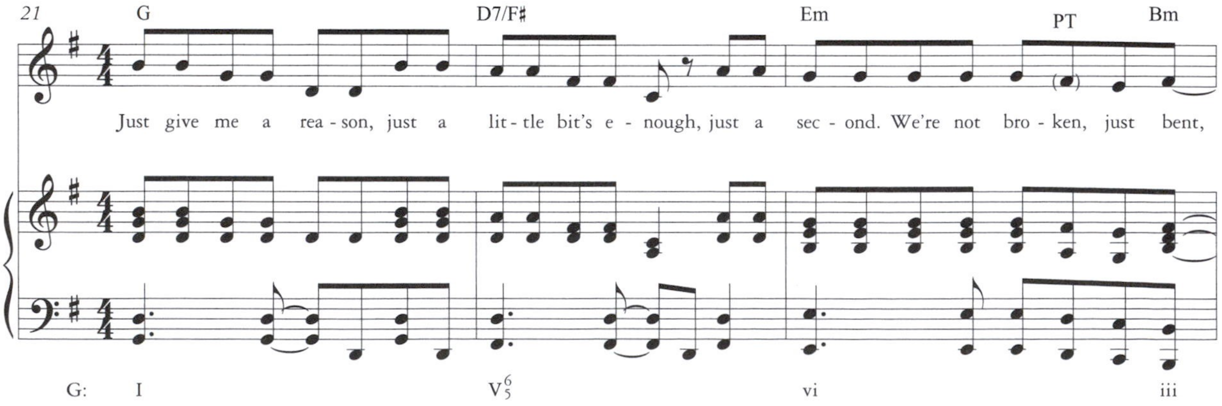

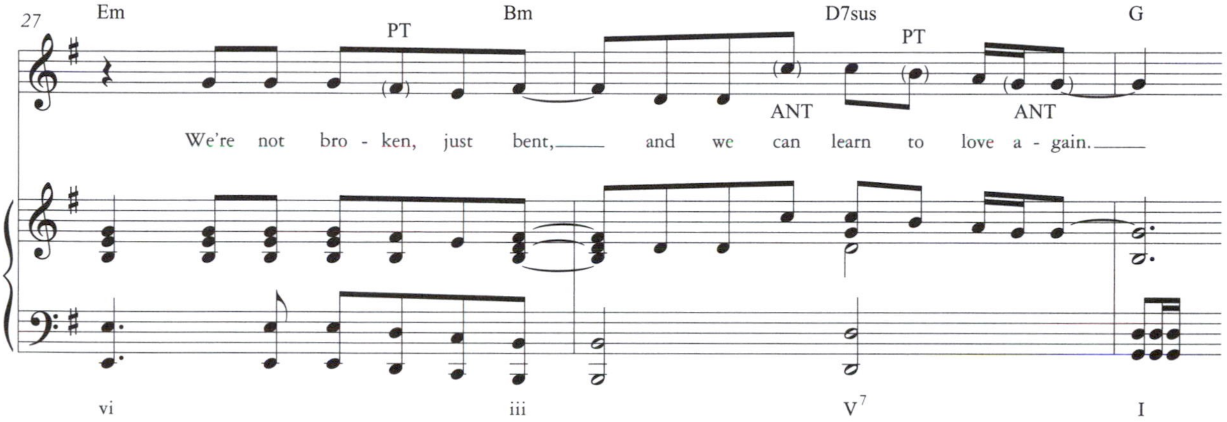

Sometimes non-chord tones are not easily identifiable and do not function as any presented in this chapter. Take for instance "So What" from Pink's *Funhouse* album. The pitches marked in parentheses do not fit within the chord: they seem to be part of a motive repeating itself as the chords change. These non-chord tones are not functioning in any of the traditional methods presented in this chapter and are used almost like a recurring pedal. These pitches are not to be included in the chord analysis and should be marked simply as non-chord tones.

VIDEO TRACK 6

Pink, "So What." Songwriters: Alecia Moore and Max Martin

Pink, "So What." Songwriters: Alecia Moore and Max Martin *(continued)*

ARTIST IN RESIDENCE

Flying through the Air

Remember the quote from the chapter opening: "Simplicity is the ultimate sophistication"? There is nothing simple about the singer Pink, either in her personal life or in her music. She is constantly raising the bar, both in the studio and in terms of live performance, so that each moment (and track) is full of surprises.

WEBSITE

VIDEO TRACK 4

During her childhood, Pink dreamed of being an Olympic gymnast (but she was kicked off the team for having a "non-team-like attitude"). Surprised? She still uses her athletic skills in her live performances; in fact, at the 2010 Grammy Awards, Pink performed "Glitter in the Air" while suspended in the air above the audience. It was the most talked about performance of the night. The crowd rewarded Pink with a standing ovation, and in an interview with CNN following the performance, Pink relayed to reporters that no one ever has another excuse to lip-sync. She had finally won the respect of her peers.

Pink takes a great deal of pride in her live performances, saying, "My shows are like group therapy," adding that the cathartic powers of performing help to tone down her temper. This power of performing has served Pink well. She has earned three Grammy Awards and more than a dozen top 10 hits, and she has sold out stadiums that have pulled in over $100 million in revenue for the singer.

Reviewing Chapter Objectives

- Define passing tone, neighbor tone, anticipation, appoggiatura, escape tone, and neighbor group (pages 191–192)
- Identify non-chord tones within a context of a musical score (pages 194–195)
- Notate specified non-chord tones when given chord progression (page 201)

EXERCISES

I. Each example below contains one non-chord tone. Give a Roman numeral analysis for the chords, and identify the non-chord tone used. Be sure to give appropriate figured bass symbols.

II. Several progressions are outlined on the staff below. Add in the correct pitches and non-chord tones to the progression. Be sure to use correct voice leading! Refer back to page 151 for basic guidelines regarding part writing.

Passing Tone, Anticipation, Appoggiatura

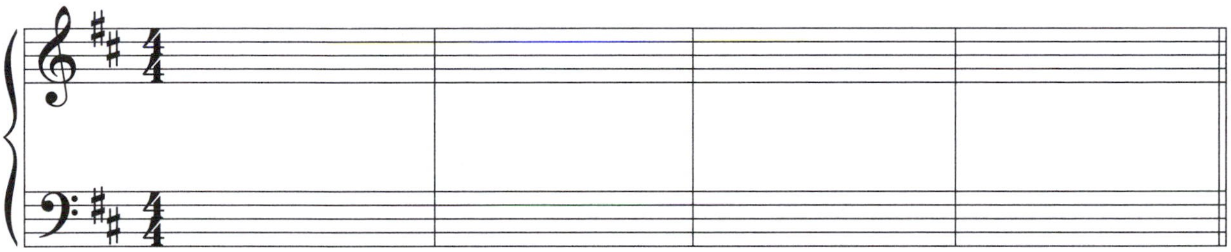

I $\quad$ I^6 $\quad$ V^7 $\quad$ vi $\quad$ ii^6 $\quad$ V^7 $\quad$ I

Escape Tone, Neighbor Group

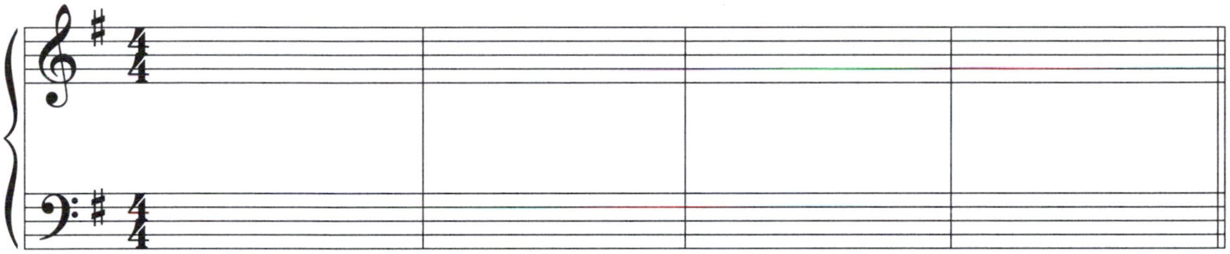

i $\quad$ iv^6 $\quad$ V^6_5 $\quad$ i $\quad$ iv^6 $\quad$ V^6_5 $\quad$ VI

Neighbor Tone, Appoggiatura, Escape Tone

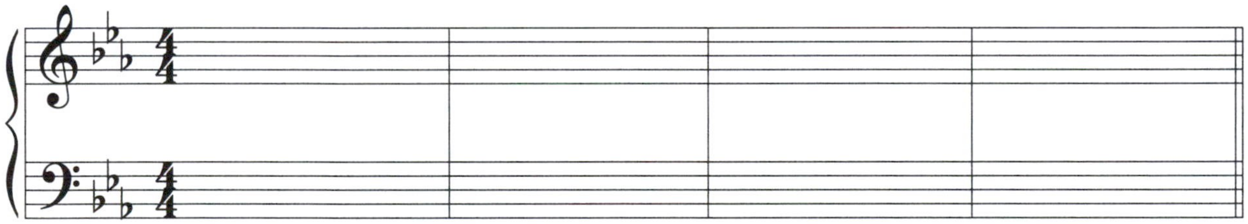

i $\quad$ vii^{o6} $\quad$ i^6 $\quad$ i $\quad$ ii^{o6} $\quad$ V^7 $\quad$ i

Anticipation, Passing Tone, Neighbor Group

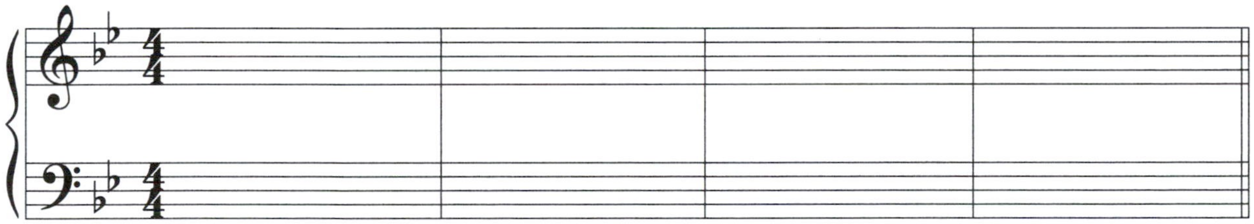

I $\quad$ V^6 $\quad$ vi $\quad$ IV $\quad$ V^4_2 $\quad$ I^6 $\quad$ I

III. A simplified version of Bach's "Aus meines Herzens Grunde" is notated below. Analyze the chords with Roman numerals and embellish the chorale with various types of non-chord tones.

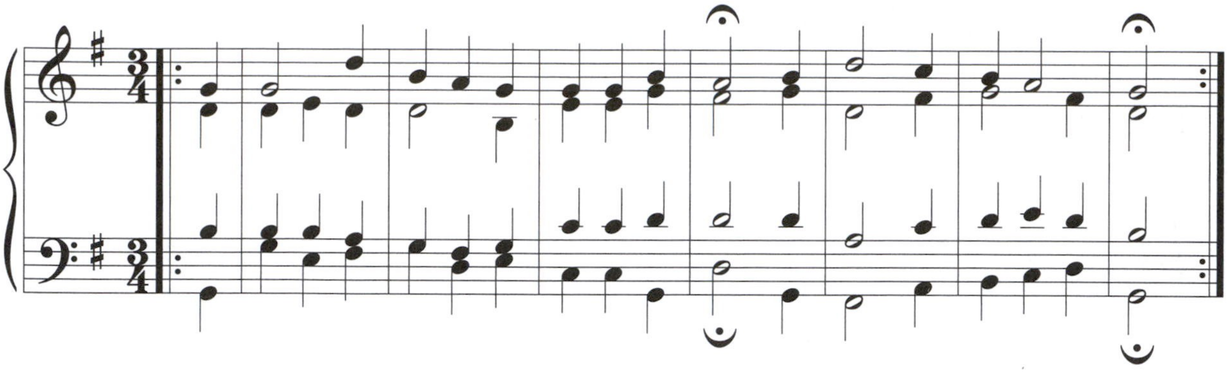

ANALYSIS

1. Return to the score excerpt from "Some Nights" on page 138. Remember how you were asked to circle the pitches not in the chord? Try to label all of the pitches you circled with the correct non-chord tone identifier.
2. Flip back to your analysis of "Batti, batti" and "Vaga luna" from Chapter 8. The non-chord tones are notated in parentheses in both of these examples. Label all of the non-chord tones used in the charts below.

Mozart, "Batti, Batti" from *Don Giovanni* page 156 (vocal line only)

Measure 1 ______ ______

Measure 2 ______

Measure 3 ______ ______

Measure 4 ______

Measure 7 ______ ______ ______

Bellini, "Vaga luna" page 161 (accompaniment line only)

Measure 6 ______

Measure 9 ______ ______

Measure 10 ______

Measure 12 ______ ______

3. Analyze the following chorale using Roman numerals and figured bass. Be sure to circle and identify any non-chord tones. Label the cadences at the end of each phrase. Do not give a Roman numeral for the chord marked with an asterisk (*). Hint: it is possible to leave out the fifth of any chord; however, this practice is mostly used with seventh chords.

VIDEO
TRACK 7

Bach, "Nun ruhen alle Wälder"

4. This excerpt is taken from Mozart's *Clarinet Quintet in A Major*, K. 581. Give a Roman numeral analysis for the entire excerpt and identify all of the non-chord tones. Remember that the clarinet in A sounds down a minor third from the written pitch.

VIDEO
TRACK 8

Mozart, "Menuetto" from *Clarinet Quintet in A Major*, K. 581, Mvt. III

Mozart, "Menuetto" from *Clarinet Quintet in A Major*, K. 581, Mvt. III *(continued)*

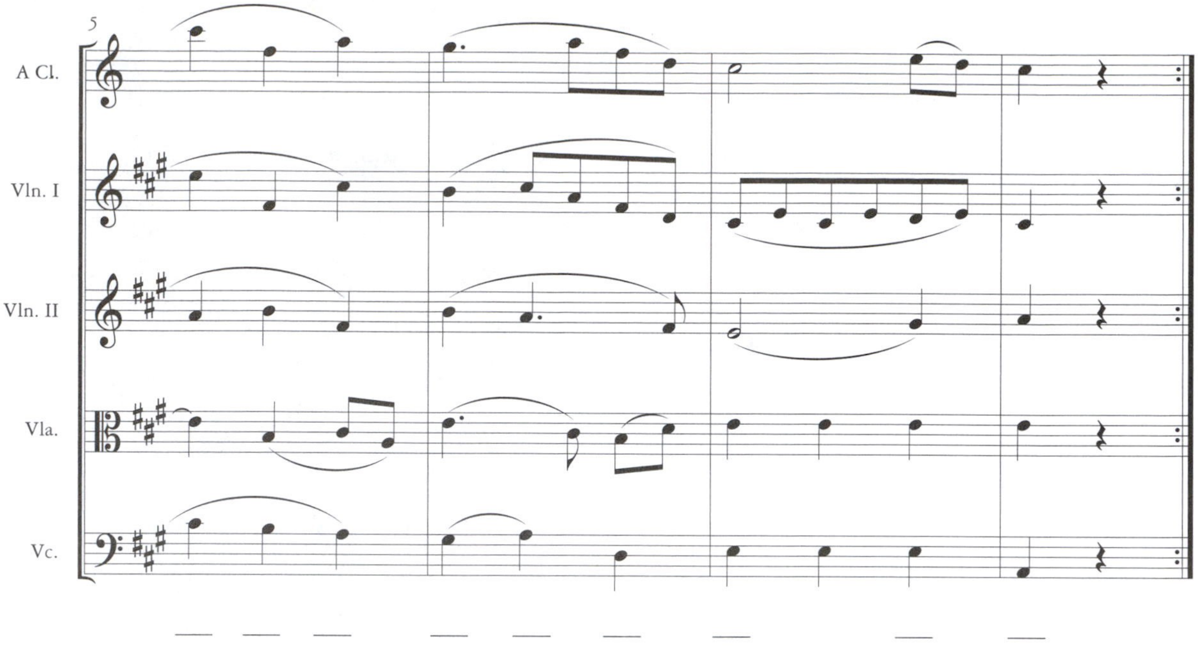

AURAL SKILLS CONDITIONING 10

Singing Chorale Phrases with Non-chord Tones

Following are three chorale phrases in four parts (soprano, alto, tenor, and bass). With your class or a small group of students, divide up into four groups and sing the examples using solfège syllables. Before you start, label the non-chord tones and cadences. The first example has been done for you.

In the final cadence, the leading tone in the alto voice leaps down to *sol* instead of resolving up to *do*. Why does the resolution still sound final when you put all the voices together?

1.

In the first beat, the soprano moves up by step from A♭ to B♭ and resolves down by leaping to the G. How would you label this non-chord tone? How does the V chord in measure 1 resolve? Why should the moving eighth notes at the beginning of measure 2 *not* be labeled as NCTs?

2.

Fmin: i V^{7} VI iv V i

The tenor leaps up from A to C♯ on beat 3 and resolves up by step to D. What is this non-chord tone called? (Hint: it is the opposite of that first NCT in example 2.) Identify the NCT in the soprano in measure 2.

3.

D: I IV$^{6}_{4}$ (Ped) I vi ii^{6} V I

Hearing Non-chord Tones in a Chorale Phrase

You will hear four progressions, each with one or two non-chord tones, performed by your instructor in the classroom or on the course website. Circle the non-chord tone(s) you hear from the choices below. Does it move by leap or step? Does it resolve by leap or step? And remember: not every eighth note is a non-chord tone!

AUDIO TRACKS CH. 10 HEARING NCT 1–4

1. Passing tone Neighbor tone Appoggiatura Escape tone
2. Passing tone Neighbor tone Appoggiatura Escape tone
3. Passing tone Neighbor tone Appoggiatura Escape tone
4. Passing tone Neighbor tone Appoggiatura Escape tone

THE FINAL NOTE: REAL-WORLD PERSPECTIVE

Jeff Watson

VICE PRESIDENT OF INTERACTIVE MARKETING AT WARNER BROTHER RECORDS

What course or courses did you take in college that best prepared you for your career? How so?

The best courses I took in both my bachelors and masters in communication were those that focus on critical thinking in the media space. I was able to get a top-down view of how media is disseminated across various cultures out outlets.

Did you ever study music formally? Lessons, music theory, composition? If so, has the study of music helped you in your career? If so, how?

While I did not study music formally, I got ground-level experience by joining bands as a signed artist (to Warner Bros Records, who turned out to be my current employer). I learned the business of the industry with the view of an artist.

Most significant learning experience of your career . . . or the "Aha" moment.

Interestingly, my failures have provided the best learning experiences. My career as a signed artist was full of mistakes and wrong choices, and it taught me what *not* to do in my career. I have learned from the errors I made and have been able to apply them to my business world.

If you could give one piece of advice to a young student interested in studying the music business, what would that be?

Intern, intern, intern! Being an intern in the music business is the best way to not only learn the basics, but (most importantly) also to make contacts that can help advance a career.

What, or who, inspired you to study music?

I am a true fan—through and through—and my musical heroes were the ones that inspired me to not only play, but also learn about the inner workings of the business. My main inspiration as a teenager was The Edge from U2. I learned guitar by listening carefully to his playing and studying his style.

CHAPTER 11

NON-CHORD TONES II

Artist in Residence: Ella Fitzgerald

Chapter Objectives

- Define suspension and retardation
- Identify suspensions and retardation with figured bass symbols
- Identify non-chord tones within a context of a musical score
- Compose a suspension and retardation when given chord progression
- Review all non-chord tones within context of musical score (jazz and classical)

Mention the name Ella Fitzgerald to many born before 1970 and you will watch their minds transported to a different time and place. The songs of Ella Fitzgerald evoke memories of smoky rooms and slow dancing on crowded floors. In an article from *The New York Times* the author describes Fitzgerald as ". . . the First Lady of Song, [she] practically invented scat and helped establish the popular standard as an art form." Listen to her rendition of the popular standard "Cry Me a River." Close your eyes while you listen and see whether you can understand why Ella Fitzgerald is called the "First Lady of Song."

WEBSITE
VIDEO TRACK 9

The middle section of this song (2:24) is altered in both key and style. The tempo is faster, and the key has modulated to D minor.[1] The main chords are all diatonic, with an occasional added six. Play through these chords on your guitar or keyboard. What exactly is an A^{7}sus?

Dmin Gmin6 A7 Dmin Gmin Gmin6 A7sus A7

SUSPENSION

The notated sus in a lead sheet symbol represents the term suspension. In both classical and popular music, the **suspension** is a non-chord tone that is "suspended" from the previous chord and resolved down in the next chord by step. It is like one pitch didn't get the memo that the harmony was changing. Let's look at the last three chords in the progression.

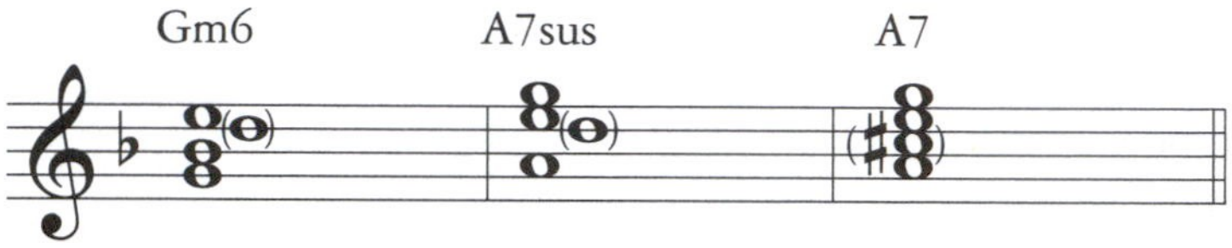

The A^{7}sus tells the performer to play a fourth above the root as a substitute for the third of the chord. The non-chord tone is resolved in the next chord: in this case, the movement from the D to C♯ in the A^7. The D in the A^{7sus} is suspended from the D found in the Gmin^6 chord.

What is so effective about suspensions, and why they are so compelling, has to do with their placement. Unlike the non-chord tones studied in Chapter 10, suspensions tend to be placed on strong beats, creating dissonance and a desired resolution in a prominent place in the melodic line.

In most popular music, the suspension is a 4–3 suspension, meaning that the fourth above the root resolves to a third above the root. However, there are other suspensions common in classical music and jazz, most notably the 9–8 suspension. Study the following examples, and play them on your keyboard. The category of suspension is based on its distance from the bass note. While in popular music, this is typically the root, the bass note may or may not be the root in all styles of music. Suspensions are *always* calculated by the distance of the suspended pitch and the note of resolution in relation to the lowest sounding pitch of the chord. Play through all of the examples of suspensions on your keyboard.

4–3

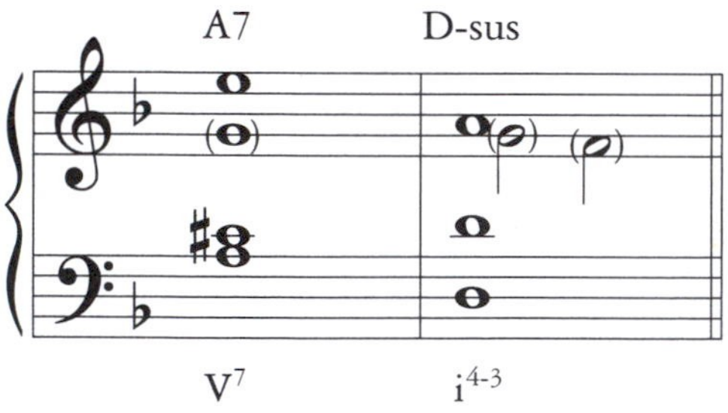

9–8

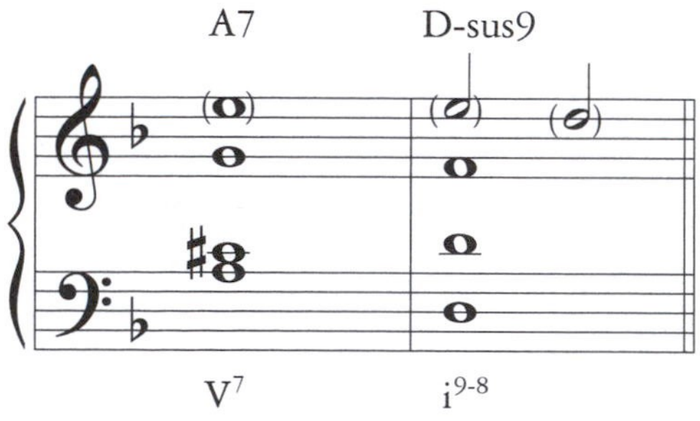

[1]See pages 282–294 for more information about modulations.

7–6

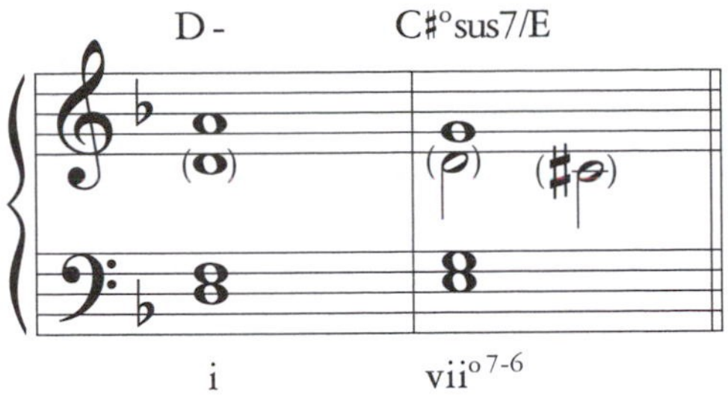

The 2–3 suspension is called the bass suspension. The numbers 2 and 3 refer to the distance between the suspension pitch (the bass) and the pitch of most dissonance, in this case the F. The 3 refers to the resulting interval in the resolution.

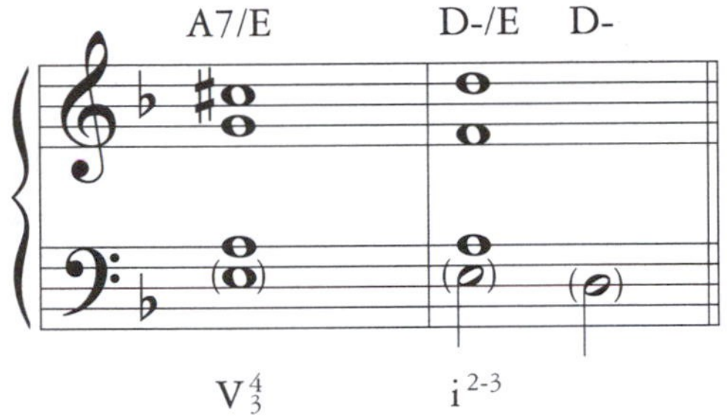

Listen to Ella Fitzgerald's rendition of "In the Still of the Night." The suspension has been marked for you in the score at measure 59. The pitch C in the melody does not fit into the G minor harmony, so it must be a non-chord tone. Which one? The pitch C is suspended from the D^7 chord and resolves down by step. The resolution occurs on the last beat of measure 59.

WEBSITE
VIDEO TRACK 10

Ella Fitzgerald, "In the Still of the Night." Songwriter: Cole Porter

VIDEO TRACK 11

An example of a 7–6 suspension is found in the song "You're the Top" from the 1934 musical *Anything Goes* by Cole Porter. The vocal line in measure 46 is notated with the pitch F supported with an E♭ major harmony. Well this isn't possible as a chord tone, right? So the F is suspended from the B♭^{7} chord and resolves down to the E♭. The distance from the bass (G) to the suspended F is a seventh, which resolves to the interval of the sixth.

Although the suspension is written in the original score by Cole Porter, Fitzgerald chooses to not hold the F over into the E♭ major chord. Because the pitch is not suspended over, no suspension can be heard in this particular performance.

Ella Fitzgerald, "You're the Top." Songwriter: Cole Porter

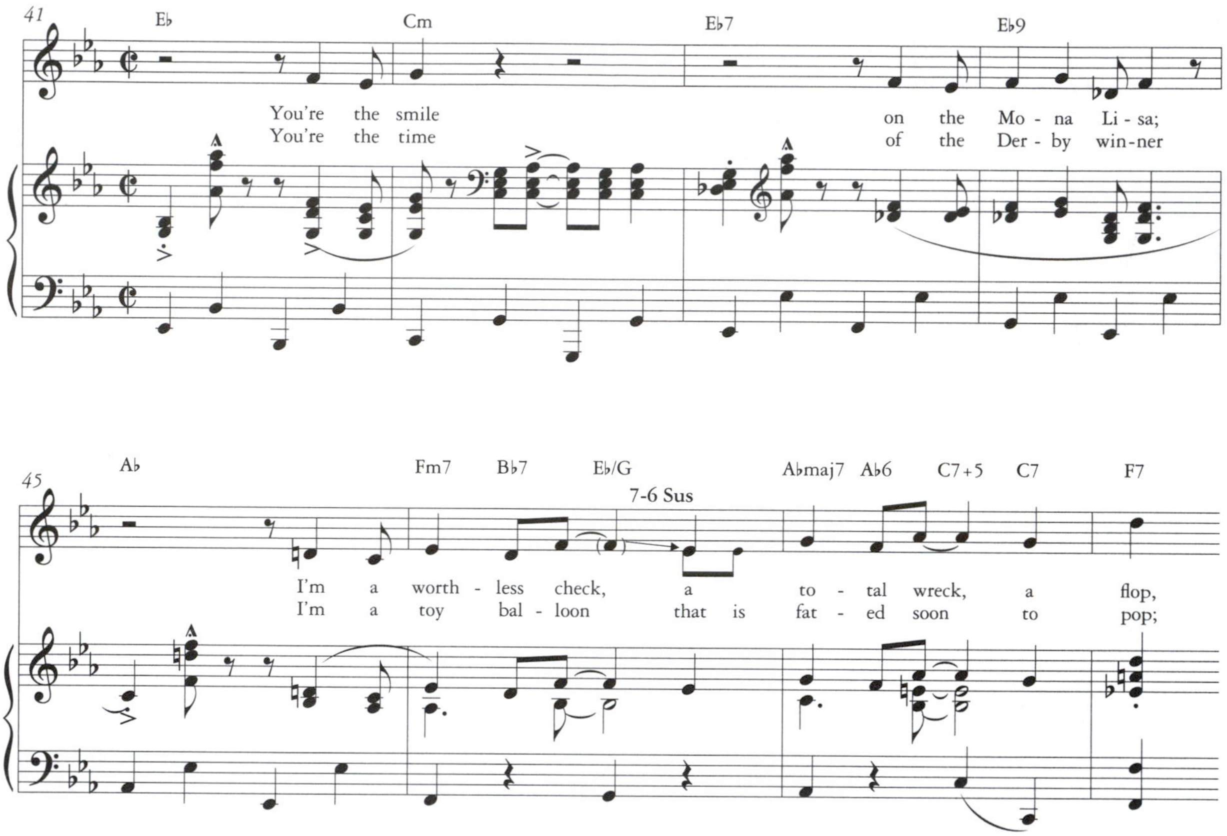

ARTIST IN RESIDENCE

First Lady of Song

They say that to properly sing the blues, you have to have lived the blues. There is no doubt that Fitzgerald's life was full of triumph and heartache, all of which can be heard in her musical performances. After her mother and father separated following her birth, Fitzgerald went to live in Yonkers, New York. It was here that she would take the train into Harlem to watch the acts at the Apollo Theater. Her love for music and performing grew into a passion.

In 1932, Fitzgerald's mother was killed in a car accident, an extremely painful experience for the young singer. In the 2 years following, she was alone and barely surviving.

In 1934, her luck changed when her name was pulled in a weekly drawing at the Apollo to perform on amateur night. A star was born, and she began to win every talent show she could find. In 4 short years, after touring with swing bands, Fitzgerald made her first recording, "A-Tisket, A Tasket." It soared immediately to number 1, where it stayed on the charts for 17 weeks. Listen to Fitzgerald's rendition of this popular nursery rhyme. Even though the basic melody is present through the entire excerpt, Fitzgerald puts her own stamp on it with her runs and improvisatory style.

WEBSITE

VIDEO TRACK 12

Fitzgerald went on to record over 200 albums, including the iconic *Ella Fitzgerald Sings the Cole Porter Songbook*, featuring the music of the great composer Cole Porter. She won 13 Grammy Awards, including Best Female Vocal Performance for *Ella Fitzgerald Sings the Irving Berlin Song Book* and Best Individual Jazz Performance for *Ella Fitzgerald Sings the Duke Ellington Song Book.*

RETARDATION

Just like the suspended note that did not get the message that the chords have moved on, a **retardation** is held over from the previous chord but resolves upward to a chord tone. The following examples indicate common retardations found in classical music. Retardations are much more common in classical music, although jazz musicians use them to "slide" up into pitches of a final cadence. There are no particular lead sheet symbols to indicate a retardation because they are most often performed in the melody line in an improvisational style.

7–8

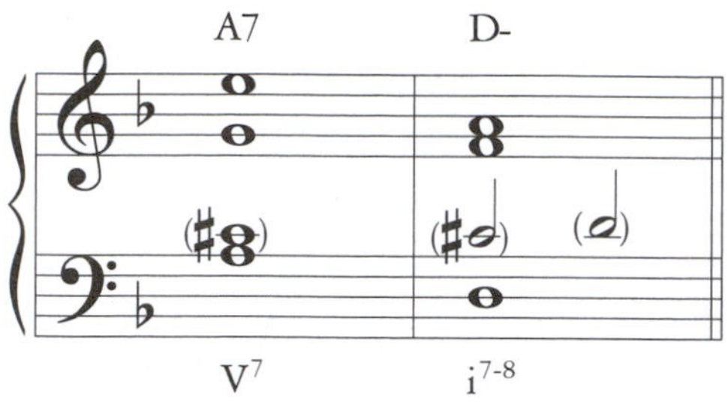

2–3

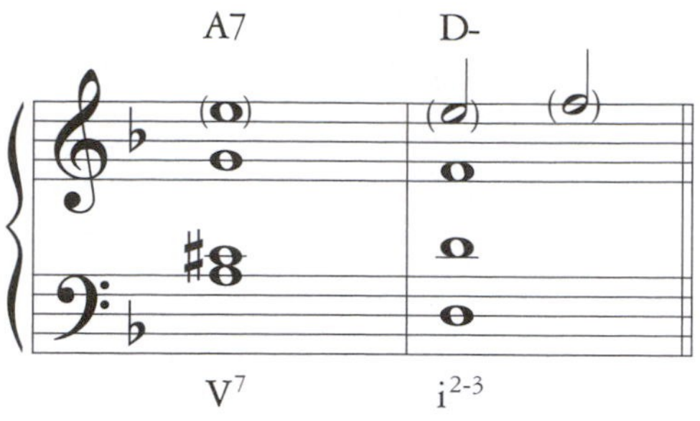

VIDEO TRACK 13

Listen to the exceptional 1957 performance of the song "Love for Sale." The original key of the piece is shown below, although Fitzgerald's rendition in this performance is dropped a fourth to the key of F major.

This excerpt includes both suspensions and retardations. In measure 34, the harmony is an A♭^{7}, but the pitch B♭ is held over from the previous E♭ chord. The non-chord tone, in this case the retardation, is approached by the same pitch and resolves up.

Ella Fitzgerald, "Love for Sale." Songwriter: Cole Porter

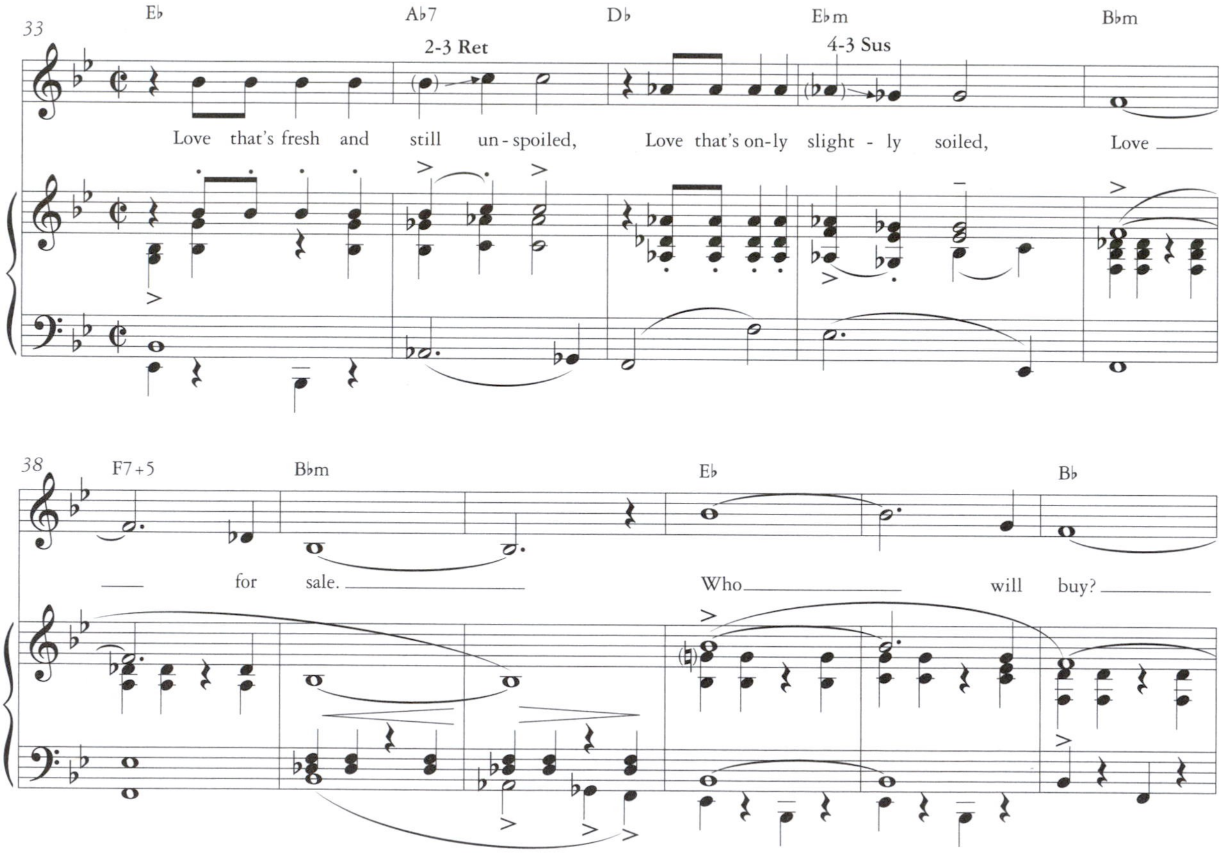

BACKSTAGE PASS

Black and White

By the late 1950s, Ella Fitzgerald was at the height of her career. She had won several Grammy Awards and was touring the country with Louis Armstrong. However, all was not rosy for a black woman in this particular decade. In 1955, Rosa Parks was arrested for refusing to give up her bus seat to a white passenger in Montgomery, Alabama. In 1957, the governor of Arkansas called in the National Guard to prevent African American students from entering the public high school. Talented or not, Fitzgerald was still a black woman touring in the Deep South. It was even reported that one television show put Vaseline on the camera lens so that viewers could not tell what race the musicians were! While on tour in Texas, a police squad barged backstage to hassle the performers. They came into Fitzgerald's dressing room, where band members, including Dizzy Gillespie and Illinois Jacquet, were shooting dice, and arrested everyone. The papers made fun of the police, reporting that "Miss Fitzgerald, wearing a décolleté gown of blue taffeta and a mink stole, was one of the most handsomely dressed women ever to visit the Houston police station." Fitzgerald said, "When we got there, they had the nerve to ask for an autograph."

She also received support from numerous celebrity fans, including a zealous Marilyn Monroe. Fitzgerald later said,

I owe Marilyn Monroe a real debt. It was because of her that I played the Mocambo, a very popular nightclub in the '50s. She personally called the owner of the Mocambo, and told him she wanted me booked immediately, and if he would do it, she would take a front table every night. She told him—and it was true, due to Marilyn's superstar status—that the press would go wild. The owner said yes, and Marilyn was there, front table, every night. The press went overboard. After that, I never had to play a small jazz club again. She was an unusual woman—a little ahead of her times. And she didn't know it.

Reviewing Chapter Objectives

- Define suspension and retardation (pages 208, 211)
- Identify suspensions and retardation with figured bass symbols (pages 208–209, 212)
- Identify non-chord tones within a context of a musical score (pages 209–210, 212–213)
- Compose a suspension and retardation when given chord progression (page 215)
- Review all non-chord tones within context of musical score (jazz and classical) (pages 216–217)

EXERCISES

I. Circle and identify the non-chord tones in the following progressions. The Roman numeral analysis has been given. Be sure to specify the type of suspension and retardation in terms of figured bass.

II. Write out the following chords on the staff. Insert a suspension of any type. Be sure that the seventh of the chord resolves down!

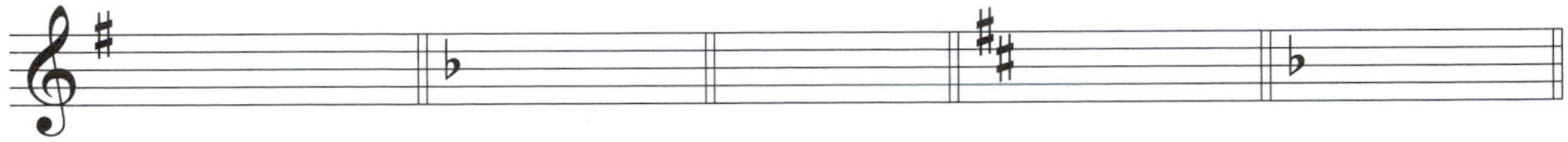

G: V^7 I Dmin: i V^6 C: V^7 vi Bmin: iv V^7 F: vi^7 IV^6

III. Complete a Roman numeral analysis for the following chorales. Be sure to circle and identify all non-chord tones. Identify the type of second inversion chords and specify the type of suspension and retardation in terms of figured bass.

D:

Fmin:

IV. Two chord progressions are given below. Using SATB voicing and smooth voice leading, correctly notate the chords on the staff and insert the non-chord tones as indicated.

Suspension, Neighbor Tone, Anticipation, Escape Tone

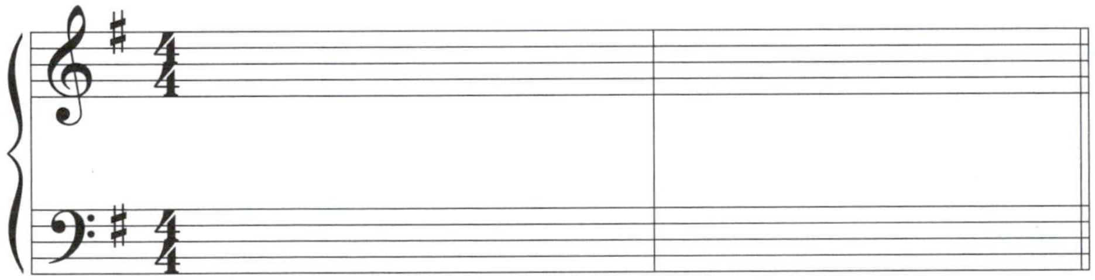

G: I ii^6 V vi IV^6 V^7 I

Retardation, Passing Tone, Appoggiatura, Neighbor Group

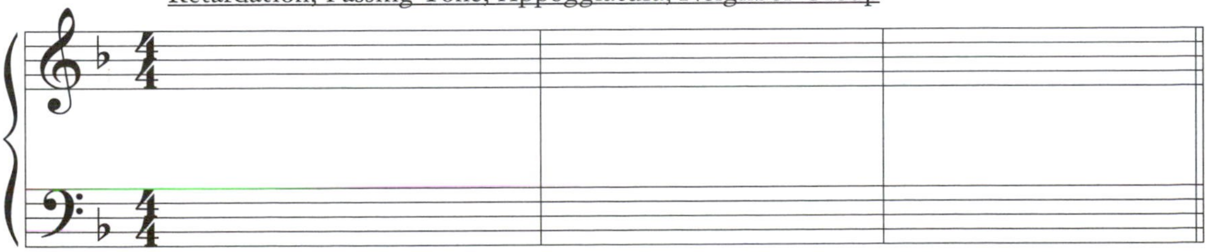

Dmin: i ii^{o6} V^6_5 i iv i^6_5 V^7 i

VIDEO TRACK 14

V. Give the lead sheet symbols for the excerpts below. Circle all pitches that are not found in the corresponding harmony, and identify each non-chord tone by type. Do not attempt a Roman numeral analysis.

Daniel Barenboim, Beethoven's *Sonata No. 8 in C Minor, Op. 13* ("Pathétique"), Mvt. III

a.

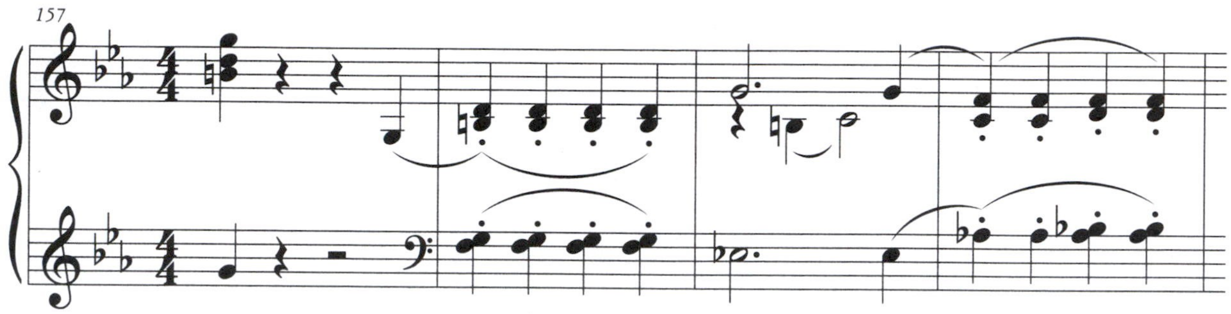

b.

ANALYSIS

VIDEO TRACKS 15 AND 16

Complete a non-chord tone analysis for the following pieces. The lead sheet symbols are given to you. Circle all pitches that are not found in the corresponding harmony, and identify each non-chord tone by type. Do not attempt a Roman numeral analysis.

In this first example, there are two extended triad chords, the Gm^9 (G–B♭–D–F–A) and C^9 (C–E–G–B♭–D). We will learn more about these in a later chapter, but for now circle the pitches that are not part of the chord and identify each.

Ella Fitzgerald, "Autumn in New York" (1934). Songwriter: Vernon Duke

Bernadette Peters, "My Romance" (1935). Songwriter: Richard Rodgers

COMPOSITION PROJECT

Composers and musicians throughout history have been fascinated with the structure of sixteen measures. In pop and jazz, this is known as the sixteen-bar blues. In musical theater, most auditions require you to have a sixteen-bar audition piece. In classical music, the sixteen-measure format most used is the double period, a phrase structure that includes four phrases in which the first three phrases end with an inconclusive cadence and the final phrase ends with a complete cadence (PAC). Most often, phrase 1 and phrase 3 are similar in terms of melodic content. Study the following phrase chart.

Melodic content	a	b	a′	c
Measure numbers	1–4	5–8	9–12	13–16
Cadences	IAC	HC	IAC	CC

Using the chart as your guide in terms of phrase structure, begin to outline a basic chord progression and melody line. Pay careful attention to the use of cadences.

There is no doubt that non-chord tones add interest to a musical line. However, it is up to you, as the composer, to decide how elaborate you would like that melody line to be. For this project, begin with a basic progression as discussed in Chapter 8. Use the following guidelines as you begin your compositional process:

- Use both root position and inverted chords. Include seventh chords as well as triads.
- Keep harmonic rhythm moving at no more than two chords per measure.
- In the melody line, include at least five different non-chord tones, at least one of which should be a suspension. Label any NCT you use.
- Analyze composition using lead sheet symbols *and* Roman numerals.

AURAL SKILLS CONDITIONING 11

Hearing Non-chord Tones: "We Are the World" and "In Remembrance"

WEBSITE
VIDEO TRACK 17

WEBSITE
VIDEO TRACK 18

In Chapter 2, you were introduced to the famous collaboration "We Are the World." Go back and listen to this original version on the YouTube channel. The last line of the first stanza ends with a very obvious suspension sung by Kenny Rogers. Watch and listen to how Rogers handles this non-chord tone. He leans into the dissonant pitch. It's pretty obvious that Rogers knows the suspended note is not a part of the chord. His interpretation makes the resolution very effective and settling. Compare the 1985 version to the more recent 2010 video. How is that same spot handled in 2010? Is it as effective, less effective, or more effective than the way in which Rogers handles the dissonance?

Listen to "In Remembrance" by Jeffery L. Ames on the YouTube channel. Start paying careful attention around 0:43, when the upper voices sing a retardation on the word "Eis." How do they perform this non-chord tone? Do they linger on it or hastily make their way to the resolution? At around 0:53, an inner voice sings a beautifully dissonant note on the "ne" of "Domine." This is actually an appoggiatura, leaping up a major third and resolving down by step. Can you identify by ear the type of cadence at 0:53? Hint: it defies our expectations. After this point, the inner voice continues down a chain of suspensions. Can you hear this tension and release? How does the dissonance in the inner voices add to the mood of the piece?

Singing Chorale Phrases with Non-chord Tones

Below are three chorale phrases in four parts (soprano, alto, tenor, and bass). With your class or a small group of students, divide up in four groups and sing the examples using solfège syllables. Identify each cadence and non-chord tone. For non-chord tones notated on a strong beat, experiment with different performance styles in order to bring out the dissonance.

Hearing Non-chord Tones in Chorale Phrases

You will hear four progressions performed by your instructor in the classroom or on the course website. Each progression includes one or two non-chord tones. Circle the non-chord tone(s) you hear. Identify the type of suspension, if applicable.

AUDIO TRACKS CH. 11 HEARING NCT 1–4

1. Passing tone   Neighbor tone   Appoggiatura   Escape tone

   Suspension (   )   Retardation

2. Passing tone   Neighbor tone   Appoggiatura   Escape tone

Suspension (   )   Retardation

3. Passing Tone   Neighbor tone   Appoggiatura   Escape tone

Suspension (   )   Retardation

4. Passing tone   Neighbor tone   Appoggiatura   Escape tone

Suspension (   )   Retardation

Other Examples for Individual Study

WEBSITE

VIDEO TRACKS 19 AND 20

1. Cambridge Singers, "The Turtle Dove"

   Pay close attention around 1:07 for a very clear bass suspension. Can you hear how the bass voices give a slight accent to the suspended pitch and decrescendo slightly on the resolution? Stunning! What do you think of this performance?

2. Martha Argerich, Ravel's *Piano Concerto in G,* Mvt. II.

   Referring to the opening of this piece, Maurice Ravel said, "That flowing phrase! How I worked over it bar by bar! It nearly killed me!" Pay special attention to the retardation around 2:10. How does Argerich handle this non-chord tone? For an extra challenge, try to identify by ear each time you hear a non-chord tone in this piano solo opening. The harmony features more extended chords and jazz sounds (as it was written in the 1930s), so it might be hard to tell what notes belong in the chord. However, Ravel places special emphasis on some resolutions, so mark where you hear a noticeable resolution.

CHAPTER 12

SECONDARY DOMINANTS

Artist in Residence: Billy Joel

Chapter Objectives

- Define chromatic chord and secondary dominant
- Recognize secondary dominants in context
- Spell secondary dominants in various keys
- Resolve secondary dominants using correct voice leading
- Compose a short song using secondary dominants

Over the past few chapters you have become familiar with diatonic chords: chords that contain pitches found within the key of a piece. But there are many instances within a song in which the harmonies include pitches not found in the key. These chromatic pitches (*chromatic*, from the Greek *chromos*, means "color") add not only variety in the qualities of chords used, but also color to the harmonies. Let's look at a commonly used progression found in both classical and popular music. Play through the progression on your guitar or keyboard.

D:	D	G	E-/G	A	D
	I	IV	ii^6	V	I

Sounds like something you would hear on the radio, right? The chords seem to flow, and by inverting the E minor chord, the bass line is relatively smooth. But what if we wanted to extend this progression? What if we wanted to add chromatic pitches that functioned in a way to create a smooth progression?

One of the most effective ways to extend a progression is through the use of a **secondary dominant chord,** a chromatic major or Mm7 chord that is used to tonicize a chord whose root is a fifth below. Any chord can be preceded by its dominant. The vii° and ii° are exceptions to this rule, but more on that later.

Using the initial progression and lead sheet symbols only, let's insert a dominant of E minor before the ii chord and a dominant seventh of A major before the V chord. The dominant of E minor is B major, and the dominant seventh of A is E^7.

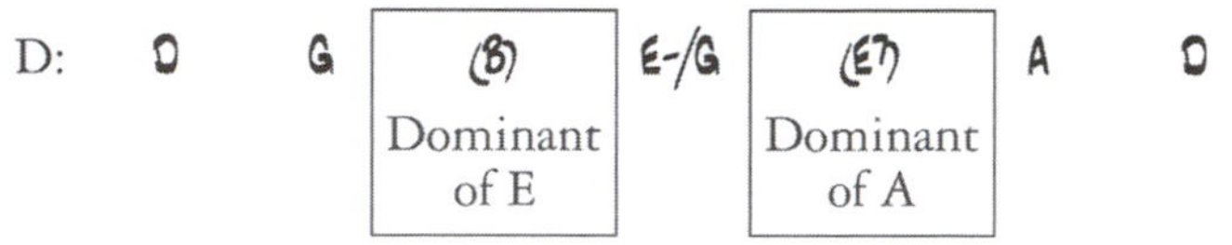

Play through the progression. The B major and E^7 both include pitches that are not diatonic to the original key of D; therefore, both chords are tonicizing, or using the key signature of the chord to the right.

Sound confusing? Let's take the pitches of the B major chord: B, D♯, F♯. You cannot explain the D♯ in the key of D, so the B must be a chromatic chord. Your first instinct should be to see whether the chromatic chord is the dominant of the chord next in the progression. B *is* the V of E minor, thus the chord is explained as a dominant of E minor, the V/E– or V/ii.[1]

Play through the following progression before studying the Roman numeral analysis.

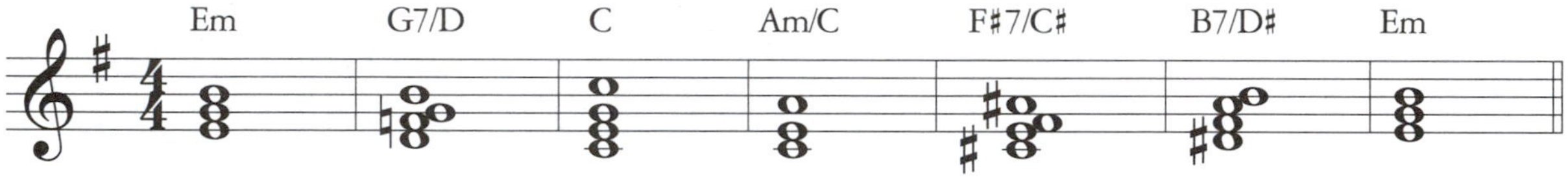

The two chords that cannot be explained diatonically in the key of E minor are the G^7 and the F♯^{7}. G^7 is the dominant of C, and F♯^{7} is the dominant of B. Both of these chromatic chords are secondary dominants because they temporarily function as a dominant seventh of their target chord, or the chord being tonicized (C major and B major).

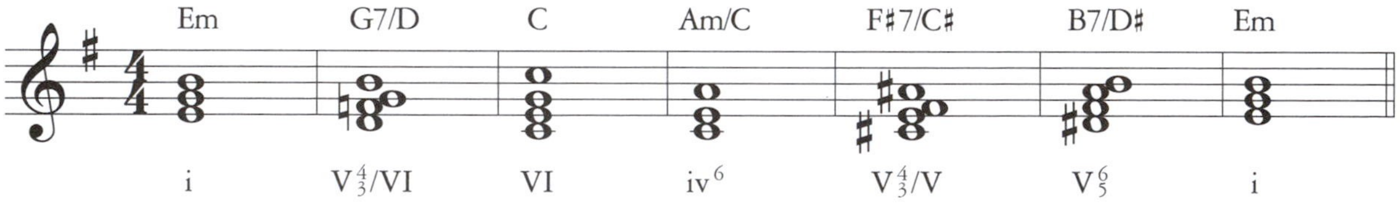

[1]In jazz music, the secondary dominant is not typically written as a V/V, V/ii, V/vi, and so forth. Instead, most jazz players opt to use Roman numerals that indicate the changes in quality only, but still refer to the chords as dominant II, dominant VI, dominant III, and so on. The D major progression presented here would be analyzed as I, IV, VI, ii, II^7, V, and I. One of the most common progressions in jazz is the I, II^7, V^7, I, where the II^7 is substituting for the ii.

ARTIST IN RESIDENCE

The Piano Man

With a career spanning over 4 decades, Billy Joel has left a legacy of piano-pounding hits. Born in the Bronx in 1949, Joel is old enough to be somebody's grandpa, but don't underestimate the impact of this living legend's career on the music industry. It all started with the household piano and some stern encouragement from his Jewish mother. From infancy, Joel thumped around on the piano often played by his father, a classically trained pianist. After 4 years, Joel's mother insisted that he start taking lessons. Joel recalls her saying, "If you're going to bang on the piano you're going to bang right." Despite name-calling and bullying from the neighborhood kids, Joel stuck with his musical passions and studied until the age of 16. Although a proficient pianist, Joel did not excel academically. He failed to complete high school and became a full-time musician determined to make it as a solo artist. After his debut album flopped, Joel moved to Los Angeles and began playing as a lounge pianist: his experiences would soon be immortalized in his iconic song "Piano Man." Released by Clive Davis under Columbia Records, the *Piano Man* album launched Joel into the commercial spotlight, where he's been ever since.

RECOGNIZING SECONDARY DOMINANTS IN CONTEXT

Joel's song "The Longest Time" peaked at number 14 on the Billboard Hot 100 on May 12, 1984. It remained on that list for a total of 56 weeks (13 months). It's pretty amazing that this song never made the top 10 on the Hot 100 considering how many a capella groups have covered it over the past decade! This short excerpt contains two secondary dominants. The lead sheet symbols are given along with the score notation. Looking at the lead sheets symbols, can you decipher what chords are diatonic and what chords are chromatic?

WEBSITE
VIDEO TRACK 21

Billy Joel, "The Longest Time." Songwriter: Billy Joel

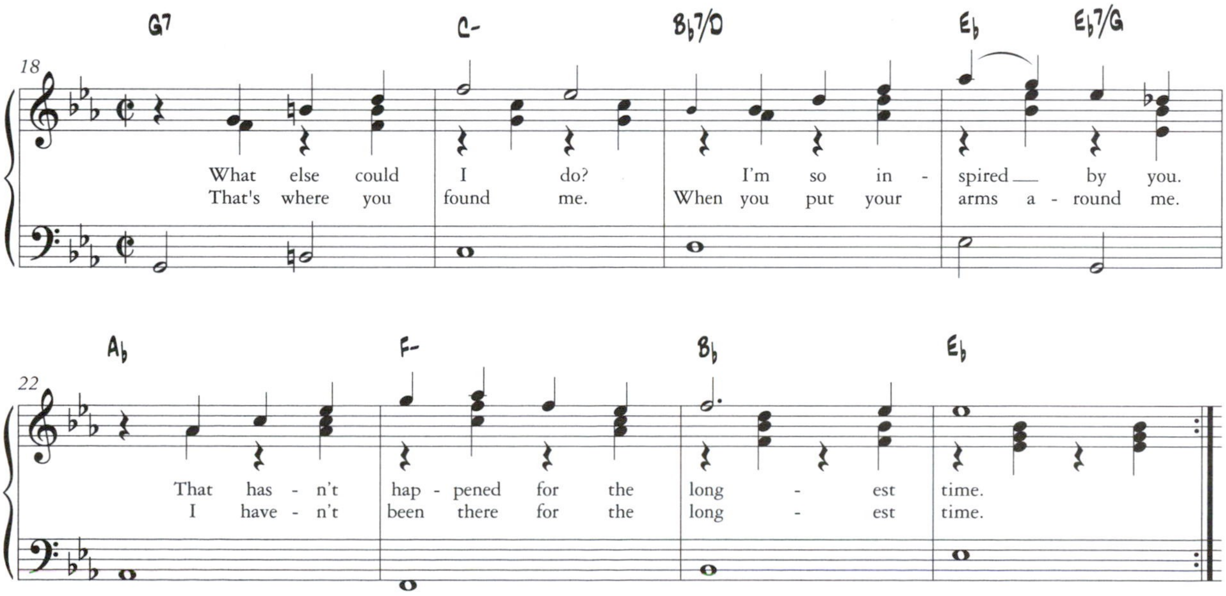

The original key of the song is E♭ major; therefore, the diatonic chords in this excerpt would be C minor (vi), B♭ major (V), E♭ major (I), A♭ major (IV), and F minor (ii). That leaves us with a G^7 and a $E\flat^7$ that can not be explained in the key of E♭.

- The G^7 chord is the dominant of C minor, and C minor is the next chord in the progression. We can label the G^7 as a V^7/C– *or* a V^7/vi (in that vi represents C, the sixth scale degree in the original key of E♭).

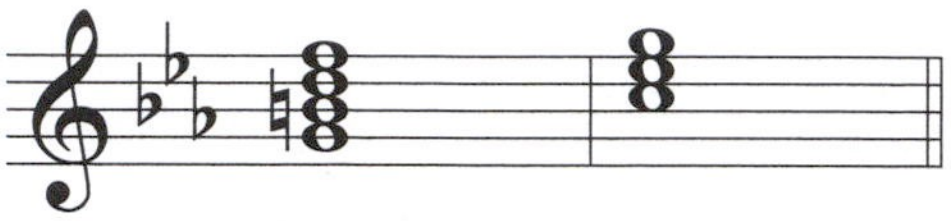

- The $E\flat^7$ chord is the dominant of A♭ major, and A♭ major is the immediate proceeding chord. We can label the $E\flat^7$ as a V^7/A♭ *or* a V^7/IV (in that IV represents the A♭, the fourth scale degree in the original key of E♭).

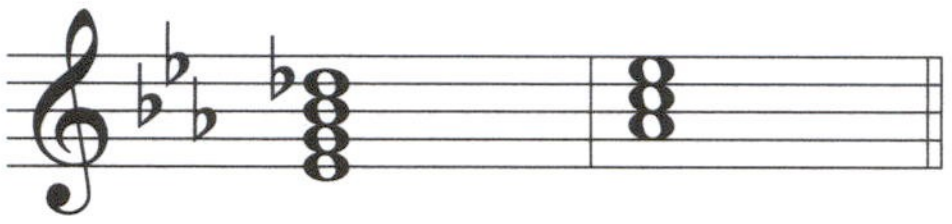

Look at the complete analysis shown below. After listening to the piece, can you see how the vi–V–I–IV–ii–V–I progression is extended with the use of secondary dominants?

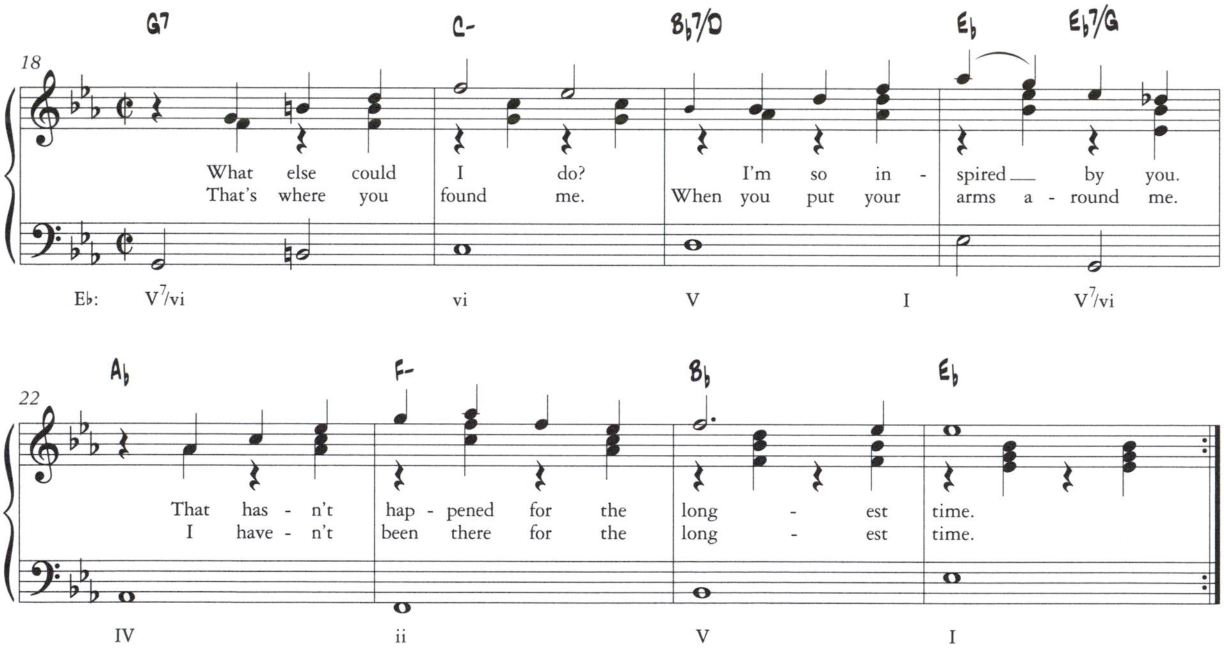

Music is a medium of emotion. Joel wrote "Lullabye (Goodnight My Angel)" (released on his 1993 album *River of Dreams*) to answer the innocent question posed by his then 7-year-old daughter: "Daddy, what happens when we die?" Because he was also separating from his wife Christie Brinkley at the time, Joel was concerned that his daughter was really asking him whether he was going to leave her.

Watch Joel's performance of "Lullabye (Goodnight, My Angel)" before reading through the analysis. Listen to the classical implications and progressions of this song. What classical elements are included on the music video? How is this sound different from that of "The Longest Time" or other hits from *An Innocent Man*?

WEBSITE
VIDEO TRACK 22

Billy Joel, "Lullabye (Goodnight, My Angel)." Songwriter: Billy Joel

"Lullabye (Goodnight, My Angel)" is composed in the key of G major. The poignant melody solidifies this key by the end of the first verse where the half cadence is extended on the D major chord. The chromatic harmonies in the first verse include C minor, G^7, and A. Let's look at each chord individually.

- The C minor is a borrowed chord, meaning that pitches are borrowed from the parallel minor (G minor). More on this in Chapter 14.
- The G^7 chord is in fact a V^7 in the key of C major. We can label this chord as a V^7/C or a V^7/IV. It resolves normally to the IV chord as expected.

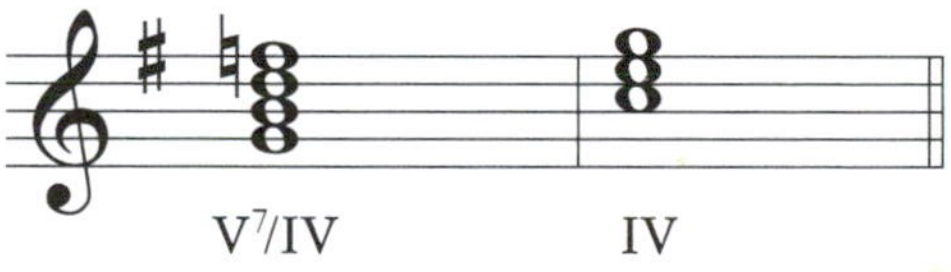

- The A major chords (Asus, A, A^7) found in measure 19 are dominants in the key of D major. We can label this chord as a V/D or a V/V. However, it does not resolve immediately to the V (D) as expected, but is interrupted by the IV chord.[2]

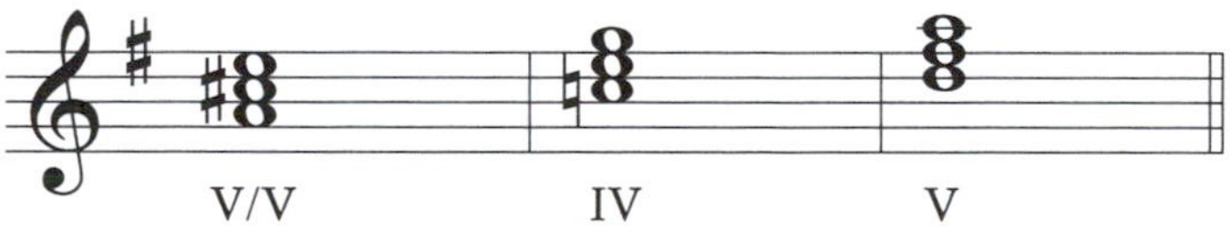

Another fan favorite, "Scenes from an Italian Restaurant" was completed by Joel during the recording process of *The Stranger* (1977). It is actually the product of several song

[2]The A major chord in measure 12 is not functioning as a secondary dominant. Play through the chords slowly in closed position. The C♯ and E are passing down to the C and E in the ii chord in measure 13.

VIDEO TRACK 23

snippets Joel was working on at the time. Composed with the image of the Manhattan restaurant Fontana di Trevi in mind, the song tells the story of high school steadies Brenda and Eddie.

The harmonies tend to change every measure with the exception of the progression toward the cadence. The first chromatic chord is G major; the B♮ cannot be explained in the key of F major. G is the dominant of C major, so the chord is analyzed as a V/V. But does it resolve directly to the V? Not exactly, but the A minor chord on "any" is best analyzed as a passing chord between the V/V and the V^6/V.

Billy Joel, "Scenes from an Italian Restaurant." Songwriter: Billy Joel

SPELLING SECONDARY DOMINANTS

How would you notate a secondary dominant if given the Roman numeral symbol? All you need to remember is that you are tonicizing, or temporarily thinking in another key!

(Ex. 1) E♭: V^7/ii

1. Start with the Roman numeral to the right of the slash. Think of that Roman numeral as the key you are tonicizing.
2. What is ii in the key of E♭ major? F minor. (Note that the quality came from the case of the Roman numeral.)
3. What is the V^7 of F minor? C^7.
4. Notate chord on staff.

(Ex. 2) b: V^6_5/VI

1. What is VI in the key of B minor? G major.
2. What is the V^6_5 of G major? D^7/F♯.
3. Notate chord on staff.

Now we can answer our question from the chapter opening. Why can we not have a secondary dominant of vii° or ii°? Because the target chord, or the chord being tonicized, actually represents a key, it is not possible to use a diminished "key" to the right of the slash.

Study the following secondary dominants notated in various keys. Practice spelling secondary dominants in various keys.

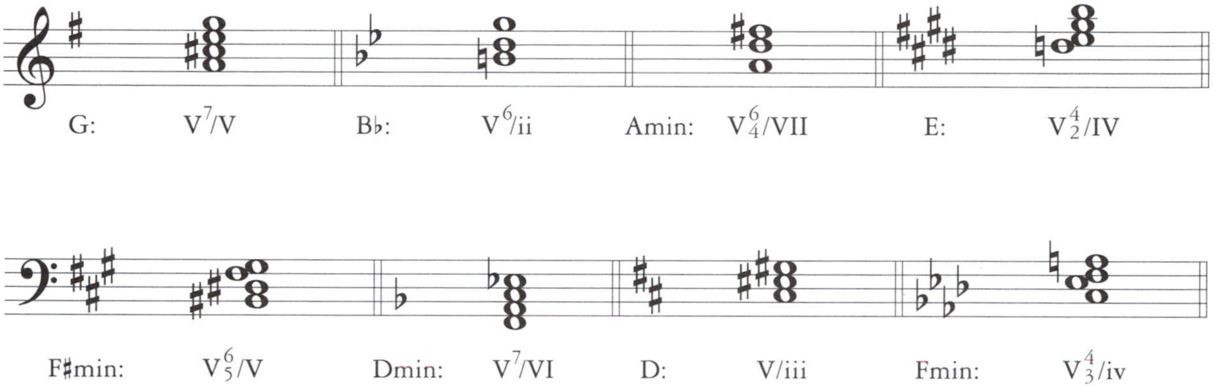

ARTIST IN RESIDENCE

Big Shot

Joel is quoted as saying, "I am no longer afraid of becoming lost, because the journey back always reveals something new, and that is ultimately good for the artist." And it's been some journey. Over the span of 3 decades, over forty of his singles have made the Billboard chart. He has sold out arenas and performed with Elton John and the Philadelphia Orchestra, winning over both popular and classical music lovers. Joel has won countless awards, including six Grammys and a Tony; has been inducted into the Songwriters Hall of Fame and the Rock and Roll Hall of Fame; and was the recipient of the 2013 Kennedy Center Honors Award. Remember the kid who dropped out of high school to pursue music? Well, he has six honorary doctorates, including one from the Manhattan School of Music.

Reviewing Chapter Objectives

- Define chromatic chord and secondary dominant (pages 221–222)
- Recognize secondary dominants in context (pages 224–226)
- Spell secondary dominants in various keys (pages 226–227)
- Resolve secondary dominants using correct voice leading (page 229)
- Compose a short song using secondary dominants (page 233)

EXERCISES

I. Given the key, analyze each chromatic chord with the correct Roman numeral. Be sure to indicate inversions with figured bass.

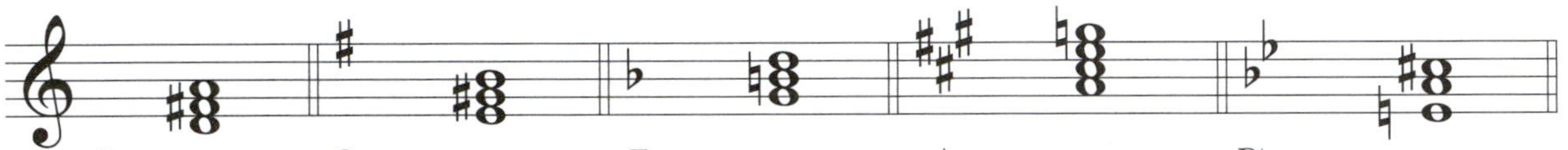

C: G: F: A: B♭:

Dmin: B: Fmin: Amin: F:

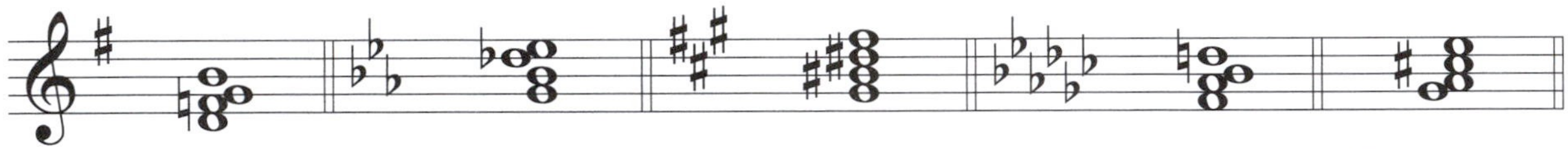

Emin: E♭: F♯min: G♭: C:

II. Given the key and Roman numeral, correctly notate the chord on the staff.

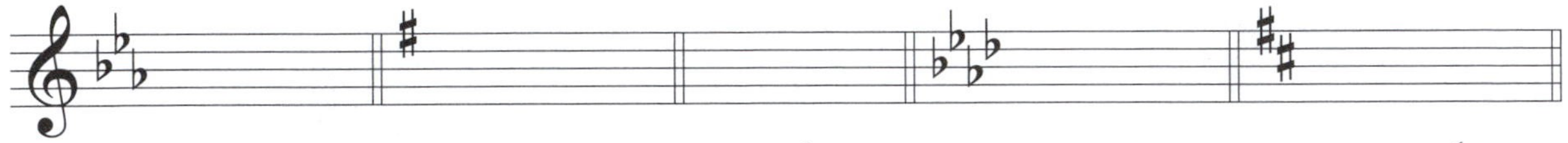

E♭: V/vi Emin: V/V C: V^6/ii A♭: V/vi Bmin: V^6_4/V

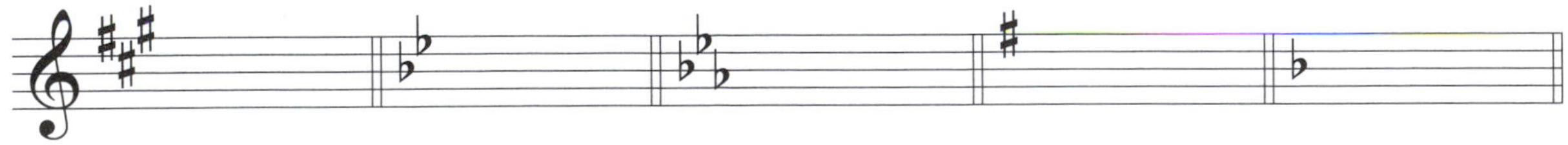

F♯min: V/VII B♭: V^7/IV Cmin: V^6_5/VI G: V^4_2/V F: V^4_3/ii

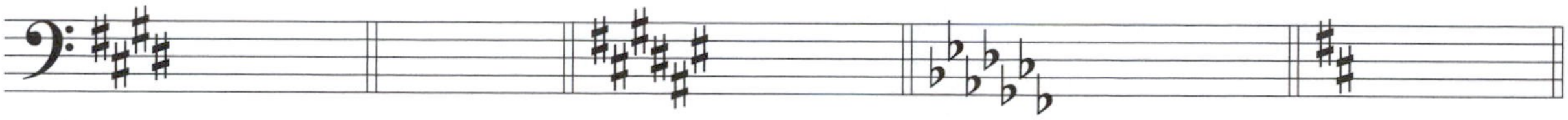

E: V^6_4/vi Amin: V/iv F♯: V^7/V C♭: V^6_5/IV D: V^4_2/ii

III. The first chord shown is a secondary dominant in the given key. Label each chord with the correct Roman numeral and resolve each chord, paying careful attention to part writing rules in terms of the seventh of the chord.

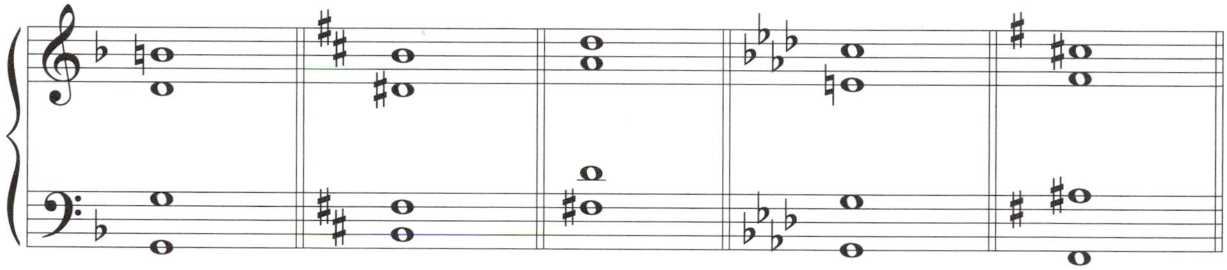

F: D: Amin: A♭: G:

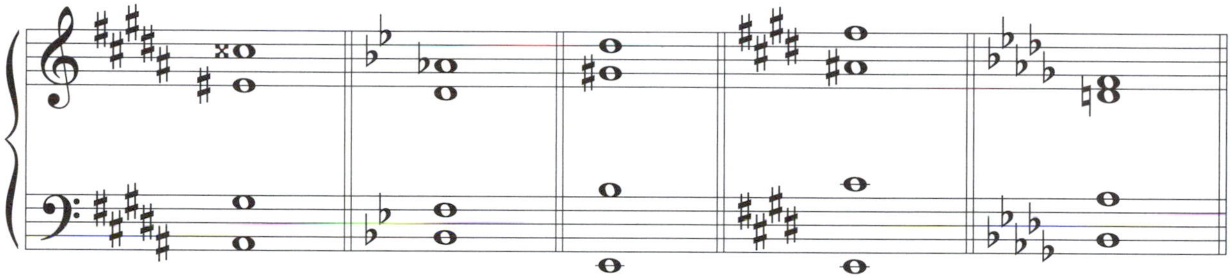

G♯min: B♭: C: C♯min: B♭min:

ANALYSIS

The song "Shameless" was released on Joel's album *Storm Front* in 1989. The album reached number 1 on the Billboard 200 chart and featured the top hit "We Didn't Start the Fire." "Shameless" didn't enjoy the success of a Joel hit, peaking at number 40; however, it became a major hit for country artist Garth Brooks in 1991, reaching number 1 on the U.S. and Canadian country charts.

WEBSITE
VIDEO TRACK 24

Using the staff paper provided, notate all of the chords used in the excerpt. After listening to the song several times, answer the following questions. Indicate which of the following chords are chromatic chords.

1. Of those, which are secondary dominants?
2. Do they resolve to the tonic of the key being tonicized?

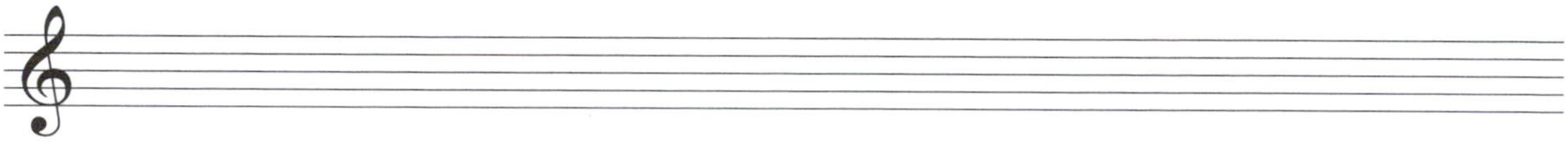

Billy Joel, "Shameless." Songwriter: Billy Joel

Complete a Roman numeral analysis for the following excerpts. Be sure to circle and identify any non-chord tones. Identify all second inversion chords and indicate inversions with the appropriate figured bass. You may find it helpful to also complete a lead sheet symbol analysis.

WEBSITE

Daniel Barenboim, Beethoven's *Piano Sonata No. 8 in C Minor, Op. 13* ("Pathétique"), Mvt. II

VIDEO TRACK 25

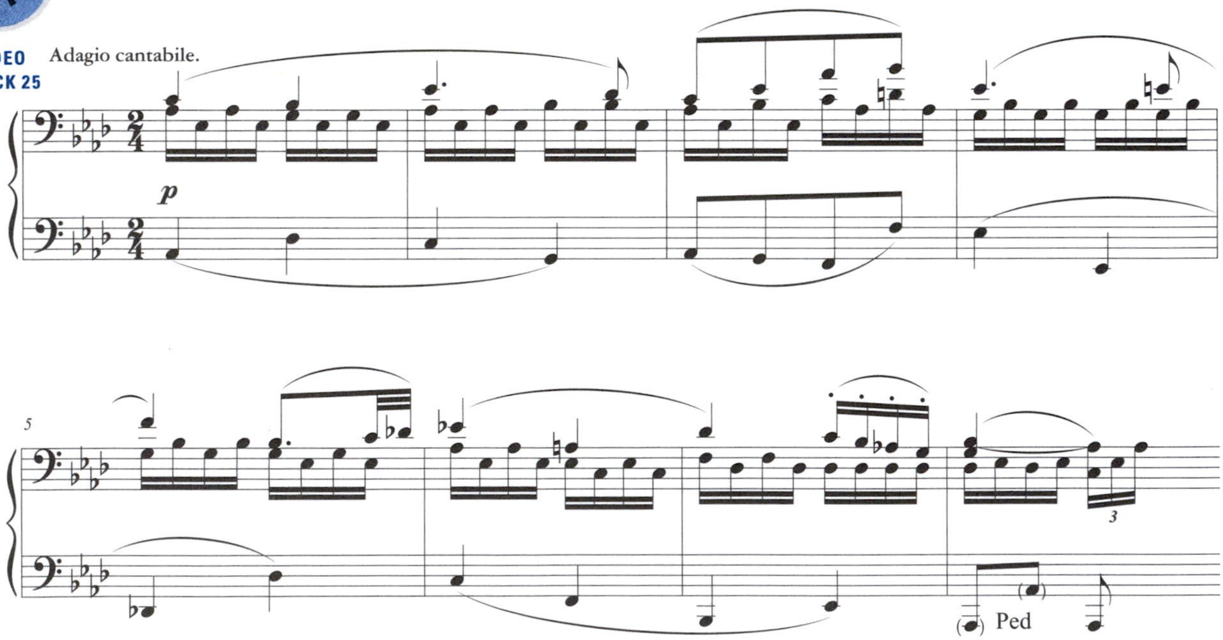

Mozart, *String Quartet in F Major, No. 5,* K. 158, Mvt. I

VIDEO TRACK 26

Mozart, *Eine Kleine Nachtmusik,* K. 525, Mvt. I

This particular excerpt is in the key of D major. All C♯s are diatonic.

VIDEO TRACK 27

VIDEO TRACK 28

Maureen Forrester, Handel's "He Was Despised" from *Messiah*

COMPOSITION PROJECT

Billy Joel on songwriting:

> I'll wake up at 4:30 in the morning with an idea and think maybe I should write this down but then think, "Nah, I'm too tired but it's so great I won't forget it." And I go back to sleep and I wake up later and I think, "Oh, what was that"—and it's gone. But not forever. It's not gone from the little mental filing cabinet that we have—it all gets filed away. Later, right in the middle of a conversation it pops back into consciousness and I'll have to go over to the piano and work it out. And that's how I do a lot of writing. It's almost like you didn't have anything to do with it. You get this feeling that somebody has done this before. And I think somebody did do it before—you did it—but you did it while you were unconscious. That's how it happens for me a lot.

What is a musical idea that pops into your head? Don't even think about it. Just sing a random melody that comes from your "musical unconsciousness" as Joel would say. Once you have the basic melodic outline written down, try to place harmonies underneath your melodic line. Be sure to use progressions discussed in previous chapters. Using your original melody, add in a few chromatic pitches. Do the added chromatic pitches form the harmonies of a secondary dominant? Provide a lead sheet, Roman numeral analysis, and melody line. Plan to perform your melody in class along with guitar accompaniment improvising on your chords.

AURAL SKILLS CONDITIONING 12 (REVIEW)

In the last eleven chapters, you had the chance to practice valuable aural skills that will better prepare you as a musician. At this point, your ear is still in the training process. Reviewing material from the past chapters is very important to the continued development of your aural skills. To challenge yourself (which is recommended after you complete the review!), see the advanced aural skills conditioning section in this chapter.

Review of Sight-Singing: Melodies Outlining the I and V Chords

The following melodies outline the tonic and dominant chords. Determine the key and the solfège for the I and V chords, and identify where these chords are outlined in the melody. Knowing this before you start will make the sight-singing more efficient and meaningful. Finally, sing the example on solfège.

1.

2.

3.

4.

5.

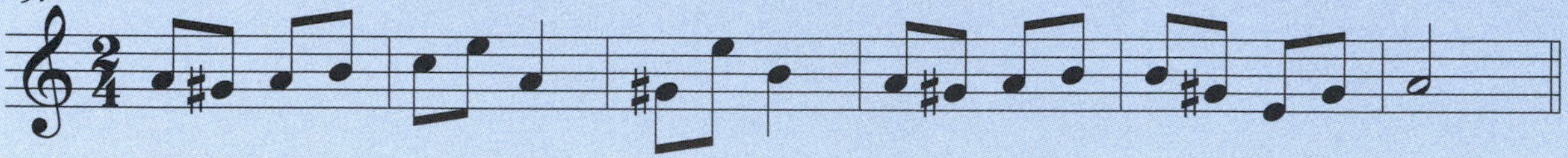

6.

Review of Melodic Dictation: Melodies Outlining the I and V Chords

AUDIO
CH. 12
MELODIC
DICTATION
1–6

You will hear six melodies performed by your instructor or on the course website. Correctly notate these melodies in terms of pitch and rhythm. These melodies are very similar to the ones you sang in the sight-singing review above. If you hear wide leaps, consider that they are more than likely outlining the I or V chord.

1.

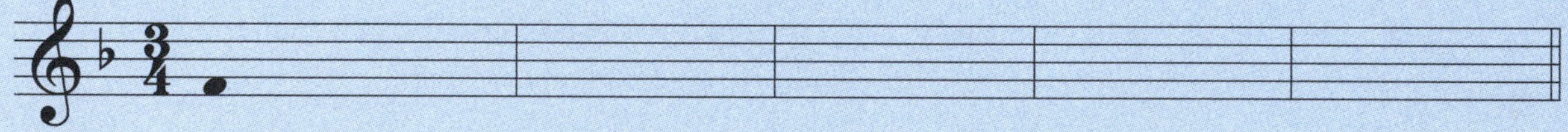

2.

3.

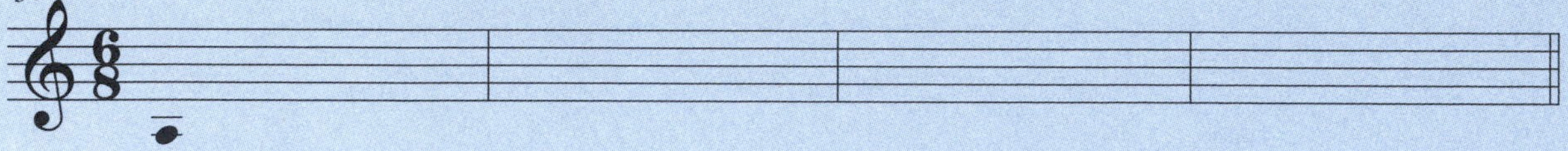

4.

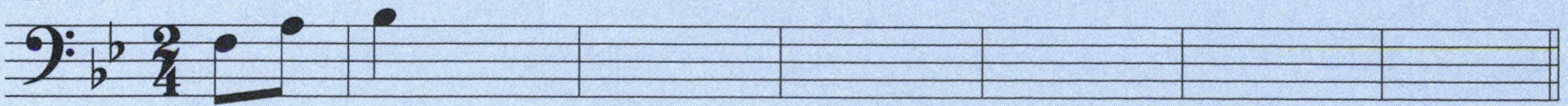

5.

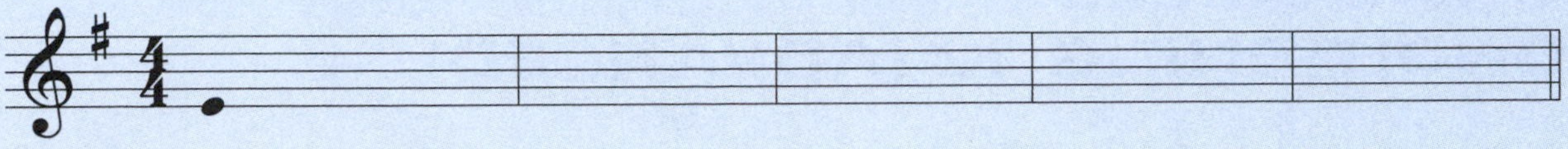

6.

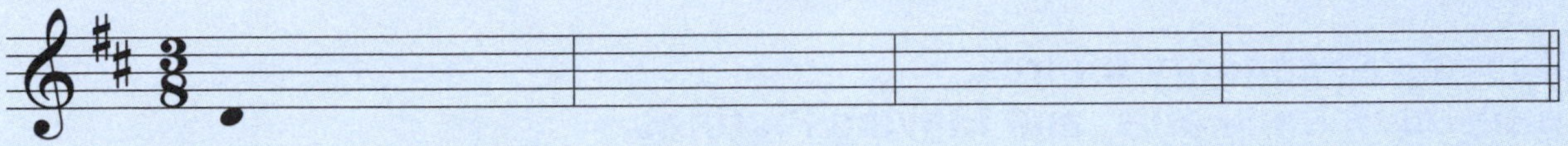

Review of Harmonic Progression: Chord Identification

Listen to the four-chord harmonic progressions performed by your instructor or on the website. Write the appropriate Roman numerals in the spaces provided below. Remember your Do-Ti test and the basics of what makes a strong harmonic progression. To review this, refer back to Chapter 8.

AUDIO TRACKS CH. 12 HARMONIC PROGRESSION 1–6

1. ________ ________ ________ ________

2. ________ ________ ________ ________

3. ________ ________ ________ ________

4. ________ ________ ________ ________

5. ________ ________ ________ ________

6. ________ ________ ________ ________

Review of Intervals: Interval Identification (All)

You will hear six intervals performed by your instructor or on the course website. Identify the interval you hear in the spaces provided below.

AUDIO TRACKS CH. 12 REVIEW OF INTERVALS 1–6

1. ______ 2. ______ 3. ______

4. ______ 5. ______ 6. ______

Now, you will hear two intervals in a row. For example, if your instructor played a major triad melodically, your answer would be: M3 m3.

See whether you can hear solfège syllables while listening to your teacher or the recorded example. Perhaps the intervals will outline a chord, like the example above. Maybe you will have to rely on your newly trained ear to tell you what intervals are being played. Write your answers in the spaces below.

AUDIO TRACKS CH. 12 REVIEW OF INTERVALS 2 1–4

1. ________ ________

2. ________ ________

3. ________ ________

4. ________ ________

AURAL SKILLS CONDITIONING 12 (ADVANCED)

SECONDARY DOMINANTS

Hearing Secondary Chords: Billy Joel, Ben Folds, and Moving Pictures

VIDEO TRACK 21

As you learned in Chapter 12, secondary chords are really just a brief tonicization in which you are temporarily thinking in a different key. Listen to Billy Joel's "The Longest Time" on the YouTube channel. Can you hear how the chords at 0:56 and 1:01 are not within the key?

VIDEO TRACK 29

Now, find Ben Folds's "The Luckiest" on the YouTube channel. As you listen, focus on the progression in the bridge around 0:51. Can you identify the one chord that isn't in the key? When does it occur?

Watch the video in which Ben Folds discusses and performs this incredibly successful song (http://www.avclub.com/video/ben-folds-discusses-and-performs-the-luckiest-64896). Beginning at 1:13, Folds can be seen singing the passage referred to above ("Where was I before the day when I first saw your lovely face?"). How does Folds play the secondary chord differently in this live performance than on the recorded track? In the interview, he says, "The subtext of the harmony of the song is that it's related to Pachelbel's Canon in D." If you can't think of how Pachelbel's most famous work sounds, play through the progression on your keyboard or guitar.

D A B- F♯- G D G A

After playing through the progression, listen to the chorus (the lyrics are "And I am, I am, I am the luckiest") and pay attention to the bass. Do you hear how the progression follows the circle of fifths similar to Canon in D?

VIDEO TRACK 30

"What About Me" by Moving Pictures spent six consecutive weeks at number 1 on the Australian charts. Listen to this track on the YouTube channel and, starting at 1:49, try to sing along with the bass line using solfège. Every chord is in root position in this section *except* the chord at 1:58. That chord is G/D in G major. (Can you hear how the bass is on *sol* here, but the lead singer is singing a *mi*?) Can you figure out the rest of the progression? Where are the chromatic chords? Are they diminished or dominant in function?

Singing Progressions with Secondary Chords

In Chapter 8, you sang the opening chord progression from Mozart's "Voi Che Sapete" on solfège, both arpeggiated and while holding out the harmony with your class. Do the same thing for the progressions below. Each of the progressions has a secondary chord. Remember that secondary chords are chromatic: they use pitches that aren't in the key. This means you'll be using some solfège syllables that aren't in a major or minor scale! Below is a chromatic scale with corresponding solfège syllables.

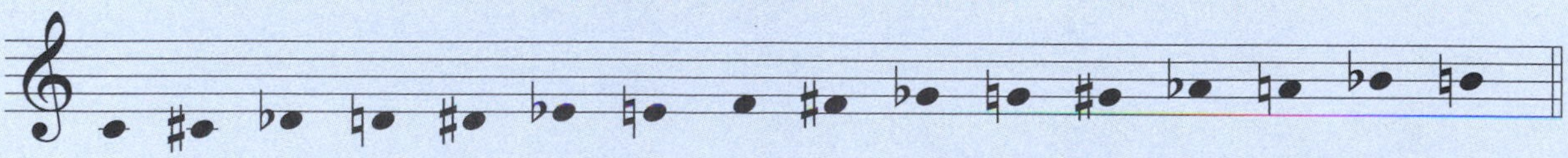

$\hat{1}$	$\sharp\hat{1}$	$\flat\hat{2}$	$\hat{2}$	$\sharp\hat{2}$	$\flat\hat{3}$	$\hat{3}$	$\hat{4}$	$\sharp\hat{4}$	$\flat\hat{5}$	$\hat{5}$	$\sharp\hat{5}$	$\flat\hat{6}$	$\flat\hat{6}$	$\flat\hat{7}$	$\hat{7}$
Do	Di	Ra	Re	Ri	Me	Mi	Fa	Fi	Sa	Sol	Si	Le	La	Te	Ti

Before you sing each progression, think about the scale degrees you'll need to sing and the chromatic solfège for each raised or lowered pitch. The first one is given for you.

1. I	V^7/IV	IV	ii	V	I
do–mi–sol	do–mi–sol–**te**	fa–la–do	re–fa–la	sol–ti–re	do–mi–sol
2. i	V^4_2/V	V^6	i	iv	i
3. I	V^7	vi	V^7/ii	ii	V
4. i	V^6_5	i	V^7/iv	iv	V
5. vi	V	IV	vii°/V	cad$^6_4$	vii°
6. vi	vi	V	IV	I	

Chord Identification: Secondary Chords

Your teacher will play a four-chord progression. Each progression includes one secondary chord. Write the Roman numerals in the spaces provided below.

AUDIO TRACKS CH. 12 CHORD ID 1–4

1. ________ ________ ________ ________

2. ________ ________ ________ ________

3. ________ ________ ________ ________

4. ________ ________ ________ ________

Singing Melodies

Using solfège, sing the melodies below. Chords are outlined in each of the melodies, and some are secondary dominants! Watch out for chromatic pitches and be aware of harmonic resolution as you sing. Use the chart of chromatic solfège pitches to help you correctly sing the pitches using solfège.

1.

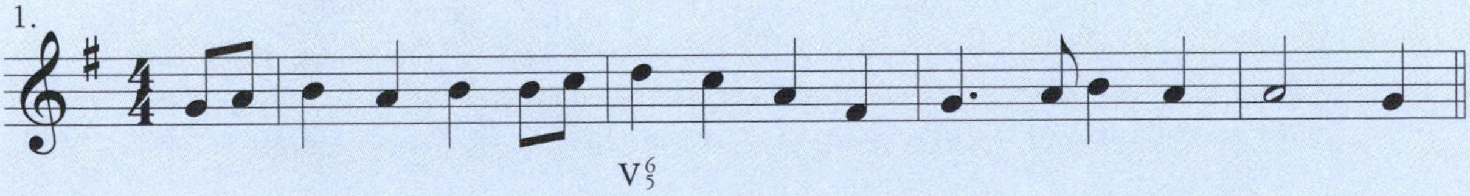

2.

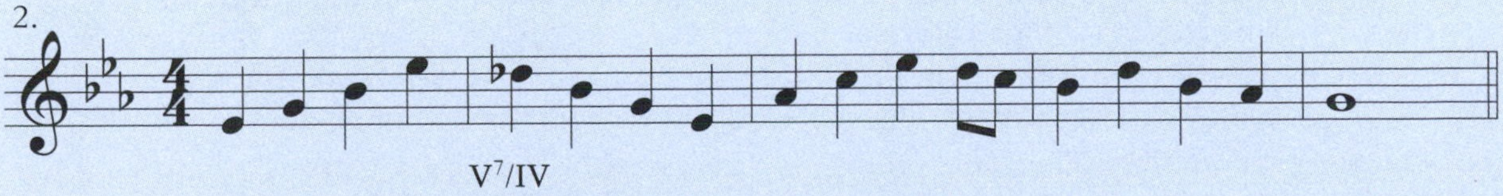

[3]Where have you heard this progression before?

3.

4.
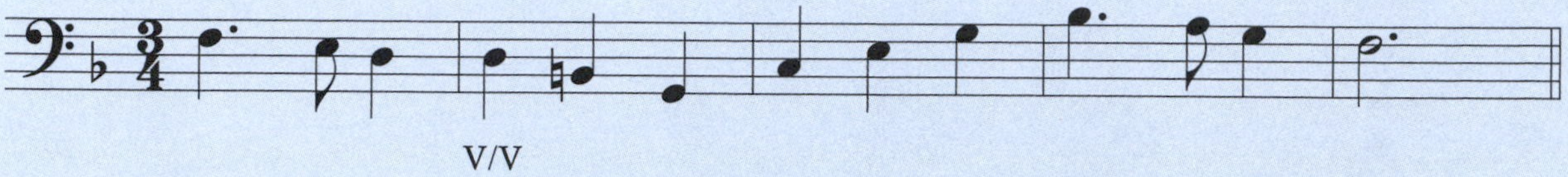

5.

6.
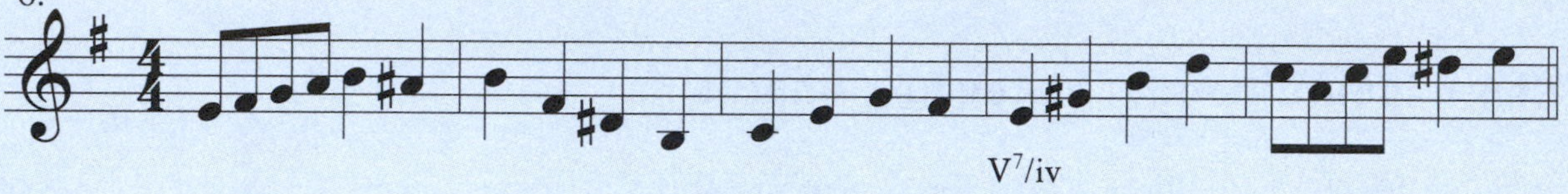

BACKSTAGE PASS

Honesty: Everyone Is So Untrue

Written by Adam Sensenbrenner

In 1989 Billy Joel filed a $90 million lawsuit against his longtime manager, Frank Weber. In what is considered to be one of the largest lawsuits against an entertainment manager, Joel cited fraud, breach of contract, breach of fiduciary duty (an obligation to act in Joel's best interest), and federal racketeering statute violations (obtaining or extorting money illegally). Weber's managerial contract gave him power of attorney and total control of Joel's business affairs. To complicate matters, Weber is Joel's former brother-in-law and at the time of the filing was also the godfather of Joel's 2-year-old daughter, Alexa Ray. Asking for $30 million in lost compensation and an additional $60 million in punitive damages, Billy Joel and his legal team brought the following accusations against Weber:

- Loans in the amount of $2.5 million were given without Joel's knowledge or authorization to various horse-breeding and real estate partnerships and other businesses controlled by Weber.
- Weber lost more than $10 million of Joel's money in investments of a highly speculative nature, many of which involved Weber's own companies.
- Weber double-billed Joel for his music videos (the videos were produced by a company owned by one of Weber's relatives), cheated him on expenses including travel and accounting fees, and mortgaged Joel's copyrights for $15 million without disclosing it on Joel's financial statements.

- Weber caused phony financial statements to be issued to Joel, which painted an unrealistic picture of Joel's finances and the value of his investments and failed to reflect liabilities, guarantees, loans, and mortgages.

Joel initiated a private investigation of Weber after detecting suspicious financial activity and fired him on August 30, 1989, after an official audit revealed major monetary discrepancies and dishonest dealings. Although he was considered one of Joel's closest friends and confidants, Weber had broken a bond of trust and integrity. Weber eventually filed for bankruptcy in 1991, and Joel was only able to recover only a small portion of his total losses.

- What preventive measures could Joel have taken to avoid being taken advantage of by Weber?
- Research the term "conflict of interest," and cite specific examples in which Weber's handlings of Joel's assets were direct conflicts of interest.
- What will you take away from Joel's experience to avoid similar pitfalls as either an artist or manager?

As illustrated by this case study, why is it important to be aware of your earnings and investments as an artist? How can you develop your business savvy as a student?

CHAPTER 13

SECONDARY LEADING TONE CHORDS

Artist in Residence: Renée Fleming

Chapter Objectives

- Define secondary leading tone chord and use correctly in a functional progression
- Recognize secondary leading tone chords in context
- Correctly notate secondary leading tone chords in various keys
- Resolve secondary leading tone chords using proper voice leading

What do dominant chords (V) and leading tone chords (vii°) have in common? The answer is in the function: they both function as dominants that typically lead to the tonic triad. After all, they share two pitches, including the leading tone! The basic principles of secondary dominants and secondary leading tone chords are exactly the same. Let's examine the progression we used in Chapter 12 to illustrate how the secondary leading tone chord works in context. Be sure to play the chords on your guitar or keyboard while you read through the discussion.

D:	D	G	E-/G	A	D
	I	IV	ii^6	V	I

Any chord, other than the vii° or ii°, can be preceded by its leading tone chord. Let's insert two **secondary leading tone chords**, a vii° of the G major chord and a vii$^{\circ 7}$ of the A major chord. The vii° of G is built on F♯ and the vii$^{\circ 7}$ of A is built on G♯. The final progression would look like this.

D:	D	F♯°7	G	E-/G	G♯°7	A	D
	I	vii$^{\circ 7}$/IV	IV	ii^{6}	vii$^{\circ 7}$/V	V	I

Play through the progression above. The F♯$^{\circ 7}$ and G♯$^{\circ 7}$ both include pitches that are not diatonic to the original key of D; therefore, both chords are tonicizing the chord to the right. Take some time to create progressions that include secondary leading tone chords. Play through the progressions on your keyboard or guitar.

ARTIST IN RESIDENCE

Ambition and Drive: The People's Diva

Called the "people's diva" by *Playbill Arts*, Renée Fleming was raised in a home surrounded by all types of music. Her parents were high school music teachers and filled the home with music in a multitude of genres. Ms. Fleming has often said that the topic at the dinner table every night was music and singing. There was no doubt in her mind that music was her destiny, whether it be in music education or performance. Even though she was accepted into Oberlin for vocal studies immediately following high school, she did not receive sufficient financial aid to attend. (Not the typical story you hear from a classical diva!) Due to financial constraints, Fleming enrolled at Crane School of Music, where she studied classical voice during the day while singing in a jazz bar at night.

As Eddie Silva stated in *Playbill Arts*, "With admirable pluck and perseverance, she found in the 'lesser' school the education and nurturance she needed. She calls the circumstances that led her to Crane 'the first great break of my career.'" Unlike many divas on the opera stage, Fleming has remained down to earth and continually thanks her mentors along the way. She is proud of her diversity and seeks to explore all styles of musical performance.

RECOGNIZING SECONDARY LEADING TONES IN CONTEXT

WEBSITE

VIDEO TRACK 31

One of Renée Fleming's signature roles is that of Violetta in *La Traviata* (Verdi, 1853). In the short excerpt from the aria "Sempre Libera," Violetta, a flirtatious debutante, is debating whether she even has the capacity to settle down with one man. The one man catching her eye at a lavish party is Alfredo; however, by the end of the aria, Violetta has proclaimed that she must always be free, or, in Italian, *sempre libera*. Alfredo is singing offstage of his love as Violetta dances around the room after the guests have left.

Study the analyzed excerpt while you listen to Fleming's performance. Begin at 9:35.

86
sier, dee vo - lar,
way, night and day,
A - mor è pal - pi-to del l'u - ni-
Now I know hap - pi-ness, deep - est e-
A♭:
89
dee vo - lar, ah! ah!
night and day! Ah!, ah, ah, ah!
ver - so.
mo - tion.
I vi vii°4/3/ii

Some key points about the example:

- The secondary leading tone chords presented in the excerpt provide a smooth bass line to extend the basic I–vi–ii progression.
- The bass line, beginning in measure 90, walks down from the A♭ to the D♭ before the cadential six-four cadence in measures 93 and 94.
- The G♭ in measure 90 is a passing tone leading to the submediant harmony in 91. It may be possible to justify a deceptive resolution of a secondary dominant; however, the bass movement is better explained as passing.
- The accidentals are not consistent, and therefore no modulation has taken place.
- The tonicization is created through secondary leading tone chords.

Premiered in Paris in 1859, Charles Gounod's opera *Faust* was not initially well received by the Paris Opera. However, it was revived in 1862 with great acclaim. Written in five acts, along with an extensive cast and ballet (added in 1869), the opera is an ambitious undertaking, typically performed only at larger opera houses. This so-called "excessiveness" can be seen in the aria "Jewel Song" from the third act. In this scene, the main character, Marguerite, is trying on jewelry and is overwhelmed by how the expensive jewels enhance her beauty. In this performance, Ms. Fleming sings the aria in a concert setting. The excerpt begins at 1:30.

WEBSITE
VIDEO
TRACK 32

Renée Fleming, Gounod's "Jewel Song" from *Faust*

The mediant triad is not often heard in music from the classical period, but it was used extensively in the later years of the romantic period. After listening to the excerpt, this particular region might sound a little unstable. That is partly due to the chromatic chords that continue until the cadence at 1:52. The pitches F𝄪 and A♯ are highly chromatic and are definitely not diatonic in the key of E! By stacking the notes in measure 21 to form F𝄪, A♯, C♯, E, we can come to the conclusion that the chord is in fact a fully diminished seventh chord. The F𝄪 is the seventh scale degree in the key of G♯, the iii in the key of E major.

Study the same motive as it appears later in the aria, this time within a broader context. How would you analyze the A♯s and B♯s used in measures 111 and 113? Look carefully at measure 123. How can these pitches be respelled in such a way as to tonicize the key of G♯ minor (iii)? Measures 123–127 are transitional in that there is a modulation to the key of B major. The concept of modulation will be discussed at length in Chapter 15.

Renée Fleming, Gounod's "Jewel Song" from *Faust*

SONG SPOTLIGHT

Classical Music to the Masses: Queens, Presidents, and the Muppets

Renée Fleming has been asked to sing for the Olympics, Super Bowl, Nobel Peace Prize ceremonies, and for important world leaders, including recent performances at the balcony of Buckingham Palace for the 2012 Diamond Jubilee Concert for Her Majesty Queen

VIDEO TRACKS 33–35

Elizabeth II and the inauguration concert for President Barack Obama. But she is just as comfortable sharing her talents with children in a collaboration with the number and pig puppets on *The Muppet Show*.

Take a few minutes to listen to the performances presented at each venue.

- Diamond Jubilee Concert at Buckingham Palace (2012), "Un bel di, vedremo" from Puccini's *Madame Butterfly*
- Inauguration of President Obama (2009), "You'll Never Walk Alone" from Rodgers and Hammerstein's *Carousel*
- *The Muppet Show* (2007), "12345" based on the melody of "Caro Nome" from Verdi's *Rigoletto*

How would you describe Ms. Fleming's stage presence? What is so compelling about her musical ability that allows those who have never cared for classical music to be mesmerized by the performance?

VIDEO TRACK 36

The opera *Tosca* by Puccini premiered in 1900 and is considered by many to be one of the great operas of the late romantic period. In this scene from the second act, the main character, Tosca, sings of her passion for music and for art in spite of her anguish that her lover is being sent to war. As you listen to the performance from the 2006 Nobel Peace Prize Concert, focus on the use of chromaticism in measures 58 and 59. The musical excerpt begins at 1:28.

Renée Fleming, Puccini's "Vissi d'arte" from *Tosca*

The A♮ seen in measure 58 is not diatonic in the key of E♭ major. So, is the chord a secondary leading tone or a secondary dominant?

Follow these steps to analyze the chord in context of the musical score:

1. Stack the chord in thirds. (F, A, C, E♭ with an escape tone on the pitch G)
2. Determine the quality of the chord. (dominant seventh chord) By definition, the chord would have to be a secondary dominant due to its quality. (V^7/?)
3. Determine the key being tonicized. F (the root of the chord being analyzed) is the fifth of what key? (B♭)
4. Determine the scale degree. B♭ is what scale degree in the key of E♭? (V)
5. Conclude the analysis. The chord at measure 58 would be analyzed as a V^7/V that resolves appropriately to the V in the last beat of the measure.

SPELLING SECONDARY LEADING TONE CHORDS

How would you write a secondary leading tone chord if given the Roman numeral symbol? Like secondary dominants, you need to remember that you are tonicizing, or temporarily thinking in another key!

(Example 1) F: vii°⁷/V

1. Start with the Roman numeral to the right of the slash. Think of that Roman numeral as the key you are tonicizing.
2. What is V in the key of F? (C major; note that the quality came from the case of the Roman numeral)
3. What is the vii^{o7} of C major? (B^{o7})
4. Insert chord on staff.

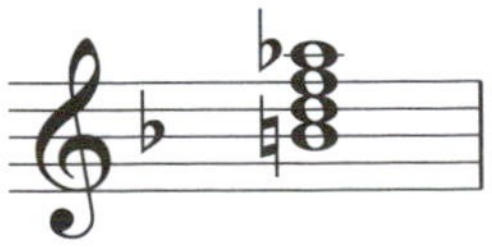

Or, you can use an even easier process:

1. Start with the Roman numeral to the right of the slash. Think of that Roman numeral as the key you are tonicizing. (C)

2. Think down a half step from the key you are tonicizing. (B)
3. Build a °7 chord on that pitch. (B^{o7})

(Example 2) G♯ minor: $vii^{ø4}_{3}$/VI

1. What is VI in the key of G♯ minor? (E major)
2. What is the $vii^{ø7}$ of E major? ($D♯^{ø7}$)
3. Notate the chord on the staff using the proper inversion.

You may have noticed that the majority of the musical examples in this chapter use fully diminished seventh chords rather than half diminished seventh chords in secondary function. This is entirely up to the composer as to what quality to use, although the fully diminished seventh is more commonly used when the target chord is minor. Play through the following progressions to hear the differences in sound quality. Notice how the 7th of the chord resolves down and the leading tone of the target chord resolves up.

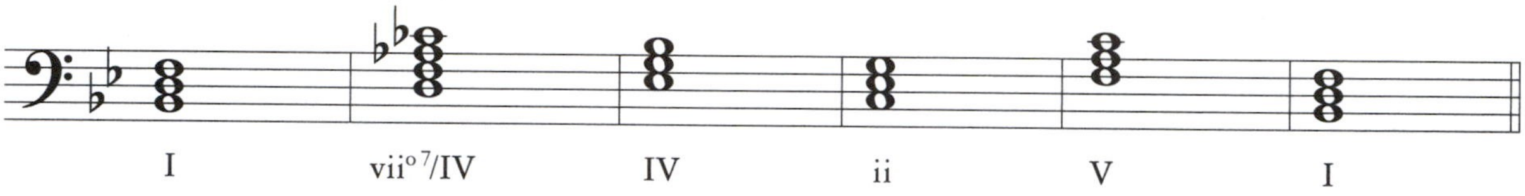

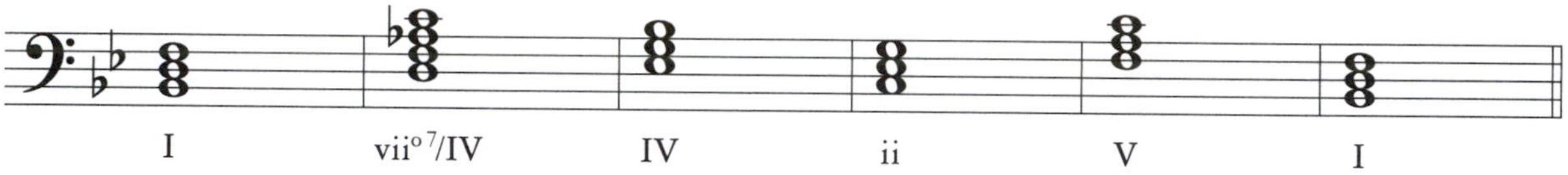

Reviewing Chapter Objectives

- Define secondary leading tone chord and use correctly in progression (page 241)
- Recognize secondary leading tone chords in context (pages 242–247)
- Correctly notate secondary leading tone chords in various keys (pages 247–248)
- Resolve secondary leading tone chords using proper voice leading (pages 248, 251)

ARTIST IN RESIDENCE

Brava!!! Honors and Awards

Renée Fleming's list of accolades and awards is extensive, including four Grammys, honorary doctorates from Juilliard and Eastman, and 2012 Singer of the Year given by the German ECHO Awards. In 2010, she was named the first ever creative consultant at Lyric Opera of Chicago. She is currently curating the creation of a world-premiere opera based on the best-seller *Bel Canto* for Lyric Opera's 2015–2016 season. Perhaps Sir George Solti said it best: "Quite apart from the sheer lyrical beauty of voice, she has an innate musicianship which makes every performance a great joy."

Year	Honors and Awards
1999	Grammy Award for Best Classical Vocal Performance for album *The Beautiful Voice*
2003	Grammy Award for Best Classical Vocal Performance for album *Bel Canto*
	Honorary membership in the Royal Academy of Music
	Honorary doctorate from the Juilliard School
2008	Polar Music Prize "in recognition of her sublime unparalleled voice and unique stylistic versatility"
2009	Grammy Award for Best Classical Vocal Performance for album *Verismo*
2011	Honorary doctorate from the Eastman School of Music
	Fulbright Lifetime Achievement Medal
2012	Victoire d'Honneur prize by France's Victoires de la Musique Classique
	Singer of the Year by the German ECHO Awards
2013	National Medal of Arts Award
	Grammy Award for Best Classical Vocal Solo

EXERCISES

I. Given the key, analyze each chromatic chord with the correct Roman numeral. Be sure to indicate inversions with figured bass symbols.

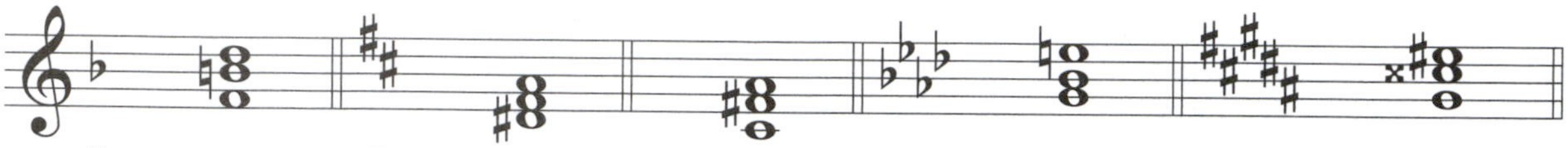

F: D: C: A♭: B:

Emin: B♭: Dmin: D♭: Amin:

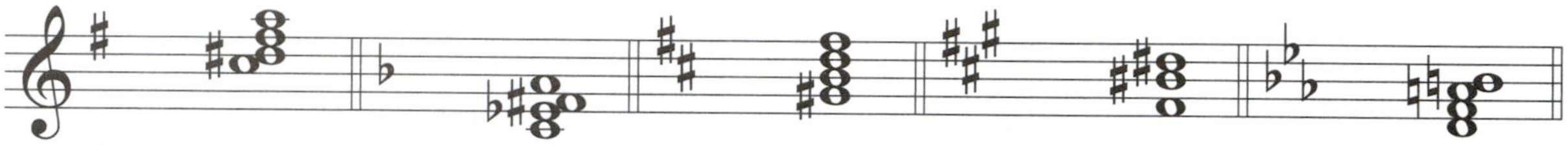

G: F: Bmin: F♯min: E♭:

II. Given the Roman numeral and figured bass symbol, notate the appropriate pitches on the staff.

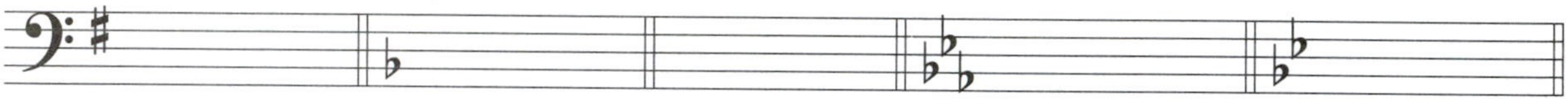

G: vii$^{\circ 6}$/vi F: vii$^{\circ 6}$/V Amin: vii$^{\circ}$/VII E♭: vii$^{\circ}{}^{6}_{4}$/iii Gmin: vii$^{ø 7}$/VI

C♯: vii$^{\circ}{}^{6}_{5}$/V A: vii$^{\circ}$/ii B♭: vii$^{\circ 6}$/vi Cmin: vii$^{\circ}{}^{4}_{2}$/VII Emin: vii$^{\circ 6}$/V

A♭: vii$^{\circ}$/ii A♭min: vii$^{\circ}{}^{6}_{4}$/iv D: vii$^{\circ 7}$/vi Dmin: vii$^{\circ}{}^{4}_{2}$/VII D: vii$^{\circ 6}$/V

III. The first chord shown is a secondary leading tone chord in the given key. Label each chord with the correct Roman numerals, and resolve each chord to the appropriate target chord. Pay careful attention to part writing rules in terms of the seventh of the chord.

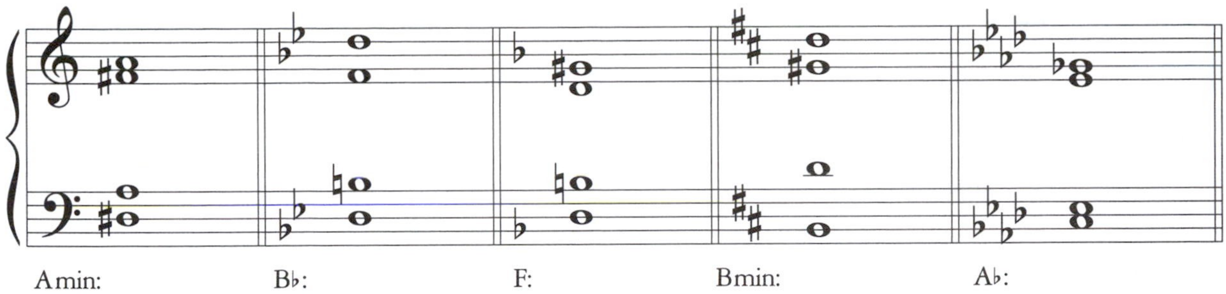

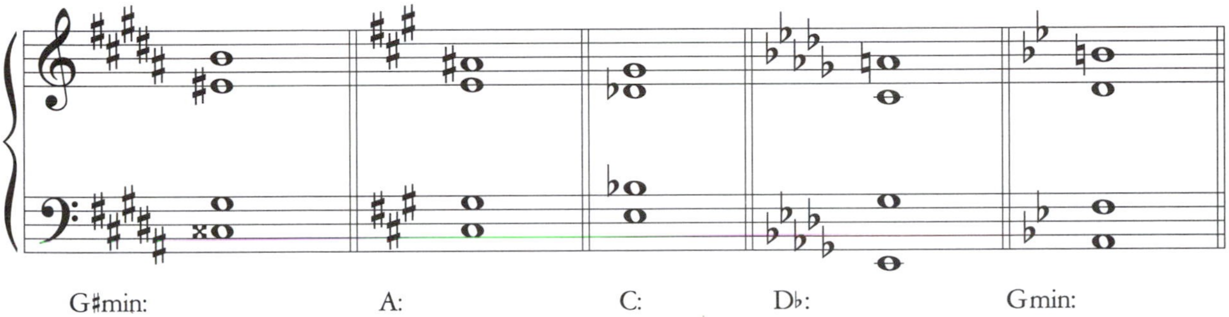

ANALYSIS

A standard in many undergraduate voice studios, "Alma del core" (early 18th century) is primarily diatonic with a scalar type melody. After listening to the excerpt, give a Roman numeral analysis for the entire example, paying careful attention to the chord in measure 83. Be sure to identify the non-chord tones within the piano and vocal line.

Antonio Caldara, "Alma del core"

"Die erwachte Rose" (1880) was rediscovered in 1958 and first performed by Elisabeth Schwarzkopf. The poem, written by Friedrich von Sallet, speaks of the beauty of the awakened rose. Where are the accidentals in this excerpt? How can you explain the function of the chromatic chord? How does it resolve? Complete a Roman numeral analysis of the entire excerpt, and identify the non-chord tones in the vocal line.

Richard Strauss, "Die erwachte Rose" from *Drei Liebeslieder*

This work was published in 1801 in a set of six string quartets (as was typical of the time) and consists of four movements. Out of the group of six, this was the last to be written and the only quartet for which no previous sketches have ever been found. Before beginning the analysis of this piece, listen carefully to the excerpt. Label each measure with lead sheet symbols. Where is the secondary leading tone chord? Does it resolve as you would expect? *Do not attempt Roman numeral analysis!*

VIDEO TRACK 37

Beethoven, *String Quartet No. 4 in C Minor, Op. 18*

Beethoven, *String Quartet No. 4 in C Minor, Op. 18 (continued)*

AURAL SKILLS CONDITIONING 13 (REVIEW)

Review of Sight-Singing: Melodies Outlining the ii and IV Chords

The following melodies outline the ii and IV chords. First, identify the key of each example. Then, determine the pitches of the ii and IV chord in the key and the solfège syllables associated with each. Sing through the melodies on solfège, paying attention to where a ii or IV chord is outlined.

1.

2.

3.

4.

5.

6.

Review of Melodic Dictation: Melodies Outlining the ii and IV Chords

Listen to the melodies performed by your instructor or on the course website. Again, these melodies are very similar to the ones you sight-sang above! Pay attention to where you hear the outlining of a ii or IV chord. Notate the melody with correct pitches and rhythm. The first pitch is *not* given to you. Try to determine the first pitch based on the key and scale degree.

REPLAY

AUDIO TRACKS CH. 13 MELODIC DICTATION 1–4

1.

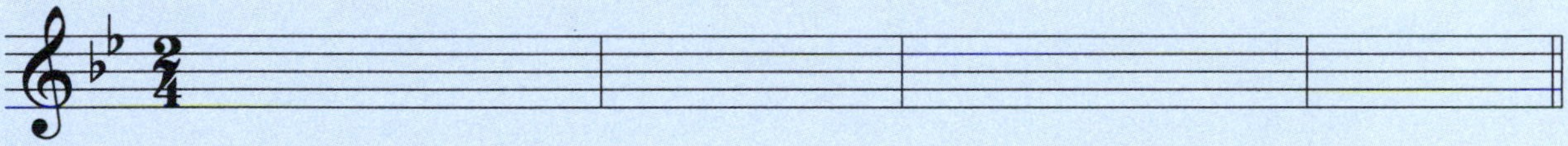

2.

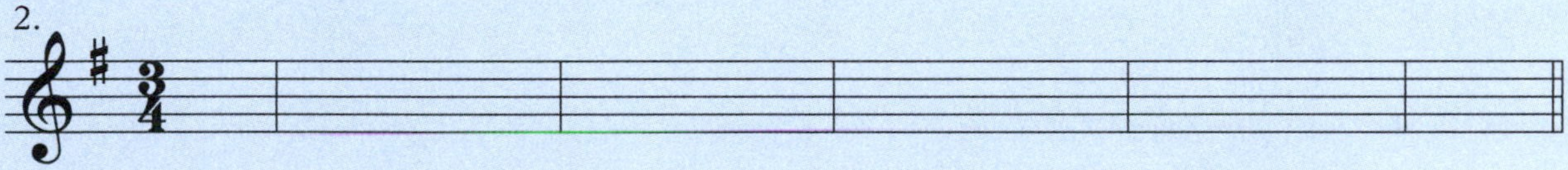

3.

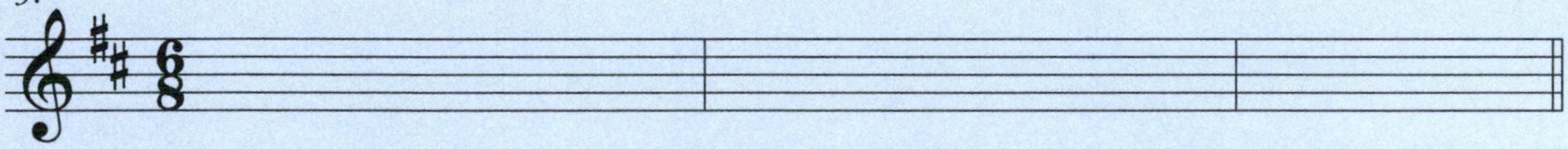

4.

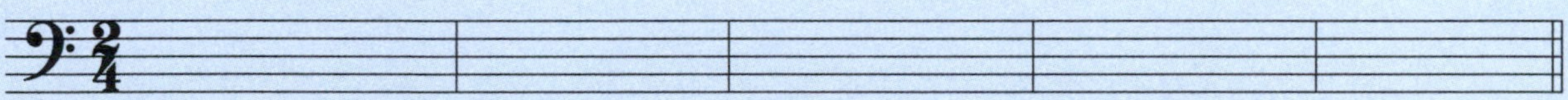

Review of Harmonic Progression: Chord Identification

Listen to the four-chord progressions performed by your instructor or on the course website. Write down the Roman numerals in the spaces below. Remember, not all of these chords will be diatonic! Remember your Do–Ti test and what constitutes a strong harmonic progression.

REPLAY

AUDIO TRACKS CH. 13 HARMONIC PROGRESSION 1–6

1. ________ ________ ________ ________

2. ________ ________ ________ ________

3. ________ ________ ________ ________

4. ________ ________ ________ ________

5. ________ ________ ________ ________

6. ________ ________ ________ ________

Review of Rhythmic Dictation

REPLAY

AUDIO TRACKS CH. 13 RHYTHMIC DICTATION 1–8

You will hear melodies performed by your instructor or on the course website. See if you can dictate the rhythm, not the pitches, in the space provided below. It might be helpful for you to quietly tap the strong beats while listening to the melody or to conduct while your instructor is playing.

1.

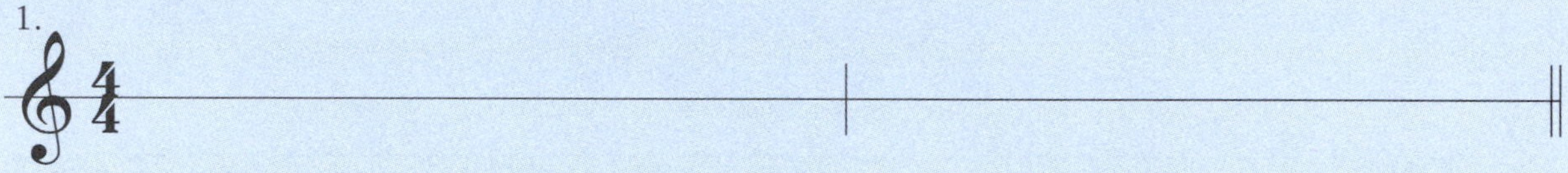

2.

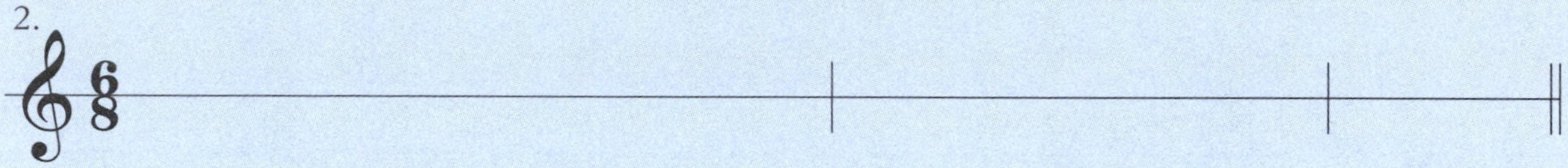

3.

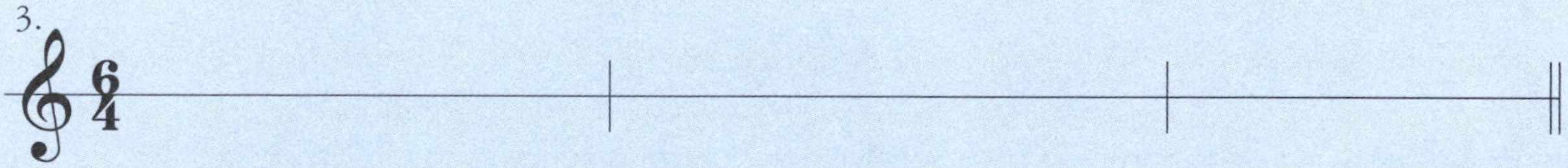

4.

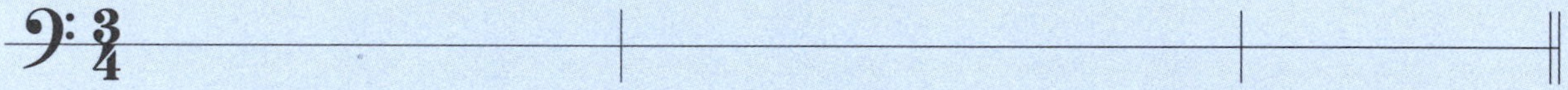

5.

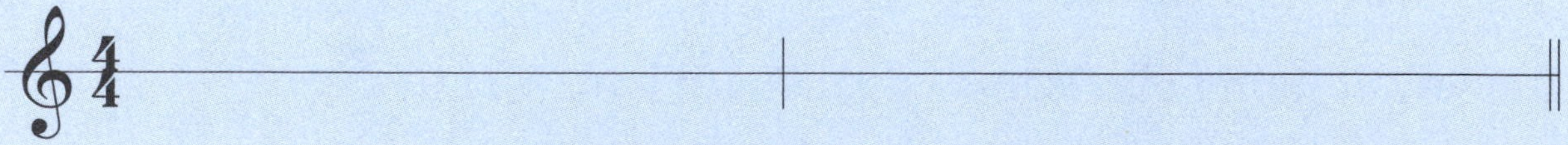

6.

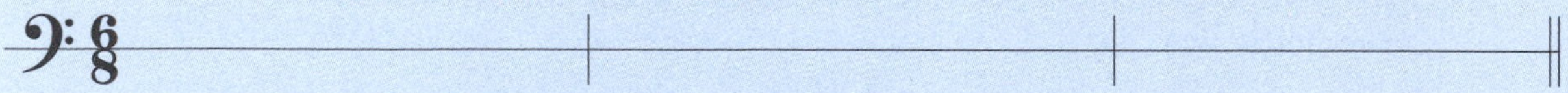

7.

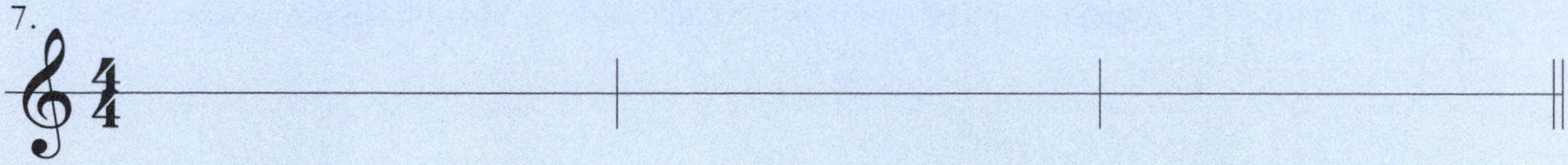

8.

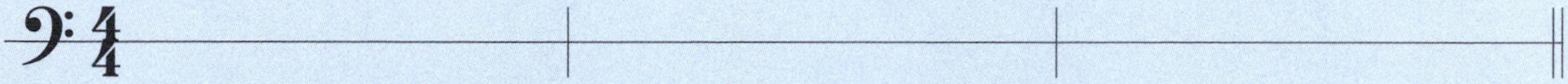

AURAL SKILLS CONDITIONING 13 (ADVANCED)

Secondary Leading Tone Chords

Play the following progression on your guitar or keyboard.

B♭: I vii^{o7}/ii ii V^7 I

Now listen to jazz great Etta James performing the American standard "Stormy Weather." Can you hear the same progression in the opening vocal line? Secondary leading tone chords are used exactly the same, whether in a Mozart aria performed by Renée Fleming or in the vocal improvisations of a jazz artist. Play the progression one more time and give extra emphasis to the B♮ in the second chord. You'll be able to hear how much power this one chromatic pitch has as it resolves up to the supertonic.

WEBSITE
VIDEO TRACK 38

Singing Secondary Leading Tone Chords

Let's practice singing secondary leading tone chords within the context of a progression. The most common secondary leading tone chords are vii^{o7}/V and vii^{o7}/ii, so we will focus on those here. (Challenge yourself to learn others as your musicianship progresses!)

Study the solfège given below, along with the chord's resolution. Notice how we have to raise the solfège syllable to reflect the leading tone of the chord being tonicized and lower the seventh in order to create a fully diminished chord! Always sing through the scale before attempting this in order to settle yourself on a clear tonic.

vii^{o7}/V	V
fi–la–do–me	sol–ti–re
vii^{o7}/ii	ii
di–mi–sol–te	re–fa–la

Now, let's try to sing these chords in the context of a progression. You can either attempt to sing these through yourself *or* you can sing together as a class with each student picking a particular solfège syllable in the opening chord and working through the progression to create the smoothest line.

I   IV   vii°7/V   cad$^6_4$ V7   I
(fi–la–do–me)

I   vi^6 vii°7/ii   ii   V$^6_5$ I
(di–mi–sol–te)

Tricky, isn't it? But what you need to notice here is that throughout the entire progression the only chord that includes a pitch outside of the key is the chromatic chord. When you listen to progressions, you can still use the Do–Ti–Re test to determine the function for all of the chords *except* the chromatic chord. If you hear a chord that seems to be outside of the diatonic key, you can label that chord as chromatic. By determining whether the chord is major or diminished and understanding its resolution, you will be able to hear the chord as either a secondary leading tone or secondary dominant chord.

Hearing Secondary Chords

REPLAY

AUDIO TRACKS CH. 13 HEARING SECONDARY 1–5

Your teacher will play a series of progressions that includes either a secondary dominant or secondary leading tone chord. Circle the type of chromatic chord you hear in the progression.

1. Secondary dominant   Secondary leading tone
2. Secondary dominant   Secondary leading tone
3. Secondary dominant   Secondary leading tone
4. Secondary dominant   Secondary leading tone
5. Secondary dominant   Secondary leading tone

Hearing Secondary Chords in Context

REPLAY

AUDIO TRACKS CH. 13 HEARING SECONDARY IN CONTEXT 1–4

Your teacher will now play a series of progressions. Try to fill in the spaces provided with the appropriate Roman numeral. A few chords are given to you to help you find your bearings.

1. i   ______   ______   VI   ______   i
2. I   ______   ______   cad$^6_4$ ______   ______
3. i   ______   i^6 ______   V^7 ______
4. I   ______   ______   ______   ______   V

THE FINAL NOTE: REAL-WORLD PERSPECTIVE

Renée Fleming

INTERNATIONAL OPERA STAR

What course or courses did you take in college, other than vocal lessons, that best prepared you for your career in performance? How so?

A career in opera is about far more than vocal technique. It requires a whole array of skills that can't be developed in a voice lesson, so there were lots of courses that helped me prepare for my career: languages, acting, and music history were all vital. Dance training was invaluable, not only for developing kinesthetic sense and moving gracefully onstage, but also because a singer's instrument is in her body. As a performer, it is important to understand the context and meaning of your art in a broader sense; so I found a course I took in the philosophy of aesthetics really beneficial.

Has the study of music theory and ear training helped you in your career? If so, how?

Absolutely. As the child of two public school voice teachers, I had a head start. Growing up, music was like air in our household. But theory and ear training are especially crucial for a classical singer. The knowledge of musical forms that I gained from studying theory has been indispensable. Understanding musical structure is as vital to jazz improvisation as it is to ornamenting a baroque aria. Ear training is also a must. A singer can't simply put her finger on a particular stop, or depress a specific key, and produce the right note. Standing alone in front of a seventy-piece orchestra, it is a great advantage to know that it's a D-minor chord that you're hearing, and that your entrance note is a major sixth above the cellos. And any successful singer will need to have the skill to learn a vast amount of music very quickly. A lot of that study will happen outside the practice room—on planes, in waiting rooms, even in the subway, reading a score. Having a solid foundation in theory has been, for me, a definite necessity.

Most significant learning experience of your career . . . or the "Aha" moment.

I prefer not to highlight one isolated learning moment. My experience has taught me that, as a musician, you will be a lifelong student. I have had "Aha" moments throughout my career, at almost every engagement. The growth continues, and the work is never finished. Finding your voice, layering and deepening interpretations, adapting to changes in your body, your life, and the world around you—this is the process, and it never stops. This need for continued study, for the ability to evolve, is becoming more and more crucial. Classical musicians (especially opera singers who work in a 400-year-old tradition), will have to respond to radical changes in the way our art is consumed and shared by audiences.

CHAPTER 14

BORROWED CHORDS

Artist in Residence: Rascal Flatts

Chapter Objectives

- Define borrowed chord and give examples of borrowed chords in various keys
- Analyze borrowed chords when given key and Roman numeral
- Correctly notate borrowed chords using appropriate accidentals
- Analyze chromatic chords found in musical scores of both classical and popular literature

WEBSITE

VIDEO TRACK 39

In 2005, the country group Rascal Flatts (Gary LeVox, Jay DeMarcus, and Joe Don Rooney) premiered the song "Bless the Broken Road." It immediately shot to number 1 on the country charts and peaked at 20 on the Adult Contemporary charts. The song went platinum and won the 2006 Grammy for Best Country Song. Take a minute to listen to the song on the YouTube channel.

Why do you think this song was so incredibly popular? It went on to be covered by many artists, including Carrie Underwood on season 4 of *American Idol*.

The chord structure of "Bless the Broken Road" is functional in every way. Using either your guitar or keyboard, play along with the first verse, using only the tonic, subdominant, dominant, and submediant (I, IV, V, vi). Written in the key of C major, the chord changes are clear and the harmonies very functional.

The following progression forms the basis for the chords in the song "Bless the Broken Road."

	C	F	G	A-	F	G	C
C:	I	IV	V	vi	IV	V	I

What if we wanted to add a few chromatic pitches to this particular progression to make it less conventional? A **borrowed chord** (sometimes called **modal mixture**) uses pitches from the parallel key in order to change the quality of various chords. Using the key of C minor, the parallel key to C major, the progression above can be changed to the following.

	C-	F-	G-	A♭	F-	G-	C-
C:	i	iv	v	♭VI	iv	v	i

While it is possible to change *every* chord in a progression to use the key signature from the parallel minor, the effect of chromaticism is, well, less effective for the listener! Play the same progression in C major, only this time substitute the A minor chord with the A♭ major chord.

	C	F	G	A♭	F	G	C
C:	I	IV	V	♭VI	IV	V	I

The fourth chord in the progression sounds extremely foreign in the key of C major, creating a slight sense of unrest or tension in the harmonic progression. Borrowed chords are used extensively in both popular and classical music for just that reason. Composers or artists insert a borrowed chord in order to have listeners raise their eyebrows a little, as if to say, "That's not what I expected." Do you want people to listen more intently? That mission can be accomplished through borrowed chords.

The following chords can all be used as borrowed chords in a song written in a major key. Notice that all the chords listed are found diatonically in a minor key.

Triads

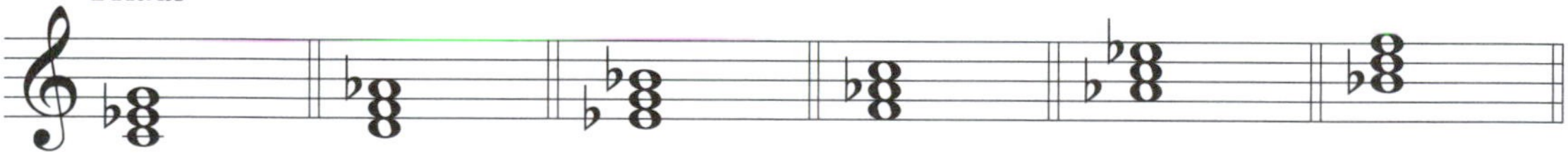

C: i ii° ♭III iv ♭VI ♭VII

7th chords

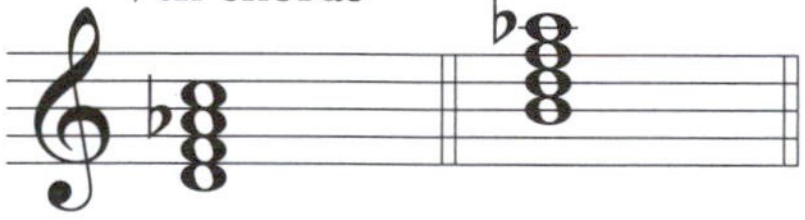

ii^{ø} vii^{o7}

Although pitches can be borrowed from either parallel major or minor keys, it is much more common for pitches to be borrowed from the minor mode. Why do you think this is? There is one exception to this statement. Music composed in the minor mode, both in classical and popular genres often conclude the composition or piece with a major tonic chord. The use of a major tonic chord at the end of a song written in a minor mode is called a picardy third.

ARTIST IN RESIDENCE

I'm Movin' On (or, better yet, Movin' Up)

Before the year 2000, the members of Rascal Flatts were background musicians for headline acts Cheryl Wright and Michael English. They were relatively well known in the Nashville studio circuit; however, it wasn't until they were introduced to Lyric Street Records that they got their first big break. According to A&R (artist and repertoire) director Doug Howard, "The vocals and harmonies, it was all there—I was just blown away. The lead singer has such a unique and compelling voice." They were immediately signed and sent to the studio to begin writing and performing. Their self-titled album was released that year and produced three top 10 hits, "Prayin' for Daylight," "I'm Movin' On," and "This Everyday Love." Rascal Flatts went on to win the Academy of Country Music Award for New Vocal Group in 2000.

Joe Don described the band's sound:

> We just really jelled because of our influences: pop, rhythm and blues, country, gospel, bluegrass roots. We've always liked to try to be different, even if we were just playing at some little dive. When someone listens to Rascal Flatts, they're going to hear a lot of harmony, a lot of funkiness because we love to groove.

THE BORROWED iv

The song "I Melt" can be found on the band's second album, *Melt*, released in 2002. Written by LeVox and non-band members Neil Thrasher and Wendell Mobley, "I Melt" peaked at number 2 on the country charts.

Study the lead sheet symbols for the chorus. The song is written in the key of E major, but the songwriters chose to insert a D major and A minor chord on the third line, neither of which are diatonic in the key of E major; however, listen to the effect that these chromatic chords have on the line! The text at this point describes the burn he feels when seeing his significant other: "the coolest thing I've ever felt." This phrase is a play on the feeling of burn. How appropriate to use a chord that is unexpected. The A minor chord is labeled as a subdominant (iv). More on the D major chord in a bit.

WEBSITE
VIDEO TRACK 40

Rascal Flatts, "I Melt." Songwriters: Gary LeVox, Wendell Mobley, and Neil Thrasher. Key: E major

E A
I melt every time you look at me that way,

E (D) B
It never fails, anytime, any place.

E (D) A/C♯ (A-/C)
This burn in me is the coolest thing I've ever felt,

E
I melt.

SONG SPOTLIGHT

Hidden under the Skin

From the album *Feels Like Today* (2004), the song "Skin" also peaked at number 2 on the country charts. The lyrics tell the story of Sarabeth, a young woman diagnosed with leukemia after noticing a small bruise on her skin. The lyrics of the chorus transport us to the prom, where we find that she has now lost all of her hair and is dancing with her boyfriend. He has lovingly shaved his head in support of his dying girlfriend.

The story recounted in the lyrics is remarkably similar to the story of a young girl named Sara Elizabeth Kennedy, although the song was not written specifically about her. The real Sara passed away from an aggressive childhood cancer in 2005. A memorial fund known as the SaraCare Fund was established after Sara Kennedy's death to provide for other young patients and their families, and also to help support healthcare providers. The song "Skin" is now often associated with Sara due to the remarkable similarities between the real Sara and the Sarabeth in the lyrics.

Powerfully written and performed, this song was "hidden" within the tracks of *Feels Like Today*: it was not listed as a separate track. There are several reasons for this, including that the band was contracted for only eleven tracks, not twelve.

VIDEO TRACK 41

The chorus of "Skin" is written in the key of A major and the chord progression focuses primarily on tonic and dominant harmonies. Listen closely to the third line of the chorus beginning with the words "And her very first love is holding her close." The use of the D minor chord (iv) at the end of the line provides a powerful reminder that all is not well with the picture given in this song. The movement from the iv to the V–I cadence at the end of the chorus brings hope once again.

THE BORROWED ♭III

VIDEO TRACK 42

The song "Why Wait" from the album *Nothing Like This* (2010) marks a return of the band to their original sound of close harmonies, large melodies, and strong vocal performances. After listening to the song on the YouTube channel, how would you describe the band's sound at this point in their career?

The ♭III chord (F major chord) at the end of the chorus interrupts the movement of the subdominant (IV) chord to the dominant (V). What a sound! The sudden shift to the F major chord prolongs the anticipation for the cadence.

Rascal Flatts, "Why Wait." Songwriters: Neil Thrasher, Tom Shapiro, and Jimmy Yeary. Key: D major

(*Chorus*)

```
D
Why wait another minute

     G                                          Dsus
For something we should have done yesterday?

D
I know a little church

      A
With a preacher who could hook us up right away

Bm
Love don't need a reason

G                        D                    G
Baby, I don't see how I could love you anymore than I do today

  (F) A7 D   Dsus  D
So why   wait
```

THE BORROWED ♭VII

Used extensively in popular music, the ♭VII can act as a substitution for either the dominant or the leading tone chord. Return back to the chord sheet for "I Melt" on page 263. The D major chord in the second line is a ♭VII that leads right into the dominant. The D major chord on the word "coolest" provides a great bass line down to the tonic chord. Look at how Rascal Flatts uses the ♭VII in the song "Unstoppable" from the album *Unstoppable* (2009). The D♭ major chord in the fourth line is not diatonic in the key, but the pitches *are* found in the parallel key of E♭ minor. Another chromatic chord in this excerpt is the G major chord found in the seventh line. Its functional purpose is to provide a smooth passing line up to the A♭ major chord; it is not a borrowed chord.

VIDEO TRACK 43

Rascal Flatts, "Unstoppable." Songwriters: Hillary Lindsey, Jay Demarcus, and James Slater. Key: E♭ major

(*Chorus*)

E♭
You find your faith has been lost and shaken

B♭
You take back what's been taken

Fm
Get on your knees and dig down deep

A♭ D♭ A♭/C
You can do what you think is impossible

E♭
Keep on believing don't give in

B♭
It'll come and make you whole again

Fm G A♭
It always will, it always does

Cm A♭
Love is unstoppable

THE BORROWED ♭VI

Although the ♭VI is used more extensively in classical music, it is often heard as a neighboring chord to the dominant or as a mediant to the tonic. The Band Perry, made up of siblings Kimberly, Reid and Neil Perry, are another country group well known for harmonies. They use plenty of chormatic chords in their music, including the ♭VI in their 2013 single "Chainsaw." The single is from the album *Pioneer* which made it to the top spot of the country charts in 2013. Study the following lyrics and chords. There are several borrowed chords used here, the ♭III, ♭VI, and the ♭VII. How can you explain the F major chord at the end of the chorus?

VIDEO TRACK 44

The Band Perry, "Chainsaw." Songwriters: Shane McAnally, Josh Osburne, and Matt Ramsey. Key: A major

A
And I got my chainsaw

D G A
Oh you know it's got to go, it's such a shame y'all

D G A C D F
But I ain't gonna be happy 'til those names fall

A
And I'm sittin' on a stump

A
Love is shady, love is tragic, it's hard to bury the hatchet

ARTIST IN RESIDENCE

Feels Like Today, Honors and Awards

Year(s)	Honors and Awards
2003–2009	Country Music Association Award, Vocal Group of the Year
2005–2009	Academy of Country Music Award, Top Vocal Group
2006	American Music Award, Artist of the Year
	Grammy Award, Best Country Song for "Bless the Broken Road"
2006–2009	American Music Award, Favorite Country Band/Duo/Group
2011	Induction into Grand Ole Opry
2012	Star on the Hollywood Walk of Fame
2014	Jim Reeves International Award

DISCOGRAPHY

- *Rascal Flatts* (2000)
- *Melt* (2002)
- *Feels Like Today* (2004)
- *Me and My Gang* (2006)
- *Still Feels Good* (2007)
- *Greatest Hits Volume 1* (2008)
- *Unstoppable* (2009)
- *Nothing Like This* (2010)
- *Changed* (2012)
- *Rewind* (2014)

Reviewing Chapter Objectives

- Define borrowed chord and give examples of borrowed chords in various keys (page 261)
- Analyze borrowed chords when given key and Roman numeral (pages 261, 267)
- Correctly notate borrowed chords using appropriate accidentals (pages 261, 268)
- Analyze chromatic chords found in musical scores of both classical and popular literature (pages 263–266, 268–269)

EXERCISES

I. Given the key, notate the correct Roman numeral for each chord. Be sure to indicate inversions with the appropriate figured bass.

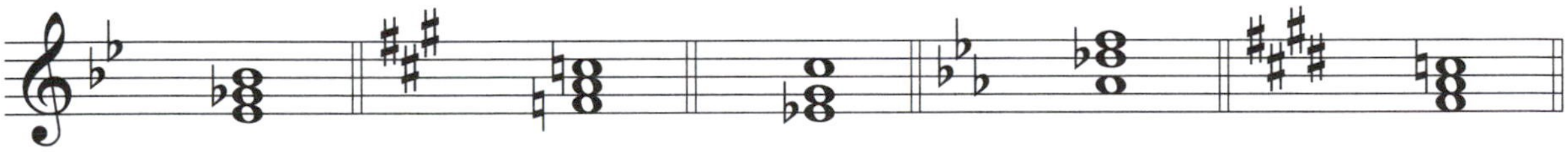

B♭: A: C: E♭: E:

D: Gmin: Amin: G♭: C:

F♯: Gmin: A: E: A♭:

II. Given the key and Roman numerals, notate the following chords. Be sure to add any necessary accidentals.

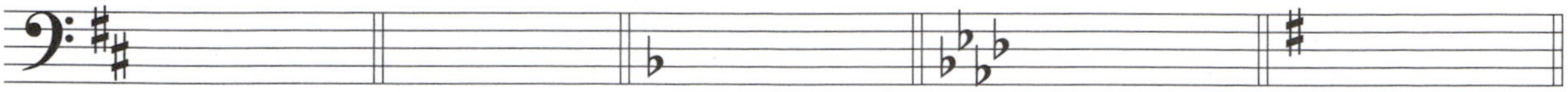

D: iv   C: ♭VI   F: i   A♭: ♭III$^{6}_{4}$ G: ii$^{\circ 6}$

F♯: ♭VII$^{6}_{4}$ E: ii$^{\circ 6}_{5}$ Cmin: picardy third   D♭: vii$^{\circ 4}_{2}$ A: V

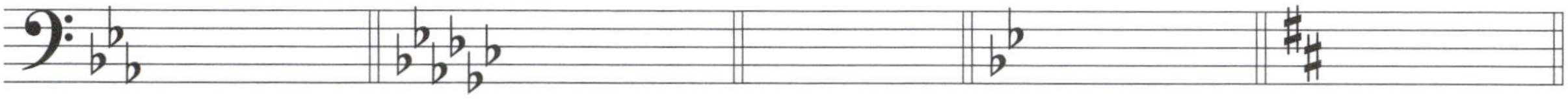

E♭: i^{6} G♭: ♭VI   Amin: IV$^{6}_{4}$ B♭: ii^{ø7} Bmin: I

ANALYSIS

For the next two examples, give a Roman numeral analysis for each chord, paying careful attention to the accidentals. Do the accidentals function as chromatic non-chord tones or do the pitches form the foundation for chromatic harmony? Identify all types of second inversion chords and circle and identify non-chord tones.

VIDEO TRACK 45

Edward MacDowell, "To a Wild Rose" from *Woodland Sketches* (1896)[1]

A:

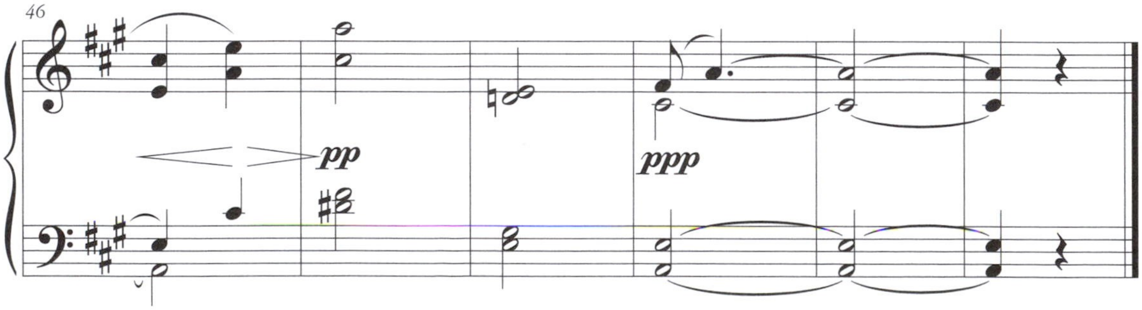

[1]The Roman numeral analysis in measure 43 could be problematic in terms of diatonic or borrowed harmonies. Explore all the options in terms of non-chord terms before determining the correct Roman numeral for analysis.

Friedrich von Flotow, "Ach, so fromm, ach so traut" from *Martha* (1847)

Translation:
So beautiful that my heart flew to her with longing;
Was wounded and inflamed by her angelic beauty
Which love has engraved in my heart, and which cannot be erased,
And the mere thought of her responding to my passion
Is able to appease the suffering which distresses me and breaks my heart!

WEBSITE
VIDEO TRACK 46

VIDEO TRACK 47

This symphony is the eighth of twelve "London Symphonies," and it is nicknamed the "Military Symphony" due in part to the trumpet fanfares and percussive aspects of the second movement. Listen carefully to the entire excerpt. How are the chromatic chords functioning in measures 239–247? Could you justify a change in key here or should the chords be analyzed as borrowed chords? Complete a Roman numeral analysis of the opening phrase in measures 226–233.

Haydn, *Symphony No. 100*, Hob.I:100, Mvt. I

229
Fl.
Ob.
Bsn.
Hn. in G
Tpt. in C
Timp.
Vln. I
Vln. II
Vla.
Vc.
Cb.

Haydn, *Symphony No. 100*, Hob.I:100, Mvt. I *(continued)*

236
Fl.
Ob.
Bsn.
Hn. in G
Tpt. in C
Timp.
Vln. I
Vln. II
p
Vla.
Vc.
Cb.

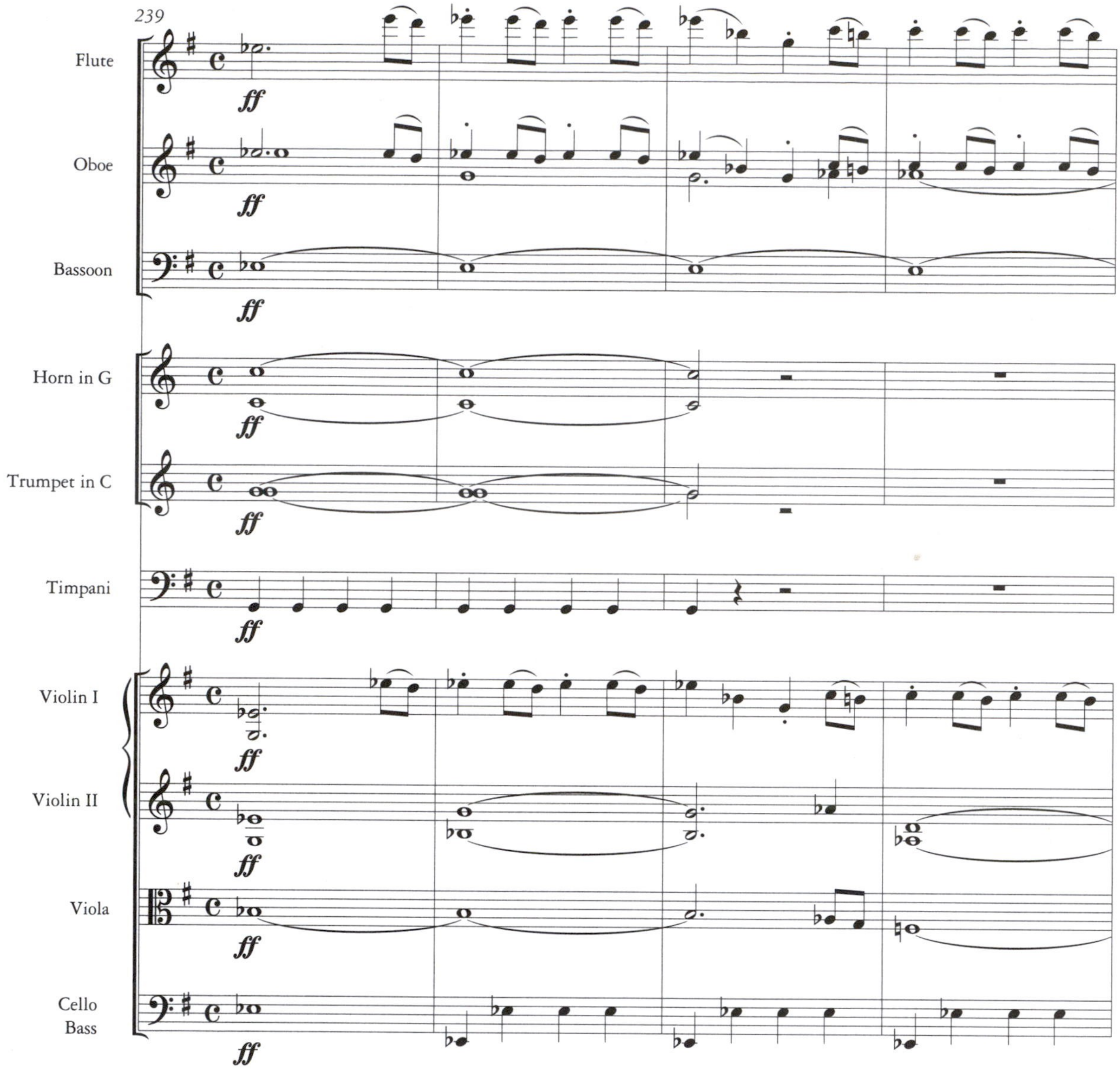
239
Flute
Oboe
Bassoon
Horn in G
Trumpet in C
Timpani
Violin I
Violin II
Viola
Cello
Bass
ff

243
Fl.
Ob.
Bsn.
Hn. in G
Tpt. in C
Timp.
Vln. I
Vln. II
Vla.
Vc.
Cb.

Haydn, *Symphony No. 100*, Hob.I:100, Mvt. I *(continued)*

AURAL SKILLS CONDITIONING 14

Borrowed Chords

As you probably realized in this chapter, borrowed chords are used extensively in popular music. That doesn't mean that you won't hear them in classical music, but it seems that songwriters are excited to introduce chromatic pitches in this manner, especially at the conclusions of cadences.

Singing Borrowed Chords

The borrowed chords most used within popular music are the ♭III (me–sol–te), iv (fa–le–do), ♭VI (le–do–me), and ♭VII (te–re–fa). Notice that in order to sing these particular chords, you must borrow solfège from the minor scale. As a class, sing through the following progressions using correct solfège.

I	vi^6	iv^6	V^7	I	
I	♭III	ii	V	I	
I	IV^6	cad^6_4	V	♭VI	
I	ii	V	♭VI	♭VII	I

HEARING BORROWED CHORDS WITHIN CONTEXT

Let's look at a few pieces from popular literature to see whether we can identify where the borrowed chord occurs. The lyrics from several well-known pop ballads are given below. While listening along to the examples on the YouTube channel, circle the lyric that is accompanied by the borrowed harmony.

Menken and Ashman, "Beauty and the Beast," (1:08–1:22)

VIDEO TRACK 48

"Ever a surprise. Ever as before, ever just as sure as the sun will rise."

Roberta Flack, "The First Time Ever I Saw Your Face," (4:45–5:19)

VIDEO TRACK 49

"Ever I saw your face, your face, your face, your face."

Righteous Brothers, "Unchained Melody," (1:28–1:41)

"Lonely rivers flow to the sea, to the sea, to the open arms of the sea, yeah."

VIDEO TRACK 50

Louis Armstrong, "What a Wonderful World," (0:10–0:30)

"I see trees of green, red roses too; I see them bloom for me and you, and I think to myself, what a wonderful world."

VIDEO TRACK 51

Now that we have a basic idea on where the chromatic chord is in each excerpt, match the following progression with the song above. You can challenge yourself to sight-sing through the progression first or play through the progression before making your decision.

1. IV	V	IV	♭III	IV	V	I			
2. I	vi	IV	iii	ii	I	V^7/vi	vi	♭VI	V
3. IV	iii	IV	iii	vi	♭VI	♭VII	I		
4. I	V	I	♭VII	I	♭VII	I			

CHALLENGING YOUR EARS: THE NEXT STEP

WEBSITE

VIDEO TRACK 52

At the end of the 20th century, Alanis Morissette was one of the top pop artists in the country. Her edgy sound and even more alternative appearance made her extremely popular to Generation X. The song "Uninvited" was recorded for the movie *City of Angels*, but was never released as a single. Her fans requested the song to be played on the radio continually, and it became a number 1 single without ever being formally released. It was even nominated for three Grammy awards in 1999. Again, the amazing thing about this is that it was *never* formally released. Listen to the song on the YouTube channel, and answer the questions below.

1. Give the solfège syllables for the opening four pitches of the introduction.
2. In terms of measures, how long does the opening motive repeat?
3. After the two-measure introduction, only three chords are used as harmonic support in measures 3–14. What is the solfège for the roots of these three chords?
4. It sounds as if the opening verse is a battle between major and minor. Would you say that the song is written in a major key with borrowed chords from the minor mode or in a minor key with borrowed chords from the major mode?

THE FINAL NOTE: REAL-WORLD PERSPECTIVE

Pat McMakin

DIRECTOR OF OPERATIONS FOR OCEAN WAY RECORDING STUDIO

Has the study of music theory and musicianship helped you in your career? If so, how?

Absolutely. When I interview perspective engineers here at Ocean Way, I always ask, "What instrument do you play?" I think there are a lot of people coming out of the studio technology education market and many of them never had a grasp of music to begin with. If you are going to record music, it is very important that you understand music in every sense of the word, including harmonics, the flow of music, how sounds are translated into frequencies. When we look at one sound masking the sound of another in a mix, you need to be able to go in and know what to take out and what to leave in.

When I started producing, I had to understand harmony. I learned most of what I know about harmony from harmony singers. I would listen and talk to them about why and how they were choosing certain notes.

How did you first become involved with music?

It was drums and seeing the Beatles on Ed Sullivan that did it for me. I saw Ringo Starr and said, "That's what I want to do." I started taking drum lessons in the third grade and I was okay. Later on, I joined the high school band and they needed someone who could read rhythms to play the sousaphone, so I was drafted from being a drummer to being a tuba player. But I had to learn on the spot how to really read notation. Later, I took some piano classes at Belmont and I'm a self-taught guitar player.

How did your previous work experience help to prepare you for this position?

I was with SONY/ATV Music for 25 years. My story is different than others', though; it's weird, because to have one job for 25 years never happens here. I came into the music business at a time of extreme growth. When I came out of school, I already had an edge because I knew how to do certain technical things. In 1982, I was hired to run a demo studio at Tree Publishing that was later purchased by Sony Music Entertainment. Record sales were just starting the increases enjoyed during the 80s so there were lots of opportunities, so 2 years later I was running three studios at the age of 28. I'll never forget that first day. To say I was nervous is an understatement. Brenda Lee was in my A room with a full film crew shooting a commercial, and I had clients in the B room. I was just thrown into it.

Eventually, I ran into clients that had producers that didn't follow through, so I started producing because people just needed help. I was literally in the studio 12 to 14 hours every day. It was a good way to learn. By the time I was 30, I had engineered or produced thirty number 1 records and had worked with Ray Charles and Dolly Parton among others.

Why do artists decide to record at Ocean Way? What makes this space so unique?

They come here because they love the room, especially studio A. But it is also about customer service. I tell my engineers, "If you think we are in any business other than customer service, then you are in the wrong business." Yes, you need your technical skills, and yes, you need to understand music. This goes for musicians too. You are in the service industry. Those that tend to thrive and do well are those that understand the needs of their client. If you are a guitar player, and you are playing on the road with Carrie Underwood, you are there to support Carrie Underwood and you are there to entertain *her* crowd. It's not about you. When I talk to some of the top session musicians in the industry, we agree that we are the tradespeople much like plumbers and electricians, putting the house together.

Do you find it important to be able to speak with engineers and musicians about the technical aspect of your craft? How important is it to be able to talk to the engineers and musicians about the musical aspect (sound, harmonies, chords, etc.) of the production?

If the musicians are happy and can hear themselves, you will get a great performance. It is a very human craft, and it is very important to talk in musical terms with the musicians and engineers.

Most significant learning experience of your career.

You just gotta learn when and how to offer suggestions. You also need to know when to be silent. I learned by getting this wrong a couple of times. But most of my experience has come from being thrown into the water way over my head and learning how to swim out.

Greatest moment of your career so far.

There's a lot of those. Just to be in the same room with Ray Charles or to have Paul Simon down the hall. And there's the day when Steve Martin was overdubbing his first bluegrass album and Dolly and Vince were in the studio. So many moments. Or turning around from the console one day and staring at Loretta Lynn and Leon Russell sitting on the sofa.

CHAPTER 15

MODULATIONS IN POPULAR MUSIC

Artist in Residence: Queen

Chapter Objectives

- Define modulation
- Recognize pivot chord modulation within the context of a popular music setting
- Recognize direct modulation within the context of a popular music setting
- Define and label sequential modulations
- Realize modulations when given Roman numerals and point of modulation
- Recognize modulations within the context of lead sheet symbols

WEBSITE VIDEO TRACK 1

Let's start this chapter by watching a video by the performance ensemble CDZA. This group of musicians from both the classical and popular sector highlights modulations found in popular songs throughout the past 3 decades. This performance proves that modulations are powerful, iconic, and in many ways epic.

A change in tonal center, called a **modulation**, requires two conditions:

- Consistent accidentals: in order for a key to truly change, accidentals must be added or deleted to indicate the new key.
- Strong cadence in the new key: typically the new key is firmly established with an authentic cadence in the new key.

Take the time to listen to several hits on the current Billboard chart. Are there instances in which the tonic seems to change as the song progresses? Challenge yourself to sing the tonic (or the syllable *do*) throughout an entire song. If the original tonic changes, the piece has modulated. Often a modulation consists of a repetition of the chorus up a half step. An "over-the-top" example of this is Beyonce's "Love on Top" in which the melody line modulates a total of four times! It doesn't have to be a half step, though: check out Johnny Cash's "I Walk the Line," in which the verse is repeated, but up a perfect fourth! Sometimes artists will include an extended bridge passage as a way to move into a new key (Ray Charles, "Georgia on My Mind"). Songs such as "All by Myself" by Celine Dion and "I Will Always Love You" by Whitney Houston incorporate modulations that seem to come out of nowhere. Listen to all of these iconic modulations, all available on the YouTube channel.

VIDEO TRACKS 2–6

CLOSELY RELATED KEYS

Often a modulation will move to a closely related key, any key that is adjacent on the circle of fifths. The relative major/minor of the original key is always a closely related key and this shift in tonal centers is very effective in modulation. For the other related keys, think of adding or removing a sharp or flat from the key signature. For instance, if the original key is E major, removing a sharp will create the key of A major and adding a sharp will create the key of B major. The keys of A major and B major (and the relative minor keys of F♯, G♯, and C♯) are all closely related keys to E major.

The following chart lists several closely related keys.

Original Key	Closely Related Major Keys	Closely Related Minor Keys
C major	F major, G major	A minor, D minor, E minor
G major	C major, D major	E minor, A minor, B minor
A minor	C major, F major, G major	D minor, E minor
E minor	G major, C major, D major	A minor, B minor
F major	B♭ major, C major	D minor, G minor, A minor
B♭ major	E♭ major, F major	G minor, C minor, D minor
D minor	F major, B♭ major, C major	G minor, A minor
G minor	B♭ major, E♭ major, F major	C minor, D minor

PIVOT CHORD MODULATION

The most common type of modulation is called a **pivot chord modulation**. In this type of modulation, a particular chord serves two functions, both in the original key and the key to which the piece is modulating.

Play the following progression on your guitar or on the keyboard. Be sure to account for the new accidental of E♯ once the key modulates to F♯!

B: B B/D♯ E F♯ G♯-
I I^6 IV V vi

ii V^7 iii Cad$^6_4$ V^7 I
F♯: G♯- C♯ A♯- F♯/C♯ C♯7 F♯

So what chords can be used as pivot chords? Look at the diatonic chords found in both B major and F♯ major. Chords shared between the two keys include B major, F♯ major, and G♯ minor; any of these chords can be the pivot chord.

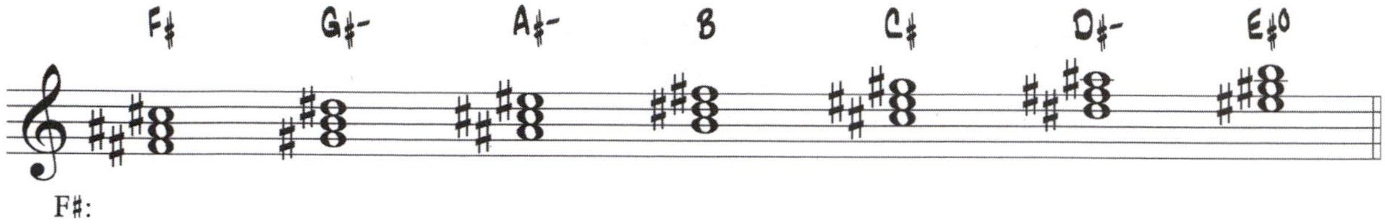

The fifth chord in the progression functions both as a submediant chord in the key of B major and a supertonic in the key of F♯ major. The sixth chord in the progression introduces the new pitch of E♯, the leading tone of the new key of F♯ major. Once the E♯ is established in the C♯ major chord, the tonal center of B is no longer valid. The strong cadential pattern at the conclusion of the progression solidifies the new key of F♯ major.

Let's create another progression using a pivot chord. Say you want to modulate from the key of C major to F major. We have plenty of chords that are diatonic in both keys (C, D–, F, and A–). Choose one to insert in your progression as your pivot, and solidify the modulation with a strong progression to the cadence in the new key.

C:	C	F/C	C	A	F			
	I	IV^6_4	I	vi	IV			
					I	ii	V^7	I
				F:	F	G-	C7	F

ARTIST IN RESIDENCE

Killer Queen

Musicians who were classically trained, fascinated with electronics in music, and trained in the art of singing the blues all came together to form the band Queen in London in 1971. Original members included the late Freddie Mercury (lead vocals, piano), Brian May (guitar, vocals), John Deacon (bass guitar), and Roger Taylor (drums, vocals). All were songwriters, arrangers, and producers of their work. Not only did the band perform their songs night after night, but also they had a vested interest in the production and arrangement of each song.

After signing with EMI in 1973, members of the band enjoyed a fast rise to the top. By 1974, they were touring in the United Kingdom, and in the United States, they had a number 1 hit with "Bohemian Rhapsody." One of the first bands to ever sell out stadiums, Queen is credited as the pioneer of stadium rock. Each concert was a true production, complete with elaborate light sequences (they were the first group to use a lighting rig) and prerecorded intro music before the band ever appeared on stage, a practice used by most touring artists today.

Year	Song (chart position)
1974	"Killer Queen" (no. 2)
1975	"Bohemian Rhapsody" (no. 1)
1976	"Somebody to Love" (no. 2)
1977	"We Are the Champions" (no. 2)
1979	"Crazy Little Thing Called Love" (no. 2)
1981	"Under Pressure" (no. 1)
1984	"RadioGaga" (no. 2)

Listen to the second phrase from the Queen hit "We Are the Champions." By measure 8 there is a strong dominant to tonic relationship between the B♭ and E♭ chord. The progression that follows in measures 10–16 is very diatonic until the sudden appearance of the C major chord in 10. By 11 we are clearly in the key of F major. The key of F is firmly established by the dominant to tonic movement in measures 10 and 11 between C major and F major. So, how did we get there? The B♭ chord functions in both keys and is our pivot chord.

VIDEO TRACK 7

Freddie Mercury, "We Are the Champions." Songwriter: Freddie Mercury

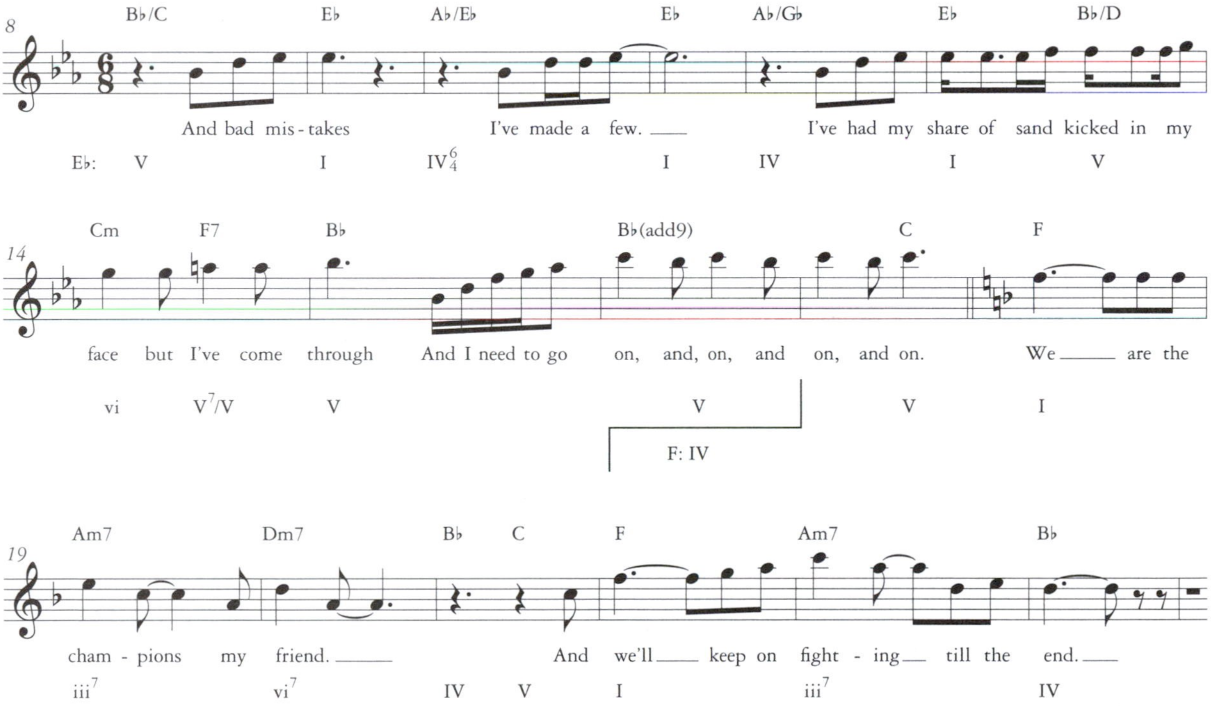

Perhaps one of the most effective pivot modulations used in popular music involves the addition of a minor seventh to the tonic triad. The addition of this one pitch transforms a tonic functioning triad into a dominant seventh chord. The addition of the seventh alters the function entirely.

This technique can be found in the powerful modulation in "Somebody to Love." The first A♭ major chord shown in the example is the final tonic triad of the opening section. There would be little doubt for the listener that the key of A♭ is firmly established by this point. However, in the next measure, the pitch G♭ is added to the tonic triad, creating a dominant seventh chord in the new key of D♭ major. Through the addition of one pitch to the tonic triad, the entire tonal center is changed.

Study the analyzed score as you listen to Queen's performance.

VIDEO TRACK 8

Freddie Mercury, "Somebody to Love." Songwriter: Freddie Mercury

DIRECT MODULATION

Listen to "Under Pressure." The piece begins in the key of D major, and the first twenty-eight measures consist of alternating tonic, subdominant, and dominant chords. Although there are a few instances of retrogression, the basic harmonic progression follows the rules of functional harmony. The strong V–I movement at the ending of the first verse solidifies the key of D major, and the tonic chord is prolonged for four measures before verse 2 begins with the text "Chippin' around."

VIDEO TRACK 9

Freddie Mercury and David Bowie, "Under Pressure." Songwriter: Freddie Mercury and David Bowie

However, the second ending offers a great deal of surprise to the listener. By measure 35 (2:12), it seems that there is a completely different tonal center. As shown below, the use of the C♮, both in the melody and in the lead sheet symbols, suggests the key of G major. The dominant chord is absent in this modulation to G major, but it is long enough for our ears to establish the shift in tonal center.

VIDEO TRACK 9

Freddie Mercury and David Bowie, "Under Pressure." Songwriter: Freddie Mercury and David Bowie

So how did we get there? D major and G major are certainly closely related keys and the modulation clearly establishes G major as the new tonal center, if nothing more than the consistent repetition of the pitch G. Following the A major chord in measure 33, the listener might expect the return of D; however, this is interrupted by the new tonic of G major. The modulation here is direct. The **direct modulation** is just that: a modulation that occurs directly after the cadence in the previous key. There are no chords that act as a pivot between these two contrasting sections.

VIDEO TRACK 9

An even bigger question might be, so how do we get back to D major? The use of modal mixture makes it difficult for us to evaluate the modality in measures 40–46 until the dominant to tonic relationship is firmly confirmed in the key of D major in measures 47–50. The C major chord in measure 40 acts as a pivot chord. The mode mixture chords provide amazing chromatic contrast!

Freddie Mercury and David Bowie, "Under Pressure." Songwriters: Freddie Mercury and David Bowie

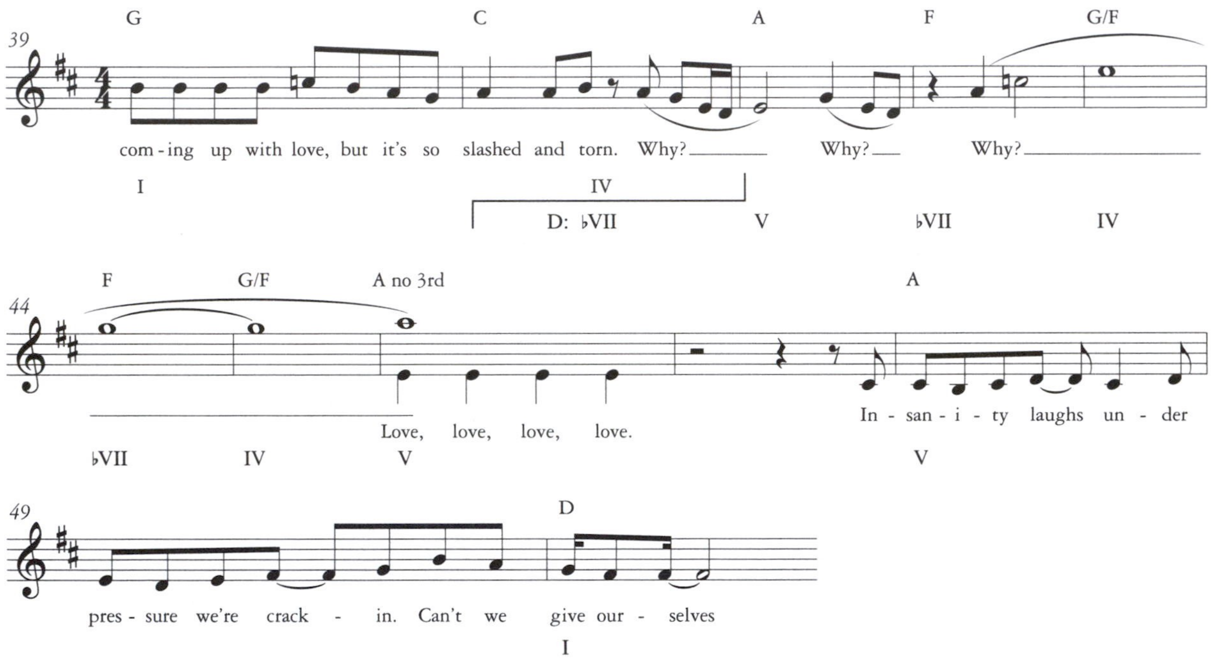

SONG SPOTLIGHT

"We Are the Champions"

VIDEO TRACK 7

Written by Freddie Mercury for the 1977 album *News of the World*, the song "We Are the Champions" reached number 2 on the UK Singles Chart and number 4 on the Billboard Hot 100 in the United States. The singable melody and optimistic lyrics have helped to make this a standard in the popular repertoire, especially in the sports arena. It has been used in numerous movies, including *High Fidelity, D2: The Mighty Ducks, What Happens in Vegas, A Knight's Tale, Kicking and Screaming, Chicken Little, You Again, Happy Feet Two, and Revenge of the Nerds*, and it has been featured in episodes of several TV series: *Friends, South Park, The Simpsons, The Sopranos, Malcolm in the Middle, The Big Bang Theory, Glee,* and *So You Think You Can Dance.*

The songs "We Will Rock You" and "We Are the Champions" are typically paired together, primarily because the two songs were released as a double A-side single. Most recently, at the 2012 Olympics Closing Ceremonies in London, Mercury's image appeared on screens while Brian May, Roger Taylor, and Jessie J performed "We Will Rock You." However, "We Are the Champions" was omitted and not performed. This created an outcry from Queen fans following the ceremonies, including one reviewer, who stated,

> The athletes who filled the floor of Olympic Stadium surely know the words to "We Are the Champions," and its emotional range suits their sacrifices and experience—from "I've paid my dues" in failures and losses, and the perseverance of "I need to go on and on and on," to the proclamation, "We are the champions my friends. And we'll keep on fighting 'til the end."

Watch the performance of the closing ceremonies after a quick search on YouTube. Why do you think the two-song set was not performed in its entirety?

SEQUENTIAL MODULATION

The opening lines of "We Are the Champions" are clearly in the key of C minor. The only two chords used in this section to accompany the vocal line are the tonic and subtonic chords. However, there is an abrupt change in measure 9. The same opening melody is now transposed up a minor third! The movement from C minor to E♭ major is a short but effective sequential modulation. In a **sequential modulation**, a melodic idea is stated at one pitch level and then restated at another pitch level.

VIDEO TRACK 7

Study the chord functions, notated by Roman numerals, in the excerpt below while listening to the song "We Are the Champions."

Freddie Mercury, "We Are the Champions." Songwriter: Freddie Mercury

PIVOT TONE MODULATION

Similar to the modulation by pivot chord, the **pivot tone modulation** includes one pitch that functions in both keys. Often the pivot pitch stands by itself, with little, if any accompaniment. The pitch is held over from the cadence in the original key and changes function as a new harmony is played underneath the pitch.

Have one student sing the following melody line while she/he is accompanied on a guitar or keyboard instrument. The pitch F♯ in measure 6 is the pivot tone to the new key of F♯ major.

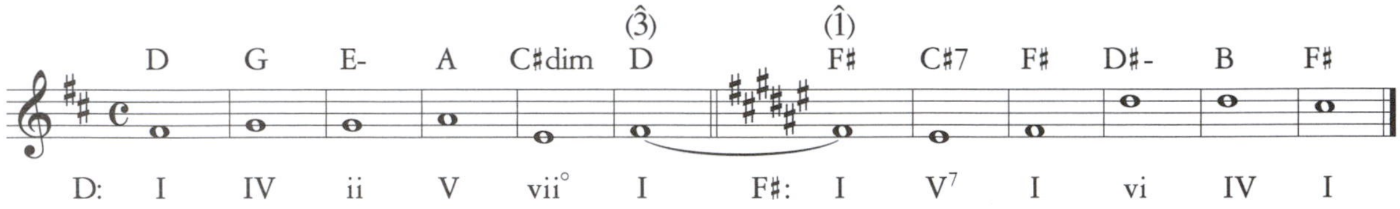

Let's see how Queen approaches this in the song "Save Me." The G held over from the final tonic suddenly changes function as it is now the subdominant pitch in the new key of D major.

VIDEO TRACK 10

Freddie Mercury, "Save Me." Songwriter: Brian May

SONG SPOTLIGHT

"Bohemian Rhapsody"

The song "Bohemian Rhapsody" is perhaps Queen's crowning achievement. Written by Mercury in 1975, it remained number 1 on the charts for 9 weeks and on the top 10 for 17 weeks. When Mercury introduced the song to the band, every single harmony part was written out, pitch by pitch. This labor of love includes 160 tracks of vocal overdubs in the chorus to create that large choral, almost operatic sound. Many told Mercury that the song was just too long for radio play. Clocking in at just under 6 minutes, EMI released the entire version a few days after it was played on local radio. The public seemed to think that Mercury was an expert in operatic composition based on this piece; however, Mercury set the record straight: "'Bohemian Rhapsody' didn't just come out of thin air. I did a bit of research, although it was tongue-in-cheek and it was a mock opera. Why not? I certainly wasn't saying I was an opera fanatic and I knew everything about it." The piece was well received and is still one of the best-selling songs of all time in the United Kingdom. Interestingly enough, through the popularity of the movie *Wayne's World*, the song found its way back to the number 2 spot on the charts 18 years later, in 1992. Transcribed for choirs, marching bands, and symphonies, most of the general public recognizes portions of this song. Why do you think this particular piece has remained so popular?

VIDEO TRACK 12

MONOPHONIC MODULATION

VIDEO TRACK 12

In this particular style of modulation, one line acts as a transition to the new key. The line is simply a single melodic line serving as transition between the two keys.

Listen to the transitional material of "Bohemian Rhapsody" starting at 3:04. Even without the score, the modulation in measure 55 is easily heard with the ear. In the following excerpt, the outlining of the C minor seventh chord in measure 55 acts as a transition to the new key of E♭. Due to the monophonic nature of the line, no pivot chord is justified here.

Freddie Mercury, "Bohemian Rhapsody." Songwriter: Freddie Mercury

OTHER MODULATIONS IN "BOHEMIAN RHAPSODY"

The excerpt below shows one example of a pivot chord in "Bohemian Rhapsody." The shift from the tonal center of B♭ major to E♭ major is solidified through the strong dominant-tonic relationship in measures 28 and 29. The borrowed v chord (F minor) functions both as an altered dominant and supertonic ii as a way to pivot between the two keys. The point of pivot is shown using Roman numerals. One could also make an argument for the pivot chord occurring on the E♭ chord. Both analyses are shown in the example below.

Freddie Mercury, "Bohemian Rhapsody." Songwriter: Freddie Mercury

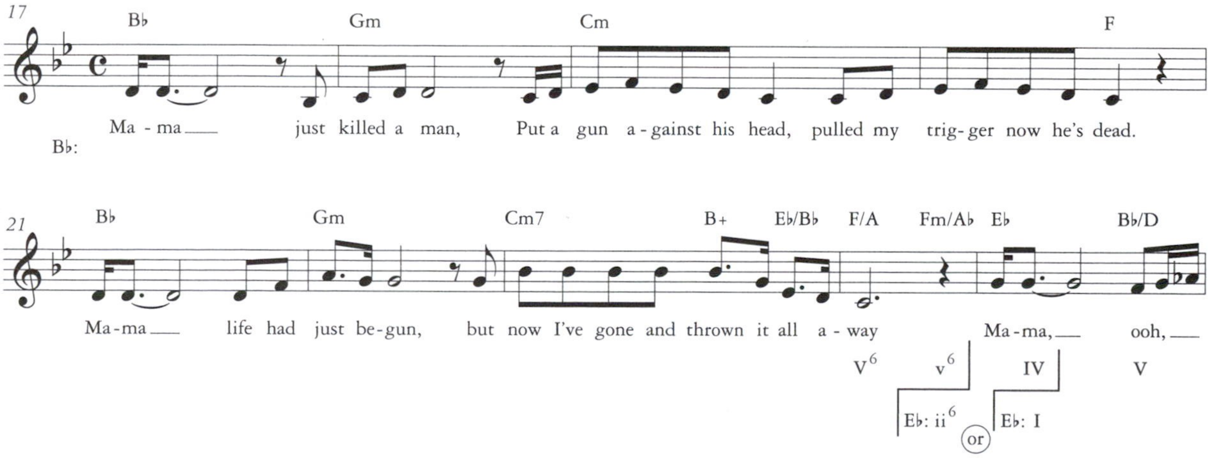

Freddie Mercury, "Bohemian Rhapsody." Songwriter: Freddie Mercury *(continued)*

Perhaps one of the more effective, yet hard to explain, modulations in "Bohemian Rhapsody" occurs in measure 42, beginning at 2:45. The transitional section is in the key of E♭ major. The chords function diatonically until the introduction of the D♭ major chord in measure 42. The D♭ chord is a borrowed chord in the key of E♭ but also can be respelled as a C♯ major chord, the chromatic mediant for the new key of A major.[1] E♭ major and A major are *not* closely related keys, but through the respelling and the mediant relationship, a modulation is achieved. The B♭ minor chord is just passing between the C♭ and A.

VIDEO TRACK 11

Freddie Mercury, "Bohemian Rhapsody." Songwriter: Freddie Mercury

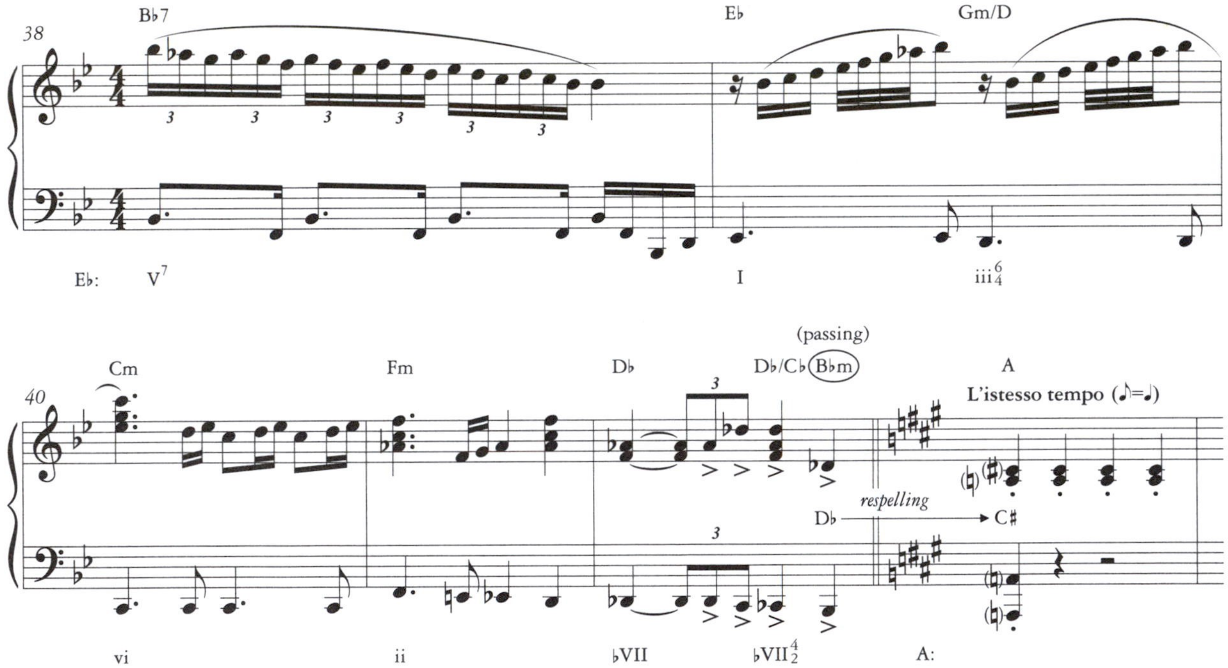

[1]A chromatic mediant relationship includes chords (or keys) whose roots are a major or minor third apart. They typically share one common tone.

BACKSTAGE PASS

Death of a Superstar

On November 25, 1991, Freddie Mercury died of bronchopneumonia resulting from AIDS. He had announced his AIDS diagnosis to the world only a day before: "The time has now come for my friends and fans around the world to know the truth, and I hope that everyone will join with me, my doctors and all those worldwide in the fight against this terrible disease." In an interview, Brian May talks about the emotional toll of Freddie's death:

> When Freddie died, it was like losing a family member, and we all handled it in different ways. For a time, I really wanted to escape from Queen; I didn't want to know about it. I think that was my grieving process. But I'm very proud of what we did together. My God, we really did go on some interesting excursions! Mostly, it makes me feel good. . . . I think about Freddie all the time, really. There certainly isn't a day where I don't have some sort of thought about him. I have been to the extremes, where I have found it very painful, and I couldn't talk about him. But I don't feel that any more. He's part of our lives, still, in a very real way. I'm not saying there aren't moments when I don't get tearful, because there are, but most of the time it's a joy.

It is hard to know what impact Mercury would have had on the music business today. Would he have reinvented himself to make his music and style more appealing as trends changed? Would he have collaborated with some of the biggest artists of this century? One thing is for certain: he influenced some of the greatest performers, including the Killers, Lady Gaga, Radiohead, and Katy Perry.

Reviewing Chapter Objectives

- Define modulation (page 282)
- Recognize pivot chord modulation within the context of a popular music setting (pages 285–286)
- Recognize direct modulation within the context of a popular music setting (page 287)
- Define and label sequential modulations (page 289)
- Realize modulations when given Roman numerals and point of modulation (page 296)
- Recognize modulations within the context of lead sheet symbols (page 297)

EXERCISES

I. Realize the following progressions using SATB voicing. Be sure to use proper voice leading rules as discussed in Chapter 8. Each progression contains a pivot chord modulation. Account for the new tonal center by inserting the correct accidentals.

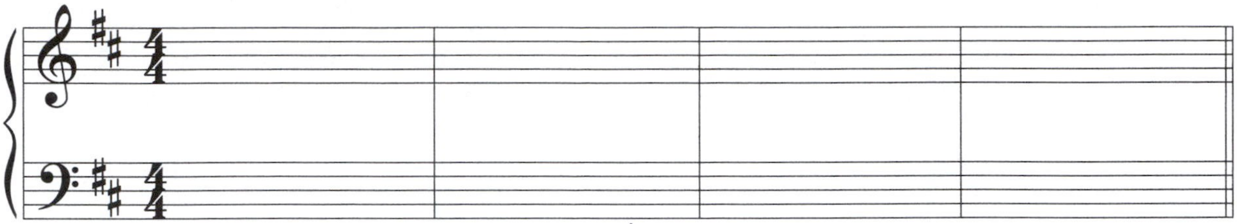

D: I IV^6 V$^6_5$ vi^6

A: ii^6 Cad$^6_4$ V^7 I

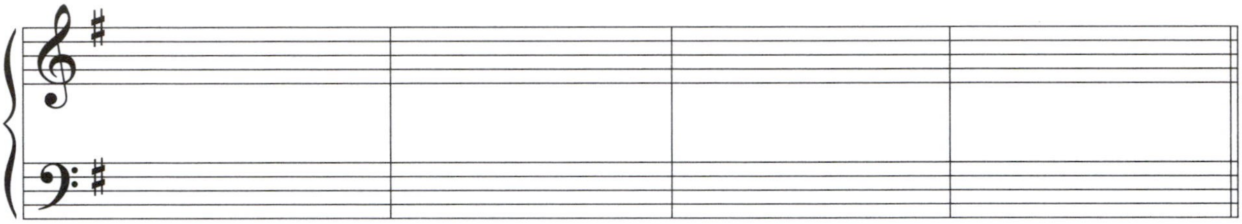

G: I ii^6 V^7 I ii

C: vi IV^6 V^7 I

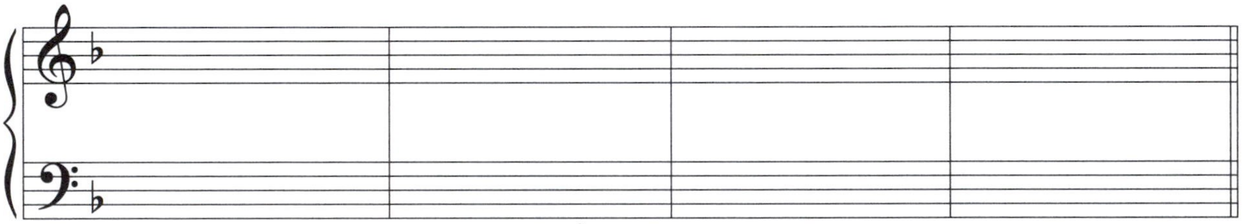

F: I IV V iii^6

Amin: i^6 ii$^{\circ 6}$ V i

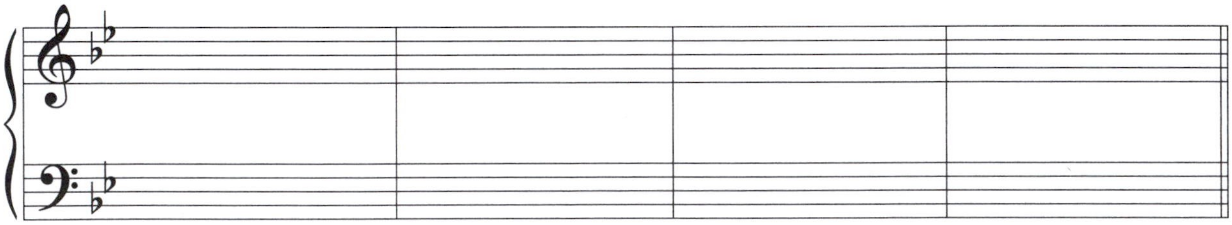

B♭: I vi^6 ii V/V

F: V Cad$^6_4$ V^7 I

A: I ii^{6} V$^{6}_{5}$ ♭VI

C: IV V^{7} I

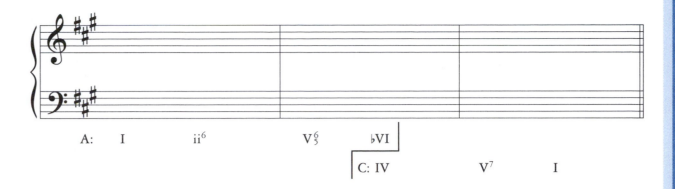

II. For each progression, write in the Roman numerals underneath the pop chords. Each progression contains a pivot chord modulation. In each progression, properly indicate the pivot chord, determine the new key, and continue the analysis in the new key. Play through each progression.

G:	G	Amin	A7	D	G♯o/B	E7	A				
	I						I				
B♭:	B♭	G-/B♭	D-	A♭/C	F	D7	G	C			
	I							I			
Dmin:	D-	Eo/G	B♭	D7	G	A-	F	G7	C		
	i								I		
D:	D	B7	E-	C♯o/E	D	G	A7	D	A/E	E7	A
	I										I
C:	C	Bo7	C	C7	F	D/F♯	G	E-	E♯o7	F♯7	B-
	I										I

ANALYSIS

Give a Roman numeral analysis for each excerpt. Identify all types of second inversion chords, and circle and identify non-chord tones. Label the point of modulation as pivot, direct, or sequential.

1. Traditional, *Flee as a Bird*

Traditional, *Flee as a Bird (continued)*

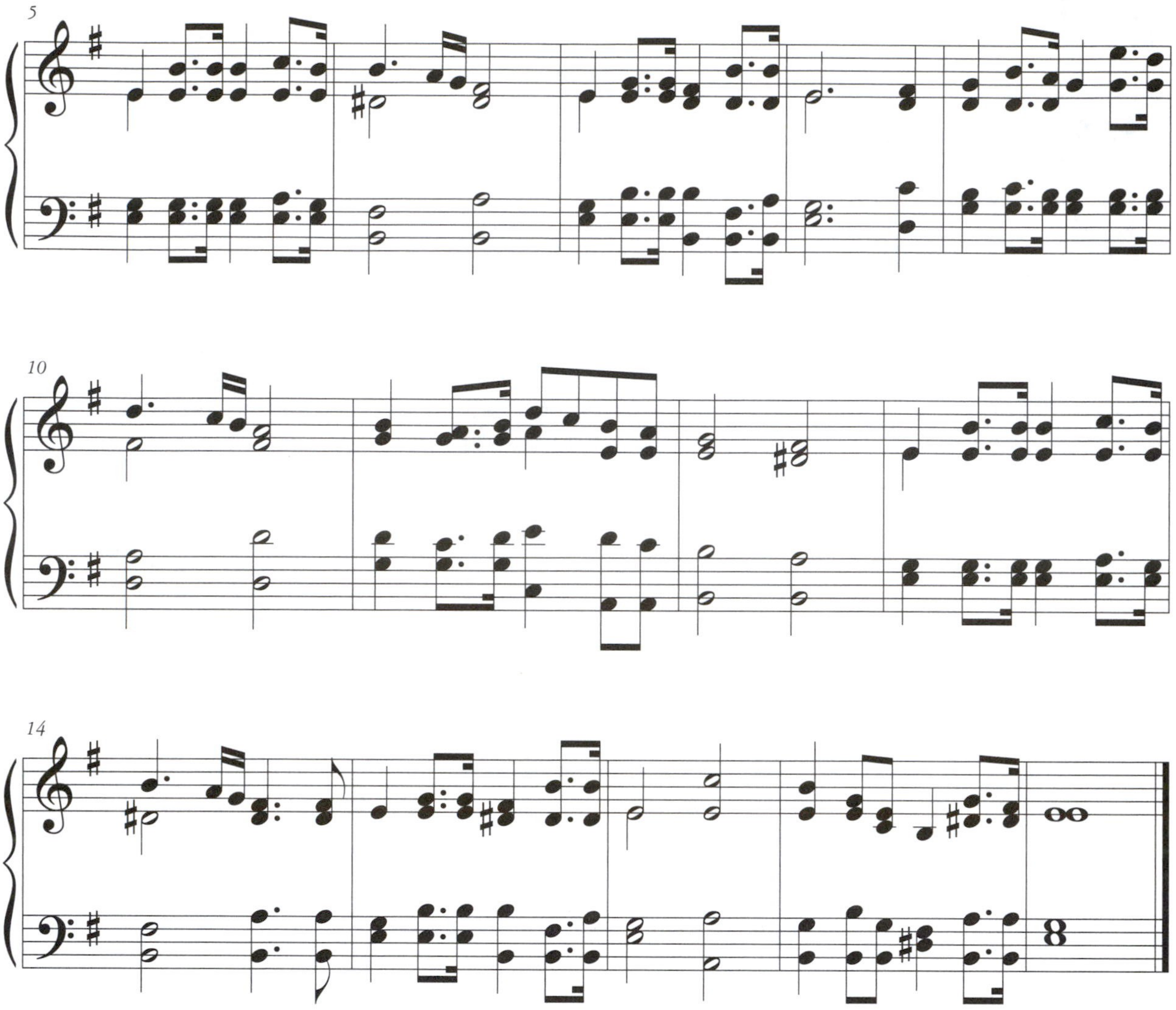

2. The Temptations, "My Girl." Songwriters: Smokey Robinson and Ronald White

VIDEO
TRACK 13

3. Felix Bernard, "Winter Wonderland"

Felix Bernard, "Winter Wonderland" *(continued)*

VIDEO
TRACK 14

4. Camille Saint-Saëns, "Le Cygne" from *Carnaval des Animaux*

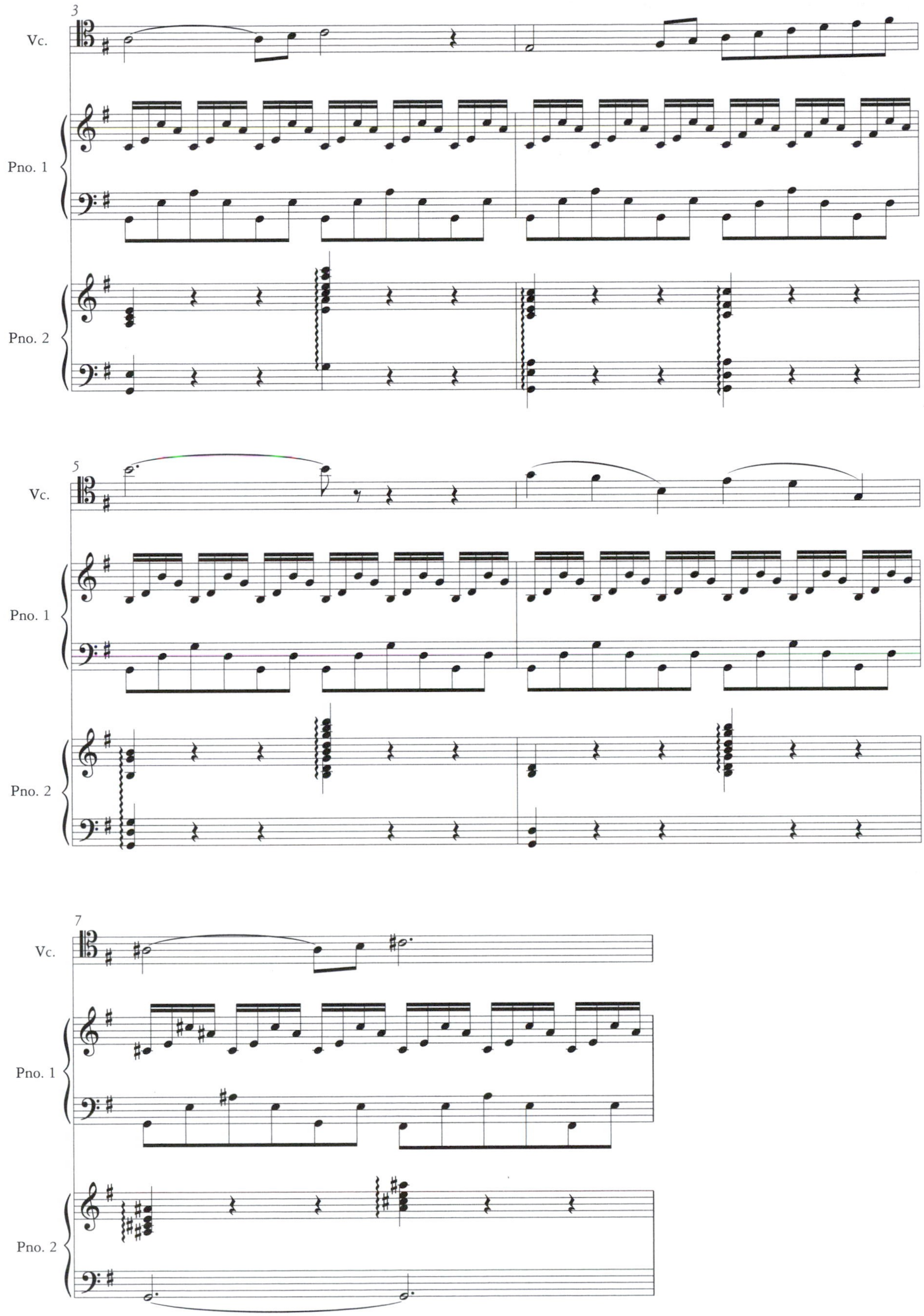
3
Vc.
Pno. 1
Pno. 2
5
Vc.
Pno. 1
Pno. 2
7
Vc.
Pno. 1
Pno. 2

Camille Saint-Saëns, "Le Cygne" from *Carnaval des Animaux (continued)*

COMPOSITION PROJECT

Throughout the past several chapters, you have learned about how chromatic chords and modulations can color a musical line. Songwriters may include a borrowed chord to emphasize a lyric while classical composers may focus on a modulation to move into a new section of a work. Take a few minutes to listen to some of the songs and compositions featured in Chapters 12–15. Is there a modulation or chromatic chord that stands out to you as extremely effective?

Using your knowledge of chord function, resolution, and modulation, compose a thirty-two-bar composition or song that includes the following:

- At least one secondary chord
- At least two borrowed chords
- One N^6 and/or Aug^6
- A modulation to a closely related key using one of the methods presented in chapter 14 and a return to the original key

Complete a lead sheet that contains both the chords and the basic melody of your song or composition. Analyze the lead sheet with Roman numerals and label all of the non-chord tones. Hand out copies of the lead sheet, and have classmates improvise on the melody and chords using a variety of styles—from Baroque to jazz to country.

AURAL SKILLS CONDITIONING 15

Modulation

Sure, we can look at a score for consistent accidentals and cadences in new keys in order to better understand modulation. But what if you are not given a score? Can you determine that a piece has modulated by trusting only your ears? Part of the challenge in mastering aural skills is keeping a sense of tonic. What if that tonic is changed halfway through the piece? The following pieces represent both classical and popular literature from a variety of time periods. As you listen to the performances on the YouTube channel, can you mark the timings for the first time you hear a change in tonal center? To even challenge yourself further, try to determine the type of modulation used at the timing you marked.

Classical Period

Haydn, *Symphony No. 33 in C Major*, Mvt. I

WEBSITE

VIDEO TRACK 15

Point of modulation: __________

Type of modulation (circle one):

pivot chord pivot tone direct sequential

Romantic Period

Gounod, "Funeral March of a Marionette"

WEBSITE

VIDEO TRACK 16

Point of modulation: __________

Type of modulation (circle one):

pivot chord pivot tone direct sequential

1970s Popular Music

Paul Williams and Kenneth L. Ascher, "The Rainbow Connection" from *The Muppet Movie*

WEBSITE

VIDEO TRACK 17

Point of modulation: __________

Type of modulation (circle one):

pivot chord pivot tone direct sequential

1980s Popular Music

Billy Ocean, "Get Outta My Dreams, Get Into My Car"

WEBSITE

VIDEO TRACK 18

Point of modulation: __________

Type of modulation (circle one):

pivot chord pivot tone direct sequential

1990s Popular Music

Celine Dion, "My Heart Will Go On" from *Titantic*

VIDEO TRACK 19

Point of modulation: __________

Type of modulation (circle one):

pivot chord   pivot tone   direct   sequential

2000s Popular Music

Idina Menzel and Kristin Chenoweth, "Defying Gravity" from the musical *Wicked*

VIDEO TRACK 20

Point of modulation: __________

Type of modulation (circle one):

pivot chord   pivot tone   direct   sequential

2010s Popular Music

Taylor Swift, "Love Story"

VIDEO TRACK 21

Point of modulation: __________

Type of modulation (circle one):

pivot chord   pivot tone   direct   sequential

THE FINAL NOTE: REAL-WORLD PERSPECTIVE

Courtney Gregg

GENERAL MANAGER AT CARNIVAL PUBLISHING

What inspired you to pursue this particular career path?

I always loved music. I was the type of person that opened up the CD and actually read who wrote every song, who the producers were. . . . I actually memorized their names. I even wrote up fake reviews for albums when I was a child. I went to my first concert (Huey Lewis and the News) at 4, and I distinctly remember asking my parents to buy me music regularly by the age of 8.

Has the study of music theory and musicianship helped you in your career? If so, how?

I've never really studied music theory, but I have a strong interest in learning it. I don't need to know it for what I currently do, but I am interested in understanding how it all works together.

What connections and experiences did you possess that helped you to acquire the position at Carnival? How did your time at *Billboard* and ASCAP help to prepare you for this position?

Relationships. It is a close-knit music community so it's more about who you know rather than what you do. I completed three internships while in college, and the final internship at ASCAP really introduced me to the people that helped me to get the position at Carnival. At *Billboard* magazine, I ended up turning down a job in ad sales to the dismay of many of my friends. I just really wanted to be involved in the music business, not just the business side. At ASCAP, I was involved in the PR program, helping with awards shows. That was great. However, there wasn't anything specific that I learned in my internships that prepared me for my job at Carnival. I had to teach myself my job.

What responsibilities do you have, and what role do you play in the company?

I started as the production coordinator, and it was my responsibility to work with labels and artists to plan studio time, hire the musicians, get the lyrics and charts together . . . things like that. As general manager, I've taken on lots of different roles. I maintain the website and work with distribution companies in terms of our publications. I work on tour presses for our artists, even though I hire outside publicists. Each week I work with radio promoters, iTunes, go after shows, conference calls with managers. . . . It's just a lot of coordinating.

We are a publishing company too, but I personally don't really pitch to Nashville. I tend to pitch to music supervisors for television. It is extremely hard because of the amount of music that is pitched to these people on a regular basis. I go to LA several times a year to stay relevant to what is happening in the television world. This is where we have been placed the most (in television). We have placed songs on shows such as *Nashville, Hart of Dixie, Army Wives*, and we have one coming out in the new Tyler Perry movie.

On Carnival's website, there is mention of a desire to make music "for people" rather than "at people." How do you go about implementing this practice and differentiating yourself from the competition?

There's a lot of music being made that feels like you are chasing something. When something becomes popular, you will see five million copycats of that same idea within the next year. So that's when you are making music at people . . . saying, "well if you like this, you are really going to like this more." Carnival has the philosophy that if we make something good and of quality, the people will listen, and we will win out in the end. We've had thirteen or so number 1 hits, but it's more than that. . . . [W]e hope that when you listen to a song written or produced by Carnival, ours really sticks out.

Most significant learning experience of your career.

I can only do so much. The artist really has to have the drive too. If I call you and say there is a 6 a.m. radio spot and you say that you need to sleep until 8 a.m., it just isn't going to work for you. When those opportunities come up and we have to say no, they will find someone to say yes. No matter how much any of us do, if you don't have that desire to do something more or different, it isn't going to work. It's just too competitive.

Greatest moment of your career so far.

There is a song in our catalogue that I was drawn to when I first started at Carnival. I was able to give this song to Miranda Lambert and it is now her current single, "All Kinds of Kinds." I've had moments like that before, but the story of the song and the lyrics just are special to me and the company. The message speaks to the mission of Carnival.

APPENDIX 1

NASHVILLE NUMBER SYSTEM

Artists in Residence: For the Fatherless and Us The Duo

Chapter Objectives

- Gain a better understanding of the notation of chords in the Nashville Number System
- Understand the rhythmic method used in the Nashville Number System
- Read through the Nashville chart while following along with a recording
- Relate the Nashville chart to Roman numerals and other traditional methods
- Gain insight into how artists use Nashville charts in studio sessions

In the recording studios and clubs of Nashville, Chicago, Atlanta, and all cities in between, a form of chord notation is emerging as the standard. While many musicians on the main stage rely on lead sheet symbols and fake book charts, artists in studio sessions find the Nashville Number System easy to read and even easier to transpose. The Nashville Number System is not a new phenomenon. Neal Matthews, a member of the Jordannaires, created the basic number system for pitches in the 1950s to help with the tedious task of writing out vocal parts. (The Jordannaires were best known for their amazing backup vocals for Elvis Presley!) It wasn't until the early 1960s that Charlie McCoy began to apply this number system to chords and the basic rhythm section.

So, what's the point of learning a new system? Harold Bradley explains: "When I became a leader it saved you 15 minutes a session if you could do the charts before the session. Back then, sometimes they didn't write the same chords to each verse." In session work, time is money, so any system that helps speed up the process is beneficial. The greatest benefit of the system is that you do not have to change the numbers in terms of a modulation. In this system, the performer is much more concerned with the sound of the chord, rather than the function within a key (as in Roman numerals).

THE BASICS OF THE NASHVILLE NUMBER SYSTEM

Chords

Each chord is assigned a number in relation to the scale degree. In this manner, the system is very similar to Roman numerals. For example, if your song is in the key of D major and you see the number 5, the chord would be an A major. Each chord quality is indicated by the symbol attached to the number. The following chart lists all of the chords in the key of D major and how the chord would be notated in the Nashville Number System.

Major	1	D
Major major seventh	$1^{\Delta 7}$	D^{M7}
Major minor seventh (dominant seventh)	5^7	A^7
Major add 6	1^6	D^6
Major add 9	1^{add9}	$D^{(add9)}$
Minor	2– or 2^{min}	E–
Minor minor seventh	2^{-7}	E^-
Augmented	5^{+7}	A^{+7}
Diminished	7°	$C\sharp-^{(\flat 5)}$
Fully diminished seventh	7^{o7}	$C\sharp-^{7(\flat 5)}$
Half diminished seventh	$7^{ø7}$	$C\sharp^{ø7}$
Dominant seventh with ♭9	$5^{7\flat 9}$	$A^{7(\flat 9)}$

You can see that two elements are given with the Nashville System—the root of the chord in terms of scale degree and the quality of the chord.

If a chord is placed in inversion, the chord is written as a fraction, with the root of the chord on the top and the bass note (scale degree) on the bottom. In the key of D major, the following chord would be played as an A^7 chord in second inversion, or A/E. If you are thinking in terms of Roman numerals, this would be a V^4_3 in the key of D major.

$\frac{5^7}{2}$ $\quad$ $5^7/2$

Let's use a progression we have seen in a previous chapter and notate it using the Nashville Number System. The opening progression from Chapter 12 is shown below along with the Nashville Number notation.

D:	I	IV	V/ii	ii^6	V^7/V	V	I
	D	G	B	E-/G	E7	A	D
	1	4	6	2-/4	2^7	5	1

The entrance of the B major chord is not a problem for the session member reading this notation. The third chord simply tells the musician to play a major chord built on the sixth scale degree.

Harmonic Rhythm

In the Nashville Number System, each chord member, unless notated differently, lasts for one full measure. Why is this? To find out, listen to a few popular country songs from billboard.com. How often does the harmony seem to change: once every measure? once every two measures? Contrary to harmonic rhythm in classical music, harmonies in popular music are typically at least one measure long.

The time signature for the piece is always given at the beginning of the chart. The following chart shows a typical progression in common time notated in the Nashville Number System.

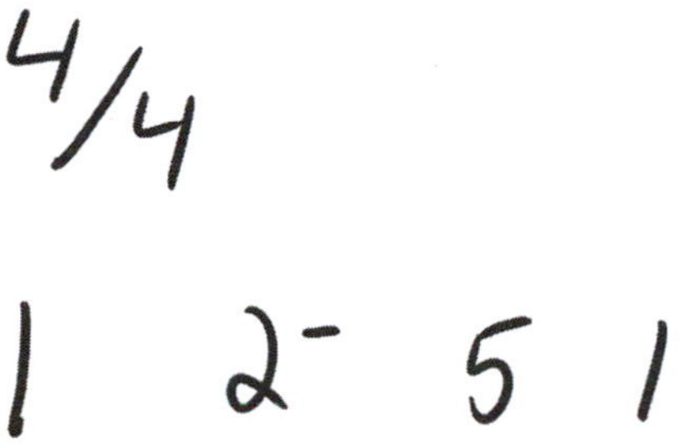

In the progression above, each chord would last for one full measure. Why do we not use slashes to show the measures in this system? Because session members are often sight-reading these charts, and a slash might be mistaken for the number 1 in a fast session read.

If more than one chord is used in a measure, split bars are used. The split bar divides the measure into beats. Study the following two examples from a song in common time. The first progression evenly splits the second measure into two half notes; however, the second progression is not evenly split, and slash marks are used to show correct harmonic rhythm.

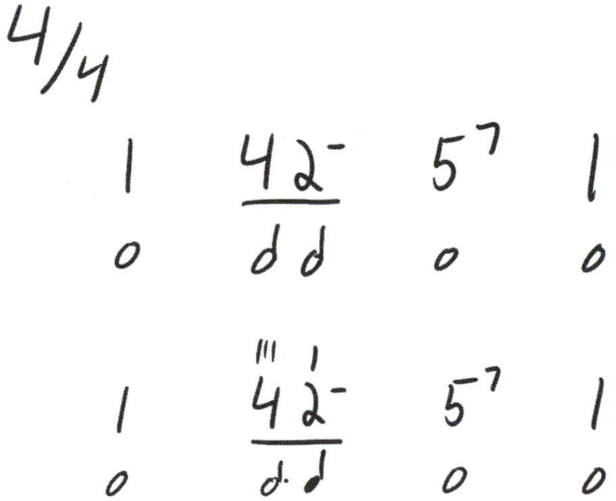

For more rhythmically complex moments in a chord progression, a box is drawn around the progression, and the rhythm is written out in traditional notation. Study the following progression.

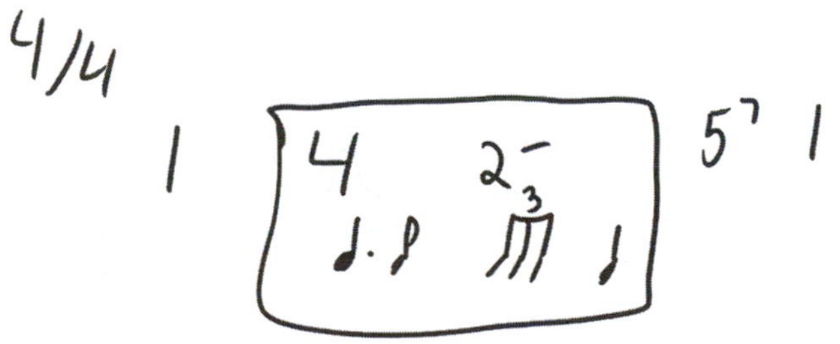

Occasionally, you will see a diamond symbol around the Nashville number. This basically means to push toward the chord, or anticipate the chord and hold. At this point, you would need to look to the band leader to follow his or her rhythm.

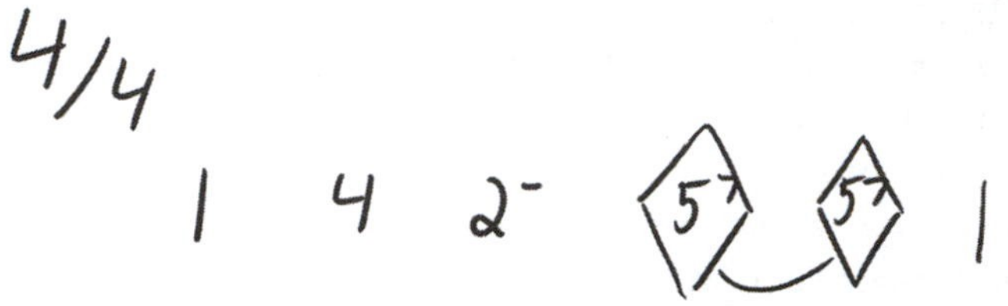

ARTISTS IN RESIDENCE

For the Fatherless, Brian Yak and Christa Yak

What inspired you to pursue music?
Brian: I just grew up singing . . . in the car, along with the radio. I guess the passion began when I started learning to play guitar and wrote my first song. I tapped into a new way to express myself.

Christa: My dad was a worship leader and songwriter, so music was always in my house. He passed away when I was 7, so music was just a great way for me to connect with my dad. I knew this is what I wanted to do . . . it is what I loved the most.

How has the study of music theory/musicianship helped in your writing?
Brian: It has made songs a lot more interesting. Say you are trying to implement a moment that you heard in another song. With mastery of theory, you can really pinpoint what is happening in the music and recreate it in your own individual way.

Christa: It helped me to hear things better. Learning chord progressions and the harmonic formulas opened my ears (and eyes) up to new ways of writing.

Can you describe your very first song-writing attempt?
Christa: It was my freshman year in college. I had just learned about common chord progressions (I–IV–V–I) and I went into a practice room, sat at the piano, and started playing progressions until I started singing a melody over the chords. I wrote a verse and never really finished it. I finally sat down years later to complete it. The song was "God in Me."

Brian: I was a freshman in high school. I wrote a cheesy love song, "Only You," to impress a girl. I played it for her, and I played it for the next 4 years in school for lots of people.

Christa: By people, do you mean girls? Wow, I'm learning so much about my husband here. You should sing it to *me* now. (lots of laughter)

What is your process in writing? Lyrics, chords, melody?
Brian: If you get lucky enough to have a melody first, go with it. If you are lucky enough to have a lyric first, go with that. Honestly, you have to follow with whatever inspires you. Sometimes you might come up with a chorus first and then go back and develop the verse.

For some reason, lyric structure is very organized. It works well when you invest both the organized and creative side while writing.

Christa: Most of my experience is with co-writing. I can never sit down and finish a song. I typically hear the melody first; it is just more natural to me. Usually when we write, Brian comes up with the chorus and we go into the co-write and finish it.

How do you plan to market this genre of music to not only the Christian market, but also expand the audience that may listen to this particular music to boost sales?
Brian: Anytime you feel brave enough to play in a bar or coffee house, you'll get your music out there. You have to be willing to go out and play live . . . often and in new environments. Our promotion is done by a publicist, and we start with churches, but we will expand to play in lots of different venues.

Christa: You need to meet people and just promote your music to a wide audience. My favorite part of this entire process is playing live.

What role do you think iTunes and Spotify play in getting your music out to the public?
Brian: You want to do whatever you have to do to get your music and message out there. If that means you earn .00001 per listen, then your music is still getting out to the public. It makes your job harder though, in that you need to do something in your songs that make people believe in your music enough to support it. You want to make your music a personal investment for your listeners.

Christa: The reality of it is that you will make little money off of iTunes, but it is still money in. I think we make .40 per download on all of our music on iTunes. I honestly could see that in 10 years CDs might not exist anymore.

What do you see for your future in terms of releasing future albums? Do you plan to stay independent or look to sign with a larger label?
Christa: We are releasing our album independently, but we are going to pursue some sort of deal after this release. The labels want to hear that you can put something together that is worth their investment before they pay attention to you.

Brian: You might be competing with eight other artists with the A&R team, so you need to find a label that is personally invested. You might sign a deal to do two records, but if your first record doesn't do well, the label will lose interest. You have to be your best promoter.

Christa: I would tell everyone that it really isn't all about a record deal. You can do a lot of these things on your own. You do need someone to help with PR and promotion. You can put your team together with people that have a personal investment in your music. Just on a side note . . . The Kickstarter and Indiegogo campaign really helped us to fund our latest album. But everyone is doing it now, whether they are qualified or not . . . so how do you set yourself apart?

Most significant learning experience of your career.
Christa: For my first EP, I didn't know about PR, radio, anything about promotion. After I released it, a lot of my family and friends bought it, but suddenly the momentum was over after the release. I didn't have anyone to help me get it out there. I didn't line up shows afterwards. So the question is, what do you do after you release the record?

Brian: You need to be in this for the long haul. My first EP only sold 500 copies, and I should have really promoted it. Now I know that if you need to sell 6,000 copies, you need to be in front of 60,000 people. My momentum is much stronger for this endeavor.

Greatest moment of your career so far.
Brian: Figuring out that we wanted to start the band For the Fatherless. To find a mission and purpose is what keeps the momentum going. For us, the best moment was when we figured out this was a life thing. It was more than a business plan, it was . . . is a calling. To have people respond to our music is a powerful experience.

Christa: For me, it is For the Fatherless. I knew it was what we were supposed to do. Since we have been performing as For the Fatherless I knew I had found my message. It changed everything.

UNDERSTANDING NASHVILLE NUMBERS IN CONTEXT: FOR THE FATHERLESS

Listen to the song "God in Me" written by Christa Yak, lead singer of For the Fatherless. Follow along with the Nashville chart.[1]

WEBSITE
VIDEO TRACK 22

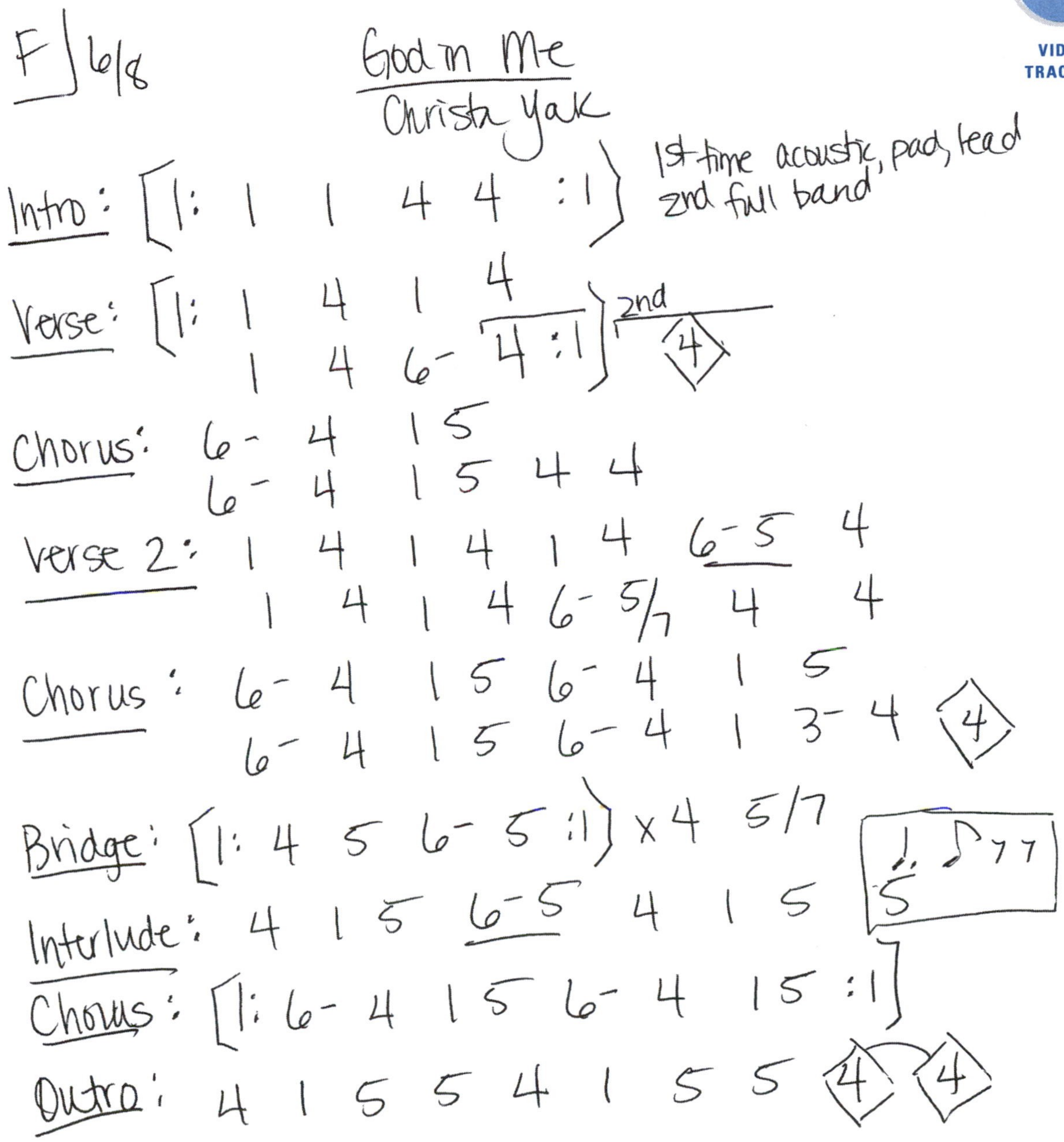

The song is written in the key of F major with a time signature of $\frac{6}{8}$.That means that each chord is going to last for six divisions or two beats (refer back to Chapter 1 for a review on the note values in compound time if needed).

The entire song is made up of four chords: F major, B♭ major, D minor, and C major. The only inversions occur in the second verse and at the end of the bridge!

Two new elements presented in this chart are the use of the repeat signs and the use of first and second endings. The intro is played twice, first acoustically and then with a full band. The first verse is repeated, ending initially with a B♭ chord for one measure, followed

[1]For definitions and descriptions of song form elements (intro, verse, bridge), refer to Appendix 2.

by a second ending with a pushed B♭ chord leading to the chorus. The fourth chord of the interlude is a split bar, meaning that the D minor chord and the C major chord notated will both last for the duration of a dotted quarter (or three division beats) each.

VIDEO TRACK 23

Listen to Brian Yak perform "Alcatraz." How is this song different in character from that presented in "God in Me"?

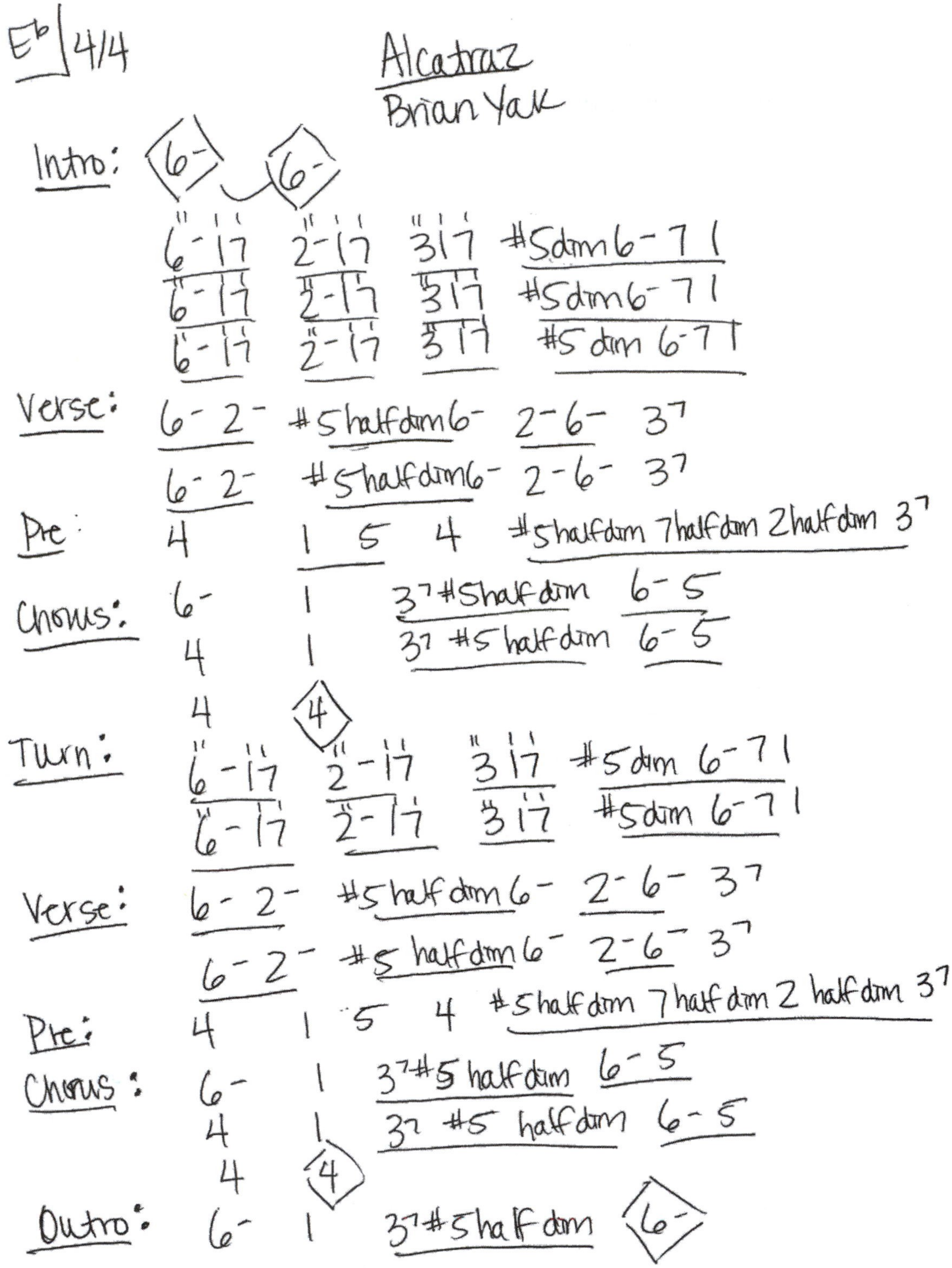

This song sounds like it is in a minor mode, but the chart shows E♭ major as the key. Why is this? Typically session members write all charts in a major key, referring all chords in relationship to the major tonic. To your ears, it might sound like the song is written in C minor, and that is correct. The 6-chord in E♭ major is C minor. As you listen, you will probably hear the 6 as the tonic chord. This is also why the ♯5dim makes perfect sense. A ♯5dim in the key of E♭ major is a B diminished chord, the leading tone of C minor. The major 3^7 is also functional; a 3 in E♭ major is G and the chord built here is the dominant seventh of C minor.

The split bars are extensive, including bars that are split into four equal beats! Study the chord progressions as well.

ARTIST IN RESIDENCE

Us The Duo, Michael Alvarado and Carissa Alvarado

Educational Background
Michael majored in music industry studies with a concentration in marketing and a minor in business. Carissa graduated high school early in order to get a jump-start on her professional acting and dancing career.

What inspired you to pursue music?
We both are inspired by three things: other musicians, a natural passion, and life events. Our love for music started by seeing and hearing others play and sing. We both tried it out and realized we enjoyed it thoroughly . . . hence, we had a natural passion for it. From there, we noticed that things continually happen in life that spur on reaction and emotions, both good and bad. We both turned to music to spill those reactions out.

How has the study of music theory/musicianship helped in your writing?

Having a good understanding of theory and musicianship can only help a songwriter. It puts you in a different level of thinking . . . one without limitations or restrictions. It's important to continually sharpen your skills, so that when you have an idea, you aren't held back by the boundaries of not knowing theory. Also, knowing theory/musicianship saves a lot of time. When you're in the creative zone, the last thing you want to do is stop and figure out the technicalities of the music. Theory paves the way for the mind to simply be creative.

What genres of music do you listen to on a regular basis? How do these other composers or artists influence your own writing?

We listen to music based on mood and quality rather than genre. To us, anything that is recorded well, has a good message, and makes you feel an emotion is worth listening to. Sometimes it's gloomy outside and we'll put on an instrumental piano and cello combo. Sometimes we're at the beach and all we want to listen to is Top 40 feel-good pop. And sometimes we're driving in traffic and blare bluegrass to lift our spirits. Through embracing every genre, we keep our minds open to new, unique melodies and song structures that continually influence our writing.

What is your process in writing? Lyrics, chords, melody?

Our process seems to change on a song-to-song basis. In general, something spurs on a melody randomly and no matter where we are (Disneyland, the mall, in bed, in the car), we immediately record it on our phones so we don't forget and come back to it later. Same thing happens with lyrics. If we get an idea, we immediately stop what we are doing, open up a notebook, and start writing without stopping. Then, one of the saved melodies might come back again in our heads and we'll pair it with the lyrics. Lastly, we pair it with chords.

On an importance scale, the chords are the least important, as they tend to just work themselves out naturally at the end. Next is the melody. While it's important to be catchy and memorable, music can't talk. Which leads us to the most important part . . . lyrics. Words have an incredible amount of power, with the ability to captivate and change people's lives in a matter of a chorus. We spend extra time on the lyrics, making sure everything makes sense, has meaning, and is exactly what we were trying to say.

What are some of the greatest challenges in the recording process? What did you learn along the way? What do you wish you had known?

The biggest thing we had to learn was how to not be over-critical. When listening back to your own voice, it's easy to never be satisfied. But, there comes a point when any artist has to step back, surrender, and say, "It's not perfect, but it's close enough." You can always record a vocal take better than the last, but if you have that mentality while recording, you may never finish or get frustrated and lose the connection to the song. Also, staying healthy is crucial. Track falsetto-intensive songs first, and leave the "screamers" for the end of the day.

How do you plan to market this genre of music to not only your YouTube fan base, but beyond?

The best way we've found to market towards people outside our fan base is to write about things that are near and dear to us, and people, somewhere, will relate. In the beginning, we tried so hard to write commercial sounding songs that would appeal to the masses and bring in more followers. As a result, the music lacked passion. Once we started writing about things that we were going through, we found other new listeners relating more and subsequently becoming fans. With our new album, we've expanded our writing to new topics, new life situations, and new emotions, and we believe that alone will expand our fan base beyond our current one.

What role do you think iTunes and Spotify play in getting your music out to the public? Has it hurt or helped your career so far?
iTunes has greatly helped. It's become a tangible music marketplace that is reputable, but also easy to penetrate. Plus, Apple is a trustworthy company, so we feel confident in placing our music in the hands of innovators. Spotify is also brilliant for the consumer, but not so much for the artist. We personally love Spotify, simply because we pay $10 a month to listen to almost every album everywhere we go. For the artist, you get paid close to nothing for it, but on the other hand, you're gaining new listeners and fans. These new listeners and fans click on your YouTube video ads, pay for concert tickets, and promote your music. Although it may not pay off at the start, it will in the long run. So, we'd say that both iTunes and Spotify have helped our career greatly!

What do you see for your future in terms of releasing future albums? Do you plan to stay independent or look to sign with a larger label?
We've been asked this question a lot. What we've learned is that the future is impossible to predict. Our main goal is to continue to write songs with a positive message, take the shows that come our way, and change people for the better with music. If in the future, a larger label or management team has the same vision as us and approaches us with the right deal, then we will assess that as it comes. As for now, we are extremely thankful to be doing what we love full time and will continue to do so for as long as we can.[2]

Most significant learning experience of your career.
Just because something is popular doesn't make it right. We've been approached with big label deals, been a part of major network television shows, and worked many times with some music industry giants. People have told us our whole life that "making it" is creating a partnership with one of these big timers, and being well-known. We've realized that most of these people have a different agenda and vision than us. They aren't seeking to spread a positive message, or to change people for the better, or to invest in relationships. And for that reason, we've chosen not to compromise what we believe in in order to become popular. Yes, it's extremely hard to turn down golden contracts on the table right in front of you, but the value of life should be based on character and not success.

Greatest moment of your career so far.
It's hard to choose just one moment. We've been blessed with so many amazing moments in our young career. From walking the red carpet at the Billboard Music Awards to appearing on *Good Morning America* in front of millions of people, we try to cherish each experience and stay in the moment. We've seen songs written in our living room go on to be included in national advertising campaigns and major motion pictures. We've been challenged more and more by each opportunity and for us it's really about the process more than the end goal. We're constantly asking ourselves—how can we improve? What can we do better to reach more people? If we get too wrapped up in these moments we can easily lose sight of our purpose—to make great music and influence people for good.

[2]Six months after this interview, Us The Duo signed to the major record label Republic Records.

VIDEO
TRACK 24

Let's take a look at one of the songs that made Us The Duo such a hit on YouTube. "I Will Wait for You" is written in the key of C, and the chords consist of I, IV, V, and vi. What is so interesting about this particular chart is the Alvarado's specific instructions on the final chorus. Follow along with the chart as you watch the music video.

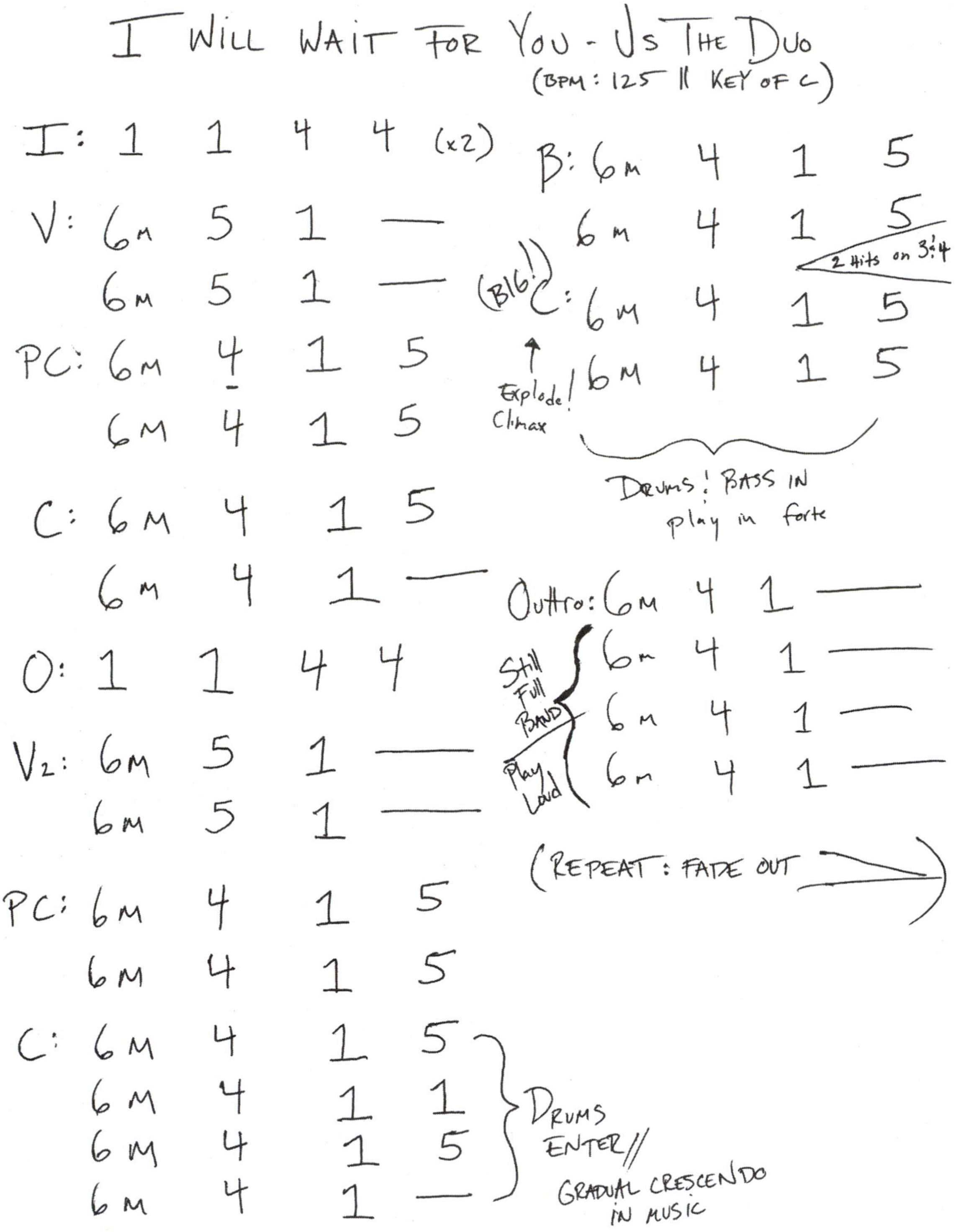

VIDEO
TRACK 25

The song "No Matter Where You Are" is the title track on Us The Duo's new album. The chords are very similar to those used in "I Will Wait for You," but the rhythms are a bit more articulated. Why is that? Is there something in the lyrics that made these changes more effective? As you listen to the performance, notice the specific dynamic markings as well.

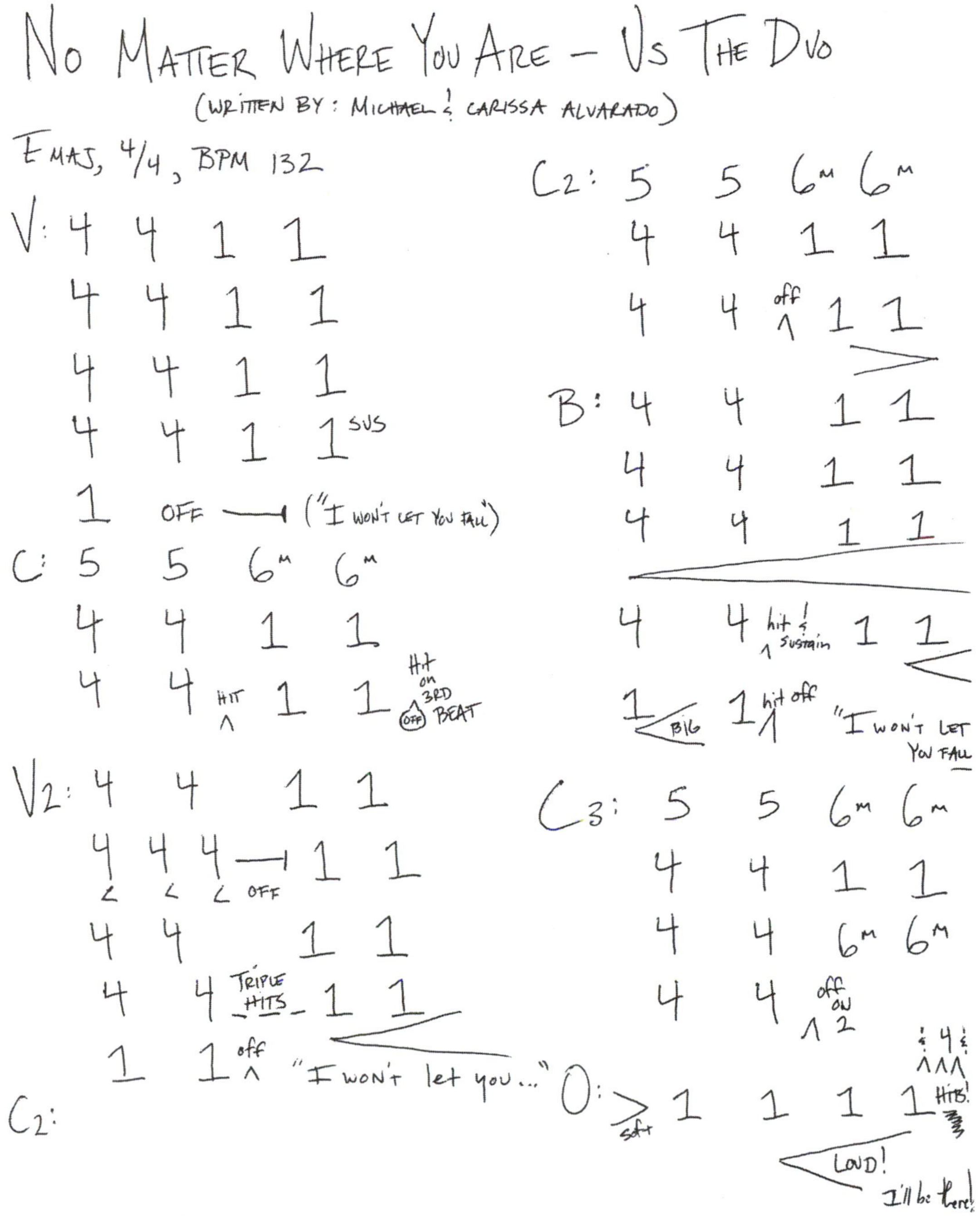
NO MATTER WHERE YOU ARE – US THE DUO
(WRITTEN BY: MICHAEL & CARISSA ALVARADO)
E MAJ, 4/4, BPM 132

V: 4 4 1 1
4 4 1 1
4 4 1 1
4 4 1 1 sus
1 OFF ("I WON'T LET YOU FALL")

C: 5 5 6m 6m
4 4 1 1
4 4 HIT ^ 1 1 (OFF) Hit on 3RD BEAT

V2: 4 4 1 1
4 4 4 OFF 1 1
4 4 1 1
4 4 TRIPLE HITS 1 1
1 1 off ^ "I won't let you..."

C2:

C2: 5 5 6m 6m
4 4 1 1
4 4 off ^ 1 1

B: 4 4 1 1
4 4 1 1
4 4 1 1
4 4 hit & sustain ^ 1 1
1 BIG 1 hit off "I won't let you fall"

C3: 5 5 6m 6m
4 4 1 1
4 4 6m 6m
4 4 off on 2 ^

O: soft 1 1 1 1 & 4 & HITS!
LOUD!
I'll be there!

Reviewing Chapter Objectives

- Gain a better understanding of the notation of chords in the Nashville Number System (page 308)
- Understand the rhythmic method used in the Nashville Number System (page 309)
- Read through the Nashville chart while following along with a recording (pages 313–314, 318–319)
- Relate the Nashville chart to Roman numerals and other traditional methods (page 318)
- Gain insight into how artists use Nashville charts in studio sessions (page 323)

EXERCISES

Answer the following questions based on the Nashville Number System charts.

WEBSITE

VIDEO
TRACK 26

For the Fatherless, "Learn to Love"

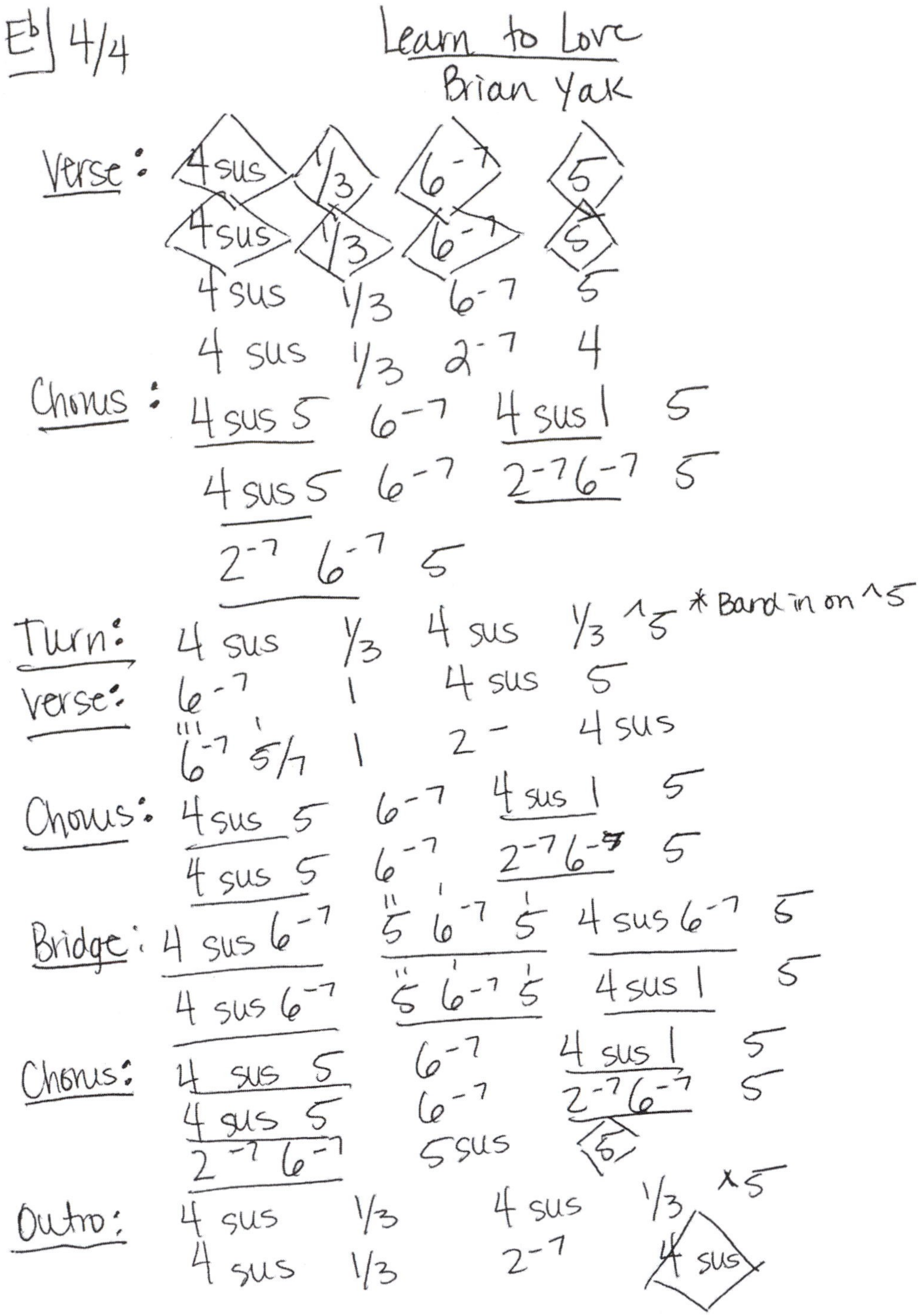

1. After listening to the song, describe the rhythm of the opening verse. Why are the holds necessary?
2. Give lead sheet symbols and Roman numerals for the entire chorus.
3. What is the purpose of the turn? How do the four measures of the turn lead into the verse?

4. Play along with the outro. How would you add in the suspensions? Give exact notation below.

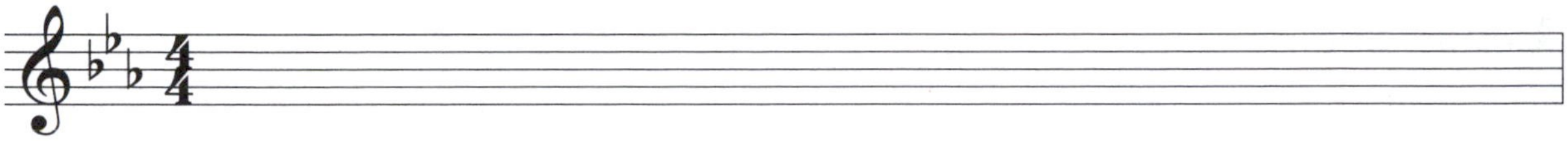

Ashton Lee, "Boulder."[3] Songwriters: Ashton Lee and Lane Caudell

VIDEO TRACK 27

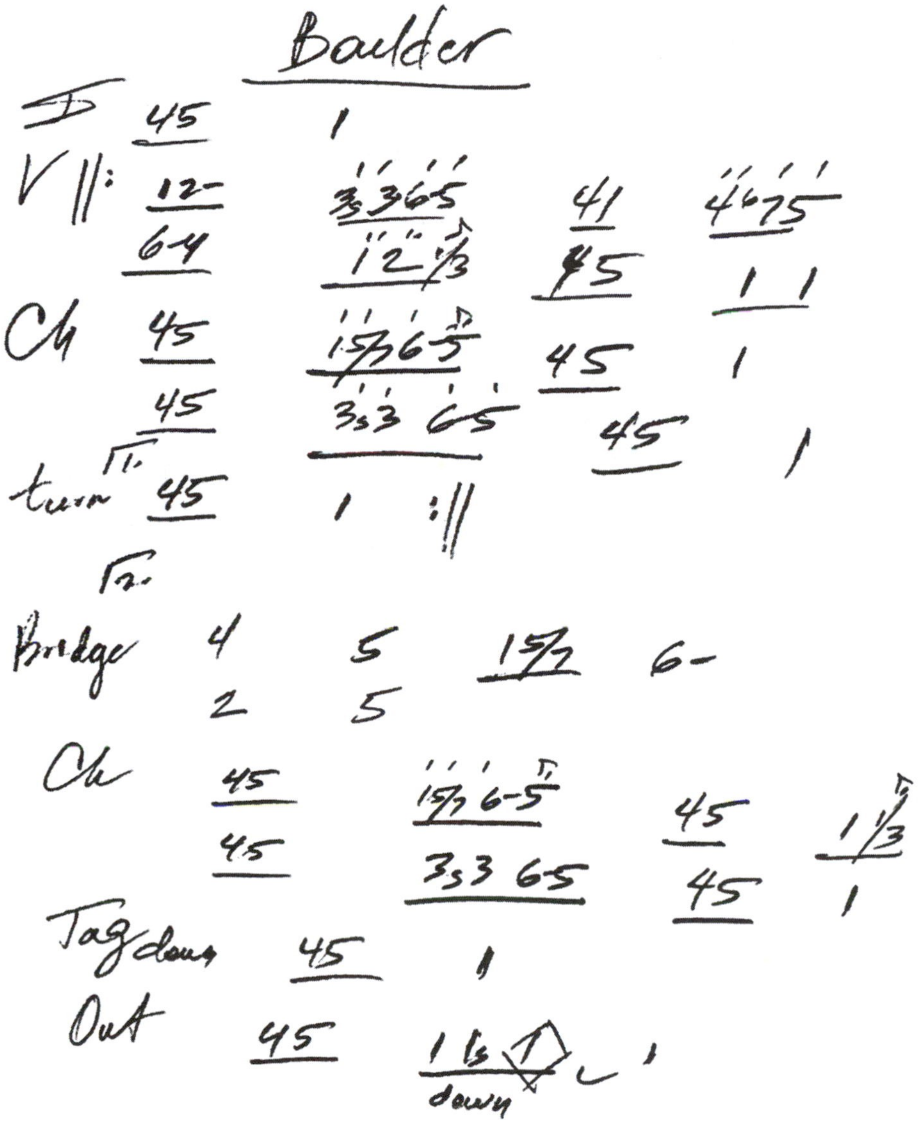

1. There is no time signature given in this chart. Determine the time signature just by listening to the song and write it in the upper left corner of the chart. The key of the song is A major.
2. The footnote mentions that the suspensions are not written into the chart. Add the word *sus* to the chords that include suspensions.
3. Give the lead sheet symbols for all of the chords in the bridge.
4. There is one borrowed chord used in the progression. Where is it? What would the Roman numeral be for the borrowed chord?

[3] In the recording, the suspensions are not written in the chart, nor is the turnaround included in the final performance.

THE FINAL NOTE: REAL-WORLD PERSPECTIVE

Ashton Lee

SINGER-SONGWRITER

What inspired you to pursue music?

Becoming a country music artist has been my dream as long as I can remember. I was born into a musical family, so I guess it was just encoded into my DNA. When I was little, my dad would sing with me as he put me to bed. Since I've never had any formal vocal training, I consider my dad to be my voice teacher. Growing up in the bluegrass world, you learn music through exposure. You develop this instinct about what sounds good and how to sing and play something that will affect people in a positive way. Now that I have an academic knowledge of music, I think this instinct is more helpful than ever in developing my style as a singer, writer, and guitarist.

Songwriting has always been a big focus for me. I have to give credit to my dad, and my guitar teacher Scott for encouraging me to write from an early age. My dad wrote some great stuff when I was younger, and that's how I learned to write. It's both an art and a craft, and I think the best songs are the ones that balance both aspects just right. I want my compositions to be listenable, enjoyable, and meaningful to musicians and non-musicians alike. Working with professional Nashville songwriters has really helped me tune in my songwriting, and I want to continue to grow as both a writer and a performer.

How did you get connected with the Cauley Music Group?

I performed with my band at a songwriter showcase put on by Split Rail Records (student-run record label) where Bob and Lane came to watch the performers and do a master class. I also performed in the master class where I made a strong enough impression for them to want to work with me. I began writing with Lane long-distance over the summer, and by the end of the summer they brought me to Nashville to record professional demos.

Describe your songwriting process for "Boulder" from start to finish.

The process for writing this song was not at all typical. I know I've never had another song develop in the way this one did. I wrote the first version of this song my senior year of high school after visiting Boulder, Colorado, over the summer. I had always loved a Garth Brooks song that included a line about Boulder, and after going there myself I decided to write a song with that area in mind. The general concept of the song and most of the musical elements from the final version came from this first song, but the structure of it was a bit too unusual. I performed the first version of the song pretty regularly. However, once I started working with my writing partner Lane, a seasoned Nashville writer, I had to change my priorities to more commercially viable compositions. Lane heard the first version of the song and saw potential for it to become a real signature song for me. We rewrote it into a tighter package—improved the storyline and structure, added a powerful bridge, etc. The result turned out to be my favorite original song. I play it with my band every show, and I think it becomes more powerful every time.

Describe your first time in the studio when you recorded your first demo, including the preparation of the NNS chart.

Getting to record demos in Nashville with top-notch studio musicians was absolutely incredible. As a music major and trained guitarist, it blew me away to see just how good these guys really are and how fast they work. The music bed for each song we cut took them about 30–40 minutes to record from the first time they heard the song to moving on to the next one. The Nashville Number Chart was written by the producer/band leader on the session. He, along with the rest of the musicians, listened to what we call a guitar-vocal (just a cell phone recording of me playing and singing) with a clipboard and blank sheet of paper, and wrote the chart from one listen. Never touched an instrument, never had any questions about the chords, even knew what key it was in.

I have tried to use my experience watching the pros work to improve the way my band works, and I think it has really helped. We use Nashville charts in our rehearsals which makes things go a lot smoother and more efficient for learning new songs. Tracking vocals in a professional setting is also an interesting process because you (and your producers) have to be very picky about each inflection, note, phrase, etc., to try to make the song as sellable as possible. It was a big, fast learning curve, but I enjoyed every minute of it.

APPENDIX 2

SONG FORM AND PERSPECTIVES FROM SONGWRITERS

Chapter Objectives

- Gain a better understanding of the process of songwriting
- Define basic terms as used in songwriting and sessions
- Answer basic questions in terms of song form when listening to songs
- Gain insight from interviews with songwriters

Can you think of a few songs that define a generation? If you were a young girl in the 1980s, one of your touchstone songs might be Cyndi Lauper's "Girls Just Want to Have Fun." If you were a teenager in a 1990s, there's nothing like "Smells Like Teen Spirit" by Nirvana to take you back. If you were growing up in the first decade of the century, Beyoncé probably had a place on your newly purchased iPod with the song "Crazy in Love." What makes these particular songs stand the test of time? Is it the lyrics? the music? the performance? There's no doubt that the lyrics play a huge role in relating the song to the listener. Interestingly enough, only one of the songs just mentioned was actually written by the artist, Kurt Cobain of Nirvana. The other two songs were written by Robert Hazard ("Girls Just Want to Have Fun") and Eugune Record ("Crazy in Love"). You've probably never even heard of Hazard or Record, but they are the ones who put the lyrics and the music into those epic songs of Lauper and Beyoncé. Behind every great song, there is a songwriter. In some cases, the writer is the performing artist, but more often than not, the songwriter or cowriter is basically unknown to the general public. Without the songwriter, there would be no lyrics to sing, so perhaps the unknown songwriter is the true hero of the music industry.

THE PROCESS OF SONGWRITING

The process of songwriting varies from writer to writer. Some accomplished songwriters have had extensive training on an instrument and/or in music theory and begin with the music. Others are more like poets, with a strong focus on the lyrics and a melody that just resides in their head. They might not possess the language to explain the melody with musical terminology as presented in this text. Let's take a quick look into the minds of the songwriters themselves for the answers in order to better understand this process.

At a recent songwriter's retreat held by LifeWay Worship in Nashville, accomplished songwriters were broken up into groups in order to cowrite. Most of the songwriters had never worked with one another, and they all described the initial awkwardness of the process. What is so compelling about the songwriting process is that each writer's method varies. Let's compare the journey of two of the rooms at the retreat.

Room 1

Immediately the four men present come to an agreement about one thing:, "There's not going to be a lot of theory here." They begin to talk about what types of song they want to write, both in terms of tempo and content. Before any lyric or melody is written, they ask one another, "Why are we here?" Everyone agrees that they want to write a song to make people think, but not one that talks down to the listener. Of the four writers in the room, two hold guitars in their hands, one has a computer on his lap, and the other is notating lyrics feverishly in his writer's book. They take one phrase, "In his name," and begin to come up with as many lyrics as they can that encompass it. At 30 minutes into the session, not one note has been written out or played on guitar.

An hour into the session, the initial plan has completely changed, and both guitars are playing through various hooks that are sung by all four men (sometimes at the same time!). Two of the writers are making comparisons to Bon Jovi's music and discussing how to write a worship song that encompasses the same feel as "Living on a Prayer." The writers begin to pace around the room, singing lines to one another, while one writer is still jotting down all of the ideas. The energy level is extremely high, and the writers decide to add in a slide to make the guitar lick a bit more bluesy, because, as they put it, "Blues is the language of men . . . it will just make the people come in." (One more writer grabs a guitar—for a total of three guitars in the room at this point. After all, who can resist a blues lick?) The lick is added, and the chorus is done. The style of the song has completely changed based on the chorus alone, so the writers agree to go back and alter the first verse. The initial goal of the song has done a 180 since the first hour. The writers are now focusing on the range of the melody, because, after all, they are looking for a song that "everyone can really sing along to."

Room 2

The setting of this room is completely different in that there are three writers sitting in a circle around a keyboard. None of the writers have ever worked together, so they spend the first few minutes learning one another's backgrounds. The conversation moves to a discussion on what songs are working in various churches. Each writer brings different experiences to the session, so there are lots of ideas here. The name Chris Tomlin is used in terms of what is popular and what works. They ask, what is happening musically that allows the worshipers to relate to his songs? They agree on a few things before a single note or lyric is written:

1. Anything more than five chords is too much.
2. A melody that is singable encourages congregational involvement.
3. The melody should be able to be sung comfortably by males and females. Always think as an alto. C–C always works.

One writer then asks, "Do you have any ideas that are killing you?" Immediately, all three writers grab their writers' books and begin to share ideas and song imageries. They agree on the idea of "Awake me" and begin to alter the thought to include phrases such as "Capture me, captivate me." After a few of the lyrical ideas are presented, one of the writers moves to the keyboard and begins to play through basic progressions while the other writers sing the lyrics with several different melodic ideas.

An hour into the session, after singing through a potential verse and chorus and sharing the excitement over the imagery created in the lyrics, one of the writers grabs her cell phone and does a quick Google search. It turns out that a song already exists with the same title, the same basic content, and similar melodic lines. It's a no-go, and the group has to start from scratch. It's back to the books, and the three writers again begin to share ideas that they have brought with them to the session. Each writer throws a title out, and the process begins all over again. They work together to paint vivid imagery while continuing to focus on simple choruses that encourage congregations to stand and sing.

TERMINOLOGY IN SONGWRITING

While the process of songwriting varies from person to person and session to session, there are terms that every writer and performer should know before beginning the journey of putting ideas and notes on paper.

Intro (Introduction) Typically 4 measures long, the intro sets up the melodic and harmonic structure and establishes the key area

Verse This tells the storyline and sets the scene (the *who*, *what*, *when*, and *where*). Typically a verse is eight or sixteen bars long. Just listen to the opening verses to "Little Rock" by Collin Raye, "I Hope You Dance" by Lee Ann Womack, or "Where Were You When the World Stopped Turning" by Alan Jackson. All of the verses in the songs set up a particular place and answer *who*, *what*, *when*, and *where*. In Jackson's case, he is asking us to answer the question *where*—and it is very effective within the context of that song.

Pre-chorus This sets up the chorus, building tension and drama in the storyline. The direction of the line—both in terms of dynamics and melody—is up, up, up! Listen to "I Need You Now" by Lady Antebellum. The last two lines before the chorus ask, "And wonder if I ever cross your mind?" followed by the realization: "It happens all the time." The opening verse focuses around the pitch G♯, while the pre-chorus centers around the pitch E, a major sixth up. We know that something is about to happen.

Chorus The chorus contains the musical hook and most often the title line. The chorus (the *why*) is repeated throughout the song. These are the moments when the volume goes up and everyone is singing along to the title line. Think of Def Leppard's "Pour Some Sugar on Me," Garth Brooks's "Friends in Low Places," or Journey's "Don't Stop Believing."

Bridge Typically found after the second chorus, the bridge contains a new chord progression or a new melodic idea. It can be in a different key and provides contrast to the verse and chorus. It normally provides the revelation and brings about the "aha" moment for the character. Check out the bridge used in Sugarland's "Stay." The chords are similar to the verse, but the melody is completely different (and so is the singer's tone). Talk about a revelation for the character! Listen to how the one lyric is changed in the final chorus to realize this revelation found in the bridge.

Hook Do you know the bass line in the opening of "Stand by Me"? You've probably sung it with the syllable "bum" several times in your life. Well, that's a hook: a melodic (or rhythmic) idea that is repeated over and over. In the case of "Stand by Me," the hook is repeated eleven times throughout the song in the bass line and is also played in the upper strings. There is not one moment of the song that doesn't contain that hook. And, for some reason, it never gets old. Another hook? Just mention the song "Lion Sleeps Tonight" and see what people begin to sing back to you.

Other Terms You Might See

Middle 8 In most cases, the middle 8 is another term for an eight measure bridge that is found between the two final choruses

Channel Another name for pre-chorus

Tag Typically found at the end of the song, the tag repeats a lyric and a progression over and over (normally with a fade). This can also be called the **outro**.

STUDYING THE SONGS

Perhaps the best way to learn about the art of songwriting is to hear from the writers themselves and to examine their music in a contextual way, studying the lyrics while you follow the notation and chords. Each writer presented in this chapter demonstrates that there is no one correct way to write a hit song. As you read through the interviews and study the music presented, ask yourself the following questions:

1. What is making this song so compelling? Is it the lyrics, melody, chords, performance . . . a combination of all of these?
2. What is the form of this song? Does it contain a bridge, a pre-chorus?
3. Does the song contain a hook? If so, is it melodic, rhythmic, lyrical?

ARTIST IN RESIDENCE

Songwriter 1: Sarah Hurst Independent Songwriter

Educational Background
B.A., Dallas Baptist University, Music Business

What inspired you to begin songwriting?

My entire family is musical, so at a very young age, I began to take piano lessons and perform with my family at local churches. I was just doing what everybody else around me was doing. When I was high school, I was compared to other family members, and I realized quickly that if I wrote my own songs, no one could compare me because the song was mine. This was a way for me to stand out. I was raised on contemporary Christian and worship music, but this music quickly became boring to me, and I needed an outlet to ease the teenage angst while I was singing. But it was much more than that. Songwriting was an eye-opener for me in that it showed me exactly what I wanted to do with my life.

Can you describe your very first songwriting attempt? How old were you?
I was 16 years old. I had written little songs all my life, but this was the first time I attempted to write a song with lyrics. It isn't my best work; it was also more like a worship song, but it was my first attempt at writing a song that was emotion led and based on personal experience. I felt that this song could really relate to teenagers at the time. Writing the song was a very fast process, and I probably wrote the song in an hour. I still stand by that song.

What is your process in writing? Lyrics, chords, melody?
Songs that I feel are my best come together at one time. All of the elements just rise together. Whenever I have words and try to put in the melody, it seems forced. The lyrics tend to dictate how the melody will naturally emerge. In terms of chord progressions, I tend to sound out the chords on the piano and then write out the melody using the guitar. Sibelius or another technology limits me in terms of my writing. . . . I tend to write on paper in my notebook, and I feel more poetic and free. I can create and embrace that creativity.

Where do you get your ideas?
From experiences. I get criticized for my songs being too sad. Whenever something bad happens, I want to (feel I must) go and create something. I need to write at all times, but I don't want to be an artist that is only known for being depressing. Sometimes it is difficult when a friend is telling me their stories. . . . I need to just listen and turn off the songwriter brain.

How did your knowledge of music theory help in your songwriting?
I love theory, and I generally wanted to learn. When I came to college, I was in a writing drought for about a year and a half. I just could not write. I had written all through high school but found the process to be almost impossible. During that time, though, I was absorbing the material I was learning in a theory class. I went through a horrible breakup my sophomore year and sat down and wrote for the first time since high school. So much had happened to me in terms of my musical knowledge by that point that I was able to really write substantial melodies by my sophomore year. My ear was now trained after sitting in those classes. The music came out so much more mature than any of my previous music. I realized I was putting all these new progressions in my music and I'm not even intending to! At this point, I was writing on guitar because I felt more artistic. However, because of my limited playing, I wasn't writing the chords that I wanted to come out. I actually had a friend to reproduce these chords with me in my charts. People could tell when songs are more mature . . . more artistic even if they don't know why.

What are some of the greatest challenges in the recording process? What did you learn along the way?
How much time do you have!!! I spent a year and a half on the album (*Fine to Wait*) that was released in 2013. I started out in practicum with eleven different engineers that each had a song of mine to record. Working with eleven different people, I was completely unprepared and not experienced. Each time I went into the studio, I was working with a different engineer with a different mindset. It was a nightmare. No one was prepared, including myself.

I started the process all over. I found the band I loved. I had one engineer that was solid. I also learned that you have no time in the studio to figure out issues like drums or song changes. You need to literally add 4 hours to everything you think will take 1 hour. Have musicians that are solid beforehand. Figure out your vision beforehand. Recording time is the time for fine tunings, not huge developments in terms of songwriting.

I've also learned how necessary it is to be professional and to be kind. If you have an attitude, the musicians will end up going with someone else regardless of your talent and skills. It makes all the difference. Humility is a huge deal.

Goals and Aspirations

I hope to support myself with performing and songwriting. I view it as a package deal, and the joy I get is really singing my own songs. My dream is to travel and take the music to people that have never heard it before.

VIDEO TRACK 28

Sarah Hurst, "The Valiant"

Verse 1

A#m
I've heard the stories of the glories of the wars

F# A#m
Long ago fought for love

Battles were gory but they sent the girls' hearts soaring

F# A#m
Cause they fought for us, Fought for us

A#m
See that man drinking, yeah he's thinking about the war

F# A#m
He finally won tonight, he's doing all right

They'll make him king and they'll teach their sons to sing

F# A#m
Songs about the valiant knight of our time

Fm7 F#
All hail the great knight's tale

Chorus:

A#m
Drink up it was a bloody fight

F#
Yeah she bled from her heart and cried out her eyes

Sarah Hurst, "The Valiant" *(continued)*

C♯
Oh he said he'd be mine and stay by my side

G♯
But he slipped away before saying goodbye

A♯m
Three cheers for your modern knight

F♯
What he lacks in honor he'll make up for in pride

C♯
Oh he came and saw and he conquered them all

F A♯m
So raise your wine for his battle cry tonight

Verse 2

A♯m
I'm tired of hearing about your naïve zealots fearing

F♯ A♯m
You and all your triumph, I've had enough

Your end is nearing they'll be hearing about another

F♯
Deadbeat good-for-nothing coward

A♯m
And they'll bow down

Fm7 F♯
And I know how the story will go

Repeat Chorus

Bridge:

C♯ G♯
Once upon a time long long long ago

F♯
There were men who fought for honor

C♯ G♯
And women they loved so

C♯ G♯
Surely if they saw the man you toast tonight

F♯
They'd shake their heads in disbelief

F
At your so called valiant knight

Last chorus:

A♯m
Drink up it's a bloody fight

F♯
Yeah she'll bleed from her heart and cry out her eyes

C♯
Oh he said he'd be mine and stay by my side

G♯ F
But he'll slip away before saying goodbye

A♯m
Three cheers for your modern knight

F♯
What he lacks in honor he'll make up for in pride

C♯
Oh he came and saw and he conquered them all

F A♯m
So raise your wine for his battle cry tonight

ARTISTS IN RESIDENCE

Songwriters 2: Jeremy Johnson and Paul Marino: Songwriters for LifeWay Music

What inspired you to pursue music?
Paul: My parents bought a piano when I was in the tenth grade, and I buried myself in the basement learning how to play and how chords worked.

Can you describe your very first songwriting attempt?
Jeremy: I was in the eighth grade and I wrote this song called "Fill Me with Your Love." It was a sweet ballad about losing a girlfriend. I was pretty much a ladies man when I sat down and sang that. (laughter)

Paul: I wrote a song called "Shine Your Light" after my sophomore year in high school. A few years later, my high school choir performed it.

On Cowriting
Jeremy: The first song we wrote together was called "Safely Home." It was actually my first cowrite. Greg Nelson had the foresight to put us together, and I've written with hundreds of others, but Paul is still my number 1 main cowriter.

Paul: In some ways our paths cross very well, especially melodically in thinking. But we are diverse in another way, so that one of us will point us in a new direction. Once you get there, you are still in a place that you love.

Jeremy: Paul has just taught me to work harder. My personality in the beginning was just to write a song and get it over with. Paul is really patient when it comes to beating things up. We're in the middle of creating a demo, and he is still over there working through a verse.

What is your process in songwriting? Lyrics, chords, melody?
Jeremy: We always go out to eat 10 minutes into the writing session. (laughter)

Paul: We always sit down and talk about the concept first. There's something that sparks the imagination to get the process going. We used to sit around the piano more, now we don't necessarily need an instrument with us to write.

Jeremy: Sometimes the instruments can be a stumbling block. We ended up sliding into a rut of something we have done before (in terms of melody). Lately, we've even written with just a drum loop or just one of us will play the instrument. When we are working on a song, we need to find it. It is like a sculptor chiseling away at a piece of granite. It's in there somewhere; we just need to reveal it. It's all about what you chip away while letting the other pieces fall to the floor.

Where did you get your concept for "Christmas in Heaven"?

Jeremy: I had the vague idea for the concept, but it all came about when I got a call asking for Christmas songs for a large country band. The song wasn't written yet, but I promised them I would have a demo to them the next day. I called Paul at 9:30 p.m. to start the process. Paul started coming up with all of these imagery pictures like "Are the mansions all covered in white?" It's one of those songs that rolled easy because we started with a good concept.

Paul: It all began with the basic imageries of Christmas, lights, trees, snow . . . so then I began to ask, What would Christmas in heaven look like? The same imagery that makes us nostalgic, will it be in heaven? I focused on that.

Jeremy: We finished the song around 1 a.m., and I made a demo and sent it on the next day. The band didn't cut it and we were pretty discouraged. Five years later, Scotty McCreery ended up recording the song.

Paul: If a really great song exists, that song will find its way. You can write all your life, but you are only going to write a handful of songs that are truly special. We get so much feedback from this song.

The response to "Christmas in Heaven."

Jeremy: Before Scotty released it, my dad took a copy of "Christmas in Heaven" to the local radio stations in Shreveport, Louisiana. The DJ said, "We get all of that from our program directors, so we can't play it." A few days passed and the DJ called and said they were going to start putting it in rotations. We knew the song was going to work because people would call to request the song over and over. This was all before it was ever released by a major artist. We knew an artist *had* to cut it.

Paul: It even had over 400,000 YouTube hits before it was ever commercially released!

Jeremy: Sometimes it just doesn't matter about the performance; it is just the song. The music and lyrics transcend the artist. Scotty heard the song on a Thursday and recorded by Monday. That never happens.

Most significant learning experience of your career.

Paul: Opportunity meets preparedness. If you wait to be inspired to write, you won't write that often and you won't be consistent. You write out of inspiration *and* discipline.

Jeremy: Every song that you write matters. They all play a part in getting you to the skill level that will allow you to write the next great song.

Greatest moment of your career so far.

Jeremy: Actually seeing a song published in the *Baptist Hymnal* and seeing that hymnal on the piano I learned to play on.

Paul: Somebody took the time to track me down to tell me that one of my songs saved their marriage. Those are the moments I personally hope for . . . because that is eternal. A gold record is temporary. That your songs move people from point A to B is significant and lasting.

VIDEO
TRACK 29

Jeremy Johnson and Paul Marino, "Christmas in Heaven"

December hasn't changed
This town looks the same
They still light that tree in the city square
There's red, white, and green shining everywhere
And I wish you were here
And I wonder—

CHORUS 1

Is the snow falling down on the streets of gold
Are the mansions all covered in white
Are you singing with angels, "Silent Night"
I wonder what Christmas in heaven is like

There's a little manger scene
Down on Third and Main
I must've walked right by it a thousand times
But I see it now in a different light
'Cause I know you are there
And I wonder

CHORUS 2

Are you kneeling with shepherds before Him now
Can you reach out and touch His face
Are you part of that glorious, holy night
I wonder what Christmas in heaven is like

REPEAT CHORUS 1

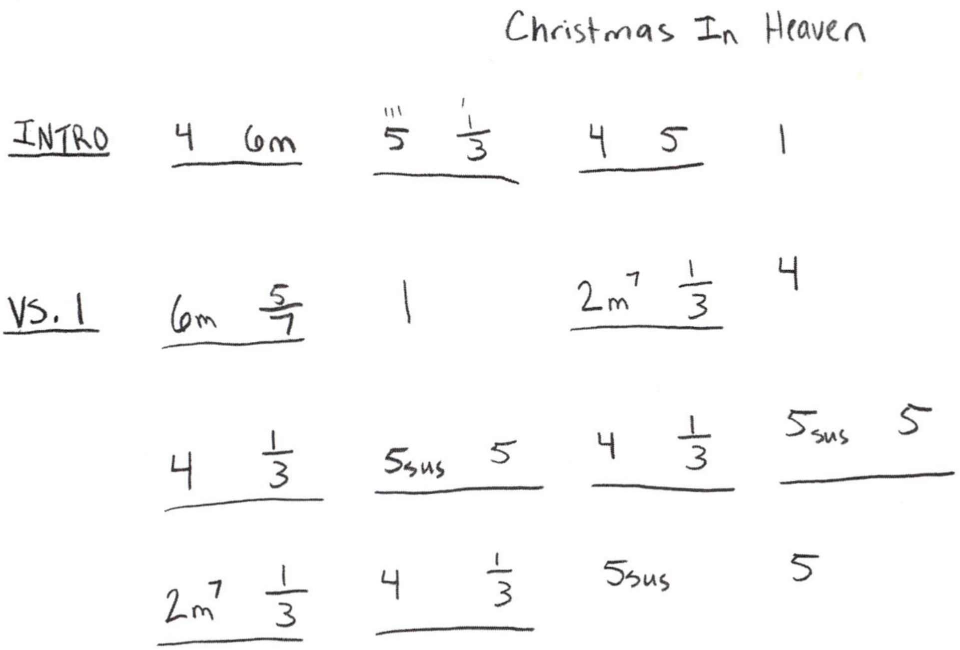

CHO $. 4 1 | 6m 4 | 4 6m | 5sus 1/3

4 1 | 2/4 5 | 4/4 6m | 2m7 | 2nd x to CODA 5sus ◇

T.A. 4 6m | 5 1/3 | 4 5 | 1

VS. 2 6m 5/7 | 1 | 2m7 1/3 | 4

4 1/3 | 5sus 5 | 4 1/3 | 5sus 5

2m7 1/3 | 4 1/3 | 5sus D.S. AL CODA

CODA ⊕ 4 | 1 37/5# | 6m 1/3 | 4²

4/6 1/3 | 4 1 5/7 | 6m | 5sus | 5sus | 5sus

CHO 4 1 | 6m | 4 6m | 5sus ◇

4 1 | 2/4 5 | 4/4 6m | 6m ◇ | 2m7 ◇ | 5sus ◇

OUT 4 6m | 5 1/3 | 4 5sus rit. | 1 ◇

ARTIST IN RESIDENCE

Songwriter 3:
James Isaac Elliott
Chair of Songwriting at Mike Curb College of Entertainment & Music Business at Belmont University
Platinum Album Award Winner

Educational Background

I got a degree in photography at Oakland Community College in Michigan. In my last semester I took a piano class and was also playing guitar. I still have the Kay guitar I bought for $50 at a music store in Pontiac.

I took a summer job working at the Grand Canyon National Park and that's where I began writing songs. I returned to Michigan and earned a B.A. in Bible and communication from John Wesley College. When I graduated, I moved to Nashville and started working in the music business. Eventually I became a television writer and feature story producer. During that time I earned an M.A. in speech, communication and theater from Austin Peay State University.

What inspired you to pursue music?

I come from a family of ten and we always had music around the house. My mom played piano and sang and my dad played guitar and banjo. We all loved music and most of us kids played in the school band. My instrument was trombone and I loved playing in the marching and concert bands. I never felt like I learned too much about music theory but I used to tell people "I can read the bass clef." I struggled sometimes academically so music really helped me get through those times. I had a really great band teacher named Mr. Mattison.

Can you describe your very first songwriting attempt? How old were you?

My earliest songs were all based around very simple melodies because I hadn't been playing guitar that long. I was heavily influenced by artists such as Willie Nelson and Bob Dylan. . . . I could see the simplicity of the melody and the chord progressions that I could learn and play. One of my earliest songs was called "Good Morning Lord". . . . very simple idea. Later, I began to collaborate with professional writers and artists and that took my music to another place.

What is your process in writing? Lyrics, chords, melody?

I think that when I first started writing, I would just play through ideas on my guitar and would try to copy and shadow songs that I really liked. Decades later, I tend to typically start with lyrics and the melody seems to come quickly. I think about rhyme and meter . . . usually once I have that, I go to the guitar and get something going.

Sometimes it takes a long time to get the lyrics exactly right. People don't understand how much time it takes to actually write a great song. It takes an enormous amount of effort. I would equate a successful songwriter to a professional athlete. It's the same amount of training and discipline.

Where do you get your ideas?

From great literature, art and paintings. I am always listening to ideas around me. There is always a story to be told, whether that be my own story or something I hear in the papers or television. You are always on the lookout for new ideas.

The art of cowriting

Sometimes writers want you to help them write up a story that they already have. That's always a nice challenge just to see what you can come up with while going back and forth. When you are a professional writer, it is just expected that you will cowrite, but it's also about finding the people you are connecting with. When you actually get something and it works, it is exciting. One of the great things about collaborating is that you get to build on each other's strengths.

I'm currently working with another writer named Jimmy Fortune. He was a longtime member of the country vocal group the Statler Brothers and he wrote several number 1 radio hits for them. He is great with melodies. I had this lyric . . . this verse, and I really didn't know where the chorus was going. He heard the verse and almost immediately came up with the chorus. I'm really excited about that. Part of the success of the cowrite is just the personalities coming from the same perspective.

Your favorite song and why.

Probably the song I am the closest to is called "My Redeemer Is Faithful and True." I had just moved to Nashville to pursue music and had left my family back in Michigan. The verse and chorus came to me as I was traveling on the 12-hour drive back to Michigan. I was thinking about my faith and my family as I drove and the lyrics just came to me.

Within that same year, I had met Steven Curtis Chapman while he was working on his first album. We worked together to finish the song and Steven added a great bridge and went on to record it on his first album. It always amazes me how the song has affected people. You never really hear all the stories, but I have heard how the song has helped people to get through a tragic situation. A new acoustic version of the song was released this year on an album called "Deep Roots" by Steven Curtis Chapman on the Cracker Barrel label . . . new audiences are hearing it for the first time.

How do you promote your songs to artists?

You must have some form of demo to play for them. If it's an artist I'm working with I may play it live or send them what we called a "work tape," a simple recording we do on our phone. Some successful writers still go in professional studios to record their songs. The demo budgets have actually gone down, so it's nice to get in there and complete a full session to demo your music. You need to showcase your songs in order to play it for people. A majority of professional songwriters today have their own recording programs, Pro Tools or Logic, that they use to record their demos.

Most significant learning experience of your career.

In recent years, I would say that teaching this lyric-writing class with Tom Douglas has been a great learning experience. Just watching Tom teach students how to dissect these lyrics . . . it is almost like watching a surgeon. The process of analyzing lyrics has been really important. I'm still excited about the songs I'm writing, but now I am really focusing on my process . . . thinking how long am I going to give to this lyric, where am I going with this. I'm always working hard at it.

VIDEO TRACK 30

James Elliott and Steven Curtis Chapman, "My Redeemer Is Faithful and True"

ARTIST IN RESIDENCE

Songwriter 4:
Tom Douglas
Songwriter
CMA and ACM Song of the Year Award Winner

Educational Background

I graduated from Oglethorpe University with a degree in economics. After graduation, I worked in real estate for a year before going back to graduate school for an MBA. I just never thought about pursuing music full time . . . I just didn't think you could make a living within the music business. But at the age of 27, I just wanted to be in or around Nashville. The pull of the songs was so strong, so I moved to Nashville and played piano on the road for a year; I was a tour manager for a few bands . . . I did various things to make a living, but really I wanted to be around the music. After a few years, I gave up on the music dream and moved to Texas to work in real estate. For the next decade or so, I no longer wrote. It took me years to regain the love of music. I gradually started writing again and had my first song recorded at the age of 41, the song "Little Rock" by Colin Raye. The song went to number 1. So that was my Red Sea moment. The seas parted, and I just walked through to the other side.

What inspired you to pursue music?

I grew up in a musical family. My father played piano and ukulele and just loved songs. Looking back, my father really taught me about songs and songwriters, including Kris Kristofferson, Hank Williams, the Beatles . . . he just loved *songs*. I have no formal musical training and am completely self-taught. When Elton John came out, I knew I *had to* learn how to play the piano.

Can you describe your very first songwriting attempt? How old were you?

I was 16 and it started as poetry and just evolved. Of course, I was just trying to impress a girl.

What is your process in writing? Lyrics, chords, melody? What was your process in writing "The House that Built Me"?

I am a lyricist first. Songwriting is hard, but writing down the song is easy. What I attempt to do is to experience the movie. I try to get to know the scene . . . what it smells like, taste like, and feels like. I want to know the backstory of the characters, who they are, where they are, what they are doing. Each song needs to include a beginning, middle, and end. My songs are mainly character driven, and honestly, I've written about the same character my entire life. The songs are just different movies. But you need to stay in the process, and you may have to make up the backstory and motivation of your character quickly. You just have to start assigning answers to blanks on the page.

My cowriter, Allen Shamblin, brought the idea for "The House that Built Me" to me. He said, "What if there was a song not about building houses, but about a house building you?" We went with it. The details in the song are from both of our experiences. It really is a metaphor of the prodigal son . . . being broken and coming back home.

Where do you get your most of your ideas?
My process is just to fill the creative tank with great literature, art, movies . . . other things that inspire me to write down things that I am interested in. The writing of the song is the last step in filling the well with forms of creativity.

Most significant learning experience of your career.
I think it is important to read all of the great literature, whether that is Hemingway or Steinbeck or Jane Austen. When I read great books, my lyric writing is at a much higher level. The greatest book on songwriting for me is *The Grapes of Wrath.*

Greatest moment of your career so far.
When I moved back to Nashville the second time, I felt like I had made it back to the starting point. I knew I had been given a second chance. I was thankful to have the past experiences that I could build on and make it better the second time.

VIDEO TRACK 31

Tom Douglas and Allen Shamblin, "House that Built Me"

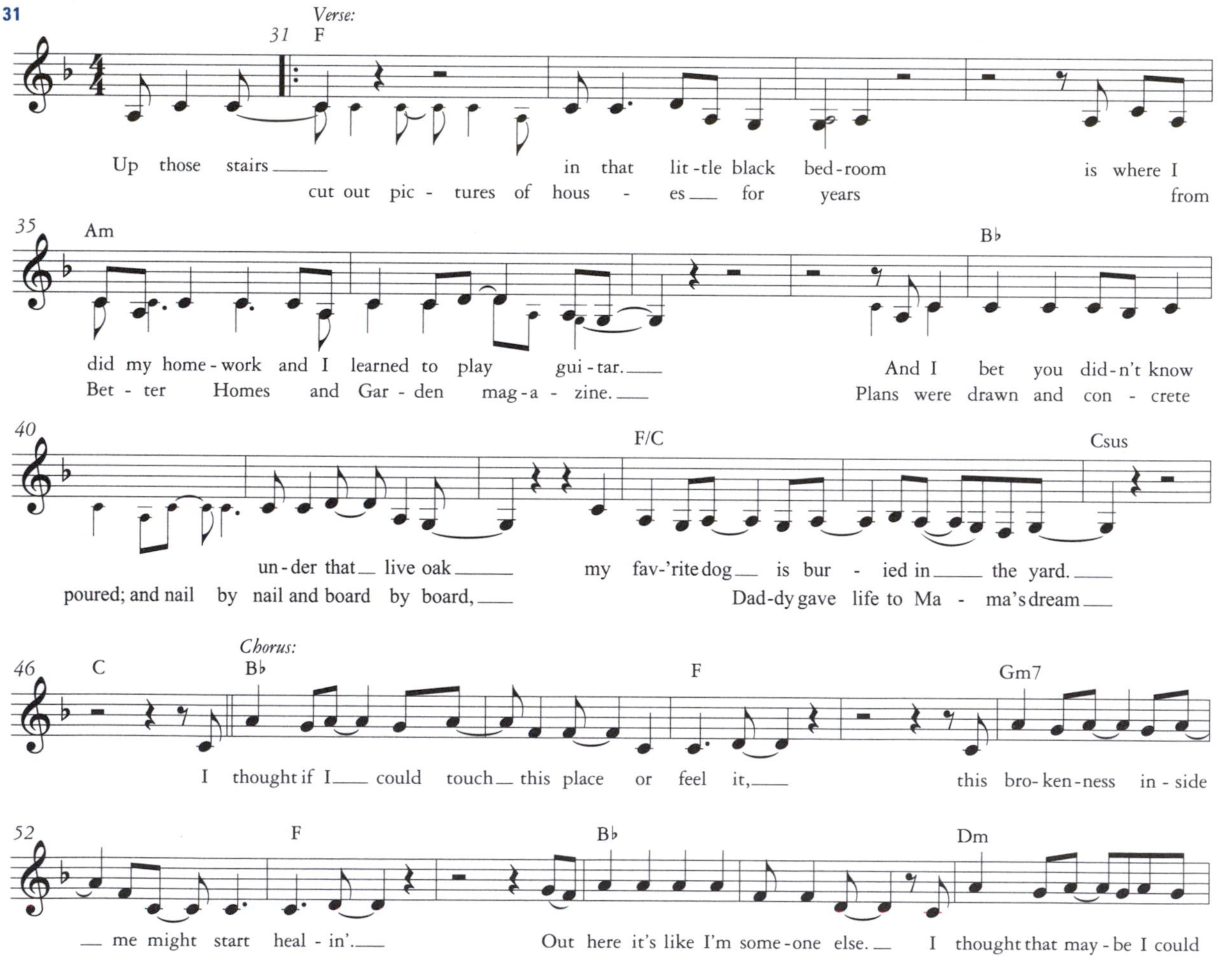

ARTIST IN RESIDENCE

Songwriter 5:
Ben Folds
Composer and Performing Artist

Educational Background

I studied at the University of Miami (percussion performance), but I didn't finish the degree. I did take some piano lessons when I was younger. I had a really keen interest in what I found out was called music theory.

When I was little, I wanted to know why something was called a certain key and why there were whole steps and half steps. When I started to figure these things out and log these ideas into my brain, I was a lot happier about making music.

Has the study of music theory and musicianship helped you in your career? If so, how?

Oh, I think it is huge. When you are composing, whether it is pop or classical music, you need brainwork. You need to understand the why. These musical moments are affecting people in the audience. If you are going to modulate all over the place, I think you kind of need to know why you did it. You don't want your feelings to become so randomized that people cannot understand them. I feel songs sound different to me once I know why and where I went.

Some people think you should just fly by the seat of your pants and that by ear you should know these things. I'm different in that I go back through my music and re-establish the basics, in order to make sense of it. As soon as I do that, I can figure out where I went off the map. I think, "I will add this to this bar and I will make this pitch a natural because it's this key." It's just simple things, and as soon as I do that, I understand where I came from and what the initial path was.

Some artists think that music theory is a threat to their creative process and I would argue very strongly that it is your friend. You need the map and you need to know the why. I'm a big fan.

Describe your typical songwriting process.

To me, a melody is everything. Melody is not open to negotiation. The melody typically comes first and a good melody usually means something. I know when a melody has a soul or when it doesn't. It takes a long time for me to apply the lyrics to the melody; I'm in the dark for quite some time on how the words are going to fit. Harmonizing the melody is far more negotiable to me. I'm open to conversation about harmony; maybe this should have an extension on this chord, maybe there shouldn't even be a chord there, those kinds of things. That, to me, is all just serving the melody. That is probably why music theory is so handy to me as a writer. If I need another option in terms of harmony, then I have a wide range of tools to choose from to help support the melody with substitution. Harmony is one of my final steps in the songwriting process.

The very last thing I do before heading into the studio is to pull notes out. It is something I am doing more and more. I ask myself, "Do I need that pitch, do I need that passing note there?" I start taking things out, subtracting elements. I find it really awesome to have the choice if it is not benefiting the song.

I find that the flowery parts can include too much information, and sometimes the musicians (and fans) are disappointed when I oversimplify things. That's because they came to know me as someone who constantly added more. I have to ignore that because my journey is to find a way to sing more succinctly than I can speak in real life.

Most significant learning experience of your career.

I've never found one more significant moment than the next. What I think is a revelation is actually an exception to the rule of my revelation the year before.

I just played at the Lincoln Center with Renée Fleming, Sara Bareilles, and Josh Groban. We've all done this quite a bit, but we are all as nervous . . . the shaking nervous, not able to focus like you need to nervous. We all thought we did about an 8/10 in terms of the performance. I guess the nerves got to us. At the last minute, we needed another singer. I asked my 14-year-old daughter, Gracie, to come up onstage and sing a harmony line with Sara. She came up and just did it. Her perspective was so different about being on the stage at the Kennedy Center with the National Symphony Orchestra. I learned so much from that . . . it's all about perspective. You have to approach every note, every song, every performance as innocently as possible.

Opposed to that is that we are imposing more and more structure. I'm trying to tell people to remember everything they have studied in their musical training but then to forget it all in order to deliver a performance with the innocence of my daughter. We also ask people to not be concerned with what someone thinks. At the same time, this caring is everything because it determines your success in your career, your songs, and your income. In order to do these things at the same time, you have to be a technical and inspired musician, a self-conscious and self-aware musician. There is a line that is very difficult to walk; it is a lifelong thing and it never gets better or easier.

Greatest moment of your career so far.

I'm really lucky that I have lots of great moments. Performing at the Kennedy Center and working with young artists at American Voices was a wonderful moment. Sometimes I have horrible failures that I file under a great moment because I realize how proud I am for having gotten through it. A lot of the great moments were when I took off work to play a gig, rented a PA system, spent all day putting it together, blew up one of the speakers, had six people show up at the gig, had to pay to play, woke up at 8 a.m. to deliver the broken PA system, and went back to wait tables by lunch. That was horrible to me when I was 23. I sucked. But now, I file that under positive. I'm glad I went through those moments, and I learned more about what I can take.

VIDEO TRACK 32

Ben Folds, "The Luckiest"

Reviewing Chapter Objectives

- Gain a better understanding of the process of songwriting (page 325)
- Define basic terms as used in songwriting and sessions (page 326)
- Answer basic questions in terms of song form when listening to songs (page 327)
- Gain insight from interviews with songwriters (pages 327–343)

COMPOSITION PROJECT

So, how does one start to write a song? Should you start with lyrics, a melody that resides in your head, or a chord progression that you have played over and over on the piano? As you have discovered in this chapter, there is no one correct way to write a song.

In groups of three or four, work together to write a song that includes lyrics, two verses, a bridge, and a chorus. Make this a collaborative effort: everyone brings something to the table before the songwriting session begins. There is no limit in terms of what theoretical concepts need to be included, but experiment with extended harmonies and chromatic chords as you write your main progression. Use this project as a way to explore everything you have learned. Include both a lead sheet and Nashville chart for the performers of your song.

APPENDIX 3

GLOSSARY

Accidentals	symbols that alter a pitch by a half or whole step
Anticipation (ANT)	a non-chord tone that arrives at the new harmony before the harmony is established in the other voices
Appoggiatura (APP)	a non-chord tone approached by a leap and resolved by a step
Bass clef	used for lower pitches, the bass clef identifies the fourth line on the staff as the placement of the pitch F; it is sometimes known as the F clef
Beam	used to connect two or more note values that contain flags; beams are equivalent to (and replace) flags
Binary form	a formal structure in which the piece of music can clearly be divided into two parts or sections
Borrowed chord	a chromatic chord that uses pitches from the parallel key in order to change the quality of various chords
Bridge	typically found after the second chorus, the bridge contains a new chord progression or a new melodic idea; it can be in a different key and provides contrast to the verse and chorus; it normally provides the revelation and brings about the "aha" moment for the character
C clefs	some of the earliest clefs in music notation that identify the location of the middle C
Cadence	final two chords composed in a musical phrase
Cadential six-four	the triad in second inversion sets up the final cadence, leading directly into the root position dominant
Channel	another name for pre-chorus
Chord	any group of pitches sounding together
Chorus	contains the musical hook and most often the title line; the chorus (the *why*) is repeated throughout the song
Chromatic pitch	any pitch that is taken outside of the scale on which a piece is based
Chromatic pivot chord modulation	a type of pivot modulation using a chord that functions in both keys; however, at least one of the pivot chords is not diatonic
Chromatic scale	arrangement of pitches in half steps within an octave
Clef	found at the beginning of each staff, it alerts the performer as to the specific placement of one pitch
Closed position	the three pitches of a triad (or chord) are as close together as possible, or within the span of an octave
Compound interval	the interval spans a space larger than an octave
Compound meter	a meter in which the main beat can be divided into three equal parts; the main beat in compound meter is always a dotted note because dotted notes divide naturally into three equal parts
Compound ternary	a three-part structure in which other large scale forms exist within one of the three sections, such as the A section having a binary structure

Concerto form	composed in such a manner as to spotlight a solo instrument, concerto form consists of two main formal sections, the solo (S) and the ritornello (R)
Continuous ternary	a simple ternary structure in which the A section contains a modulation to another key or concludes with something other than a PAC in the original key
Deceptive cadence	a dominant chord that moves to a chord other than I, most often the submediant
Diatonic pitch	any pitch that is taken from the scale on which a piece is based
Direct modulation	a modulation that occurs directly after the cadence in the previous key; in this type of modulation, there is no transition or pivot chord and a new section of music immediately begins in a new key
Dotted note (dot)	extends the value of a note or rest by one-half of its original value
Enharmonic pitches	pitches that sound the same but are spelled differently
Escape tone (ET)	a non-chord tone approached by a step and resolved by a leap
Figured bass	a shorthand notation involving the use of numbers to indicate the intervals of the pitches above the bass in order to show inversions
First inversion	the third of the triad (or chord) is the lowest sound pitch
French augmented sixth (Fr^{+6})	an augmented sixth chord that is made up of the same pitches as the It^{+6}, but with the addition of $\hat{2}$, or re
German augmented sixth (Ger^{+6})	an augmented sixth chord that is made up of the same pitches as the It^{+6}, but with the addition of the $\flat\hat{3}$ (me)
Grand staff	grouping together of bass and treble staves
Half cadence	a cadence in which the phrase ends on the unstable dominant harmony; the dominant harmony can be approached by the ii, IV, or I
Half step	in Western music, the shortest distance between two pitches; it involves two adjacent keys on the keyboard
Harmonic interval	the two pitches of the interval are sounded simultaneously
Harmonic minor scale	a natural minor scale in which the $\hat{7}$ is raised in order to create the half step relationship between the leading tone and the tonic
Harmonic progression	a series of chords leading toward a cadence; the progression is based upon relationships between the tonic, subdominant, and dominant harmonies
Hook	a melodic (or rhythmic) idea that is repeated over and over
Imperfect authentic cadence (IAC)	an authentic cadence in which the soprano voice of the I chord is notated with a $\hat{3}$ or $\hat{5}$, the first chord is a vii°, or any chord is in inversion
Interval number	interval size, which can be determined by counting the letters between the two pitches
Intervals	the distance between two pitches
Intro (Introduction)	typically 4 measures long, the intro sets up the melodic and harmonic structure and establishes the key area
Inverted interval	the lower pitch of the original interval becomes the higher pitch
Italian augmented sixth (It^{+6})	an augmented sixth chord that contains the pitches le, do, fi and functions as a subdominant chord; the resolution is also similar in that it resolves to a dominant chord (or the cadential six-four)
Key signature	a symbol given at the beginning of any tonal piece; it tells the performer what scale the piece is based on and what accidentals to use
Lead sheet notation (or pop chord symbols)	a modern musical score that shows the lyrics, the basic chords, and sometimes, but not always, the vocal melody; lead sheet symbols are shorthand for writing out triads and chords using letter symbols
Ledger lines	extend the staff up or down to accommodate pitches outside the standard five-line staff
Major scale	consists of seven different pitches, where the half steps lie between the third and fourth scale degrees and the seventh and eighth scale degrees

Melodic interval	the two pitches of the interval are sounded in succession
Melodic minor scale	a natural minor scale with a raised $\hat{6}$ and $\hat{7}$ on the ascent
Meter	the grouping of strong and weak beats into a recurring pattern
Middle 8	in most cases, the middle 8 is another term for an eight-measure bridge that is found between the two final choruses
Modal mixture	the use of pitches from the parallel key in order to change the quality of various chords
Modulation	a change in tonal center
Monophonic modulation	a type of modulation in which one line acts as a transition to the new key; the line is simply a single melodic line serving as transition between the two keys
Natural minor scale	a minor scale based on the intervallic makeup of WHWWHWW
Neapolitan chord (N^6 or N)	a major chord built on the lowered second scale degree; functioning as a subdominant harmony, the Neapolitan is usually found in first inversion and resolves to the V or a cadential six–four pattern
Neighbor group (NG)	two non-chord tones that embellish a pitch as a lower *and* an upper neighbor
Neighbor tone (NT)	a non-chord tone used to embellish a single pitch a step above or below
Non-chord tone or **embellishing tone**	a pitch outside of the harmony, used to embellish the melody
Octave	an interval formed when the same pitch is repeated up one register, such as F4 to F5
Open position	the pitches of a triad (or chord) span a space larger than an octave
Outro	typically found at the end of the song, the tag repeats a lyric and a progression over and over (normally with a fade)
Parallel keys	two keys that share the same tonic, but use different key signatures
Passing six-four	the lowest pitch of the triad acts as a passing tone in order to move from a root position chord to a chord in first inversion
Passing tone (PT)	a non-chord tone that fills the interval between two different chord tones
Pedal six-four	the lowest pitch of the triad acts as a "pedal" common tone between two chords in root position; most often the chord is a IV^6_4
Perfect authentic cadence (PAC)	a cadence that includes a root position V and I chord; within the I chord, the tonic must be present in the soprano voice
Perfect intervals	the intervals of the 1, 4, 5, and 8
Period	a combination of phrases into a larger structural unit, much like a written sentence; often periods are made up for two phrases: the first phrase is called the antecedent, and the second phrase is called the consequent; the antecedent always concludes with a weaker cadence than the PAC that concludes the consequent
Phrase	a complete music thought; typically made up of two, four, or eight measures and must conclude with a cadence
Phrase group	a group of phrases in which the conclusive cadence is not present
Pivot chord modulation	in this type of modulation, a particular chord serves two functions, both in the original key and the key to which the piece is modulating
Pivot tone modulation	a type of modulation that includes one pitch that functions in both keys; often the pivot pitch stands by itself, with little, if any accompaniment; the pitch is held over from the cadence in the original key and changes function as a new harmony is played underneath the pitch
Plagal cadence	a cadence in which the subdominant harmony moves directly to the tonic, bypassing the dominant all together
Pre-chorus	sets up the chorus, building tension and drama in the storyline; the direction of the line, both in terms of dynamics and melody is up
Prime	another name for unison
Relative keys	keys that share the same key signature but have different tonics

Retardation a non-chord tone that is held over from the previous chord but resolves upward to a chord tone

Rondo form a formal design comprised of a recurring section alternating with contrasting sections; rondo movements tend to be separated into five or more parts so that the alternation between the restatement and contrasting sections can be more clearly realized

Rounded binary a formal structure that includes a return of the material from the A section at the conclusion of the B section; as a result, there is a tendency for the organization of the phrases to be more symmetrical

Scale an arrangement of pitches into a series of half and whole steps

Scale degree the numbered position of individual pitches within a scale

Second inversion the fifth of the triad (or chord) is the lowest sound pitch

Secondary dominant chord a chromatic major or Mm7 chord that is used to tonicize a chord whose root is a fifth below

Secondary leading tone chord a chromatic chord of diminished or half diminished quality that is used to tonicize a chord whose root is a half step above

Sectional ternary a simple ternary structure in which the A section ends with a PAC in the original key

Sequential modulation a type of modulation in which a melodic idea is stated at one pitch level and then restated at another pitch level

Seventh chord a triad with the addition of another third, or a seventh above the root

Simple meter a meter in which the main beat can be divided into two equal parts; the top number of a time signature in simple meter will always be 2, 3, or 4

Simple ternary a three-part structure in which each section consists of a phrase or period design; each section falls short of having another form within it

Solfège refers to the syllables assigned to the scale degrees of major and minor keys

Sonata form emerged logically from the rounded binary concept, the original simplicity of the style growing gradually more complex; the three main components of a composition in sonata form are the exposition, the development, and the recapitulation

Staff a grid of five lines and four spaces

Suspension a non-chord tone that is "suspended" from the previous chord and resolved down in the next chord by step

Tag typically found at the end of the song, the tag repeats a lyric and a progression over and over (normally with a fade). This can also be called the **Outro**.

Tempo the speed of the beat

Ternary form a formal structure in which the piece of music can clearly be divided into three parts or sections; this style of formal design includes a statement, a contrast, and a restatement

Tie connects two noteheads of the same pitch. Tied pitches are held for the duration of both pitches, but only the first pitch is struck.

Time signature pair of numbers that indicate the meter, what note value = 1 beat, and the number of beats per measure

Treble clef used for higher pitches, the treble clef identifies the second line on the staff as the placement of the pitch G; it is sometimes identified as the G clef

Triad chord made up of three pitches; most common is the tertian triad

Verse tells the storyline and sets the scene (the *who*, *what*, *when*, and *where*); typically a verse is eight or sixteen bars long

Whole step comprised of two half steps

APPENDIX 4

TIMINGS FOR YOUTUBE CHANNEL

PLAYLIST 1

Chapter 1

The Shining—opening scene

The Truman Show—Mozart, *Sonata No. 11 in A Major,* K. 331, Mvt. III (1:21–2:05)

The King's Speech—Beethoven, *Symphony No. 7, Op. 92,* Mvt. II (1:09–1:42)

Life Is Beautiful—Offenbach, "Belle Nuit" from *Les Contes d'Hoffman* (1:28–1:47)

Oceans 11—Debussy, "Clair de Lune" from *Suite Bergamasque,* Mvt. III (0:54–1:22)

Shawshank Redemption—Mozart, "Sull'aria" from *Le Nozze di Figaro* (1:21–2:24)

Titanic—Sarah Flower Adams, "Nearer My God to Thee" (0:06–1:06)

The Pianist—Chopin, "Ballade No. 1 in G Minor" (0:23–1:02)

2001 Space Odyssey—Johann Strauss, *The Blue Danube* (1:33–2:11)

YouTube Symphony Orchestra plays Britten's *The Young Person's Guide to the Orchestra*

Chapter 2

Playing For Change, "Stand by Me" (Entire Selection)

The Aristocats—"Arpeggios" (Entire Selection)

Willie Nelson and Norah Jones, "Baby It's Cold Outside" (0:00–0:42)

Mark O'Connor, "Emily's Reel" (1:51–2:04)

Various Artists, "We Are the World" (0:25–0:53) (3:06–3:20) (3:55–4:29)

Various Artists, "We are the World 25 for Haiti" (Entire Selection)

The Three Tenors, "Nessun Dorma" from Puccini's *Turandot* (0:40–1:49)

Chapter 3

Lang Lang and Metallica, "One" (0:00–1:45)

Rachmaninoff, *Preludes, Op. 23, No. 5* (0:00–0:19)

Schubert, *Fantasy in F Minor,* D. 940 (0:00–0:48)

Liszt, "La Campanella" from *Grandes etudes de Paganini* (0:33–1:07)

Vivaldi's *The Four Seasons* in various commercials

Chapter 4

Adele, "Rolling in the Deep" (Entire Selection)

Adele, "Rumour Has It" (2:47–3:27)

Adele, "Set Fire to the Rain" (0:47–1:17)

Adele, "Someone Like You" (1:14–1:48)

Adele's 2012 Grammy performance of "Rolling in the Deep" (Entire Selection)

Taylor Swift, "You Belong with Me" (0:37–1:05)
Rodgers and Hammerstein, "You'll Never Walk Alone" (1:03–1:20)
George Gershwin, "Summertime" from *Porgy and Bess* (0:00–0:15)
John Williams, "Theme from *Jaws*" (0:00–0:14)
Adele, "Skyfall" (1:23–1:51)

Chapter 5

Candice Glover, "I Who Have Nothing" (Entire Selection)
Kelly Clarkson, "Because of You" (0:41–1:10)
Chris Daughtry, "What About Now" (0:03–0:25)
Phillip Phillips, "We've Got Tonight" (0:00-0:15)
Carrie Underwood, "Inside Your Heaven" (0:00–0:36) Live Version
Carrie Underwood, "Inside Your Heaven" Studio Version (Entire Selection)
Phillip Phillips, "Home" (0:33–0:42)
Kelly Clarkson, "Stronger" (0:00–0:24)
Jackie Evancho, Gounod's "Ave Maria" (0:00–0:46)

Chapter 6

Joshua Bell and Nathan Gunn, Rachmaninoff's "O, Cease Thy Singing, Maiden Fair, Op. 4, No. 4" (0:52–1:20)
Joshua Bell and Kristin Chenoweth, Rodgers and Hart's "My Funny Valentine" (2:31–3:06)
Joshua Bell, Debussy's "La Fille aux Cheveux de Lin" (0:00–0:39)
Joshua Bell and Josh Groban, "Love Theme" from *Cinema Paradiso* (0:49–1:28)
Joshua Bell, ["Stop and Hear the Music"] (Washington D.C. metro experiment)
George Gershwin, "I Loves You Porgy" from *Porgy and Bess* (2:32–2:58)
Joshua Bell, Saint-Saëns's "Le Cygne" from *Carnaval des Animaux* (0:27–0:46)
Bruno Mars, "When I Was Your Man" (0:10–0:36)
Joshua Bell, "Somewhere" (live performance) (0:00–0:34)
Joshua Bell, Tchaikovsky's *Violin Concerto* (0:35–1:29)

Chapter 7

Elvis Presley, "Don't Be Cruel" on *The Ed Sullivan Show* (Entire Selection)
Elvis Presley, "Hound Dog" on *The Milton Berle Show* (Entire Selection)
Elvis Presley, "All Shook Up" (0:06–0:45)
Elvis Presley, "Love Me Tender" (0:11–2:36)
Elvis Presley, "Return to Sender" (0:09–1:22)
Fun., "We Are Young" (0:40–1:29)
Fun., "Some Nights" (1:03–1:34)
Sarah Hurst, "To the Moon" (Entire Selection)
Elvis Presley, "Can't Help Falling in Love" (0:22–0:52)
The Beatles, "Across the Universe" (0:48–1:10)

Chapter 8

Cecilia Bartoli, Pergolesi's "Se tu ma'mi" (0:23–0:43)
Cecilia Bartoli, Giordani's "Caro mio ben" (0:23–1:06)
Cecilia Bartoli, Mozart's "Voi che sapete" from *Le Nozze di Figaro* (0:02–0:40)
Cecilia Bartoli, Bellini's "Vaga luna" (0:27–1:00)
Maria Callas, Puccini's "O mio babbino caro" from *Gianni Schicchi* (1:07–1:52)

Cecilia Bartoli, Rossini's "Non piu mesta" from *La Cenerentola* (0:11–1:46)
Leonard Bernstein, "Maria" from *West Side Story* (0:00–0:45)

Chapter 9

Jackson 5, "I Want You Back" (Entire Selection)
Michael Jackson, "Ben" (0:06–0:35)
Michael Jackson, "Billie Jean" (Entire Selection)
Michael Jackson, "Thriller" (Entire Selection)
Michael Jackson, "Man in the Mirror" (2:43–2:52) (0:48–1:11)
Michael Jackson, "Black or White" (2:40–3:01)
Taylor Swift, "Love Story" (2:44–3:00)
King's College, Mozart's "Ave Verum Corpus" (0:05–0:33)
Universitäts Chor Müchen, Mendelssohn's "Die Nachtigall" (0:46–1:37)
The Beatles, "Hey Jude" (0:00–1:30)
Jackson 5, "I'll Be There" (Entire Selection)
Renée Fleming, "Lo, How a Rose E'er Blooming" (Entire Selection)
Ben Folds, "Still Fighting It" (Entire Selection)
Elgar, "Nimrod" from *Enigma Variations* (Entire Selection)
Gabe Dixon Band, "Disappear" (Entire Selection)
Diamond Rio, "You're Gone" (Entire Selection)

PLAYLIST 2

Chapter 10

Pink, "There You Go" (Entire Selection)
Destiny's Child, "Bills, Bills, Bills" (Entire Selection)
Pink, "Get the Party Started" (0:22–0:47)
Pink, "Glitter in the Air" 2010 Grammy performance (1:01–1:31)
Pink and Nate Ruess, "Just Give Me a Reason" (0:50–1:12)
Pink, "So What" (0:33–1:05)
Bach, "Nun Ruhen Alle Wälder" (0:00–0:17)
Mozart, "Menuetto" from *Clarinet Quintet in A Major,* K. 581, Mvt. III (0:00–0:20)

Chapter 11

Ella Fitzgerald, "Cry Me a River" (2:24–2:47)
Ella Fitzgerald, "In the Still of the Night" (1:25–1:54)
Ella Fitzgerald, "You're the Top" (1:10–1:23)
Ella Fitzgerald, "A Tisket, a Tasket" (Entire Selection)
Ella Fitzgerald, "Love for Sale" (0:40–1:14)
Daniel Barenboim, Beethoven's *Sonata No. 8 in C Minor, Op. 13* ("Pathétique") Mvt. III (3:29–3:32 and 4:22–4:36)
Ella Fitzgerald, "Autumn in New York" (0:06–0:32)
Bernadette Peters, "My Romance" (1:01–1:27)
Various Artists, "We Are the World" (0:42–0:51)
Jeffrey L. Ames, "In Remembrance" (Entire Selection)
Cambridge Singers, "The Turtle Dove" (Entire Selection)
Martha Argerich, Ravel's *Piano Concerto in G*, Mvt. II (Entire Selection)

Chapter 12

Billy Joel, "The Longest Time" (0:55–1:08)

Billy Joel, "Lullabye (Goodnight, My Angel)" (Entire Selection)

Billy Joel, "Scenes from an Italian Restaurant" (0:48–1:15)

Billy Joel and Garth Brooks, "Shameless" (0:00–1:10)

Daniel Barenboim, Beethoven's *Sonata No. 8 in C Minor, Op. 13* ("Pathétique") Mvt. II (0:00–0:38)

Mozart, *String Quartet in F Major, No. 5,* K. 158, Mvt. I (0:00–0:10)

Mozart, *Eine Kleine Nachtmusik,* K. 525, Mvt. I (0:50–0:58)

Maureen Forrester, Handel's "He Was Despised" from *Messiah* (6:25–6:45)

Billy Joel, "The Longest Time" (0:45–1:07)

Ben Folds, "The Luckiest" (0:20–1:05)

Moving Pictures, "What About Me" (1:45–2:06)

Chapter 13

Renée Fleming, Verdi's "Sempre Libera" from *La Traviata* (9:35–9:48)

Renée Fleming, Gounod's "Jewel Song" from *Faust* (1:31–1:35) (3:32–3:52)

Renée Fleming, Puccini's "Un Bel Di, Vedremo" from *Madame Butterfly* (Entire Selection)

Renée Fleming, "You'll Never Walk Alone" from Rodgers and Hammerstein's *Carousel* (Entire Selection)

Renée Fleming, "1234" on *The Muppet Show* (Entire Selection)

Renée Fleming, Puccini's "Vissi d'arte" from *Tosca* (1:28–2:09)

Beethoven, *String Quartet No. 4 in C Minor, Op. 18* (0:08–0:24)

Etta James, "Stormy Weather" (0:00–0:45)

Chapter 14

Rascal Flatts, "Bless the Broken Road"

Rascal Flatts, "I Melt" (0:56–1:24)

Rascal Flatts, "Skin"

Rascal Flatts, "Why Wait" (1:13–1:41)

Rascal Flatts, "Unstoppable" (0:55–1:23)

The Band Perry, "Chainsaw" (1:15–1:45)

Edward MacDowell, "To a Wild Rose" (1:42–2:09)

Friedrich von Flotow, "Ach, so fromm, ach so traut" from *Martha* (0:54–1:26)

Haydn, *Symphony No. 100,* Hob.I:100, Mvt. I (6:42–7:08)

Menken and Ashman, "Beauty and the Beast" (1:08–1:22)

Roberta Flack, "The First Time Ever I Saw Your Face" (4:45–5:19)

Righteous Brothers, "Unchained Melody" (1:28–1:41)

Louis Armstrong, "What a Wonderful World" (0:10–0:30)

Alanis Morissette, "Uninvited"

PLAYLIST 3

Chapter 15

CDZA, "Epic Key Changes" (Entire Selection)

Beyoncé, "Love on Top" (1:30–3:05)

Johnny Cash, "I Walk the Line" (0:00–1:25)

Ray Charles, "Georgia on My Mind" (2:40–3:55)
Celine Dion, "All by Myself" (2:00–2:55)
Whitney Houston, "I Will Always Love You" (2:40–3:25)
Queen, "We Are the Champions" (0:05–0:51)
Queen, "Somebody to Love" (1:33–2:04)
Queen, "Under Pressure" (0:30–1:24) (2:01–2:20) (2:14–2:38)
Queen, "Save Me" (0:25–0:58)
Queen, "Bohemian Rhapsody" (3:03–3:26) (0:56–1:45)
Film clip from *Wayne's World* (Entire Selection)
Felix Bernard, "Winter Wonderland" (0:30–0:55)
Camille Saint-Saëns, "Le Cygne" from *Carnaval des Animaux* (0:00–1:02)
Haydn, *Symphony No. 33 in C Major,* Mvt. I (Entire Selection)
Gounod, "Funeral March of a Marionette" (Entire Selection)
Paul Williams and Kenneth L. Ascher, "The Rainbow Connection" from *The Muppet Movie* (Entire Selection)
Billy Ocean, "Get Outta My Dreams, Get Into My Car" (Entire Selection)
Céline Dion, "My Heart Will Go On" from *Titanic* (Entire Selection)
Idina Menzel and Kristin Chenoweth, "Defying Gravity" from *Wicked* (Entire Selection)
Taylor Swift, "Love Story" (Entire Selection)

Appendix 1

For the Fatherless, "God in Me" (Entire Selection)
For the Fatherless, "Alcatraz" (Entire Selection)
Us The Duo, "I Will Wait for You" (Entire Selection)
Us The Duo, "No Matter Where You Are" (Entire Selection)
For the Fatherless, "Learn to Love" (Entire Selection)
Ashton Lee, "Boulder" (Entire Selection)

Appendix 2

Sarah Hurst, "The Valiant" (Entire Selection)
Scotty McCreery, "Christmas in Heaven" (Entire Selection)
Steven Curtis Chapman, "My Redeemer Is Faithful and True" (0:14–1:04)
Miranda Lambert, "House that Built Me" (1:00–3:01)
Ben Folds, "The Luckiest" (0:00–4:20)

SUPPLEMENTAL CHAPTERS

Online Chapter 1

Debussy, *La Mer*
Barbara Hendricks, Fauré's "Après un Rêve" (1:00–1:58)
Barbara Hendricks, Fauré's "Chanson D'amour" (0:04–0:46)
Walter Gieseking, Debussy's *Prelude No. 4 from Book I, Op. 28* (0:02–0:51)
Barbara Hendricks or if unavailable, Elly Ameling, Fauré's "Automne" (1:56–2:33)
Walter Gieseking, Debussy's "Arabesque No. 1" (0:01–0:34)
Bernadette Peters, Hart and Rodgers's "My Romance" (Entire Selection)
Debussy, *La Cathédrale Engloutie* (0:00–1:19)
Ravel, "Pavane pour une Infante Defunte" (0:00–0:58)

Billie Holiday, "Prelude to a Kiss" (0:07–0:37)
Judy Garland, "Cottage for Sale" (0:23–1:37)
Fred Astaire and Ginger Rogers, "Cheek to Cheek" (0:07–0:54)

Online Chapter 2

Beethoven, *Cello Sonata No. 3 in A Major, Op. 69*, Mvt. I (4:12–4:31)
Robert Schumann, *Cello Concerto in A Minor, Op. 129*, Mvt. I (6:52–7:09)
Edward Elgar, *Cello Concerto in E Minor, Op. 85*, Mvt. IV (1:40–1:56)
Felix Mendelssohn, *Cello Sonata No. 2, Op. 58*, Mvt. I (7:35–7:45)
Beethoven, *Piano Sonata No. 8 in C Minor Op. 13* ("Pathétique") Mvt. III (0:50–1:06)
Robert Schumann, *Cello Concerto in A Minor, Op. 129*, Mvt. I (3:14–3:37)
Beethoven, *Sonata for Piano and Cello No. 3 in A, Op. 69*, Mvt. I (8:12–8:20)
Beethoven, *Sonata for Piano and Cello No. 3 in A, Op. 69*, Mvt. III (7:16–7:30)
Brahms, *Sonata for Cello and Piano No. 2, Op. 99*, Mvt. III (0:00–0:15)
Chopin, *Nocturne in C♯ Minor No. 20* (0:25–1:07)
Haydn, *String Quartet No. 5 in F Minor, Op. 20*, (0:00–0:16)
Mozart, "Lacrymosa" from *Requiem* (0:00–1:08)
Beethoven, *Piano Sonata No. 14 in C♯ Minor*, "Moonlight" (4:45–5:19)

Online Chapter 3

Bernstein, "Tonight" from *West Side Story* (Entire Selection)
Bernstein conducting the *William Tell Overture* (Entire Selection)
Bernstein conducting the overture to *Candide* (Entire Selection)
Mozart, *Symphony No. 25* in G Minor, K. 183, Mvt. I (2:08–2:24) (0:38–0:58)
Bernstein, "I Feel Pretty" from *West Side Story* (1:11–1:38)
Mozart, *Symphony No. 35 in D Major*, K. 385, Mvt. I (1:57–2:10)
Bernstein, Chichester Psalms, Mvt. II (1:30–1:54)
Haydn, *Symphony No. 98, Hob.I:98*, Mvt. III (20:28–20:49)
Mozart, *Symphony No. 41 in C Major*, K. 551, Mvt. I (1:02–1:30) and (3:06–3:28)
Mozart, *Symphony No. 41 in C Major*, K. 551, Mvt. III (0:00–0:25)
Mozart, *Symphony No. 35 in D Major*, K. 385, Mvt. III (1:11–1:30)

Online Chapter 4

Robert Schumann, "Wilder Reiter" (Entire Selection)
Bach, *Goldberg Variation No. 9*, BWV 988 (Entire Selection)
Mozart, *Piano Sonata No. 11 in A Major*, K. 331, Mvt. I (Entire Selection)
Chopin, *Etude in E Major, Op. 10, No. 3* (Entire Selection)
Handel, "He Was Despised" from *Messiah* (Entire Selection)
Beethoven, *Piano Sonata No. 8 in C Minor, Op. 13* ("Pathétique") Mvt. II (Entire Selection)
Haydn, *Piano Sonata in D Major*, Hob.XVI:37, Mvt. I (Entire Selection)
Mozart, *Horn Concerto No. 4 in E-flat Major*, K. 495, Mvt. I (Entire Selection)

SELECTED BIBLIOGRAPHY AND SOURCES CONSULTED

Chapter 1

"GRAMMY.com: The Official Site of Music's Biggest Night." *GRAMMY.* http://www.grammy.com.

"Hot 100 and Other Billboard Charts." *Billboard*, January 1955–present.

Neal, Jocelyn R. *Country Music: A Cultural and Stylistic History*. New York: Oxford University Press, 2013.

Rojek, Chris. *Pop Music, Pop Culture*. Cambridge, UK: Polity Press, 2011.

Sarath, Ed. *Music Theory through Improvisation: A New Approach to Musicianship Training.* New York: Routledge, 2010.

Sorce, Richard. *Music Theory for the Music Professional: A Comparison of Common-Practice and Popular Genres*. New York: Ardsley House, 1995.

Wadhams, Wayne. *Inside the Hits*. Boston: Berklee Press, 2001.

Chapter 2

Dyer, Richard. "Luciano Pavarotti, 71; Tenor Transcended Opera World." *Boston Globe*, September 7, 2007. http://www.boston.com/ae/music/articles/2007/09/07/luciano_pavarotti_71_tenor_transcended_opera_world/?page=full.

Tyler-Ameen, Daoud. "The Worst Ideas of 2010: We Are the World 25." *NPR*. http://www.npr.org/blogs/therecord/2010/12/21/132214278/the-worst-ideas-of-2010-we-are-the-world-25.

Chapter 3

Greenstreet, Rosanna. "Lang Lang: I'd Play the Piano at 5am." *The Guardian* (London), May 13, 2011. http://www.theguardian.com/lifeandstyle/2011/may/14/lang-lang-piano-china-father.

Grow, Kory. "Metallica and Lang Lang Become 'One' at the Grammys." *Rolling Stone*, January 26, 2014.

"Lang Lang." *Lang Lang*, accessed March 23, 2014. http://langlang.com/en.

"Lang Lang International Music Foundation." *Lang Lang Foundation*, accessed March 23, 2014. http://langlangfoundation.com.

Von Rhein, John. "17-Year-Old Sub Steals the Show at Ravinia Gala." *Chicago Tribune*, August 16, 1999.

Chapter 4

Adkins, Adele. "Defining Moments." *Spinner.* AOLRadio, December 23, 2010.

Levine, Nick. "Exclusive: Adele Aimed to 'Surprise' with Tedder Song." *Digital Spy*, January 19, 2011. http://www.digitalspy.com/music/news/a298869/adele-aimed-to-surprise-with-tedder-song.html.

Love, Ryan. "Adele Explains Brits Tears." *Digital Spy*, February 16, 2011. http://www.digitalspy.com/music/news/a304126/adele-explains-brits-tears.html.

Montgomery, James. "Adele's Vocal Surgery: An Expert Weighs In." *MTV News*, November 1, 2011. http://www.mtv.com/news/articles/1673568/adele-vocal-surgery-expert.jhtml.

Chapter 5

Halperin, Shirley. "'American Idol' Finale's Ratings Free Fall: What Went Wrong." *Hollywood Reporter*, May 17, 2013. http://www.hollywoodreporter.com/idol-worship/american-idol-finales-ratings-free-524775.

Smith, Grady. "How Phillip Phillips' Song 'Home' Was Chosen for the Olympics." *Entertainment Weekly*, August 9, 2012. http://music-mix.ew.com/2012/08/09/how-phillip-phillips-home-was-chosen-for-olympics/.

Chapter 6

Campbell, Margaret. "Bell, Joshua." In *Grove Music Online/Oxford Music Online*. February 2, 2002. http://www.oxfordmusiconline.com/subscriber/article/grove/music/42214.

Cutruzzula, Kara. "Joshua Bell on Messing Up His First Violin Competition." *Newsweek*, January 1, 2012. http://mag.newsweek.com/2012/01/01/joshua-bell-on-messing-up-his-first-violin-competition.html.

"Joshua Bell: Review Quotes." *Joshua Bell*, accessed September 11, 2014. http://www.joshuabell.com/review-quotes.

Laitz, Steven G. *The Complete Musician: An Integrated Approach to Tonal Theory, Analysis, and Listening*, 3rd ed. New York: Oxford University Press, 2012.

Weingarten, Gene. "Pearls before Breakfast: Can One of the Nation's Great Musicians Cut through the Fog of a D.C. Rush Hour? Let's Find Out." *Washington Post*, April 8, 2007. http://www.washingtonpost.com/wp-dyn/content/article/2007/04/04/AR2007040401721.html.

Chapter 7

Doss, Erika Lee. *Elvis Culture: Fans, Faith, & Image*. Lawrence: University Press of Kansas, 1999.

Szatmary, David P. *Rockin' in Time: A Social History of Rock-and-Roll*, 4th ed. Upper Saddle River, NJ: Prentice Hall, 2000.

Torr, James D. *Elvis Presley*. San Diego: Greenhaven Press, 2001.

Chapter 8

Henahan, Donal. "Review/Music; Mezzo Sings Entirely Mozart." *New York Times*, July 19, 1990. http://www.nytimes.com/1990/07/19/arts/review-music-mezzo-sings-entirely-mozart.html.

Hoelterhoff, Manuela. *Cinderella & Company: Backstage at the Opera with Cecilia Bartoli*. New York: Alfred A. Knopf, 1998.

Holland, Bernard. "The Met's New 'Cosi,' with Bartoli's Debut." *New York Times*, February 10, 1996. http://www.nytimes.com/1996/02/10/arts/music-revi-w-the-met-s-new-cosi-with-bartoli-s-debut.html.

Loomis, George. "Cecilia Bartoli at Salzburg." *New York Times*, May 22, 2013. http://www.nytimes.com/2013/05/22/arts/22iht-loomis22.html?_r=0&adxnnl=1&adxnnlx=1384975636-iwo23k6L0+pp4xpxiJvRVA.

Smith, Patrick. "Review of Cecilia Bartoli's *If You Love Me*." *Opera News* 58, no. 7 (1993): 33.

Chapter 9

Jackson, Michael. *Moonwalk*. New York: Doubleday, 1988.

Jefferson, Margo. *On Michael Jackson*. New York: Pantheon Books, 2006.

"Michael Jackson Biography." *Rolling Stone,* accessed September 11, 2014. http://www.rollingstone.com/music/artists/michael-jackson/biography.

Taraborrelli, J. Randy. *Michael Jackson: The Magic, the Madness, the Whole Story, 1958–2009.* New York: Grand Central, 2009.

Chapter 10

Edwards, Gavin. "A Darker Shade of Pink." *Rolling Stone*, September 17, 2009.

Gundersen, Edna. "Pink Learns 'The Truth about Love.'" *USA Today*, September 18, 2012. http://usatoday30.usatoday.com/life/music/story/2012/09/18/pink-learns-the-truth-about-love/57797248/1.

Kim, Chris. "Fun.'s Nate Ruess Admits It's 'Hard to Argue' with Pink." *MTV News*, January 2, 2013. http://www.mtv.com/news/articles/1700614/pink-just-give-me-a-reason-fun-nate-ruess.jhtml.

Chapter 11

"Ella Fitzgerald: The Official Site of the First Lady of Song." *Ella Fitzgerald*, accessed September 11, 2014. http://www.ellafitzgerald.com.

Jefferson, Margo. "Ella in Wonderland." *New York Times*, December 29, 1996. http://www.nytimes.com/1996/12/29/magazine/ella-in-wonderland.html.

Chapter 12

"Billy Joel." *Billy Joel*, accessed September 11, 2014. http://www.billyjoel.com.

Chapter 13

"Renée Fleming." *Renée Fleming*, accessed September 11, 2014. http://www.reneefleming.com.

Silva, Eddie. "La Diva Renée." *Playbill Arts*, September 13, 2010. http://www.playbillarts.com/features/article/8455.html.

Chapter 14

"Rascal Flatts, 'Why Wait'—Story behind the Lyrics." *The Boot*, November 24, 2010. http://theboot.com/rascal-flatts-why-wait-lyrics.

"SaraCare: It Comes from the Heart." *SaraCare*, accessed September 23, 2013. http://saracare.org/.

Chapter 15

Chappell, Bill. "Olympics Closing Ceremony: Both Well-Received and Anger-Inducing." *NPR*, August 13, 2012. http://www.npr.org/blogs/thetorch/2012/08/13/158693657/olympics-closing-ceremony-both-well-received-and-anger-inducing.

Hutchinson, Lydia. "The Story behind Queen's 'Bohemian Rhapsody.'" *Performing Songwriter*, accessed September 11, 2014. http://performingsongwriter.com/freddie-mercury-queen-bohemian-rhapsody.

Mercury, Freddie, and Greg Brooks. *Freddie Mercury: A Life, in His Own Words*. London: Mercury Songs, 2006.

Neil, McCormick. "Brian May Interview: Freddie Is in My Thoughts Every Day." *Telegraph*, March 9, 2011. http://www.telegraph.co.uk/culture/music/rockandpopmusic/8371458/Brian-May-interview-Freddie-is-in-my-thoughts-every-day.html.

Appendix 1

Williams, Chas. *The Nashville Number System*, 7th ed. N.p.: Chas. Williams, 2005.

Appendix 2

Kachulis, Jimmy, and Jonathan Feist. *The Songwriter's Workshop*. Boston: Berklee Press, 2005.

Perricone, Jack. *Melody in Songwriting: Tools and Techniques for Writing Hit Songs*. Boston: Berklee Press, 2000.

Online Chapter 1

"Barbara Hendricks." <http://www.barbarahendricks.com>.

Dubal, David. *The Art of the Piano: Its Performers, Literature, and Recordings.* 3rd ed. Pompton Plains, N.J.: Amadeus Press, 2004. Print.

Ligon, Bert. *Jazz Theory Resources: Tonal, Harmonic, Melodic, & Rhythmic Organization of Jazz.* Milwaukee, WI: Hal Leonard, 2001.

Swafford, Jan. *The Vintage Guide to Classical Music.* New York: Random House, 1992.

"Walter Gieseking." *Walter Gieseking*, accessed October 24, 2014. http://www.allmusic.com/artist/walter-gieseking-mn0000659476/biography.

Online Chapter 2

Godell, Tom. "Review." *American Record Guide* Nov. 1994: 5, 8.

"Jacqueline du Pre, Noted Cellist, Is Dead at 42." *New York Times* 20 Oct. 1987, sec. Obituaries. Page B.5 http://www.nytimes.com/1987/10/20/obituaries/jacqueline-du-pre-noted-cellist-is-dead-at-42.html.

Potter, Tully. "Du Pré, Jacqueline." *Grove Music Online. Oxford Music Online.* Oxford University Press.

Wilson, Elizabeth. "Jacqueline du Pré: A 60th year Anniversary celebration." *BBC Music Magazine* Feb. 2005: 22–26.

Online Chapter 3

Atkinson, Brooks. "Review of West Side Story." *New York Times* 27 Sept. 1957.

Henahan, Donald. "Leonard Bernstein, 72, Music's Monarch, Dies." *New York Times* 15 Oct. 1990, sec. Obituaries. Page A.1. http://query.nytimes.com/gst/fullpage.html?res=9D0CE0DA1F3DF936A25753C1A966958260.

Laird, Paul R., and David Schiff. "Bernstein, Leonard." *Grove Music Online. Oxford Music Online.* Oxford University Press.

Online Chapter 4

Bie, Oskar, E. E. Kellett, and Edward W. Naylor. *A History of the Pianoforte and Pianoforte players.* New York: Da Capo Press, 1966.

Zaslaw, Neal. *Mozart's Symphonies: Context, Performance Practice, Reception.* Oxford, Oxfordshire: Clarendon Press, 1989.

CREDITS

PHOTO CREDITS

p. 1: AP Photo/Mel Evans; **p. 23:** Karen Will Rogers / Nashville; **p. 25:** AP Photo, File; **p. 29:** Anthony Quintano (Quintanomedia.com), CC BY 2.0; **p. 37:** AP Photo/Mark J. Terrill; **p. 40:** photo by Alan Light (CC BY 2.0); **p. 46:** Portrait by Mitch Weiss; **p. 49:** May S. Young (CC BY-SA 2.0); **p. 53:** © Featureflash | Dreamstime.com; **p. 59:** © Featureflash | Dreamstime.com; **p. 71:** AP Photo/Joel Ryan, file; **p. 74:** © Sbukley | Dreamstime.com; **p. 79:** Karen Blue (CC BY-SA 2.0); **p. 92:** © Lucy Clark | Dreamstime.com; **p. 109:** Photo by Jeremy Denton, courtesy of Gregg Lohman; **p. 111:** Alexduff (CC BY-SA 3.0); **p. 115:** © Laurence Agron | Dreamstime.com; **p. 129:** Courtesy of Library of Congress (LC-USZ62-115589); **p. 134:** Courtesy of Library of Congress (LC-DIG-ppmsca-19959); **p. 143:** Courtesy of Layng Martine Jr. and BMI; **p. 146:** GINIES/SIPA/Newscom; **p. 153:** SCHROEWIG/R.R./picture-alliance / SCHROEWIG/R.R/Newscom; **p. 172:** © Imagecollect | Dreamstime.com; **p. 177:** Bernie Ilson, Inc., public relations, New York (public domain via Wikimedia Commons); **p. 179:** AP Photo; **p. 190:** Photo by Jason Merritt / EdStock / iStock; **p. 194:** © Yakub88 | Dreamstime.com; **p. 199:** © Yakub88 | Dreamstime.com; **p. 207:** Courtesy of Library of Congress (LC-USZ62-114744); **p. 211:** © Aija Lehtonen | Dreamstime.com; **p. 221:** Anthony Correia / Shutterstock.com; **p. 227:** © Aaron Settipane | Dreamstime.com; **p. 240:** Photo by Michael Loccisano / EdStock / iStock; **p. 245:** Photo by Chip Somodevilla / EdStock / iStock; **p. 249:** Photo: Andreas Praefcke (PD via Wikimedia Commons); **p. 260:** © Sbukley | Dreamstime.com; **p. 262:** AP Photo/Mark Humphrey; **p. 263:** Courtesy of Norma Kennedy and the SaraCare Foundation; **p. 266:** Bob James (CC BY 2.0); **p. 280:** Courtesy of Patrick McMakin; **p. 282:** AP Photo; **p. 291:** marka / Marka / Superstock.com; **p. 311:** Photo by Kellie Mueller, courtesy of Brian and Christa Yak; **p. 315:** Photo by Jeremy Cowart; **p. 322:** Marshall Hurley/Amicus Photo; **p. 327:** Meredith Bacon Photography, courtesy of Sarah Hurst; **p. 332:** © Copyright 2007 Van Ness Press, Inc. (ASCAP) (admin. by LifeWay Worship c/o Music Services, www.musicservices.org). All rights reserved. Used by permission; **p. 336:** Photo by David Herrera, courtesy of James Issac Elliott; **p. 339:** Courtesy of Tom Douglas; **p. 341:** © Carrienelson1 | Dreamstime.com

TEXT CREDITS

p. 59: Rosanna Greenstreet, first published in *The Guardian*; **p. 53:** from "Metallica and Lang Lang Become 'One' at the Grammys" by Kory Grow, RollingStone.com, February 13, 2014. Copyright © Rolling Stone LLC 2014. All Rights Reserved. Used by Permission; **p. 180:** from Michael Jackson's online biography, RollingStone.com, August 25, 2009. Copyright © Rolling Stone LLC 2009. All Rights Reserved. Used by Permission; **p. 295:** © Neil McCormick / The Daily Telegraph

MUSIC CREDITS

(alphabetical by song title)

Alcatraz

Used by permission of Christa and Brian Yak.

All Shook Up

Words and Music by Otis Blackwell and Elvis Presley

Baby, It's Cold Outside

By Frank Loesser

Because Of You

Words and Music by Kelly Clarkson, David Hodges and Ben Moody

Words and Music by KELLY CLARKSON, BEN MOODY and DAVID HODGES

Ben

Words by Don Black
Music by Walter Scharf

© 1971, 1972 (Renewed 1999, 2000) JOBETE MUSIC CO., INC.
This arrangement © 2014 JOBETE MUSIC CO., INC.
All Rights Controlled and Administered by EMI APRIL MUSIC INC.
All Rights Reserved International Copyright Secured Used by Permission
Reprinted by Permission of Hal Leonard Corporation

Black Or White

Words and Music by Michael Jackson
Copyright © 1991 Mijac Music
This arrangement Copyright © 2014 Mijac Music
All Rights Administered by Sony/ATV Music Publishing LLC, 424 Church Street, Suite 1200, Nashville, TN 37219
International Copyright Secured All Rights Reserved
Reprinted by Permission of Hal Leonard Corporation

Bohemian Rhapsody

Words and Music by Freddie Mercury
© 1975 (Renewed 2003) QUEEN MUSIC LTD.
This arrangement © 2014 QUEEN MUSIC LTD.
All Rights for the U.S. and Canada Controlled and Administered by GLENWOOD MUSIC CORP.
All Rights for the world excluding the U.S. and Canada Controlled and Administered by EMI MUSIC PUBLISHING LTD.
All Rights Reserved International Copyright Secured Used by Permission
Reprinted by Permission of Hal Leonard Corporation

Boulder

Lyric sheet and Nashville chart reproduced by permission of Cauley Music Group. "Boulder," written by Ashton Lee and Lane Caudell. Song published by Bodell Music, a division of Cauley Music Group, LLC.

Chainsaw

Words and Music by Josh Osborne, Shane McAnally and Matt Ramsey
Copyright © 2013 UNIVERSAL MUSIC CORP., SMACK INK, WANT A FRESH ONE MUSIC and MATTHEW RAMSEY PUBLISHING DESIGNEE
This arrangement Copyright © 2014 UNIVERSAL MUSIC CORP., SMACK INK, WANT A FRESH ONE MUSIC and MATTHEW RAMSEY PUBLISHING DESIGNEE
All Rights for SMACK INK Controlled and Administered by UNIVERSAL MUSIC CORP.
All Rights Reserved Used by Permission
Reprinted by Permission of Hal Leonard Corporation

Written by Josh Osborne, Shane McAnally and Matt Ramsey
Songs of Black River (ASCAP), a division of Black River Entertainment LLC / One Little Indian Creek Music (ASCAP) (admin. By Black River Entertainment LLC.
All rights reserved. Used by permission.
© 2014 Sonic Geo Music (ASCAP) admin by Calhoun Enterprises. Used by permission.

Christmas in Heaven

Written by Jeremy Johnson/Paul Marino
© 2008 VAN NESS PRESS, INC. (ASCAP) (Admin by Music Services). All rights reserved.
Used by permission.

Emily's Reel

Copyright © 2000 Mark O'Connor Musik International (administered by Conexion Entertainment Group) Copyright Renewed

International Copyright Secured All Rights Reserved Used by Permission.

Get The Party Started

Words and Music by Linda Perry

Copyright © 2001 Sony/ATV Music Publishing LLC and Stuck In The Throat Music

This arrangement Copyright © 2014 Sony/ATV Music Publishing LLC and Stuck In The Throat Music

All Rights Administered by Sony/ATV Music Publishing LLC, 424 Church Street, Suite 1200, Nashville, TN 37219

International Copyright Secured All Rights Reserved

Reprinted by Permission of Hal Leonard Corporation

Glitter In The Air

Words and Music by Alecia Moore and Billy Mann

© 2008 EMI BLACKWOOD MUSIC INC., PINK INSIDE PUBLISHING, SONY/ATV MUSIC PUBLISHING LLC and TURTLE VICTORY

This arrangement © 2014 EMI BLACKWOOD MUSIC INC., PINK INSIDE PUBLISHING, SONY/ATV MUSIC PUBLISHING LLC and TURTLE VICTORY

All Rights for PINK INSIDE PUBLISHING Controlled and Administered by EMI BLACKWOOD MUSIC INC.

All Rights for SONY/ATV MUSIC PUBLISHING LLC and TURTLE VICTORY Administered by SONY/ATV MUSIC PUBLISHING LLC, 424 Church Street, Suite 1200, Nashville, TN 37219

All Rights Reserved International Copyright Secured Used by Permission

Reprinted by Permission of Hal Leonard Corporation

God in Me

Used by permission of Christa and Brian Yak.

Home

Words and Music by Greg Holden and Drew Pearson

Copyright © 2011, 2012 Fallen Art Music, Drewyeah Music and CYP Two Publishing

This arrangement Copyright © 2014 Fallen Art Music, Drewyeah Music and CYP Two Publishing

All Rights for Fallen Art Music Administered by Songs Of Razor & Tie d/b/a Razor & Tie Music Publishing, LLC

All Rights for Drewyeah Music and CYP Two Publishing Administered by Downtown DMP Songs/Downtown Music Publishing LLC

All Rights Reserved Used by Permission

Reprinted by Permission of Hal Leonard Corporation

Words and Music by DREW PEARSON and GREG HOLDEN

© 2012 DREWYEAH MUSIC (BMI), CYP TWO PUBLISHING (BMI) and FALLEN ART MUSIC

All Rights for DREWYEAH MUSIC (BMI) and CYP TWO PUBLISHING (BMI) Administered by DOWNTOWN DMP SONGS (BMI)/DOWNTOWN MUSIC PUBLISHING LLC

All Rights for FALLEN ART MUSIC Administered by SONGS OF RAZOR & TIE d/b/a RAZOR & TIE MUSIC PUBLISHING, LLC

All Rights Reserved

Used by Permission of ALFRED MUSIC

Hound Dog

Words and Music by Jerry Leiber and Mike Stoller
Copyright © 1953 Sony/ATV Music Publishing LLC
Copyright Renewed
This arrangement Copyright © 2014 Sony/ATV Music Publishing LLC
All Rights Administered by Sony/ATV Music Publishing LLC, 424 Church Street, Suite 1200, Nashville, TN 37219
International Copyright Secured All Rights Reserved
Reprinted by Permission of Hal Leonard Corporation

The House That Built Me

Words and Music by Tom Douglas and Allen Shamblin
Copyright © 2009 Sony/ATV Music Publishing LLC, Tomdouglasmusic and Built On Rock Music
This arrangement Copyright © 2014 Sony/ATV Music Publishing LLC, Tomdouglasmusic and Built On Rock Music
All Rights on behalf of Sony/ATV Music Publishing LLC and Tomdouglasmusic Administered by Sony/ATV Music Publishing LLC, 424 Church Street, Suite 1200, Nashville, TN 37219
All Rights on behalf of Built On Rock Music Administered by ClearBox Rights
International Copyright Secured All Rights Reserved
Reprinted by Permission of Hal Leonard Corporation

© Copyright 2004. Built On Rock Music/ASCAP (admin. By ClearBox Rights)/Sony/ATV Tree Publishing/BMI. All rights reserved. Used by permission.

I Loves You, Porgy (from "Porgy and Bess")

from PORGY AND BESS
Music and Lyrics by George Gershwin, DuBose and Dorothy Heyward and Ira Gershwin
© 1935 (Renewed) NOKAWI MUSIC, FRANKIE G. SONGS, DUBOSE AND DOROTHY HEYWARD MEMORIAL FUND and IRA GERSHWIN MUSIC
This arrangement © 2014 NOKAWI MUSIC, FRANKIE G. SONGS, DUBOSE AND DOROTHY HEYWARD MEMORIAL FUND and IRA GERSHWIN MUSIC
All Rights for NOKAWI MUSIC Administered by IMAGEM SOUNDS
All Rights for IRA GERSHWIN MUSIC Administered by WB MUSIC CORP.
All Rights Reserved Used by Permission
Reprinted by Permission of Hal Leonard Corporation

Words and Music by GEORGE GERSHWIN, DU BOSE and DOROTHY HEYWARD and IRA GERSHWIN
© 1935 (Renewed) IRA GERSHWIN MUSIC, DU BOSE AND DOROTHY HEYWARD MEMORIAL FUND and GEORGE GERSHWIN MUSIC All Rights on behalf of IRA GERSHWIN MUSIC Administered by WB MUSIC CORP.
All Rights Reserved
Used by Permission of ALFRED MUSIC

I Melt

Words and Music by Gary Levox, Wendell Mobley and Neil Thrasher
Copyright © 2001, 2002 Sony/ATV Music Publishing LLC, Warner-Tamerlane Publishing Corp., Major Bob Music Co., Inc. and Reservoir Media Music
This arrangement Copyright © 2014 Sony/ATV Music Publishing LLC, Warner-Tamerlane Publishing Corp., Major Bob Music Co., Inc. and Reservoir Media Music
All Rights on behalf of Sony/ATV Music Publishing LLC Administered by Sony/ATV Music Publishing LLC, 424 Church Street, Suite 1200, Nashville, TN 37219

All Rights on behalf of Reservoir Media Music Administered by Reservoir Media Management, Inc.
International Copyright Secured All Rights Reserved
Reprinted by Permission of Hal Leonard Corporation

Words and Music by WENDELL LEE MOBLEY, NEIL THRASHER and GARY LEVOX
© 2002 WARNER-TAMERLANE PUBLISHING CORP. (BMI), MAJOR BOB MUSIC CO., INC. (ASCAP),
SONY/ATV TUNES LLC DBA CROSS KEYS
PUBLISHING (ASCAP) and ONALY MUSIC, A DIV. OF TERACEL (ASCAP)
All Rights Reserved
Used by Permission of ALFRED MUSIC

I Will Wait for You

Written by Michael and Carissa Alvarado. Reproduced by permission.

In the Still of the Night (from "Rosalie")

Words and Music by COLE PORTER
© 1937 (Renewed) CHAPPELL & CO., INC.
All Rights Reserved
Used by Permission of ALFRED MUSIC

Inside Your Heaven

Words and Music by Savan Kotecha, Per Nylen and Andreas Carlsson
© 2005 EMI BLACKWOOD MUSIC INC., OH SUKI MUSIC, UNIVERSAL MUSIC PUBLISHING AB and ANDREAS CARLSSON PUBLISHING AB
This arrangement © 2014 EMI BLACKWOOD MUSIC INC., OH SUKI MUSIC, UNIVERSAL MUSIC PUBLISHING AB and ANDREAS CARLSSON PUBLISHING AB
All Rights for OH SUKI MUSIC Controlled and Administered by EMI BLACKWOOD MUSIC INC.
All Rights for UNIVERSAL MUSIC PUBLISHING AB in the United States and Canada Controlled and Administered by UNIVERSAL - POLYGRAM INTERNATIONAL PUBLISHING, INC.
All Rights for ANDREAS CARLSSON PUBLISHING AB in the United States and Canada Controlled and Administered by WB MUSIC CORP.
All Rights Reserved International Copyright Secured Used by Permission
Reprinted by Permission of Hal Leonard Corporation

Words and Music by ANDREAS CARLSSON, PER NYLEN and SAVAN KOTECHA
© 2005 WB MUSIC CORP., ANDREAS CARLSSON PUBLISHING AB, UNIVERSAL MUSIC PUBLISHING AB and OH SUKI MUSIC
All Rights on behalf of itself and ANDREAS CARLSSON PUBLISHING AB Administered by WB MUSIC CORP.
All Rights Reserved
Used by Permission of ALFRED MUSIC

Just Give Me A Reason

Words and Music by Alecia Moore, Jeff Bhasker and Nate Ruess
© 2012 EMI BLACKWOOD MUSIC INC., PINK INSIDE PUBLISHING, SONY/ATV MUSIC PUBLISHING LLC, WAY ABOVE MUSIC, WB MUSIC CORP., FBR MUSIC and BEARVON MUSIC

Learn to Love

The Longest Time

Love for Sale (from "The New Yorkers")

Love Me Tender

Love Story

Words and Music by Taylor Swift

Love Theme

from CINEMA PARADISO
Music by Andrea Morricone

The Luckiest

Words and Music by BEN FOLDS

Lullabye (Goodnight, My Angel)

Words and Music by Billy Joel

Man In The Mirror

Words and Music by Glen Ballard and Siedah Garrett

My Funny Valentine (from "Babes in Arms")

Words by Lorenz Hart
Music by Richard Rodgers

Rights for the Extended Renewal Term in the U.S. Controlled by Williamson Music, a Division of Rodgers & Hammerstein: an Imagem Company and WB Music Corp.
International Copyright Secured All Rights Reserved
Reprinted by Permission of Hal Leonard Corporation

Words by LORENZ HART
Music by RICHARD RODGERS
© 1937 (Renewed) CHAPPELL & CO., INC.
All Rights for the Extended Renewal Term in the U.S. Controlled by WB MUSIC CORP. and WILLIAMSON MUSIC CO.
All Rights Reserved
Used by Permission of ALFRED MUSIC

My Girl

Words and Music by William "Smokey" Robinson and Ronald White
© 1964, 1972, 1973, 1977 (Renewed 1992, 2000, 2001, 2005) JOBETE MUSIC CO., INC.
This arrangement © 2014 JOBETE MUSIC CO., INC.
All Rights Controlled and Administered by EMI APRIL MUSIC INC.
All Rights Reserved International Copyright Secured Used by Permission
Reprinted by Permission of Hal Leonard Corporation

My Redeemer Is Faithful And True

Words and Music by James Isaac Elliott and Steven Curtis Chapman
Copyright © 1987 by Universal Music-Careers, Birdwing Music, Sparrow Song and Greg Nelson Music
This arrangement Copyright © 2014 by Universal Music-Careers, Birdwing Music, Sparrow Song and Greg Nelson Music
All Rights for Birdwing Music, Sparrow Song and Greg Nelson Music Administered at EMICMGPublishing.com
International Copyright Secured All Rights Reserved
Reprinted by Permission of Hal Leonard Corporation

Copyright © 1987 Birdwing Music (ASCAP) Sparrow Song (BMI) Greg Nelson Music (BMI) (adm. at CapitolCMGPublishing.com) / Universal Music-Careers (BMI)
International Copyright Secured. All Rights Reserved. Used by Permission.

My Romance

from JUMBO
Words by Lorenz Hart
Music by Richard Rodgers
Copyright © 1935 by Williamson Music and Lorenz Hart Publishing Co.
Copyright Renewed
This arrangement Copyright © 2014 by Williamson Music and Lorenz Hart Publishing Co.
All Rights in the United States Administered by Williamson Music, a Division of Rodgers & Hammerstein: an Imagem Company
All Rights outside of the United States Administered by Universal - PolyGram International Publishing, Inc.
International Copyright Secured All Rights Reserved
Reprinted by Permission of Hal Leonard Corporation

No Matter Where You Are

Written by Michael and Carissa Alvarado. Reproduced by permission.

Return To Sender

Words and Music by Otis Blackwell and Winfield Scott
Copyright © 1962; Renewed 1990 Elvis Presley Music (BMI)
This arrangement Copyright © 2014 Elvis Presley Music (BMI)
All Rights for Elvis Presley Music Administered by Imagem Music LLC d/b/a Songs Of Imagem Music
International Copyright Secured All Rights Reserved
Reprinted by Permission of Hal Leonard Corporation

Rumour Has It

Words and Music by Adele Adkins and Ryan Tedder
Copyright © 2011 MELTED STONE PUBLISHING LTD. and WRITE 2 LIVE PUBLISHING
This arrangement Copyright © 2014 MELTED STONE PUBLISHING LTD. and WRITE 2 LIVE PUBLISHING
All Rights for MELTED STONE PUBLISHING LTD. in the U.S. and Canada Controlled and Administered by UNIVERSAL - SONGS OF POLYGRAM INTERNATIONAL, INC.
All Rights for WRITE 2 LIVE PUBLISHING Administered by KOBALT MUSIC PUBLISHING AMERICA, INC.
All Rights Reserved Used by Permission
Reprinted by Permission of Hal Leonard Corporation

Save Me

Words and Music by Brian May
© 1980 QUEEN MUSIC LTD.
This arrangement © 2014 QUEEN MUSIC LTD.
All Rights for the U.S. and Canada Controlled and Administered by BEECHWOOD MUSIC CORP.
All Rights for the world excluding the U.S. and Canada Controlled and Administered by EMI MUSIC PUBLISHING LTD.
All Rights Reserved International Copyright Secured Used by Permission
Reprinted by Permission of Hal Leonard Corporation

Scenes From An Italian Restaurant

Words and Music by Billy Joel
Copyright © 1977 (Renewed 2005), 1978 IMPULSIVE MUSIC
This arrangement Copyright © 2014 IMPULSIVE MUSIC
All Rights Administered by ALMO MUSIC CORP.
All Rights Reserved Used by Permission
Reprinted by Permission of Hal Leonard Corporation

Set Fire To The Rain

Words and Music by Adele Adkins and Fraser Smith
Copyright © 2011 MELTED STONE PUBLISHING LTD. and CHRYSALIS MUSIC LTD.
This arrangement Copyright © 2014 MELTED STONE PUBLISHING LTD. and CHRYSALIS MUSIC LTD.
All Rights for MELTED STONE PUBLISHING LTD. in the U.S. and Canada Controlled and Administered by UNIVERSAL - SONGS OF POLYGRAM INTERNATIONAL, INC.
All Rights for CHRYSALIS MUSIC LTD. in the U.S. and Canada Administered by CHRYSALIS MUSIC GROUP, INC., A BMG CHRYSALIS COMPANY
All Rights Reserved Used by Permission
Reprinted by Permission of Hal Leonard Corporation

Shameless

Words and Music by Billy Joel
Copyright © 1989 JOELSONGS
This arrangement Copyright © 2014 JOELSONGS
All Rights Administered by ALMO MUSIC CORP.
All Rights Reserved Used by Permission
Reprinted by Permission of Hal Leonard Corporation

So What

Words and Music by Alecia Moore, Max Martin and Johan Schuster
© 2008 EMI BLACKWOOD MUSIC INC., PINK INSIDE PUBLISHING and MARATONE AB
This arrangement © 2014 EMI BLACKWOOD MUSIC INC., PINK INSIDE PUBLISHING and MARATONE AB
All Rights for PINK INSIDE PUBLISHING Controlled and Administered by EMI BLACKWOOD MUSIC INC.
All Rights for MARATONE AB Administered by KOBALT MUSIC PUBLISHING AMERICA, INC.
All Rights Reserved International Copyright Secured Used by Permission
Reprinted by Permission of Hal Leonard Corporation

Some Nights

Words and Music by Jeff Bhasker, Andrew Dost, Jack Antonoff and Nate Ruess
Copyright © 2012 Sony/ATV Music Publishing LLC, Way Above Music, Rough Art, Shira Lee Lawrence Rick Music, WB Music Corp., FBR Music and Bearvon Music
This arrangement Copyright © 2014 Sony/ATV Music Publishing LLC, Way Above Music, Rough Art, Shira Lee Lawrence Rick Music, WB Music Corp., FBR Music and Bearvon Music
All Rights on behalf of Sony/ATV Music Publishing LLC, Way Above Music, Rough Art and Shira Lee Lawrence Rick Music Administered by Sony/ATV Music Publishing LLC, 424 Church Street, Suite 1200, Nashville, TN 37219
All Rights on behalf of FBR Music and Bearvon Music Administered by WB Music Corp.
International Copyright Secured All Rights Reserved
Reprinted by Permission of Hal Leonard Corporation

Words and Music by NATE RUESS, JEFF BHASKER, ANDREW DOST and JACK ANTONOFF
©2012 WB MUSIC CORP., FBR MUSIC, BEARVON MUSIC, SONY/ATV MUSIC PUBLISHING LLC,
WAY ABOVE MUSIC, ROUGH ART and SHIRA LEE LAWRENCE RICK MUSIC
All Rights on behalf of itself, FBR MUSIC and BEARVON MUSIC Administered by WB MUSIC CORP.
All Rights on behalf of SONY/ATV MUSIC PUBLISHING LLC, WAY ABOVE MUSIC,
ROUGH ART and SHIRA LEE LAWRENCE RICK MUSIC
Administered by SONY/ATV MUSIC PUBLISHING LLC, 8 Music Square West, Nashville, TN 37203
All Right Reserved
Used by Permission of ALFRED MUSIC

Somebody To Love

Words and Music by Freddie Mercury
© 1976 (Renewed 2004) QUEEN MUSIC LTD.
This arrangement © 2014 QUEEN MUSIC LTD.

All Rights for the U.S. and Canada Controlled and Administered by BEECHWOOD MUSIC CORP.

All Rights for the world excluding the U.S. and Canada Controlled and Administered by EMI MUSIC PUBLISHING LTD.

All Rights Reserved International Copyright Secured Used by Permission

Reprinted by Permission of Hal Leonard Corporation

Someone Like You

Words and Music by Adele Adkins and Dan Wilson

Copyright © 2011 MELTED STONE PUBLISHING LTD., CHRYSALIS MUSIC and SUGAR LAKE MUSIC

This arrangement Copyright © 2014 MELTED STONE PUBLISHING LTD., CHRYSALIS MUSIC and SUGAR LAKE MUSIC

All Rights for MELTED STONE PUBLISHING LTD. in the U.S. and Canada Controlled and Administered by UNIVERSAL - SONGS OF POLYGRAM INTERNATIONAL, INC.

All Rights for CHRYSALIS MUSIC and SUGAR LAKE MUSIC Administered by CHRYSALIS MUSIC GROUP INC., A BMG CHRYSALIS COMPANY

All Rights Reserved Used by Permission

Reprinted by Permission of Hal Leonard Corporation

Stronger (What Doesn't Kill You)

Words and Music by Greg Kurstin, Jorgen Elofsson, David Gamson and Alexandra Tamposi

© 2011 EMI APRIL MUSIC INC., KURSTIN MUSIC, UNIVERSAL MUSIC PUBLISHING MGB SCANDINAVIA, BMG GOLD SONGS and PERFECT STORM MUSIC GROUP AB

This arrangement © 2014 EMI APRIL MUSIC INC., KURSTIN MUSIC, UNIVERSAL MUSIC PUBLISHING MGB SCANDINAVIA, BMG GOLD SONGS and PERFECT STORM MUSIC GROUP AB

All Rights for KURSTIN MUSIC Controlled and Administered by EMI APRIL MUSIC INC.

All Rights for UNIVERSAL MUSIC PUBLISHING MGB SCANDINAVIA in the United States and Canada Administered by UNIVERSAL MUSIC - CAREERS

All Rights for BMG GOLD SONGS Administered by BMG RIGHTS MANAGEMENT (US) LLC

All Rights for PERFECT STORM MUSIC GROUP AB Administered by SONY/ATV MUSIC PUBLISHING LLC, 424 Church Street, Suite 1200, Nashville, TN 37219

All Rights Reserved International Copyright Secured Used by Permission

Reprinted by Permission of Hal Leonard Corporation

To the Moon

Reproduced by permission of Sarah Hurst Music.

Under Pressure

Words and Music by Freddie Mercury, John Deacon, Brian May, Roger Taylor and David Bowie

© 1981 EMI MUSIC PUBLISHING LTD., TINTORETTO MUSIC and QUEEN MUSIC LTD.

This arrangement © 2014 EMI MUSIC PUBLISHING LTD., TINTORETTO MUSIC and QUEEN MUSIC LTD.

All Rights for EMI MUSIC PUBLISHING LTD. in the U.S. and Canada Controlled and Administered by SCREEN GEMS-EMI MUSIC INC.

All Rights for TINTORETTO MUSIC Administered by RZO MUSIC

All Rights for QUEEN MUSIC LTD. in the U.S. and Canada Controlled and Administered by BEECHWOOD MUSIC CORP.

Reprinted by Permission of Hal Leonard Corporation

Written by David Bowie, John Deacon, Brian May, Freddie Mercury, Roger Taylor
Reprinted by permission of Tintoretto Music (BMI) administered by RZO Music, Inc.

Unstoppable

Words and Music by Jay DeMarcus, Hillary Lindsey and James Slater
Copyright © 2008, 2009 Sony/ATV Music Publishing LLC, Eileensong, Raylene Music, State One Music America and Me You And The Piano Songs
This arrangement Copyright © 2014 Sony/ATV Music Publishing LLC, Eileensong, Raylene Music, State One Music America and Me You And The Piano Songs
All Rights on behalf of Sony/ATV Music Publishing LLC and Eileensong Administered by Sony/ATV Music Publishing LLC, 424 Church Street, Suite 1200, Nashville, TN 37219
All Rights on behalf of Raylene Music Administered by BPJ Administration, P.O. Box 218061, Nashville, TN 37221-8061
International Copyright Secured All Rights Reserved
Reprinted by Permission of Hal Leonard Corporation

Words and Music by JAMES SLATER, JAY DeMARCUS and HILLARY LINDSEY
© 2010 RESERVOIR MEDIA MANAGEMENT, INC., ENGLISH IVY MUSIC (BMI), ME YOU AND THE PIANO SONGS (BMI), SONY/ATV TREE PUBLISHING (BMI), EILEENSONGS (BMI) and RAYLENE MUSIC (ASCAP)
All Rights for RESERVOIR MEDIA MUSIC (ASCAP), ENGLISH IVY MUSIC (BMI), ME YOU AND THE PIANO SONGS (BMI) Administered by RESERVOIR MEDIA MANAGEMENT, INC.
RESERVOIR MEDIA MUSIC (ASCAP) Administered by ALFRED MUSIC
All Rights for SONY/ATV TREE PUBLISHING (BMI) and EILEENSONGS (BMI) Administered by SONY/ATV SONGS LLC, 8 Music Square West, Nashville, TN 37203
All Rights for RAYLENE MUSIC (ASCAP) Administered by Becky Pommer-Jones Administration, P.O. Box 218061, Nashville, TN 37221
All Rights Reserved
Used by Permission of ALFRED MUSIC

The Valiant

Reproduced by permission of Sarah Hurst Music.

We Are The Champions

Words and Music by Freddie Mercury
© 1977 (Renewed 2005) QUEEN MUSIC LTD.
This arrangement © 2014 QUEEN MUSIC LTD.
All Rights for the U.S. and Canada Controlled and Administered by BEECHWOOD MUSIC CORP.
All Rights for the world excluding the U.S. and Canada Controlled and Administered by EMI MUSIC PUBLISHING LTD.
All Rights Reserved International Copyright Secured Used by Permission
Reprinted by Permission of Hal Leonard Corporation

We Are The World

Words and Music by Lionel Richie and Michael Jackson
Copyright © 1985 by Brockman Music, Brenda Richie Publishing and Mijac Music
This arrangement Copyright © 2014 by Brockman Music, Brenda Richie Publishing and Mijac Music

All Rights on behalf of Mijac Music Administered by Sony/ATV Music Publishing LLC, 424 Church Street, Suite 1200, Nashville, TN 37219
All Rights Reserved Used by Permission
Reprinted by Permission of Hal Leonard Corporation

We Are Young

Words and Music by Jeff Bhasker, Andrew Dost, Jack Antonoff and Nate Ruess
Copyright © 2011, 2012 Sony/ATV Music Publishing LLC, Way Above Music, Rough Art, Shira Lee Lawrence Rick Music, WB Music Corp., FBR Music and Bearvon Music
This arrangement Copyright © 2014 Sony/ATV Music Publishing LLC, Way Above Music, Rough Art, Shira Lee Lawrence Rick Music, WB Music Corp., FBR Music and Bearvon Music
All Rights on behalf of Sony/ATV Music Publishing LLC, Way Above Music, Rough Art and Shira Lee Lawrence Rick Music Administered by Sony/ATV Music Publishing LLC, 424 Church Street, Suite 1200, Nashville, TN 37219
All Rights on behalf of FBR Music and Bearvon Music Administered by WB Music Corp.
International Copyright Secured All Rights Reserved
Reprinted by Permission of Hal Leonard Corporation

Words and Music by NATE RUESS, JEFF BHASKER, ANDREW DOST and JACK ANTONOFF
© 2012 WB MUSIC CORP., FBR MUSIC, BEARVON MUSIC, SONY/ATV MUSIC PUBLISHING LLC,
WAY ABOVE MUSIC, ROUGH ART and SHIRA LEE LAWRENCE RICK MUSIC
All Rights on behalf of itself, FBR MUSIC and BEARVON MUSIC Administered by WB MUSIC CORP.
All Rights on behalf of SONY/ATV MUSIC PUBLISHING LLC, WAY ABOVE MUSIC, ROUGH ART and SHIRA LEE LAWRENCE RICK MUSIC
Administered by SONY/ATV MUSIC PUBLISHING LLC, 8 Music Square West, Nashville, TN 37203
All Right Reserved
Used by Permission of ALFRED MUSIC

What About Now

Words and Music by David Hodges, Ben Moody and Josh Hartzler
© 2006 EMI BLACKWOOD MUSIC INC., 12:06 PUBLISHING, ZOMBIES ATE MY PUBLISHING, SMELLSLIKEMETAL PUBLISHING, DWIGHT FRYE MUSIC INC., BUG MUSIC and 7 MONTHS OF SHADOWS PUBLISHING
This arrangement © 2014 EMI BLACKWOOD MUSIC INC., 12:06 PUBLISHING, ZOMBIES ATE MY PUBLISHING, SMELLSLIKEMETAL PUBLISHING, DWIGHT FRYE MUSIC INC., BUG MUSIC and 7 MONTHS OF SHADOWS PUBLISHING
All Rights for 12:06 PUBLISHING Controlled and Administered by EMI BLACKWOOD MUSIC INC.
All Rights for 7 MONTHS OF SHADOWS PUBLISHING Administered by BUG MUSIC
All Rights Reserved International Copyright Secured Used by Permission
Reprinted by Permission of Hal Leonard Corporation

Words and Music by BEN MOODY, DAVID HODGES and JOSH HARTZLER
© 2006 FSMGI (IMRO), SMELLSLIKEMETAL PUBLISHING (BMI), 7 MONTHS OF SHADOWS PUBLISHING (BMI), BUG MUSIC, INC. (BMI), 12 06 PUBLISHING (BMI) and EMI BLACKWOOD MUSIC, INC. (BMI)
All Rights for FSMGI (IMRO) and SMELLSLIKEMETAL PUBLISHING (BMI)
Administered by STATE ONE MUSIC AMERICA (BMI)
All Rights Reserved
Used by Permission of ALFRED MUSIC

When I Was Your Man

Words and Music by Bruno Mars, Ari Levine, Philip Lawrence and Andrew Wyatt

Words and Music by PHILIP LAWRENCE, ANDREW WYATT, BRUNO MARS and ARI LEVINE

Why Wait

Words and Music by Tom Shapiro, Neil Thrasher and James Yeary

Words and Music by JIMMY YEARY, NEIL THRASHER and TOM SHAPIRO
© 2010 BLACK TO BLACK SONGS/OLE, BMG GOLD SONGS, FEET IN THE CREEK MUSIC,
EMI BLACKWOOD MUSIC, INC. and PIANO WIRE MUSIC LLC
All Rights for BLACK TO BLACK SONGS/OLE Administered by OLE MEDIA MANAGEMENT LP
All Rights Reserved
Used by Permission of ALFRED MUSIC

Winter Wonderland

Words by DICK SMITH
Music by FELIX BERNARD
© 1934 (Renewed) WB MUSIC CORP.
All Rights Reserved
Used by Permission of ALFRED MUSIC

You Belong With Me

Words and Music by Taylor Swift and Liz Rose
Copyright © 2008 Sony/ATV Music Publishing LLC, Taylor Swift Music, Potting Shed Music and Barbara Orbison World Publishing
This arrangement Copyright © 2014 Sony/ATV Music Publishing LLC, Taylor Swift Music, Potting Shed Music and Barbara Orbison World Publishing
All Rights on behalf of Sony/ATV Music Publishing LLC and Taylor Swift Music Administered by Sony/ATV Music Publishing LLC, 424 Church Street, Suite 1200, Nashville, TN 37219
All Rights on behalf of Potting Shed Music and Barbara Orbison World Publishing Administered by BMG Rights Management (US) LLC
International Copyright Secured All Rights Reserved
Reprinted by Permission of Hal Leonard Corporation

Words and Music by LIZ ROSE and TAYLOR SWIFT
© 2012 WARNER-TAMERLANE PUBLISHING CORP. (BMI), ORBISON MUSIC LLC (BMI) and TAYLOR SWIFT MUSIC (BMI)
All Rights Reserved
Used by Permission of ALFRED MUSIC

You'll Never Walk Alone

from CAROUSEL
Lyrics by Oscar Hammerstein II
Music by Richard Rodgers
Copyright © 1945 by Williamson Music, a Division of Rodgers & Hammerstein: an Imagem Company
Copyright Renewed
This arrangement Copyright © 2014 by Williamson Music, a Division of Rodgers & Hammerstein: an Imagem Company
International Copyright Secured All Rights Reserved
Reprinted by Permission of Hal Leonard Corporation

You're the Top (from "Anything Goes")

Words and Music by COLE PORTER
© 1934 (Renewed) WB MUSIC CORP.
All Rights Reserved
Used by Permission of ALFRED MUSIC

INDEX OF MUSICAL EXAMPLES

POPULAR SONGS LISTED BY BOTH ARTIST AND SONGWRITER

INDEX